TULAGI
PACIFIC OUTPOST OF BRITISH EMPIRE

TULAGI

PACIFIC OUTPOST OF BRITISH EMPIRE

CLIVE MOORE

PRESS

PACIFIC SERIES

Published by ANU Press
The Australian National University
Acton ACT 2601, Australia
Email: anupress@anu.edu.au

Available to download for free at press.anu.edu.au

ISBN (print): 9781760463083
ISBN (online): 9781760463090

WorldCat (print): 1119375474
WorldCat (online): 1119375535

DOI: 10.22459/T.2019

This title is published under a Creative Commons Attribution-NonCommercial-NoDerivatives 4.0 International (CC BY-NC-ND 4.0).

The full licence terms are available at creativecommons.org/licenses/by-nc-nd/4.0/legalcode

Cover design and layout by ANU Press.

Front cover image: Painted by Brett Hilder in 1960, this depicts deputy commissioner Charles Woodford (soon to be the first Resident Commissioner) at Gavutu Island in 1897. He arrived on HMS *Rapid*, which rendezvoused with Burns Philp & Co.'s SS *Titus*. Brett Hilder (1911–81) joined Burns Philp & Co. as a midshipman in 1927 and served on its ships in Asia and the Pacific. During World War II, he taught navigation to Australian air crews and joined the Royal Australian Air Force. He became a ship's master and finally Burns Philp's Commodore of the Fleet, often sailing on the Sydney–Solomon Islands run. He began to paint as a hobby during the war and became an accomplished artist. The painting is housed in the Noel Butlin Archives Centre, The Australian National University. Burns Philp and Company (Sydney Office and Branches), N115-503, photograph of painting of SS *Titus* at Gavutu 1897, by Brett Hilder, 1960.

This edition © 2019 ANU Press

Contents

List of maps, figures and plates vii
List of tables. xix
Acronyms and abbreviations. xxi
A note on nomenclature xxiii
Acknowledgements xxv
Introduction 1
1. Protecting Solomon Islanders. 27
2. A 'very arduous task': Charles, Arthur and Frank 71
3. Administration: Pop, Spearline and the poodle 137
4. Chinatown, the club, hotels and the 'black hole'. 199
5. Mildewed elegance, houses and servants. 245
6. '… a pity you didn't wing him': Gender, sexuality and race 285
7. Silk, white helmets and Malacca canes. 315
8. Evacuation, invasion and destruction 373
Bibliography. 415
Index 447

List of maps, figures and plates

Maps

Map A.1 Modern Solomon Islands, showing Tulagi in Central Province and Honiara, the new capital, on Guadalcanal. xxvii

Map A.2 The Gela (Nggela or Florida) Group, 1930s. xxvii

Map A.3 Settlement on Tulagi Island in the 1930s xxviii

Map 1.1 The Tulagi enclave in the early 1940s, based around Tulagi and Gavutu harbours off Gela Sule 31

Map 1.2 European Pacific administrative boundaries, 1886 62

Map 1.3 European Pacific administrative boundaries, 1910 67

Map 2.1 Tulagi's commercial area, circa 1922. 117

Map 4.1 'No. 2', the commercial area on Tulagi, circa 1934. 216

Map 8.1 Tulagi in 1942, showing the trenches and gun emplacements 374

Figures

Figure 3.1 Tulagi's new prison, 1919 172

Figure 3.2 The new Tulagi Hospital, 1914 179

Figure 7.1 The third residency, 1934 320

Plates

Plate I.1 Tulagi viewed from the harbour, 1972 2

Plate I.2 Tulagi, looking into the harbour from the old prison area, 2013 2

Plate I.3 Tulagi Harbour, 2013. 3

Plate I.4 Tulagi docks, 2007 3

Plate I.5 Tulagi market on the harbour beach front, 2007. 5

Plate I.6 A house built over the water at Tulagi, 2013. 6

Plate I.7 The view down the stairs from the Resident Commissioner's residency in the 1910s 7

Plate I.8 The view from the top of the stairs that once led to the Resident Commissioner's home, 2013. The outline of the original path is still evident 8

Plate I.9 The first section of the residency stairs, 2013 13

Plate I.10 One of the many sets of concrete steps on Tulagi that once formed the entrances to government buildings, 2013. 14

Plate I.11 An attempt at heritage identification on Tulagi. A Ministry of Provincial Government and Institutional Strengthening sign outside the old prison, 2013. 14

Plate I.12 The remains of the prison cells on Tulagi, 2007 15

Plate I.13 The Solomon Tayo Ltd fish cannery on Tulagi in the 1970s. 16

Plate I.14 Inside the Solomon Tayo Ltd fish cannery on Tulagi in the 1970s. 16

Plate I.15 Vanita Motel, Tulagi, 2007. 18

Plate I.16 Walking towards the cutting through the central ridge, past the Telekom building, Tulagi, 2007. 18

Plate I.17 The author at the cutting through the ridge, Tulagi, 2007... 19

Plate I.18 Christ the King Cathedral, Anglican Diocese of Central Solomons, Tulagi, 2007 20

Plate I.19 The Anglican Mothers' Union building, Tulagi, 2007..... 20

LIST OF MAPS, FIGURES AND PLATES

Plate I.20 The sign for the Seventh-day Adventist Church on Tulagi, showing steps cut into the rock, 2013 21

Plate I.21 The remains of the strongroom at Levers Pacific Plantations Ltd headquarters on Gavutu, being used as a house, 2007 22

Plate I.22 The remains of the Levers Pacific Plantations Ltd wharf at Gavutu, 2007... 22

Plate I.23 One of the Japanese tunnels on Tulagi, constructed during their occupation of the island in 1942, photographed in 2013.. 23

Plate I.24 Fishing boats anchored in Tulagi Harbour, 2007 26

Plate 1.1 A hand-coloured lantern slide of the Gela Group, probably from a 1906 photograph 29

Plate 1.2 View from the end of Sandfly Passage, looking out to Guadalcanal, 1973................................... 30

Plate 1.3 A panoramic view from Port Purvis showing Gavutu and Tulagi islands in the distance, 1906................... 30

Plate 1.4 Longapolo village, Gela Group, 1906 33

Plate 1.5 Kombe village, Gela Group, 1906 33

Plate 1.6 Reverend Alfred Penny from the Melanesian Mission travelling by whaleboat in the Gela Group, 1870s 34

Plate 1.7 St Barnabas's College, Norfolk Island, where the early Gela pastors were trained, 1870s 35

Plate 1.8 Siota Melanesian Mission house, Gela Group, 1906 35

Plate 1.9 The Melanesian Mission's *Vaukolu* congress at Honggo village, Gela Group, 1906 37

Plate 1.10 The Melanesian Mission's *Vaukolu* congress at Honggo, 1906....................................... 38

Plate 1.11 The crowd listening to proceedings at the Melanesian Mission's *Vaukolu* congress at Honggo, 1906 38

Plate 1.12 The Melanesian Mission church at Longapolo village, Gela Group, 1906 39

Plate 1.13 The Melanesian Mission church at Kombe, Gela Group, 1906 40

ix

Plate 1.14 View of Bungana Island, the site of an early Melanesian Mission school, and the Tulagi lighthouse, Gela Group, 1906 ... 40

Plate 1.15 Gavutu Island, viewed from Halvo, showing fishing platforms, 1906 ... 43

Plate 1.16 Charles Woodford at Aola, Guadalcanal, 1890 ... 45

Plate 2.1 Tulagi viewed from Gavutu, 2007 ... 73

Plate 2.2 The first residency, built in 1898 on Tulagi's central ridge ... 75

Plate 2.3 The first two homes of the Resident Commissioner ... 75

Plate 2.4 The back of Woodford's second residency, built in 1905, showing the gardens ... 76

Plate 2.5 *Lahloo*, the first government yacht, anchored off Arundel Island ... 77

Plate 2.6 Tulagi Harbour and Mulallie Creek ... 78

Plate 2.7 The scene from Tulagi ridge, looking towards Gavutu, in the mid-1910s ... 81

Plate 2.8 Tulagi's first hospital, built in 1913 ... 81

Plate 2.9 BP's SS *Minindi* at the wharf, Makambo Island ... 84

Plate 2.10 BP's Makambo Island, showing the rail system that transported supplies to and from the wharf. Tulagi is in the background ... 85

Plate 2.11 Makambo Island from the beach, with the manager's house at the top ... 85

Plate 2.12 The main store area on Makambo Island ... 86

Plate 2.13 BP's SS *Mataram* sailing from Tulagi Harbour for Sydney ... 86

Plate 2.14 A man in a canoe, from an early Burns Philp & Co. advertisement for tourism in Solomon Islands ... 89

Plate 2.15 A woman in a grass skirt, from an early Burns Philp & Co. advertisement for tourism in Solomon Islands ... 90

Plate 2.16 Tulagi, with the port and customs office in the foreground ... 95

Plate 2.17 A trade store on Tulagi ... 96

LIST OF MAPS, FIGURES AND PLATES

Plate 2.18 Charles Woodford, Deputy Commissioner, 1896,
    and Resident Commissioner, 1897–1915. 99
Plate 2.19 The wharves at Levers' headquarters, Gavutu Island,
    1907 107
Plate 2.20 Levers' headquarters, Gavutu Island, 1914. 108
Plate 2.21 Chinatown during the first half of the 1910s 115
Plate 2.22 Solomon Islanders were constant visitors to the
    Tulagi enclave. 122
Plate 2.23 Solomon Islanders on Tulagi wharf 122
Plate 2.24 Prisoners maintaining a path on Tulagi, 1930s. 123
Plate 2.25 Inspection of an armed constabulary guard of honour,
    Tulagi Club, 1930s. 127
Plate 2.26 This photograph shows labourers typical of those who
    passed through Tulagi. 129
Plate 2.27 Two constables from the armed constabulary, Tulagi 135
Plate 2.28 Solomon Islanders manning a large rowing boat
    in Tulagi Harbour, 1930s 136
Plate 3.1 A tinted photograph of Tulagi, viewed from the harbour,
    circa 1935 139
Plate 3.2 The cutting through the central ridge was constructed
    in 1918 using prisoners and indentured labourers 143
Plate 3.3 The completed cutting, showing the bridge over the top . . 144
Plate 3.4 The bridge over the cutting enabled easy contact between
    all residents on the ridge. 145
Plate 3.5 The Treasury and Customs House, Tulagi, 1930s. 152
Plate 3.6 Pop Johnson, Treasurer, Collector of Customs and
    Registrar of Shipping, 1919–42 158
Plate 3.7 Spearline Wilson worked in the Lands Department
    from 1919 to 1942. 161
Plate 3.8 The armed constabulary barracks and offices, Tulagi 167
Plate 3.9 The armed constabulary on their daily parade 167

xi

Plate 3.10 Inspection of an armed constabulary guard of honour, Tulagi. 168

Plate 3.11 An armed constabulary canoe in the canoe shed on Tulagi, 1930s 170

Plate 3.12 Tulagi Prison, 1930s 171

Plate 3.13 The wireless station, built in 1915 on a flat area on the outer coast of Tulagi. 173

Plate 3.14 The 'native' ward, Tulagi Hospital, 1930s. 181

Plate 3.15 Jessie Watt worked as a nurse at Tulagi Hospital in 1923, before she married Spearline Wilson. 182

Plate 3.16 Dr Nathaniel Crichlow in old age 183

Plate 3.17 The Tulagi waterfront with the Lands Department building in the foreground 191

Plate 3.18 Government offices on the Tulagi waterfront 191

Plate 3.19 The Post Office, Tulagi. 192

Plate 4.1 Tulagi in the 1930s, showing Elkington's Hotel on the left on the top of the ridge 202

Plate 4.2 Elkington's Hotel, Tulagi 203

Plate 4.3 The Tulagi Club, 1920s 207

Plate 4.4 The Tulagi Club, 1930s. Shutters and sides have been added to enclose the verandah 207

Plate 4.5 The Tulagi cricket ground, 1935 209

Plate 4.6 The Tulagi cricket ground, 2 April 1939 209

Plate 4.7 A tennis court, next to the Tulagi Club 212

Plate 4.8 The Tulagi golf course and the Tulagi Club 212

Plate 4.9 The two wireless station masts and the golf course, 1930s. . . . 213

Plate 4.10 Chinatown in the 1930s, with BP's Makambo Island in the background 215

Plate 4.11 The main street of Chinatown, 1938 215

Plate 4.12 Chinatown in the 1930s, with identification of the leases added from Map 2.1 (1922). 218

LIST OF MAPS, FIGURES AND PLATES

Plate 4.13 Solomon Islands leaf houses and a substantial Chinese house built over the water in Chinatown 221

Plate 4.14 Solomon Islands leaf houses built over the water in Chinatown, and a Chinese trading vessel 221

Plate 4.15 A branch of Jiang Jieshi's (Chiang Kai-shek's) Chinese Nationalist Party, the Guomindang (Kuomintang or KMT) operated on Tulagi from 1925. The building dates from about 1927 223

Plate 4.16 Malaita's district officer William Bell, who was assassinated in 1927. 228

Plate 4.17 *Auki*, district officer William Bell's ship 229

Plate 4.18 HMAS *Adelaide* and HMAS *Sydney* in Tulagi Harbour . . 238

Plate 4.19 The government ships *Ranadi* and *Hygenia* at Tulagi wharf, late 1920s 238

Plate 4.20 Labourers being fed during the expedition to Kwaio, Malaita. 240

Plate 4.21 A member of the 1927 expedition shaking hands with a Kwaio man 241

Plate 4.22 Prisoners on Tulagi. 243

Plate 5.1 The second residency in the 1910s. 248

Plate 5.2 Florrie Woodford at the back gate of the residency. 249

Plate 5.3 Florrie and Charles Woodford having tea on the residency verandah in the 1910s 249

Plate 5.4 Spearline and Jessie Wilson's home, with the wireless station and the golf course in the background 253

Plate 5.5 Spearline and Jessie Wilson's home in the centre, with a neighbouring house to the right. 253

Plate 5.6 Pop and Agnes Johnson's home, 1930s. 254

Plate 5.7 The manager's house on Gavutu in 1907, showing canvas sheeting on one side that could be let down to shield the verandah from rain. 255

Plate 5.8 Spearline and Jessie Wilson and their Irish setter 257

Plate 5.9 This living room is in the district officer's house at Auki, Malaita, in the 1910s, during the tenancy of Thomas and Mary Edge-Partington 258

Plate 5.10 BP's Makambo Island, 1930s. 260

Plate 5.11 A staff cottage on Makambo Island 260

Plate 5.12 Fish were always on the menu 262

Plate 5.13 These cattle are on Tulagi. Most plantations also had herds that were used to keep down vegetation around coconut palms, and for food 263

Plate 5.14 Jessie Wilson at the beach with a house servant and one of her children 269

Plate 5.15 The Wilson family servants with Michael James Wilson and Andrea Gordon Wilson. 274

Plate 6.1 Spearline Wilson and his son Alexander ('Sandy') Robert, aged eight months 287

Plate 6.2 Spearline and Jessie Wilson's children on Tulagi: Andrea Gordon (born 1931) and James Michael (born 1928), with their 'red Indian' tent. 288

Plate 6.3 James Wilson on a garden bench at the family home in Tulagi. 289

Plate 6.4 Jessie Wilson and her daughter Andrea Gordon visiting Sydney. 289

Plate 6.5 Pop and Agnes Johnson on Tulagi in the 1930s 291

Plate 6.6 Agnes and Pop Johnson and their daughter Dorothy 292

Plate 6.7 The marriage of Jack Lotze to Dorothy Johnson, Tulagi, 1931. 293

Plate 6.8 Jack and Dorothy Johnson and an unknown woman 293

Plate 6.9 Frank Wickham, who married three local women and had six children 301

Plate 6.10 Fred Campbell in 1913 while he was Commandant of the Armed Constabulary, playing tennis at Auki, Malaita, with Mary Edge-Partington and Captain Hancock of HMS *Sealark*. . 302

Plate 6.11 Pop Johnson is in the centre of the photograph 312

Plate 7.1 The cooks at the squadron of the Legion of Frontiersmen's outing to Guadalcanal, 1914 317

Plate 7.2 The participants in the squadron of the Legion of Frontiersmen's outing, 1914. 317

Plate 7.3 The armed constabulary marching with drums and bugles . . 318

Plate 7.4 The Tulagi Harbour in 1938, looking towards the port and Chinatown 318

Plate 7.5 The Tulagi beachfront in 1939. 319

Plate 7.6 The third residency, completed in 1934, showing the armed constabulary guard house 320

Plate 7.7 Anglican mission house at Bungana Island, 1906. 323

Plate 7.8 The Anglican Melanesian Brothers when Charles Fox was a member, circa 1938. 323

Plate 7.9 The Anglican headquarters at Siota in the 1930s 324

Plate 7.10 The Anglican Christ the King Church, built on Tulagi in 1937 324

Plate 7.11 St Luke's Cathedral at Siota, dedicated in 1928 326

Plate 7.12 The altar of St Luke's Cathedral, Siota, when first built . . 326

Plate 7.13 The final ornate structure of the altar of St Luke's Cathedral, in the 1930s 326

Plate 7.14 Jack Barley and Stanley Annandale at a picnic in the Gela Group, 1910s. 338

Plate 7.15 Pop Johnson, his children and friends at a picnic on Tulagi 338

Plate 7.16 Jessie Wilson accompanied her husband on several surveying trips 340

Plate 7.17 Spearline Wilson and friends 341

Plate 7.18 James Basil Hicks, Agnes Johnson, Dorothy Lotze, Vic Sheridan and a friend. 344

Plate 7.19 High commissioner Sir Eyre Hutson visiting Tulagi in 1927 352

Plate 7.20 The new Anglican headquarters at Taroaniara, in the early 1940s. 354

Plate 7.21 The bishop's house at Taroaniara, in the early 1940s. 355

Plate 7.22 The seafront on Tulagi's inner side, in the 1930s 356

Plate 7.23 Samuel Alasa`a was involved in a court case and spent a short time in prison on Tulagi in the 1920s. 358

Plate 7.24 Shem Irofa`alu worked as a cook at the single officers' quarters on Tulagi 359

Plate 7.25 Silas Sitai from Santa Ana was a clerk in the office of the Resident Commissioner on Tulagi 360

Plate 7.26 Salana Ga`a (Maega`asia) from west Kwara`ae, Malaita, worked on Tulagi as a *haus boi* and an orderly for two resident commissioners 361

Plate 7.27 As a teenager, Jonathan Fifi`i from east Kwaio, Malaita, worked as a *haus boi* on Tulagi 362

Plate 8.1 A Japanese fishing boat at Tulagi, 1936 376

Plate 8.2 Japanese fishermen on Tulagi, 1936. 377

Plate 8.3 Martin Clemens and men from the BSIP Defence Force . . 378

Plate 8.4 Members of the Japanese garrison on Tulagi, 1942. 397

Plate 8.5 A camouflaged Japanese truck on Tulagi, August 1942 . . . 397

Plate 8.6 A Japanese 13 mm gun on Tulagi. 398

Plate 8.7 A Japanese plan of their flying boat facilities at Gavutu–Tanambogo 398

Plate 8.8 A Solomon Islander trading on Tulagi, 1940s 399

Plate 8.9 A devastated Gavutu Island and the causeway to Tanambogo Island, 1942 401

Plate 8.10 The causeway between Gavutu and Tanambogo islands, 1942 401

Plate 8.11 Smoke from the American bombing on Tulagi, 7 August 1942. 402

Plate 8.12 This photograph was taken after the Americans bombed Tulagi on 7 August 1942 402

Plate 8.13 Makambo Island being bombed, with Tanambogo Island burning in the background. The main Makambo wharf and the settlement area are visible. 403

Plate 8.14 The remains of Chinatown, with Makambo in the background, August 1942 405

Plate 8.15 Japanese and Korean prisoners-of-war on Tulagi, August 1942 405

Plate 8.16 An American machine-gun post on Tulagi. 406

Plate 8.17 An American cargo ship at Tulagi wharf, 1944. 407

Plate 8.18 Tulagi cricket ground turned into a tent town for the Americans 407

Plate 8.19 The US Navy Marine Corps Cemetery on Tulagi, on the edge of the former cricket ground. After the war, bodies were exhumed and returned to the United States. 408

Plate 8.20 The marines' shower on the beach, Tulagi, May 1943 . . . 408

Plate 8.21 American ships gathered at Tulagi in March 1945 on their way to the Battle of Okinawa 409

List of tables

Table 2.1 Indentured labour in Solomon Islands, 1913–40 131
Table 3.1 Deputy commissioner, resident commissioners
 and military governors, 1896–1948 141
Table 3.2 The Tulagi civil service establishment, 1925–26 150
Table 3.3 Tulagi Hospital admissions, 1914–21 184
Table 5.1 The Judicial Commissioner's living expenses, 1925 267

Acronyms and abbreviations

A/RC	Acting Resident Commissioner
ACOM	Anglican Church of Melanesia
ANU	The Australian National University
ANUA	The Australian National University Archives
AWA Ltd	Amalgamated Wireless (Australasia) Ltd
BM	British Museum
BP	Burns Philp and Company
BSIP	British Solomon Islands Protectorate
BSIP *AR*	British Solomon Islands Protectorate *Annual Reports*
BSIPNS	*British Solomon Islands Protectorate News Sheet*
CO	Colonial Office
CSR	Colonial Sugar Refining Company Limited
HC	Western Pacific High Commissioner
HMAS	His Majesty's Australian Ship
HMCS	His Majesty's Royal Colonial Ship
LNMTNG *AR*	League of Nations Mandated Territory of New Guinea *Annual Reports*
MAC	Minutes of the Advisory Council
NASI	National Archives of Solomon Islands
NBAC	Noel Butlin Archives Centre, The Australian National University
NSW	New South Wales
PIM	*Pacific Islands Monthly*
PIYB	*Pacific Islands Year Book*

PMB	Pacific Manuscripts Bureau
RAAF	Royal Australian Air Force
RC	Resident Commissioner
RNAS	Royal Navy Australia Station
SCL	*Southern Cross Log*
SS	steamship
SSEM	South Sea Evangelical Mission
UQFL	Fryer Library, University of Queensland
US	United States of America
WPHC	Western Pacific High Commission
WPHCA	Western Pacific High Commission Archives
WPHCG (S)	*Western Pacific High Commission Gazette (Supplement)*

A note on nomenclature

One difficult issue is how to spell Solomon Islands geographic and personal names, which over decades have been written in multiple ways. Glottal stops and extra guiding letters in words to indicate pronunciation—such as 'ng', 'ngg' and 'mb', which are single consonant sounds—are difficult to render. Europeans have trouble hearing glottal stops, particularly at the beginning of words, and Solomon Islanders seldom use them at all when they write words. Often, words have been spelt incorrectly and the wrong spellings then become so common they are regarded as normal, and spellings also change over decades. For instance, I have chosen to use Gela, not Ngela or Nggela, as this is how modern usage has evolved. Generally, to write 'ng', 'nd' or 'mb' at the beginning of words is simply to add an unnecessary letter. Even so, I am not always consistent and have on occasion bowed to contemporary and official usage. I have used Mboli as the name of the passage between Gela Pile and Gela Sule islands and Mbokonimbeti as the original name of Sandfly Island, as this is still the usual practice. Solomon Islanders are aware of these sounds and manage to pronounce words correctly, no matter how they are spelt. I have left personal names as I found them and likewise names on early maps.

When individuals were always known by nicknames (for instance, Pop Johnson, Spearline Wilson or Monty Masterman), I have used their Christian names for the first mention and then only their nicknames. Chinese names also present a problem as they are written in many ways. On the first occasion the name appears, I have placed a standard pinyin form in brackets after the version found in the sources unless they are identical with modern forms. In subsequent usage, I have continued to use the original form.

I have converted most units originally in the imperial measuring system to the metric system: 1 acre is 0.404 hectares, 1 mile is 1.609 kilometres, 1 foot is 30.5 centimetres and 1 gallon is 4.546 litres. Ton has been retained, as tonne (0.984207 of a ton) is not an exact equivalent. I have followed the convention of not placing a 'the' before 'Solomon Islands'. For stylistic reasons, on occasions I have also used 'Solomons' as the short form for Solomon Islands.

Acknowledgements

This book has been researched and written over more than a decade and is a companion to my *Making Mala: Malaita in Solomon Islands, 1870s–1930s*, published in 2017 by ANU Press. Both books cover virtually the same period. This book would not have been possible without the research presented in the digital *Solomon Islands Historical Encyclopaedia, 1893–1978*, first published in 2013. I am also working on a history of Honiara, which replaced Tulagi as the capital. They are all part of the same extensive research and writing project.

Many people have helped me along the way by answering my often naive questions, reading drafts or offering information, photographs and maps: David Akin, Frédéric Angleviel, Transform Aquorau, Helen Barrett, Cyril Belshaw, Judy Bennett, Hendry Billy, Terry M. Brown, Ben Burt, Peter Cahill, Christopher Chevalier, Alexandra Clemens, Peter Flahavin, Jonathan Friedlander, Graeme Golden, Geoffrey Gray, Martin Hadlow, Ian Hogbin, Johnson Honimae, Lyn Innes, Ross Johnston, Sir Peter and Lady Margaret Kenilorea, Sir Nathan Kere, Mei-Fen Kuo, Doreen Küper, David Lawrence, Brij Lal, Hadley Leung, Morris Low, Brian MacDonald-Milne, Steve Mullins, Doug Munro, Lot Page, Joan Presswell, Sir Henry Quan, Max Quanchi, Rhys Richards, Paul Roughan, John Smith, Ian Tedder, Paul Turnbull, Isobel Wallace, Peter Williams and Jeff Wilmott. My thanks to them all. I 'inherited' my colleague Ralph Shlomowitz's large collection of research materials on labour and health in the British Solomon Islands Protectorate (BSIP). I thank him for being so thorough so many years ago. Thanks are also due to the staff of the Solomon Islands National Archives and the Special Collections section of the Libraries and Learning Services, University of Auckland, which houses the Western Pacific Archives.

Several descendants of early European residents made family records and information available, which provided significant new sources on Tulagi: Suzanne Ellis, granddaughter of Frederick (Pop) and Agnes Johnson; Kate Broadhurst, granddaughter of Alexander Herbert (Spearline) and Jessie Wilson; Ian Elkington, grandson of Tom and May Elkington; and Justin Nielsen, great-great grandson of Lars Nielsen. I would also like to thank the staff of The Australian National University Archives, Ben Burt at the British Museum, Abraham Hauriasi of the Anglican Church of Melanesia and the US National Archives and Records Administration for access to images. Beatrice Yell and Tania Hilder, daughters of Captain Brett Hilder, gave permission for the use of the cover image, painted by their father in 1960. Burns Philp & Co., the owners of the painting, also gave permission for its use. Annika Korsgaard was generous with her Tulagi sources and photographs. Chi Kong Lai provided the standard pinyin form of Chinese names. Robert Cribb provided two of the maps and Vincent Verheyen has been a valued part of the project, responsible for much of the cartography. It has been a pleasure to work with Stewart Firth at the Pacific Editorial Board at The Australian National University and Emily Hazlewood and other staff at ANU Press.

I have translated key financial figures into modern-day currency equivalents using Thom Blake's online Australian historical monetary data conversion and current Solomon Islands dollar conversion rates. These modern equivalents have many variables and can be regarded as only approximate.

Clive Moore
The University of Queensland
August 2019

ACKNOWLEDGEMENTS

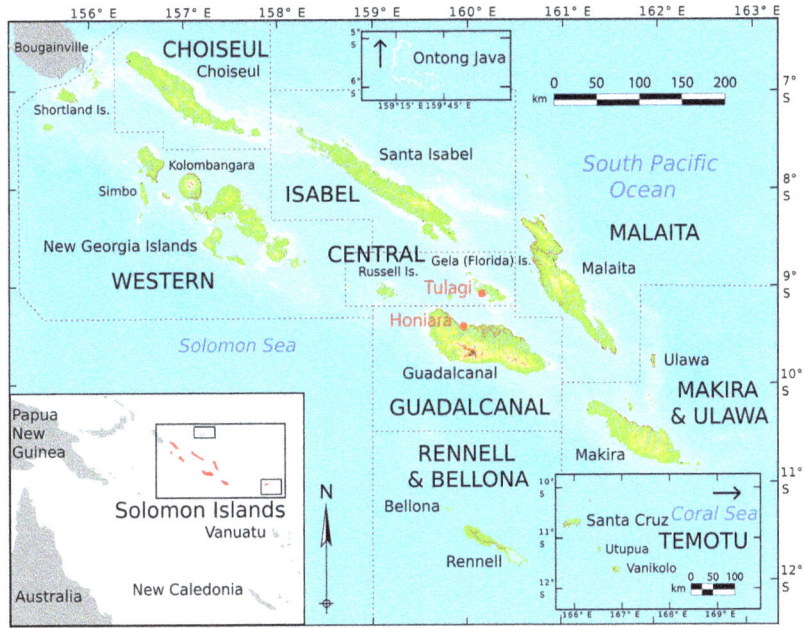

Map A.1 Modern Solomon Islands, showing Tulagi in Central Province and Honiara, the new capital, on Guadalcanal

Source: Cartography by Vincent Verheyen.

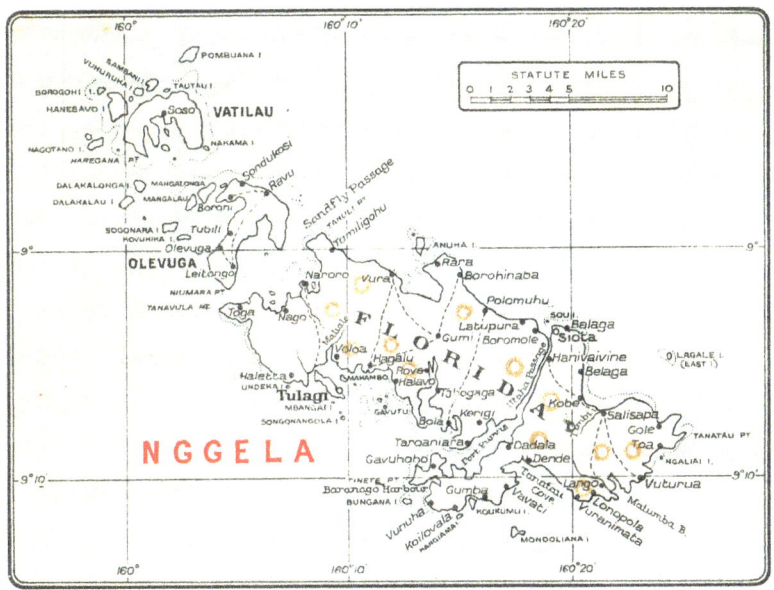

Map A.2 The Gela (Nggela or Florida) Group, 1930s

Source: H.E.C. Robinson Pty Ltd, Map of Solomon Islands, 1930s.

xxvii

TULAGI

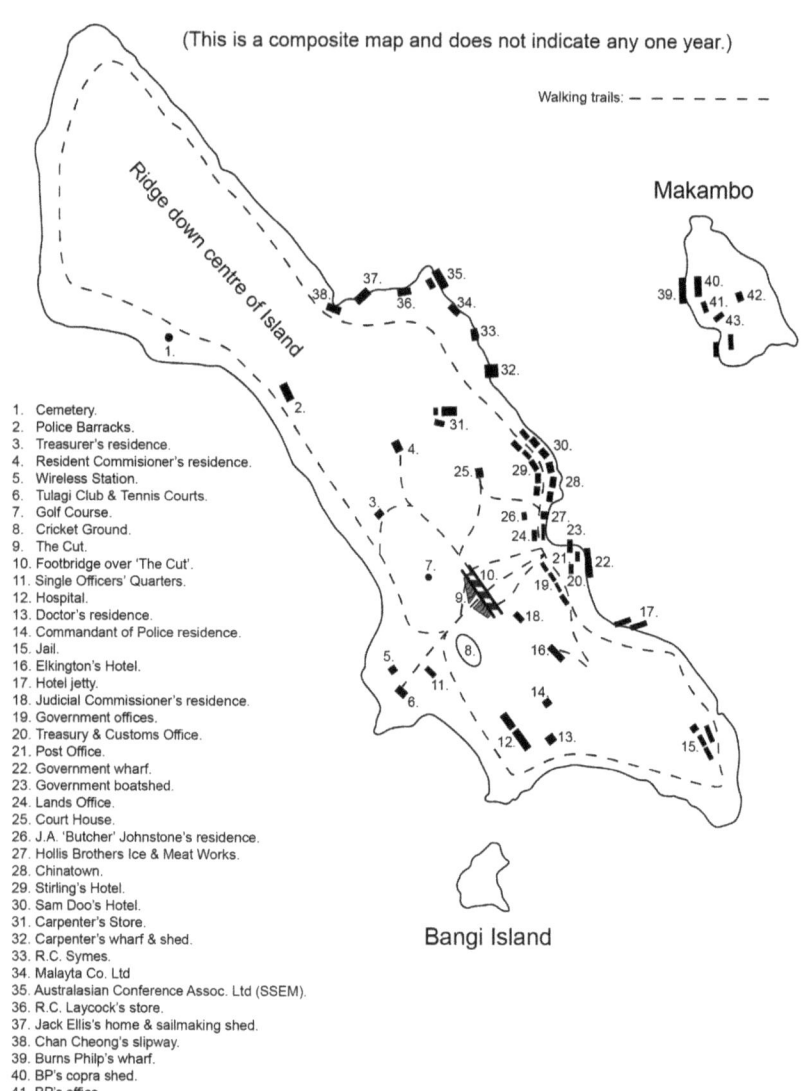

1. Cemetery.
2. Police Barracks.
3. Treasurer's residence.
4. Resident Commisioner's residence.
5. Wireless Station.
6. Tulagi Club & Tennis Courts.
7. Golf Course.
8. Cricket Ground.
9. The Cut.
10. Footbridge over 'The Cut'.
11. Single Officers' Quarters.
12. Hospital.
13. Doctor's residence.
14. Commandant of Police residence.
15. Jail.
16. Elkington's Hotel.
17. Hotel jetty.
18. Judicial Commissioner's residence.
19. Government offices.
20. Treasury & Customs Office.
21. Post Office.
22. Government wharf.
23. Government boatshed.
24. Lands Office.
25. Court House.
26. J.A. 'Butcher' Johnstone's residence.
27. Hollis Brothers Ice & Meat Works.
28. Chinatown.
29. Stirling's Hotel.
30. Sam Doo's Hotel.
31. Carpenter's Store.
32. Carpenter's wharf & shed.
33. R.C. Symes.
34. Malayta Co. Ltd
35. Australasian Conference Assoc. Ltd (SSEM).
36. R.C. Laycock's store.
37. Jack Ellis's home & sailmaking shed.
38. Chan Cheong's slipway.
39. Burns Philp's wharf.
40. BP's copra shed.
41. BP's office.
42. BP's manager's house.
43. BP's bachelor quarters.

Map A.3 Settlement on Tulagi Island in the 1930s

Source: Based on Graeme Golden's map (Golden 1993), with new cartography by Vincent Verheyen.

Introduction

Tulagi Island is one of more than 900 islands and atolls in the modern Solomon Islands nation—a beautiful tropical archipelago stretching over 1,400 kilometres in the eastern Coral Sea off north-eastern Australia, neighboured by Papua New Guinea, Nauru, Tuvalu, Vanuatu and Fiji. The major islands in the nation form a double chain that begins south of Buka and Bougainville (an autonomous region of Papua New Guinea) and converges again at Makira (San Cristobal). The largest islands—Choiseul, Isabel, Guadalcanal, Malaita and Makira—vary from 150 to 190 kilometres in length and 20 to 50 kilometres in width. The island of New Georgia is a smaller, but still substantial, part of an island group of the same name. On Guadalcanal, Mount Popomaneseu reaches 2,355 metres—higher than any of Australia's mountains. To the south, separated by 400 kilometres of ocean, the Santa Cruz Group, Reef Islands, Vanikolo, Tikopia and other more scattered islands and atolls are also part of the modern nation. The islands have been inhabited for many thousands of years. The indigenous cultures of Solomon Islands are all quite closely related and similar, although remarkably diverse linguistically. The people participated in and did not separate themselves from their natural environment and spirit world. Then, in 1893, they became a British protectorate, centred on Tulagi.

Within the Gela Group, Tulagi nestles close to the larger Gela Sule. This small group of islands, now within Central Islands Province, is typical of many Solomon Islands, replete with rugged mountainous interiors, crystal-clear streams, sandy beaches, mangroves and fringing reefs. Tulagi is approximately 320 hectares in size, 5 kilometres long and 0.8 kilometres wide. It was originally covered by rainforest. Aligned north-west to south-east, the island has a steep stony central ridge extending its full length, varying in height up to 120 metres and flattened at each end. A coastal rim allows easy access to all areas. The island receives rainfall of 2,230 to 3,800 millimetres per year and there are natural springs and a safe, commodious inner harbour. A walk around the island takes about two hours.

Plate I.1 Tulagi viewed from the harbour, 1972
Source: Brian Taylor Collection.

Plate I.2 Tulagi, looking into the harbour from the old prison area, 2013
Source: Annika Korsgaard Collection.

INTRODUCTION

Plate I.3 Tulagi Harbour, 2013
Source: Annika Korsgaard Collection.

Plate I.4 Tulagi docks, 2007
Source: Clive Moore Collection.

Tulagi was the capital of the British Solomon Islands Protectorate (BSIP) from 1897 until 1942. It was a town, albeit small, as well as an enclave of islands. Tulagi, Gavutu and Makambo islands were at the enclave's core, with Bungana a little further away, housing an Anglican school and the lighthouse that guided ships to the port. Two new sites were added in the early 1940s: the Anglican headquarters was shifted from Siota to Taroaniara, across the harbour on Gela Sule, and Tanambogo was joined to Gavutu as part of a seaplane base. During World War II, the Tulagi enclave was heavily bombed by the Japanese and the Americans, erasing 45 years of colonial history.

Once the decision was made in 1945 not to rebuild Tulagi and to move the administrative headquarters to Guadalcanal, to what became Honiara, Tulagi was no longer central to Solomon Islands. A great deal is missing from the history of the nation without an understanding of the Tulagi enclave. Most Solomon Islanders are aware of where Tulagi is and that it was once the capital, but they know nothing more. Before the war, Tulagi was part of the lives of tens of thousands of Solomon Islanders, particularly men and youths who passed through on indentured or casual labour contracts. It was the only town most of them knew and the focus of a new system of government they did not understand, which claimed control over them. It was a European and a Chinese town imposed on to the indigenous communities. Although the number of Solomon Islanders in the Tulagi enclave was as large as that of the expatriates, they were never able to make it their own in the way they have in recent times with Honiara, Gizo, Auki or Noro. Neither Tulagi nor Honiara has a history written about it and this book aims to restore old Tulagi to modern Solomon Islands.

INTRODUCTION

Plate I.5 Tulagi market on the harbour beach front, 2007
Source: Clive Moore Collection.

Plate I.6 A house built over the water at Tulagi, 2013
Source: Annika Korsgaard Collection.

When Richard Kane, the third Resident Commissioner, arrived in 1921, he held a function at the residency that was attended by 78 Europeans. The *Planters' Gazette* proudly announced that this was 'perhaps the largest assembly of white people ever congregated together in the Solomons'.[1] About 50 were from the enclave, where they lived alongside a Chinese population of around the same number. In its last days just before the Pacific War, the enclave's permanent population was around 600—300 foreigners, one-third of European origin and most of the remainder Chinese; and 300 Solomon Islander residents—made up of police, hospital staff and patients, prisoners, clergy, clerks, labourers and servants. Although eclipsed by Suva, Tulagi enclave was the second-largest urban settlement under Western Pacific High Commission (WPHC) jurisdiction before the Pacific War. Nevertheless, compared with Honolulu—the largest Pacific Island city, which had a population of almost 15,000 in the 1870s, including several hundred foreigners, and grew to become a major city of almost 180,000 by 1940—the Tulagi enclave was tiny.[2]

---

1   *Planters' Gazette*, 3 August 1921, 4.
2   Daws 1967; Daws 2006; Daws and Hymer 2008; Johnson and Turnbull 1991.

INTRODUCTION

Plate I.7 The view down the stairs from the Resident Commissioner's residency in the 1910s

The hospital, built in 1913, is on the right near the path and Gavutu Island can be seen in the background.

Source: British Museum, George Rose's photographs in the Thomas Edge-Partington Photographic Collection.

Plate I.8 The view from the top of the stairs that once led to the Resident Commissioner's home, 2013. The outline of the original path is still evident
Source: Annika Korsgaard Collection.

Of the neighbouring urban centres, only the Ocean (Banaba) Island headquarters settlement in the Gilbert and Ellice Islands Crown colony and Port Vila in the New Hebrides Condominium were smaller. The argument presented in this book is that Tulagi's size and the smallness of its overall foreign population have a lot to do with the way in which colonial legacies played out. Several Melanesian urban centres operated during the same years as Tulagi: Thursday Island, Port Moresby, Samarai, Rabaul, Levuka, Suva and Nouméa. The equivalent north-east Australia urban centre was 350-hectare Thursday Island just off Cape York, which was Queensland's administrative base in Torres Strait and which began in the 1870s, replacing moribund Somerset on Cape York. In the late 1890s and early 1900s, 1,500 people lived on Thursday Island, and during the first decades of the twentieth century, the island became a substantial urban base with a population several times that of the Tulagi enclave.[3] Similar to Tulagi, the settlement spilled over on to neighbouring islands and, as

---

3   Thursday Island's population was 1,515 in 1903, 1,079 in 1922 and 1,047 in 1934. Information from Steve Mullins, 9 July 2018, and Ian Townsend, 19 September 2018. See also Singe 1979; Mullins 1995.

a pearling port, it had a substantial European, Japanese, Malay, Filipino and Singhalese (Sri Lankan) population, along with Torres Strait Islanders and other Pacific Islanders. As many people lived on the pearling luggers and schooners anchored near Thursday Island as lived on the island itself. There have been several histories of Torres Strait and its people, but none concentrates on Thursday Island. There was also a string of Queensland coastal towns on the Coral Sea, within easy distance of Tulagi.

Neighbouring Australian Papua had two urban centres during the Tulagi years. Port Moresby included a substantial local Motu-Koita population within its boundaries, and late nineteenth-century Chinese, Malay and Filipino traders had married into the nearby coastal Papuan community.[4] There were very few urban Asian settlers during the first half of the twentieth century because they had been blocked by the White Australia Policy. When World War I began, Port Moresby had a foreign population of 453 Europeans. In 1921, it was home to 577 Europeans, 190 of them female; then during the 1930s the town shrank back to just over 300 Europeans.[5] In 1939, legend has it that there were only three Chinese in Papua—all in Port Moresby and all involved in tailoring and a laundry. Australian Papua's second town was Samarai on Dinner Island, just off the mainland in China Strait in the east, which was established in the 1880s. Samarai covered 25 hectares and, with its white crushed-coral paths and a profusion of flowering shrubs, it physically resembled Tulagi, although no Asians lived there. Samarai was also an enclave, with a London Missionary Society mission on adjacent Kwato Island (which seceded in 1917 under its founder Charles Abel)[6] and the town's cemetery on the mainland. Its port trade was three times the size of Port Moresby's, and there were around 100 European residents in 1907 and 293 in 1919.[7] Port Moresby has attracted the attention of historians, while Samarai has been almost ignored.

German New Guinea was the northern neighbour of the BSIP. Captured by Australia in 1914, it became a League of Nations mandated territory administered by Australia.[8] Rabaul (originally Simpsonhafen), the capital, on New Britain's Gazelle Peninsula, was a substantial Pacific settlement. In the 1920s, Rabaul had a European population of around 300, who

---

4   Dutton 1985, 149–94.
5   Oram 1976, 13, 38; Stuart 1970.
6   Wetherell 1996.
7   Oram 1972, 1028–29; Quanchi 2006.
8   Mackenzie 1987.

were outnumbered by the Chinese residents. Around 200 indigenous police and 300 contract labourers also lived in barracks there. Rabaul had roads, cars and trucks, a newspaper, schools, a movie theatre, a race track and a prosperous large Chinatown and market. The town was beautiful, its rich volcanic soil supporting prolific gardens, with the whiff of sulphur from the surrounding volcanoes always in the air. There were grand mansions around the bay in the late German period, belonging in particular to leading traders and plantation owners.[9] The total European population of Kokopo and Rabaul—the two main urban centres on the Gazelle Peninsula—was around 2,000. The Germans had encouraged Chinese migration and, after 1921, as a mandated territory, the strictures of Australia's White Australia Policy did not apply. Rabaul's Chinese population increased from 1,000 in 1914 to 1,300 in the 1920s and to 2,000 by 1940.[10] Although the town has attracted the attention of historians because of its volcanic activity, its significance in two world wars and its Chinese community, there is only one historical overview.[11]

The most significant urban centre in the south-west Pacific was Suva. Between 1877 and 1952, Fiji was the administrative centre of the British Pacific and, like Solomon Islands, Fiji had two capitals. In the 1870s, Fiji already had a substantial settler society of 3,000 Europeans. The small multiracial beachside community of Levuka became the main town. From meagre beginnings in the 1820s and 1830s, Levuka in the 1840s had a population of about 50 foreigners. The town began to flourish during a cotton boom in the 1860s and reached a population of 1,250 in 1869, peaking at 2,670 in 1872, and then declining to 500 by 1886.[12] Suva replaced Levuka as the capital in 1882, becoming a sizeable town. It was described by a visitor in the 1910s as 'a large English town, with two banks, several churches, dental surgeons, a large gaol, auctioneers, bookmakers, two newspapers, and all the other apparatuses of civilization'.[13] There were substantial government buildings and the magnificent Grand Pacific Hotel, built in 1914—equalled in the region

---

9   Epstein 1969, 27; Robson 1965; Hernsheim 1983; Neumann 1992.
10   League of Nations Mandated Territory of New Guinea *Annual Reports* [hereinafter LNMTNG AR], 1925; 1935; 1940. These statistics were provided by Peter Cahill, Brisbane, 24 January 2016. See also Johnson and Threlfall 1985, 68, 79; Cahill 2012, 113; Inglis 1972.
11   Threlfall 2012; Stone 1994; Aplin 1980; Neumann 1996; Johnson and Threlfall 1985; Cahill 2012; Townsend 2017.
12   Ralston 2014, 103, 216; Young 1966, 385; Young 1984; Young 1988; Quanchi 1977; Anonymous (by people of Levuka) 2001.
13   Quoted in Scarr 1984, 79.

only by the Queen's Hotel in Townsville in north Queensland. Fiji in the 1920s and 1930s had an indigenous population of around 90,000, with Indo-Fijians (originally labour immigrants) numbering only a few thousand less than the Fijians. Suva in 1921 had a population of 13,982, with 6,449 living in the central town and 6,342 in the suburbs. There were 1,753 Europeans in Suva, 1,436 of whom lived in the central town.[14] The Fiji European and part-European community numbered around 8,000 in the 1930s, along with 1,700 Chinese, who were concentrated in Levuka and Suva, with outposts in rural areas. They sold basic necessities from small stores and often married into the indigenous community.[15] After indenture ended in 1920, the Indian labourers became farmers on leased land and shopkeepers. Most were still engaged in agricultural work, but rather than a Chinatown or Indian quarter, Suva developed regional multiracial trading areas. The shops provided general merchant services, plus tailoring, laundering, boot-making, jewellery manufacture and outreach through hawking.[16] Government policy kept the Indians separate from the Fijians. Despite its importance, Suva has not been the subject of a single historical study on its growth.

The first foreigner to settle on nearby New Caledonia was a British trader in 1851. The French were anxious to gain Pacific territory and settled Port-du-France in 1854—renamed Nouméa in 1866—after which a small number of free settlers arrived. However, the French used New Caledonia as a penal colony from the 1860s to the 1890s—much to the disgust of the east coast Australian colonialists, who had managed to end the importation of British convicts there. Just over 30,000 male and female convicts were sent to New Caledonia. Nouméa grew slowly, from a population of 4,000 in 1890 and 8,700 in 1911 to 11,000 in 1936. This included French ex-convicts and free settlers, Metis (mixed race), Asian workers and Kanaks, whose overall number declined in the 1920s.[17]

14 Statistics provided by Brij Lal, 14 July 2018.
15 Lal 1992, 63–65. See also Lal 2016.
16 Scarr 1984, 35; Lal 1992, 76.
17 There are histories of many aspects of Nouméa, although there is no overriding history of the city, which now has a population of 100,000. I have been unable to obtain any early statistics. Amiot and Terrier 2007; Association Salomon 2008; Cauville et al. 2006; Daly 2002; Barbançon et al. 2004; Delathière 2000; Delathière 2004; Kakau 1998; Moyen 2004; Patarin 1997; Rolland 2002. Frédéric Angleviel and Max Quanchi helped provide the statistics.

Tulagi was the poor cousin, with only basic services available, no newspaper and too few students to warrant a primary school. This study of Tulagi provides an understanding of the origins of modern Solomon Islands. It also enables a close analysis of race, sex and class, and the process of British colonisation and government in the late nineteenth and early twentieth centuries. Because of the destruction caused by the Pacific War, researching Tulagi is a historical detective story pieced together from fragments. The hardest thing to retrieve in writing this book has been an understanding of how and why Solomon Islanders reacted to what they saw and experienced at Tulagi. I hope that, in a small way, I have helped to elucidate their side of the story, while also advancing study of British imperialism in the Pacific.

Tulagi today

Today, Tulagi is a ghost of its former self. While it is clearly an interesting island—and it remains the urban centre for a province—very little of the protectorate's first capital is still visible, except for the cutting through the central ridge made in 1918, remnants of the police and prison compounds (including cells) and the concrete foundations of what were once large buildings. Concrete steps that once led up to the front of the Resident Commissioner's house now ascend to empty space. The beautifully tended tropical gardens and the white coral paths have long gone.

Plate I.9 The first section of the residency stairs, 2013
Source: Annika Korsgaard Collection.

Plate I.10 One of the many sets of concrete steps on Tulagi that once formed the entrances to government buildings, 2013

Source: Annika Korsgaard Collection.

Plate I.11 An attempt at heritage identification on Tulagi. A Ministry of Provincial Government and Institutional Strengthening sign outside the old prison, 2013

Source: Annika Korsgaard Collection.

Plate I.12 The remains of the prison cells on Tulagi, 2007
Source: Clive Moore Collection.

After the war, there were suggestions that a new capital should be established on Gela Sule, which would have utilised the commodious harbour. However, in October 1945, the BSIP Advisory Council agreed to shift the capital to a site centred on Point Cruz and the Mataniko River on Guadalcanal, which was already in use as an American military base and, since 1943, had also housed the remnant protectorate government. The advantages of inheriting a fully built town next to airfields and plains suitable for agriculture were too large to ignore. Despite initial reticence from the 'old hands', by mid-1949, Tulagi was almost deserted.[18] Even the post office closed that year, when the central district headquarters moved to Honiara. Tulagi went into decline, although its wartime docks and slipways remained in use until new port facilities were established in Honiara in the 1950s and 1960s. Tulagi was sustained by the Solomon Taiyo Limited fish cannery, from the early 1970s until the 1980s, followed by National Fisheries Development Limited.

---

18   *Pacific Islands Monthly* [hereinafter *PIM*], January 1948, May 1949; Douglas 2004, 41.

Plate I.13 The Solomon Tayo Ltd fish cannery on Tulagi in the 1970s
Source: Clive Moore Collection.

Plate I.14 Inside the Solomon Tayo Ltd fish cannery on Tulagi in the 1970s
Source: Clive Moore Collection.

Today, it is a provincial headquarters town and a pleasant but sleepy diving destination with a plentiful supply of World War II wrecks to lure tourists and Honiara's expatriates on weekends. There are a couple of small hotels, dive centres and eco-lodges and a marketplace on the beach, administrative buildings, a Telekom building, McMahon Community High School, a hospital and a few scattered houses. An Anglican presence remains, in the form of the Mothers' Union and Women's Resources Centre and the Christ the King Cathedral and house. The ruins of the fish cannery remain on the sheltered inner coast. During the 2010s, the Sasape area was revitalised with a government slipway—now a joint venture between the Solomon Islands National Provident Fund and Silent World Shipping and Logistics Limited, an Australian company. Clustered at the south-eastern tip of the island is a public housing precinct for government workers. Gavutu and Makambo islands—the old commercial headquarters for Levers Pacific Plantations Limited (known as Levers)[19] and Burns Philp and Company (BP)—are close by across the harbour. Makambo carries little evidence of its commercial past and when I visited Gavutu it was deserted except for a couple of caretakers. Gavutu was renamed Dolphin Island in the 1990s and 2000s, during an attempt to farm and export dolphins to theme parks around the world. There is a derelict house high on a hill and empty dolphin-holding ponds—witness to this disastrous enterprise. Only two remnants of Levers' long tenancy remain. One is the company's strongroom, which in 2007 was in use as a rather odd and airless residence. The other is the slowly subsiding but still grand concrete wharf. Most of the wartime causeway to Tanambogo is still there.

---

19 The original company was Levers Pacific Plantations Limited (1902, United Kingdom), which became Levers Pacific Plantations Proprietary Limited (1928, Australia). The usual short form is Levers or Lever Brothers.

Plate I.15 Vanita Motel, Tulagi, 2007
Source: Clive Moore Collection.

Plate I.16 Walking towards the cutting through the central ridge, past the Telekom building, Tulagi, 2007
Source: Clive Moore Collection.

Plate I.17 The author at the cutting through the ridge, Tulagi, 2007
Source: Clive Moore Collection.

Plate I.18 Christ the King Cathedral, Anglican Diocese of Central Solomons, Tulagi, 2007
Source: Clive Moore Collection.

Plate I.19 The Anglican Mothers' Union building, Tulagi, 2007
Source: Clive Moore Collection.

Plate I.20 The sign for the Seventh-day Adventist Church on Tulagi, showing steps cut into the rock, 2013
Source: Annika Korsgaard Collection.

Honiara, which replaced Tulagi as the capital, has been a constant presence in my life for over 40 years, and although Tulagi is close by, these days it is off the normal shipping routes. Twice I have visited Savo Island, Tulagi's neighbour—once in my youth, climbing up almost boiling streams into the smouldering sulphurous crater of the volcano. I have taken many voyages to Malaita, passing through Mboli Passage in the Gela Group, close to Tulagi. My only visit to Tulagi was for a few days in 2007. To get there I travelled on a small coastal trading vessel piled high with passengers and cargo. To return to Honiara, I hitched a ride with a speedboat full of divers who had spent the weekend exploring various wartime wrecks. It was enough to make me curious about Tulagi's past. There was no local knowledge of the fascinating history of the Tulagi enclave. There was no historical literature available on Tulagi, not even a pamphlet for the tourists and divers who venture there. I left disappointed. However, the trip whetted my appetite to try to find out more about the early settlement. Since then, there appears to be a new interest emerging to understand the history of Tulagi and there has been talk of rebuilding the residency as a tourist destination.

Plate I.21 The remains of the strongroom at Levers Pacific Plantations Ltd headquarters on Gavutu, being used as a house, 2007
Source: Clive Moore Collection.

Plate I.22 The remains of the Levers Pacific Plantations Ltd wharf at Gavutu, 2007
Source: Clive Moore Collection.

Plate I.23 One of the Japanese tunnels on Tulagi, constructed during their occupation of the island in 1942, photographed in 2013
Source: Annika Korsgaard Collection.

Tulagi may yet rise again as a port and transport hub. There are proposals from the Central Islands Provincial Government for it to become a transhipping port for international cargo liners distributing cargo to the smaller Pacific countries, such as Tuvalu, Kiribati and other nations in Micronesia.[20] The characteristic that made Tulagi great for half a century—its sheltered extensive harbour—may once more become an asset to the nation and neighbouring countries. As well, during the 2010s, successive national governments have announced a desire to promote Solomon Islands as a tourist destination. Let us hope Tulagi features in this new policy, as the former capital is an important part of Pacific and local history. Tulagi is a short trip from Honiara and deserves to be visited more regularly. My hope is that, as Solomon Islands grows as a tourist destination, Tulagi, which was on the early Pacific tourist and shipping routes from the 1900s, will regain its rightful place as a beautiful and historical Pacific port and town.

Tulagi: Pacific Outpost of British Empire has several aims. It is a study of the British Empire in the Pacific, but it is also a local urban history that seeks to understand what colonial life was like in the island enclave. The book is also a contribution to heritage studies and the national estate in terms of the historical, physical and built environment and social fabric of Solomon Islands. I have tried to evoke place and time and to understand how Tulagi functioned as a community, including its foibles and eccentricities. Chapter 1 situates Tulagi within British imperialism in the Pacific, along with the prior European trading and missionary bases in the Gela Group, and includes a sketch of the background of Charles Woodford, the first Resident Commissioner. Because Tulagi was a British protectorate, we need to understand the legal framework and the strengths and limitations of being largely a public service town with trading companies and a small Chinatown tacked on. Chapter 2 concentrates on the early days of Tulagi—roughly from 1897 to 1915, the year Woodford retired. Chapter 3 covers the 1920s—Tulagi's middle years—concentrating on the establishment of government departments and an examination of the administrative staff and their duties. Chapter 4 stays with the 1920s, dealing with other aspects of the Tulagi enclave as it developed into a port and trading complex involving major Australian, British, Fijian-based and Chinese merchant houses. The chapter looks at social institutions and extends the discussion of Chinatown begun in

---

20   *Solomon Star*, 9 June 2015.

Chapter 2. It also covers the Kwaio attack on Malaita's District Officer in 1927 and the subsequent government-sponsored retribution. The debacle that followed was Tulagi's most critical emergency before the Pacific War.

Chapters 5 and 6 detail the domestic and social scenes, covering the lives of expatriate women within the Tulagi enclave. The chapters explore what it was like to run a household and to live in the Tulagi enclave. The 1920s and 1930s produced discriminatory legislation, which raises questions about the relationships between white women and indigenous men in Pacific colonies, moral panic and other power relationships. Earlier historians of Fiji and Papua New Guinea have argued that white women formed fundamentally different relationships with the indigenous people than did white men. European women lived on Tulagi over many decades. Some had independent lives, although the majority were there because of their husbands' positions. Hitherto unknown similarities with the social scenes in Port Moresby, Rabaul and Suva have been uncovered. Chapter 7 concentrates on assessing the final years—the flourishing settlement of the 1930s, which was cut short by war in 1942. This chapter brings together many strands that surface in the preceding chapters and fits Tulagi into the wider picture of the colonial Pacific and British imperialism. Chapter 8 examines the British defences against the Japanese, the evacuation and the destruction of the capital of the protectorate. European, Chinese and Solomon Islander residents, and visitors, are interwoven throughout. Tulagi's history since 1942 is not covered, except in the photographs within this introduction.

The final stages of writing this book came after my retirement from decades of teaching and research in universities. I am experiencing a slowly developing sense of liberation. My own voyage away from academic life caused me to reassess the style of the book. It is full of characters and eccentricity. Alongside the book's more serious moments, it can also in part be read as a ripping yarn. Although I have provided a web of references, in a quest for readability, I have kept academic debates out of the text. They will not be relevant to most readers, although those who wish to mine the reference notes and bibliography can do so easily.

Plate I.24 Fishing boats anchored in Tulagi Harbour, 2007
Source: Clive Moore Collection.

The illustrations will also help Solomon Islanders, visitors and others interested in Solomon Islands and Pacific and colonial history to understand the early centrality of Tulagi to the history of the nation. This book is an attempt to restore Tulagi to the people of Solomon Islands. My apologies for any misinterpretations and imperfections.

1

Protecting Solomon Islanders

> When I first visited the Solomons in 1886, to make zoological collections, there were only about two white men living ashore. Three small trading schooners from 100 to 200 tons each made voyages from Sydney, the round voyage out & home occupying from 5 to 9 months, according as they filled up for copra. During my first visits between 1886 & 1889 was sixteen months without letters from England, as nobody seemed to know how letters should be addressed and arrived back to me sent via Fiji.
>
> — Charles Woodford, 1919[1]

Before the protectorate was proclaimed, the people of Solomon Islands lived in hundreds of small kinship-based groups with no single overarching authority. Only the chiefs on the small Polynesian Outliers could be said to have been autonomous local leaders whose hereditary status and power the British might have recognised. Social units were divided into villages and hamlets. Creating a series of urban centres, albeit small, and choosing one as the capital were decisive British actions in keeping with Western traditions. This chapter provides background on the establishment of the British protectorate over these diverse peoples and explains why Tulagi was chosen as the capital. The chapter surveys aspects of the preexisting European presence—the Anglican Melanesian Mission, the various foreign trading ventures and the participation by Gela people in the movement of labour to overseas colonies—all of which helped make Tulagi a sensible

---

1   Pacific Manuscripts Bureau [hereinafter PMB], Woodford Papers and Photographs, 1021, H. Monckton and E.P. Monckton, C.M. Woodford, and F.M. Woodford, Correspondence, British Solomon Islands, 1909–28, C.M. Woodford to R.P. Brown Johnson, 27 March 1919.

choice. Context is also provided on the way British colonialism evolved in the Western Pacific. Choosing a protectorate as the legal form of British territory in the islands shaped the way colonialism developed right through to independence in 1978. The chapter also introduces Charles Woodford, the man responsible for selecting Tulagi as the capital and for running the administration until 1915.

Four centuries earlier, in 1568, Spanish explorer Álvaro de Mendaña y Neira named the main island of the Gela Group Isla de Flores (Island of Flowers) and recorded that the islands were thickly populated.[2] The name 'Florida' remains in occasional use and is often still found on maps. There are two passages through the group. Mboli Passage divides the two largest islands, Gela Sule and Gela Pile. The third main island is Mbokonimbeti or Sandfly Island, which is separated from Gela Sule by Sandfly Passage.[3] The smaller Mangalonga, Vitilau (Buena Vista), Hanesavo and Kombuana islands are to the north-west. Tulagi, Gavutu and Makambo—the three islands that made up the core of the Tulagi enclave—nestle close to Gela Sule, and there are also many other smaller islets. The islands have mountainous spines and ridges and many areas of bare plains covered with coarse grass, which was burnt regularly to enable forest clearance— more like similar areas of Guadalcanal's dry north coast than the heavily forested and wetter Isabel or Malaita.[4]

Tulagi was the capital of the BSIP between 1897 and 1942. In 1942, the Japanese southern push in World War II (also known as the Pacific War) overran the northern and central islands of the archipelago. The British retreated and, after a short Japanese interregnum, the Allies—primarily the United States—gained control of Tulagi. Because the Pacific War destroyed the infrastructure of the Tulagi enclave, the WPHC had to make decisions about the site of the postwar capital. At the end of the war, the WPHC decided to develop a new capital on Guadalcanal. There were three reasons for the choice. First, Tulagi was typical of other small Pacific towns such as Levuka and Samarai, which began in the nineteenth century when transport was by ship. They were located on narrow strips of coastal land or small islands, which later proved unsuitable for expansion into modern cities, which required space for urban development and

---

2   Jack-Hinton 1969, 51; Amherst and Thomson 2010, 146.
3   Fox 1955, 3.
4   Roe 1993, 17.

airfields. These old Pacific towns became anachronisms—colonial backwaters from another era. The second reason related to the new American facilities available on Guadalcanal, which stretched along the northern coast from Point Cruz east to airfields constructed on Levers' Kukum estate. The American infrastructure—five airfields and a large military base—made the choice of Honiara logical. Third, Honiara abuts Guadalcanal Plains, the largest area of flat land in the nation and one of the largest areas of well-watered land suitable for agriculture in any Pacific island country. The move to Honiara was inevitable and, as a result, Tulagi forever lost its centrality as the main government and commercial base for Solomon Islands.

Plate 1.1 A hand-coloured lantern slide of the Gela Group, probably from a 1906 photograph

Source: British Museum (BM), Melanesian Mission Collection.

TULAGI

Plate 1.2 View from the end of Sandfly Passage, looking out to Guadalcanal, 1973
Source: Brian Taylor Collection.

Plate 1.3 A panoramic view from Port Purvis showing Gavutu and Tulagi islands in the distance, 1906
Source: National Archives of Solomon Islands (NASI), Anglican Church of Melanesia (ACOM) Collection, J.W. Beattie Collection.

Tulagi and the Gela Group

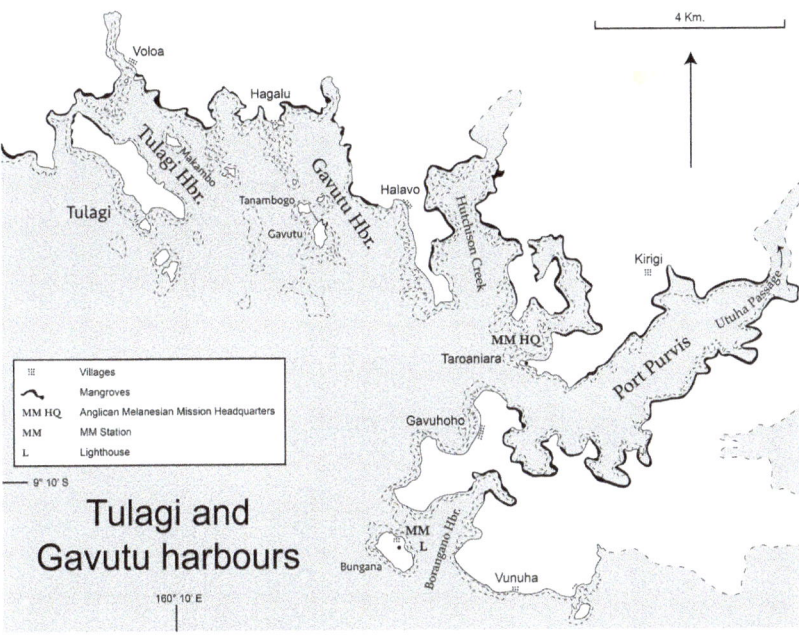

Map 1.1 The Tulagi enclave in the early 1940s, based around Tulagi and Gavutu harbours off Gela Sule

Between Gela Sule and Gela Pile, Port Purvis and Utuha (also Utaha) or Mboli Passage led through to Siota, the early headquarters of the Anglican Melanesian Mission. Tulagi, Gavutu and Makambo formed the core area, with an Anglican base and, from 1911, a school on Bungana Island, plus a lighthouse. In the early 1940s, Taroaniara on Gela Sule became the new Anglican headquarters, with an interregnum during the Japanese invasion in 1942, then continuing until 1945. In 1941, Tanambogo Island was joined to Gavutu as part of a seaplane base.

Source: Cartography by Vincent Verheyen.

Charles Woodford had multiple motivations in 1896 when he chose Tulagi as the WPHC headquarters for the BSIP. European port communities in the Pacific Islands often owed their origins to traders and missionaries, with the government bases added later.[5] The situation in the Gela Group was similar, as the trading station on neighbouring Gavutu Island preceded the settlement on Tulagi and Christianity was well established in the group, where missionary 'occupation' dated back

---

5   Ralston 2014.

to the 1860s. These neighbouring trading and missionary bases made establishing Tulagi much easier, as did the participation of Gela men in the external labour trade, which, after a rough beginning in the early 1870s, also assisted by exposing the Gela people to labour away from home and its recompense in the form of 'trade goods'—the products of European technology. The Tulagi enclave became the centre of commercial activity in the protectorate and Tulagi Island became the centre for the administration of all laws and regulations, licences, labour recruiting, land acquisition and policing. Thousands of labourers were signed on there or passed through when they ended their contracts. Tulagi became the first official port of entry in the protectorate, which forced overseas shipping to make the island their initial port of call. The laws and regulations all emanated from Tulagi and, apart from the district officers, all the protectorate government's staff lived there. The island became the centre of an important port complex for the Melanesian islands. However, Tulagi was always an extension of the WPHC, which had its headquarters in Suva, Fiji.

The Gela language has three dialect variations and has its origins in Austronesian—the language family widely dispersed throughout maritime South-East Asia, Madagascar and the islands of the Pacific Ocean, comprising about one-fifth of the world's languages. Austronesian speakers arrived in Solomon Islands several thousand years ago. Bughotu, an Austronesian language from Isabel Island, was also spoken in the small islands around Buena Vista to the north-west. The Gela Group is positioned geographically between Isabel, the Russells, Malaita, Guadalcanal and Savo. Its people have longstanding language, kinship, trade and raiding relationships with these surrounding islands. The Gela language is understood and spoken on Savo and in Russell Islands, where the main languages are of earlier (non-Austronesian) origin. It is also understood on the southern coast of Isabel and along the northern coast of Guadalcanal, which has strong kinship links with the Gela people. Central-west Malaita also has a complex relationship with residents of the Gela Group. The inhabitants of the artificial islands in Malaita's Langalanga Lagoon obtained shells for wealth manufacture from Gela and the Gela people also traded pigs with the Langalanga.

Plate 1.4 Longapolo village, Gela Group, 1906
Source: NASI, ACOM Collection, J.W. Beattie Collection.

Plate 1.5 Kombe village, Gela Group, 1906
Source: NASI, ACOM Collection, J.W. Beattie Collection.

The first sustained contact between European explorers, traders and whalers and the peoples of Solomon Islands began in the late eighteenth and early nineteenth centuries. The earliest substantial foreign contact with Gela came later, when the Anglican Melanesian Mission began taking young men away to be trained as pastors. After a few years, they were returned for a few months' break, then picked up again for further education. The full process took around seven years. Bishop John Patteson first visited Gela in 1862, a year after his consecration. In 1866, Charles Sapibuana from Gela was one of the last pupils to be taken to Kohimarama, the Melanesian Mission's early headquarters in Auckland, New Zealand. Kohimarama failed because its climate was too cold for men and women from tropical islands and it was too far away for easy communications with home. The next year, Sapibuana was transferred to the new headquarters at St Barnabas's College on Norfolk Island. Charles Brooke and Joe Atkin—both ordained on Norfolk Island in 1867—first visited Mboli Passage that year. From 1868, Brooke was based at Mboli for a few months each year. Conversions were slow because of hostilities caused in the early 1870s by kidnapping of labour for plantations in Queensland and Fiji, which led to the *Lavinia* massacre in 1872.[6]

Plate 1.6 Reverend Alfred Penny from the Melanesian Mission travelling by whaleboat in the Gela Group, 1870s
Source: Penny (1888: 176).

---

6   The crew of the trading schooner *Lavinia* was massacred at Gela in 1872 while the ship was anchored at Tiba collecting bêche-de-mer. The captain was away in a boat and some crew members were ashore. All onshore were killed. Pathea, an early Melanesian Mission student who had travelled to New Zealand, was one of the leaders of the attack. Another participant, Musua, was the brother of Charles Sapibuana. Moore 2013, entry for *Lavinia* Massacre; *Southern Cross Log* [hereinafter *SCL*], 15 August 1898, 5.

Plate 1.7 St Barnabas's College, Norfolk Island, where the early Gela pastors were trained, 1870s
Source: Penny (1888: 30).

Plate 1.8 Siota Melanesian Mission house, Gela Group, 1906
Source: NASI, ACOM Collection, J.W. Beattie Collection.

Brooke was joined by New Hebrideans Tom Ulgau from Mota Island and Walter Woser from Motlav Island. All three learned the Gela language and Brooke wrote a detailed description of life on Gela between 1867 and 1874, before he retired to England in disgrace for sexual misdeeds.[7] The first Gela-language prayer book was published in 1873. Permanent village schools were established, a few years later, at Polomuhu (in Mboli Passage), with Dudly Laukoma as pastor, and at Langgo (in the Gaeta district on the south-western coast of Gela Sule), where Charles Sapibuana was the pastor. Reverend Alfred Penny, who replaced Brooke in 1876, conducted the first baptisms on Gela in 1879.[8] Anglican missionaries made further progress after a violent incident involving HMS *Sandfly* in 1880, when three English sailors were beheaded at Gaeta. Britain sent HMS *Emerald* and HMS *Cormorant* on a savage punitive expedition, destroying villages, canoes and crops and strategically sparing only Langgo village. Bishop John Selwyn helped negotiate an end to naval retaliation. He convinced 'bigman' Kalekona to give up the culprits; three were executed, although Kalekona's son Vuria, who had also been involved, was spared. Kalekona was humiliated. The British wrath was remembered, and the mission prospered from it.[9]

Kalekona converted to Anglicanism in 1882, advising his people to destroy ancestral sacred objects. Sapibuana's congregation grew to 115, and he became a deacon in 1882—the first Solomon Islander to reach this level in the Melanesian Mission. Penny learnt the Gela language and translated the four Gospels and the Book of Acts. By 1884, there had been 600 baptisms in the Gela Group, rising to 1,000 two years later. The mission claimed in 1896 that 3,500 out of a total Gela population of 4,000 had become Christians.[10] While the depth of the widespread conversion can be doubted, and 'backsliding' was obvious 10 years later, it was a significant change. One consequence was that the power of the local bigmen was partly usurped by the Norfolk Island–trained mission pastors who often overstepped their authority.[11] To counter this, Reverend John H. Plant, who replaced Penny in 1887, introduced a *Vaukolu* or 'meeting', which functioned as an annual assembly for Anglican leaders

---

7   Brooke 1881; Golden 1993, 31.
8   Penny 1887, 181–84.
9   Moore 2013, entry for Sandfly Passage, Nggela, incident, 1880; Whiteman 1983, 140–41; Lawrence 2014, 149–52.
10 Whiteman 1983, 142.
11 Lawrence 2014, 142–46.

throughout the central Solomons. In selecting the Gela Group as the centre for administration of the protectorate, the WPHC was aware of the progress of missionary work and the beginnings of a process of collective consultation. The *Vaukolu* continued to operate into the early twentieth century, although by then its purpose was more social than administrative. The protectorate government took it over and quietly sidelined its communal parliamentary functions. By 1908, its membership was limited to chiefs, priests, pastors and teachers.[12]

Plate 1.9 The Melanesian Mission's *Vaukolu* congress at Honggo village, Gela Group, 1906
Source: NASI, ACOM Collection, J.W. Beattie Collection.

---

12 Hilliard 1978, 95; Fox 1958, 42–43, 184; *SCL*, January 1901, 113, October 1902, 59; Whiteman 1983, 143–44.

Plate 1.10 The Melanesian Mission's *Vaukolu* congress at Honggo, 1906
Source: NASI, ACOM Collection, J.W. Beattie Collection.

Plate 1.11 The crowd listening to proceedings at the Melanesian Mission's *Vaukolu* congress at Honggo, 1906
Resident commissioner Charles Woodford is seated at the table, wearing his uniform and pith helmet.
Source: NASI, ACOM Collection, J.W. Beattie Collection.

Another advantage of Gela was St Luke's School, the first permanent educational institution in the protectorate, which was established at Siota at the northern end of Mboli Passage. Reverend Richard Comins purchased land for the school in 1893. It opened three years later and, by the next year, had 47 male students.[13] The pattern—one that continued in many Solomon Islands schools—was for students to work in gardens to produce food before and after attending classes. Comins ran the school for half the year and Dr Reverend Henry Welchman took over during the other half. English, rather than Mota (the usual lingua franca of the diocese), was used. The school's site was unhealthy—too close to swamps and mangroves—and four years after it opened a dysentery epidemic killed 11 students and made Welchman very ill. The school was closed.

Plate 1.12 The Melanesian Mission church at Longapolo village, Gela Group, 1906
Source: NASI, ACOM Collection, J.W. Beattie Collection.

13 Fox 1958, 178–79; Hilliard 1978, 92, 96, 150.

Plate 1.13 The Melanesian Mission church at Kombe, Gela Group, 1906
Source: NASI, ACOM Collection, J.W. Beattie Collection.

Plate 1.14 View of Bungana Island, the site of an early Melanesian Mission school, and the Tulagi lighthouse, Gela Group, 1906
Source: NASI, ACOM Collection, J.W. Beattie Collection.

The Gela Group (along with Isabel Island) was the most fully Christian (Anglican) area in Solomon Islands. Even today, Central Islands Province remains 80 per cent Anglican. In 1895, Siota became the first headquarters of the Melanesian Mission in Solomon Islands. A few years later, the Gela Group had 33 schools and almost 100 pastors and teachers. There were about 20 white missionaries based at Siota, mostly priests and pastors or lay teachers, as well as two indigenous deacons—Reuben Bula and Alfred Lobu—supervised by Reverend C.W. Browning. Siota, Honggo and Bungana (close to Tulagi) became the main Gela mission bases. Tulagi was supported by the neighbouring Anglican developments. Each augmented the other.[14]

Foreign traders had also been operating in the central Solomons since the 1860s and 1870s. Joseph ('Portuguese Joe') Emmanuel traded around the Gela Group and Savo during the final decades of the nineteenth century, as did Norwegians Lars Nielsen and Oscar Svensen. Nielson was the best-known Gela trader. He was shipwrecked in Bougainville Strait in about 1875, as was Frank Wickham, another long-time resident of the Solomons, who is mentioned in Chapter 6.[15] Both men worked for trader Alexander Ferguson[16] at Roviana Lagoon, New Georgia, until each struck out on his own. Between 1877 and 1880, Nielsen traded for Ferguson on Savo Island. He and his partners later purchased 8.4-hectare Gavutu Island, as well as nearby Bara Island.[17]

Gela people began trading local produce in return for Western manufactured goods. Once the mission and commercial bases began, and the Tulagi enclave was established, the surrounding Gela Islanders became the primary providers of local foodstuffs—vegetables, fruit, pigs and fish—for the European and Chinese communities. Dozens of Gela villages and hamlets were within easy reach of Tulagi. The foreign presence was a 'windfall' for the Gela people because it gave them access to large quantities of European goods. By contrast, nearby Malaita had no direct access to trade goods until its men entered the external Pacific labour trade from the 1870s and 1880s.[18] Just as the Melanesian Mission bases and the traders familiarised Gela people with foreign ways, so too did

---

14   Fox 1958, 60, 68, 225–26. Siota was destroyed by the Japanese during the war.
15   Golden 1993, 68–70, 195–96, 206–08.
16   ibid., 198–201.
17   ibid., 68; Bennett 1987, 25, 82.
18   Moore 2007.

proximity to Tulagi, Gavutu, Makambo and Bungana. The local people began to produce their own copra, selling it to traders, and, during the 1930s when copra prices were low, Gela villagers also collected and sold trochus shell.[19]

Woodford was very familiar with the Gela Group. In 1888, while a naturalist, he chose Gavutu as one of the bases for his explorations and travelled on Nielsen's ketch *Amelia*. Nielsen built up his trading station and small copra plantation on Gavutu, where he lived with his Malaitan wife. There was a store and a comfortable house. He also purchased other trading vessels and had a contract to supply coal and water to British naval ships—services that were soon extended to commercial ships. By 1897, Nielsen had added to the existing slender sand causeway joining Gavutu to neighbouring Tanambogo Island, which protected his harbour and increased his access to land. He became prosperous, and owned a 25-ton schooner, *Narova*, and a 15-ton cutter, *Rubiana*.[20] Nielsen helped all the early Christian missions to become established. One of the early photographs from Gavutu—said to have been taken in 1890—is of Nielsen, bearded and middle-aged, with his employees working in the background. In 1897, Gavutu was well established, with a comfortable house in a fenced paddock, a small copra plantation and shed, a trading boat and a causeway to Tanambogo.[21] Oscar Svensen (also known as Captain Marau), the other prominent Norwegian trader, purchased Gavutu and other assets from Nielsen in 1903.[22] Florence Young, from the Queensland Kanaka Mission (which later became the South Sea Evangelical Mission/Church), first visited Tulagi and Gavutu in 1904 and provided a description of Gavutu. Svensen had installed 18 huge open water tanks, used to provision ships. His house had two levels under an unlined single gable-shaped ripple-iron roof. The ground floor contained a store, with three rooms above, all of which had lead floors to stop water leakage into the commercial area below. The core of the house was surrounded by wide verandahs and nearby there was a palm-leaf kitchen

---

19   Bennett 1987, 246.
20   Lawrence 2014, 187.
21   ibid., 187.
22   Golden 1993, 68–70; Bennett 1981. Nielsen became unwell, sold his properties and returned to Norway. In about 1902, he offered to sell his holdings to Burns Philp and Company (BP) for £2,500, which they declined. He then sold out to Oscar Svensen for £3,000. The next year, Svensen offered the Nielsen properties to BP for £10,000, which they also declined, later regretting their reticence when Svensen sold his total assets to Levers for £40,000. BP lost its commercial advantage and in 1908 hurriedly purchased nearby Makambo Island.

with an earthen floor.²³ Several early photographs of Gavutu indicate that the trading station grew rapidly and became an established commercial venture with a substantial timber wharf.²⁴

Plate 1.15 Gavutu Island, viewed from Halvo, showing fishing platforms, 1906
Source: NASI, ACOM Collection, J.W. Beattie Collection.

As already noted, the Gela Group also supplied labour for indenture in overseas colonies, particularly Queensland and Fiji. Given the population of the group in the late nineteenth century was estimated to be between 4,000 and 5,000, the 2,069 Gela labour contracts for work in Queensland between the 1870s and 1900s involved a large segment of the total male population. To sustain these numbers, it seems likely that there was once a substantially higher population, followed by decline late in the nineteenth century as contact accelerated and new diseases were introduced. Only 86 Gela labourers were contracted to work in Fiji, mainly in the late 1870s and 1880s. Most of the Gela labourers enlisted during the 1880s and

23 Young, F. 1926, 145.
24 BM, Thomas Edge-Partington Photographic Collection, Album 4, Dscn 1021, 1022, Album 6, Dscn 1115, 1126; Beattie 1909; National Library of Australia [hereinafter NLA] 1909, Photographs R32 Sundry 1.11, Solomon Islands 11, Coaling Station, Gavutu Island.

1890s worked for three years before returning.[25] After a rough beginning with the *Lavinia* and *Sandfly* massacres, the labour recruiters found Gela largely peaceful and were able to go ashore to collect food, water and wood to refresh their supplies. Gela's men continued to serve as labourers— in the Tulagi enclave and on the plantations that developed within the protectorate; 659 Gela labourers were indentured between 1913 and 1940, which is low compared with their earlier participation in the Queensland labour trade.[26] Presumably, this means they had satisfactory alternative sources of income because of their proximity to mission bases, plantations that were developed in the group and the Tulagi enclave.

Charles Morris Woodford

The choice of Tulagi as the protectorate's headquarters by the first Resident Commissioner, Charles Morris Woodford, made good sense. Woodford deliberately lobbied for the creation of his own position within the WPHC. Young, intelligent, fit and seasoned to life in the Pacific and particularly Solomon Islands, Woodford was the perfect choice for the first permanent British official. Born in Kent, England, in 1852, the son of a prosperous wine and spirits merchant, Woodford attended Tonbridge, an exclusive school not far from his hometown of Milton. His talents as a collector of natural history specimens began to emerge while he was still at school and, like many boys in the age of empire, he showed interest in the expansion of the British Empire in Africa and further afield. After school he was absorbed into the family business, until he departed for the Pacific to pursue a future as a procurer of natural history specimens for museums and rich private collectors back in England.[27] At the age of 30, he arrived in Fiji, in March 1882. Woodford worked as a government agent on board the labour vessel *Patience* on a trip to the Gilbert and Ellice islands, where they repatriated 45 Gilbertese who had been incorrectly dropped off on Malekula Island in the New Hebrides by a German vessel out of Samoa. He also held a minor position in the WPHC's Treasury.[28]

---

25   Price with Baker 1976; Siegel 1985.
26   Shlomowitz and Bedford 1988; Penny 1887, 122–49.
27   Lawrence 2014, 9–23.
28   ibid., 27–30; Scarr 1967, 263.

Plate 1.16 Charles Woodford at Aola, Guadalcanal, 1890
Source: Pacific Manuscripts Bureau (PMB), AU PMB PHOTO 56-21 (ANUA 481-1A-21).

Woodford returned to England, sold his Pacific butterfly collection and began, with the assistance of the Royal Geographical Society in London, to prepare for a trip to Solomon Islands as a naturalist. He was back in Fiji in February 1886. In April, he joined the *Christine*, a small labour trade schooner working around the New Hebrides and Solomon Islands. The ship visited several islands in the New Hebrides, then sailed north to Uki ni masi (usually known as Uki), Santa Ana, Makira, Ulawa, Malaita, Guadalcanal and Alu—the last being the largest of the Shortland Islands. They arrived at Uru and Sinalagu harbours on east Malaita not long after a series of attacks on labour trade vessels that had incurred naval reprisals.[29] However, the *Christine* experienced no difficulties along the east coast and then moved on to Malu'u in the north and to Coleridge Bay (Fauaabu) in the north-west. From June to August, Woodford remained on Alu, then transferred to Fauro Island in the same group, remaining there until mid-September. His trip was cut short by fever, although he also spent two weeks on Guadalcanal before returning to Australia, from where he sent his new collection home to England.

Woodford returned again to Solomon Islands in January 1887. He spent two weeks at Roviana Lagoon, New Georgia, followed by six months at Aola on Guadalcanal's north-east coast. From there he made three unsuccessful attempts to explore the high central mountains. He left for Australia and England in September 1887, having collected 20,000 specimens on the two trips. He was back in the Solomons again in mid-1888, spending another two weeks at Roviana Lagoon, three months in the Gela Group and one month at his Aola house. His rationale changed during these trips. Alongside natural history collecting, he began to allocate more time to exploration and anthropology, even replotting parts of Mendaña's 1568 expedition route. Woodford then returned to Fiji. Motivated by the British and German annexations in east New Guinea in 1884, and adjustments to the south-eastern German New Guinea border in 1886, he began a campaign to have Britain take formal possession of the remainder of Solomon Islands. His book *A Naturalist among the Head-Hunters* was well received and became one of the two standard early English-language texts on Solomon Islands, along with Henry Guppy's 1887 book *The Solomon Islands and Their Natives*, based on his 1881 and 1884 voyages on HMS *Lark*.[30] Woodford's book was part of his campaign.

---

29 These were *Borealis* (1880), *Janet Stewart* (1882), *Helena* (1884) and *Young Dick* (1886). Lawrence 2014, 78–79; Fowler 1969; Keesing 1986.
30 Guppy 1887; Woodford 1890.

In 1889, Woodford married Florence (Florrie) M. Palmer, the daughter of a pastoral family from Bathurst, New South Wales. They moved to London, where he worked for a stockbroker, which did not suit his ambitions any more than being a wine and spirits merchant. Bored with settled life, he made up his mind in 1893 to return to the Pacific. He applied to the Marquess of Rippon, the new Secretary of State for the Colonies, to become the Resident or Deputy Commissioner of the newly proclaimed British Solomon Islands Protectorate. He had the support of Lord Amherst of Hackney (who was editing the first English translation of Mendaña's voyage diaries), the president of the Royal Geographical Society and a Royal Navy captain whom he knew from his Pacific adventures. The British Government, which was not ready to install any official representative, rebuffed Woodford, who then wrote to high commissioner Sir John Thurston in Suva offering to privately fund an official appointment. Thurston refused his request because he doubted Woodford's administrative abilities and suspected that his real intention was to extend his lucrative work as a naturalist in the Solomons. Woodford then tried another direct approach to Rippon.

Knowing that it was only a matter of the right timing, and never one to give up easily, Woodford decided to move his family to Australia in October 1894, and then returned to Fiji, where he could lobby directly. By this time, there was rivalry between Germany and Britain in Samoa, which, with WPHC staffing changes, led to Woodford being appointed as acting Consul and Deputy Commissioner in Apia. He hoped this would be his proving ground for the BSIP position. In April 1896, he was employed to assist in the High Commissioner's office. At this time, a dispatch was sent to London protesting the lack of a salary for a BSIP resident commissioner. With all the hallmarks of a Woodford-authored document, it argued that the Gilbert and Ellice Islands Protectorates were already self-supporting, which meant that money could be released to be spent in the Solomons. As well, it said that the minimal costs of administration could be met by the proceeds of trading licences; only a small police force was needed and the Resident Commissioner's salary was already covered by a local WPHC vote of money. The proposal was endorsed by Thurston, who was then in Sydney, urged on by a personal visit from Woodford on his way to the Solomons.[31] The Colonial Office acquiesced at last.

---

31   Scarr 1967, 262–63; Lawrence 2014, 135–68.

Jurisdictional imperialism

The shape of the modern Solomon Islands nation is an artefact of British, German and French colonialism. Eventually, and only after agreement with Germany and France, Britain assumed legal control of the southern section of the Solomon Archipelago, as well as the Santa Cruz Group and surrounding islands. The situation in the Pacific was extremely complex, requiring some innovative decisions and the manipulation of boundaries. Solomon Islanders seldom question the nature of the British intervention in their islands, but in fact it was an occupation without permission, and the territorial shape of the modern nation-state relates to haphazard political circumstances. The British acknowledged indigenous landownership within the protectorate, at the same time as adopting processes that enabled alienation of large areas.

In colonisation, gaining legal control of the land and people was paramount, although the motivations and legal mechanisms differed. The examples of Australia, New Zealand, New Caledonia and Fiji will suffice to show the very different approaches. In Australia, all land was claimed by the Crown as *terra nullius*, ignoring the rights of approximately 1 million Indigenous people. It took until the Mabo and Wik judgments of the High Court in the 1990s for this legal anomaly to be overturned. After a long period of denial, many modern Australians now accept that their continent was invaded by the British and that settlement was not a peaceful process. In New Zealand, the 1840 Treaty of Waitangi signed by Māori chiefs gave Britain control of the North Island. Although much dishonoured by the British, the treaty provided the basis for subsequent land and political negotiations. The less populous South Island of New Zealand was also secured for settlement. New Caledonia became a French territory in 1853, with the same status as a province in metropolitan France. Control was extended to the neighbouring Loyalty Islands in 1864, which became a dependency of the territory. France wanted a strategic port near Australia and a place to establish a convict colony as well as a settler society. New Caledonia provided a substantial Western Pacific presence to augment their early exploration and existing Christian missions, trading stations and plantations. It was a large island and a valuable asset, but in the process of acquisition the indigenous people were dispossessed of their land and placed on to 'native reserves'. Neighbouring Fiji was 'ceded' to Britain in 1874 by Cakabau, a leading chief, which led to the establishment of a Crown colony—partly to appease the small settler society there, but also because it suited wider British plans in the Pacific Islands. Fijian interests were safeguarded: large areas of their land were made inalienable and a Fijian administration was established, which led to establishment of the annual Council of Chiefs, alongside plans for the economic development of some areas.

The same intensity of land acquisition did not occur in most other Western Pacific Island groups. Usually the process combined some acknowledgement of indigenous land rights with the enabling of economic development by foreigners. This was the situation in Solomon Islands, where Britain established a protectorate and large areas were alienated from customary landowning groups. Eighty-five years after the protectorate was proclaimed, Solomon Islanders became independent and most land is now under the control of extended families in local areas, not the state. Much of the alienated land was returned to the people, including some quite outrageous foreign land acquisitions, such as 999-year leases. It could be argued that this retention of local indigenous ownership was the result of being a protectorate, rather than a Crown colony. Today, by and large, Solomon Islanders do not think in terms of British invasion and conquest in the way that First Nation Australians do. This may be because they never had to deal with a settler society or importation of large numbers of foreign labourers. During the colonial years, Solomon Islanders were of course aware that their islands had been taken over and they resented the fact. Nevertheless, because they had no central indigenous political core, it was difficult for them to protest in any organised manner. Britain declared a protectorate over their islands for reasons related to British interests, emanating from Australasian settler societies and the Crown colonies in British New Guinea and Fiji. However, if Britain had not taken this action it is highly likely that either Germany or France would have claimed the islands.

There is nothing particularly 'natural' about the territory included in the modern Solomon Islands nation-state. The north of the Solomon Archipelago—Buka and Bougainville (the largest island) plus a few neighbouring atolls—was claimed by Germany and remains part of Papua New Guinea. The Solomon Islands nation-state covers the southern section of the archipelago, from Shortland Islands down to Makira, and includes the Santa Cruz Group and adjacent islands, which are separated from the south of the Solomon Archipelago by 400 kilometres of ocean. Geographically and culturally, Temotu Province is more closely allied to the islands that became the New Hebrides Condominium—now modern

Vanuatu. In the 1880s, and for the next 20 years, there was a possibility that, using Port Moresby as the headquarters, Britain would annex a huge arc of Melanesian islands stretching east and south to include both Solomon Islands and the New Hebrides. The Australian east coast colonies were in support, although they were unwilling to help pay the costs. Similar proposals surfaced again at various times, and were last revived in the 1950s and 1960s when the future of Netherlands New Guinea (now Indonesia's Papua provinces), Solomon Islands and the New Hebrides were under international discussion.[32]

The colonial partition of Melanesia depended on accommodating British, German and French trading, labour recruiting and missionary interests, as well as colonial arrangements made in other parts of the world. Geographic common sense seldom applied, although it did in the choice of Tulagi as the site for the protectorate's headquarters. Tulagi was centrally located and had an excellent harbour. There was already a considerable missionary and trader presence in the Gela Group, while another obvious option, the New Georgia Group, which had an early whaling and trading presence, was not central to the islands that fell between the German claims to the north and the French claims to the south. Woodford was ready and waiting for the task, and he had Tulagi in mind as the protectorate's new capital.

Although the British Empire was never a formal legal entity, Britain had several methods of adding territory. Originally, British law had no provisions regarding protectorates. If a new territory was settled, it became part of the British dominions and the common law and statute law of England applied to the settlers. If the territory was obtained by conquest, its original laws remained in force until they were changed. This could be done without local consent, using an order in council. But neither category applied to areas such as Solomon Islands, which were not formally part of the Crown's dominions, even if the islands were recognised as being under Britain's sphere of influence. In the Pacific Islands, European powers cooperated by recognising one another's spheres of influence and then slowly made these into 'legal' entities. Before the use of protectorates, new British territory could be annexed or ceded (as in Fiji) or settled (as in Australia and New Zealand). The fourth and much favoured method during the nineteenth century was through proclaiming protectorates.

---

32 Waters 2016.

The protectorate concept evolved between the 1840s and the 1890s, allowing various degrees of British involvement as local circumstances required. Quite simply, it was a solution to the need for a cheap method of colonial control. British law came to recognise protectorates—usually tribal territories—and protected states, where Britain introduced a form of local internal self-government based on an existing government. In both cases, Britain controlled defence and external relations. Protectorates continually evolved and, by the twentieth century, there was no longer a clear difference between the ways protectorates and Crown colonies were administered. The path was not always the same—for instance, some began as protectorates and became Crown colonies. The difference between the two was extremely blurred in the BSIP. One person in a good position to know this was Colin Allan, the last Governor of the BSIP, between 1976 and 1978. A New Zealander, he first arrived in the BSIP as a cadet officer in 1945 and progressed rapidly through the ranks. In 1952, he took leave to complete legal training and was put in charge of the Special Lands Commission into customary land, the report from which was published in 1957. Allan concluded that Solomon Islanders believed that the government had exceeded its powers in dealing with land alienation:

> In connection with this question, it must be emphasised that while today it is generally believed that no difference exists between a 'colony' and a 'protectorate', the fact remains that for Solomon Islanders the two possess very different meanings and implications. As they see it, a Protectorate is a country under the protection of an alien, yet friendly and benevolent power, which protects and administers the people in accordance with their own wishes and interests. A colony, on the other hand, is a territory whose resources and people are enslaved and exploited in the sole interest of the colonising power. Implicit in the term 'colony' for them is the loss of all land interests. This attitude was given full expression during the political troubles of 1946–1952, is still extant, and regardless of how naive it might be held to be, it is one which cannot be lightly disregarded.[33]

---

33   Allan 1957, 56.

Allan is playing with words and, as the author of the only major land report since the 1920s, he was not about to concede that the BSIP Government had misinterpreted land law in regard to protectorates. Nevertheless, he does point to a basic truth: a protectorate is not a Crown colony; they are legally quite distinct. Allan also said:

> In later years all minerals and exploitation thereof have been reserved to the Crown. Legislation has been enacted to appropriate land required for public purposes. There have thus been steady inroads upon native land interests, and the precise limits to which legislation can go has never been clear. This has caused some concern to successive Commissioners of Lands.[34]

It is an interesting thought that the alienation of some land in the BSIP might have been illegal.

British acts of parliament and orders in council

All through the nineteenth century, Britain grappled with how to administer areas with indigenous tribal organisation that had been brought under international legal jurisdiction. It came up with the concept of the protectorate, legalised under the *Foreign Jurisdiction Act*. Whenever the Foreign Office wanted to extend British authority, it was normally done either by amending the Act or, more commonly, by an order in council under the Act. British protectorates were an evolving legal form, an indication of British territorial interest—initially, just enough to discourage other European nations from making territorial claims. They were not outright annexations or claims of sovereignty, as occurred with Crown colonies.

BSIP colonial officials were guided by several types of laws and regulations—some standard across the empire, some relating only to the WPHC and still others created within the protectorate. While BSIP officials could lobby for modifications when the system appeared to be unworkable or in need of revision, they were always bound by precedent and had little room to manoeuvre. They could always be overruled by the Western Pacific High Commissioner. A basic understanding of the

---

34   ibid.

status of Solomon Islands as a British protectorate, rather than a Crown colony or a settler colony, helps us to understand Tulagi, its functions and its society.

Areas such as New Guinea and Solomon Islands were regarded as 'uncivilised' and without states, which meant that in theory they could only become protectorates. However, British New Guinea—culturally similar to Solomon Islands—began as a protectorate in 1884 and became a Crown colony in 1888, creating a local precedent, as did another neighbouring area, the Gilbert Islands Protectorate and the Ellice Islands Protectorate, both of which began in 1892, were administered as one and became a single Crown colony in 1916.[35] Protectorates became a means of placing all British subjects and foreigners within a territory under effective legal control, without any commitment to acquire the territory as a colony. As Edward Wolfers suggests:

> They were, in a sense, no more than legal fictions to allow for a type of indirect rule over areas in which the British government did not presently wish to become involved in the day-to-day business of internal administration.[36]

Britain also had existing sovereign territories close by. Founding a penal settlement in the Crown colony of New South Wales in 1788 was part of much wider British strategic plans. As they developed—all carved out of New South Wales—the eastern Australian and New Zealand colonies[37] were utilised as a convenient British doorstep to the Pacific. Sydney grew into a prosperous port and in the early decades the colony's economic focus was on the Pacific more than the inland, until the pastoral industry expanded. Early food supplies for Sydney were brought from Tahiti, and New Zealand and Fiji were settled from eastern Australia. Sydney became a Pacific port where marine products from the islands were sold. On a small scale, recruitment of Pacific labour for use in New South Wales began in 1847. At first, settlement spread south and north along the east coast, then in the 1810s, it moved west over the coastal ranges behind Sydney. Pastoralism spread north during the 1840s and 1850s into the northern districts of New South Wales, which became the Colony of Queensland in 1859. Queensland's interests extended into New Guinea and the

---

35 Joyce 1971, 99–104.
36 Wolfers 1971, 2.
37 The North Island and about half of the South Island were initially part of New South Wales. In 1825, when Van Diemen's Land (Tasmania) became a separate colony, the border was altered so that only the top half of the North Island was included in New South Wales.

islands around the Solomon and Coral seas. Once the Queensland labour trade began in the 1860s, the islands closest to Australia were at first loosely incorporated into the British Pacific, and then, increasingly, more formally. Allied to this was the dislike by British Australasian colonists of French and German neighbours in the Pacific.

The ships of the Royal Navy Australia Station (RNAS), which had been based in Sydney since the 1820s, patrolled around Australia, New Zealand and the Western Pacific. Until 1859, the eastern boundaries of the RNAS were 185 degrees west (including Tonga, Niue and Samoa) and 10 degrees south (cutting through Torres Strait and Solomon Islands). In 1864, the boundary was extended west to include the Cocos and Christmas islands, although the northern boundary still cut through Torres Strait. The boundary was extended in 1872, east as far as the Cook Islands and north to include Micronesia and all of New Guinea.[38] The reality was that there were never many ships attached to the RNAS and, at best, they visited parts of the main islands once or twice a year, usually to investigate reports of 'outrages'. The British Navy had no power to arrest indigenous perpetrators of an act of violence against foreigners or take them for trial in Fiji or the Australasian colonies. The only recourse was to treat any attack as a formal act of war. This led to 'commodore justice'—the bombardment of villages and often the punishment of innocent people not directly involved in the incident. Any other solution, such as executing the offending persons, left the naval captain open to charges of murder.[39] The temporary answer to judicial problems, arrived at in 1888, was to appoint some of the naval commanders as deputy commissioners. This gave them limited magisterial powers to act on behalf of the WPHC.

The establishment of a British protectorate required a physical visit by a senior officer and some show of compliance by the indigenous leaders in any newly acquired region. In areas such as Solomon Islands, with no substantial hereditary chieftainships, the acceptance of protectorate status was of dubious legality. The neighbouring Gilbert and Ellice islands were made into British protectorates with far more validity, since there were Gilbertese and Tuvaluan hereditary leaders. Even as a single Crown colony, they were still administered by a WPHC resident commissioner until just before independence, when the two island groups were split.[40]

---

38   Bach 1986, frontispiece map.
39   ibid., 247–49.
40   Munro and Firth 1986; Johnston 1973; Newbury 1973; McIntyre 1967; Macdonald 1982.

By the 1890s, when the BSIP was proclaimed, issues relating to establishing criminal and civil jurisdiction had been solved. A protectorate confirmed Britain's control over its own subjects in the protected areas, with protectorate functions expanded to include general administrative and regulatory powers over citizens of other nations and indigenous inhabitants. As historian Ross Johnston concluded:

> It was a compromise between the extremes of annexation and disregard of the area. It offered an indefinite means of control, a somewhat shadowy amount of jurisdiction and administration, but it was sufficient to satisfy at least the more direct demands for the protection of British subjects and of 'helpless savages'. But this solution—jurisdictional imperialism—was reached only very slowly and by faltering steps.[41]

Extraterritorial jurisdiction laws were much easier to establish over protected states that had existing significant government structures recognisable in European terms. In dealing with many parts of Africa and the Pacific Islands, legal advisers to the British Government had to break new ground. They were also subservient to the interests of both the Colonial Office and the Foreign Office, which were less concerned with legal theory than with the practical convenience of governing with few staff, providing legal justification for what had or was about to happen within various spheres of interest and minimising financial costs. They often requested supporting legislation to provide a legal basis for already established policy. Even so, the French and German colonial legal systems were more workable, which was to the disadvantage of Britain.[42]

Britain made a series of moves between 1872 and 1877 to extend British control in the Pacific, mainly over British subjects in areas not under formal claim. First, to protect Pacific Islanders from depredations by its subjects, Britain tried unsuccessfully to apply existing imperial antislavery Acts and passed new Acts, particularly the *Pacific Islanders Protection Act*s of 1872 and 1875. These Acts were motivated initially by the murder of Anglican Bishop John Patteson on Nukapu in the Reef Islands in September 1871 and the notorious incidents of kidnapping and massacre on the brig *Carl* in August 1872, plus other illegal incidents in the Queensland and Fiji labour trades.[43] The intention was to bolster

---

41   ibid., 22.
42   ibid., 29–30.
43   Carter 1999.

the Queensland *Polynesian Labourers Act* of 1868 (the term Melanesia was not then in use)[44] and to regulate the labour trade. The Queensland Act was adopted by the British Consul in Levuka for use in Fiji and there was a substantial new territorial claim. Fiji became a Crown colony in 1874—an assertion of British sovereignty, although, in Fiji, Britain always acknowledged the continued partial sovereignty of Fijians.

When the future status of Fiji was discussed during the early 1870s, the way in which wider control over the Pacific Islands could be achieved was also under consideration. Issues discussed were a Pacific court of justice with civil and criminal jurisdiction over British subjects and how it would relate to the existing court system operating in the Australian and New Zealand colonies, and to laws relating to the Admiralty. The enabling legislation that created the WPHC was in the form of an August 1877 order in council under the *Foreign Jurisdiction Act*. This listed many Pacific Islands by name and included:

> all other islands in the Western Pacific Ocean not being within the limits of the colonies of Fiji, Queensland, or New South Wales, and not being within the jurisdiction of any civilized Power.

Solomon Islands was one of these areas. The order in council also applied to British subjects on British-registered vessels within the area. One of the primary reasons for the formation of the WPHC was to manage the Pacific labour trade, which was criticised as being a new form of slavery, although slavery had been abolished in all British territories in a rolling process between 1807 and 1833. Accusations in the 1860s and 1870s that slavery was flourishing in the Pacific and involved British subjects were an embarrassment in London. While the British Government grappled with how to control its Pacific interests, in 1877, WPHC plans were put forward for a series of deputy commissioners resident in the New Hebrides, Solomon Islands, New Guinea and the Caroline and Gilbert islands. These were dismissed in Britain as being well beyond the available budget. Nevertheless, the WPHC became the main administrative and legal mechanism used to oversee later British interests in the Pacific Islands. To use the words of historian David McIntyre, it was 'an experiment in providing order and jurisdiction without assuming [British] sovereignty'.[45]

---

44 'Polynesia' was defined in Queensland Acts as including Fiji, New Caledonia, any of the Loyalty, the New Hebrides, Banks or Solomon islands or any island in the Pacific Ocean not being in her majesty's dominions and not within the jurisdiction on any civilised power. 'Melanesia' was not in common use.
45 McIntyre 1960, 285.

Over time, the purpose of the WPHC became more defined, particularly after the 1884–85 Berlin Conference clarified European spheres of influence in the Pacific. Back in 1875–77, when the Crown Colony of Fiji and the WPHC were being shaped, Britain had ideas that the role of the Governor of Fiji and High Commissioner would include being 'commander' of the Pacific 'tribes'.[46] Almost two decades later, in 1893, another order in council vested the High Commissioner with executive and legislative powers and limited his jurisdiction to territories under formal British control. The WPHC became a unique oceanic territory that governed protectorates, small British Pacific territories such as Pitcairn Island (a colony), half a condominium (the New Hebrides) and eventually also one Crown colony (the Gilbert and Ellice Islands).[47] Administered from the Crown Colony of Fiji and covering a huge area of the Western Pacific, the WPHC worked closely with the British Royal Navy. The title of high commissioner was rare in the British Empire. In 1854, the Governor of the Cape Colony was made High Commissioner for South Africa— responsible for certain affairs beyond the frontier. Another example was in the Palestine and Transjordan mandated territories after 1928. The usual term used elsewhere was chief commissioner. Once high commissioner became the standard term used for British Commonwealth diplomatic representatives, the use of the same term for the head the WPHC became misleading. Nevertheless, the title lasted until the 1970s.

Although the title and territory of the Western Pacific high commissioners were grand, their small team had no real access to most of the islands they were supposed to administer. There was a high commissioner (the Governor of Fiji), a chief judicial commissioner (Fiji's Chief Justice) sitting in the High Commissioner's Court and provision to appoint special, deputy and resident commissioners. The High Commissioner had the power to exclude any British subject from a protected area for two years if they committed a breach of the 1872 or 1875 Acts or were considered dangerous to peace and good order. The Australasian colonies

---

46 Scarr 1967, 36.
47 Initially, the WPHC appointed deputy commissioners for Tonga, Samoa, New Guinea, New Britain and the New Hebrides, with two RNAS officers appointed as roving deputy commissioners. Once colonial territories were under more formal claim, the WPHC governed the protectorates/ colony of Gilbert and Ellice Islands (proclaimed in 1892 and 1916, respectively), the BSIP (proclaimed in 1893), the British half of the New Hebrides Condominium (1906), Samoa (1879; initially just Apia, until separation into American Samoa and Western Samoa in 1900), Tonga (from 1900, it was a 'protected state' like the Ionian Islands and Zanzibar, with a consul and Britain in charge of foreign affairs) and Pitcairn Islands (a colony from 1838 and under the WPHC from 1898).

also had the power to intercede in the Pacific, although this right was rather vague and untested, except for Queensland's control over British New Guinea in the 1880s and 1890s at gubernatorial level.

Whalers had operated in the Solomon Archipelago since the 1790s, with their presence declining by the 1860s. European traders sailed there from Sydney in the 1860s, 1870s and 1880s, mostly to buy copra (dried coconut), ivory nuts (from sago palms), bêche-de-mer (also known as trepang or sea cucumbers) and 'tortoise shell' (actually turtle shell).[48] In the early 1870s, the labour trade to Queensland and Fiji—then operating in the Loyalty Islands and New Hebrides—moved north into the Solomons. Controls hit legal problems in the late 1860s with failed naval prosecutions of British subjects over breaches of existing laws and the non-applicability of anti-slavery laws to the Pacific labour trade. Attempts to protect the islanders from unscrupulous British subjects—particularly those from New South Wales, Queensland and Fiji—were failing. One improvement was that from 1870 to 1871, each labour vessel of British origin carried a government agent to supervise the recruiting process. Although these agents varied considerably in their reliability, they became the most constant British Government presence in the archipelago until the protectorate was established, even though their legal authority was limited to their ship and the ship's boats.[49] During the 1860s and into the 1870s, Admiralty powers were still being circumvented by Australian colonial courts.[50]

A different system unfolded in the New Hebrides, where the colonists were French and British. The French Government viewed the New Hebrides as a natural extension of its New Caledonia territory and its Loyalty Islands dependency. The British Consul in New Caledonia monitored French expansion and Australian colonists watched closely, not keen on having French neighbours. The transportation of convicts to eastern Australia ceased in 1853, which meant that British Australians with their new representative governments were not happy when French convicts were sent to New Caledonia between the 1860s and 1897. Neither power was willing to cede the New Hebrides to the other and eventually, after an initial Anglo-French agreement in 1878 guaranteeing continued independence and neutrality, the unsatisfactory Anglo-French Joint Naval

---

48   Bennett 1987, 21–102.
49   ibid.; Corris 1973; Moore 1985.
50   Mortensen 2000; Hunt 2007.

Commission was established in 1888. This lasted until 1906, when the New Hebrides became a condominium—an unusual form of government that continued until the islands became independent as Vanuatu in 1980. From 1902, both France and Britain maintained resident officials in Port Vila.[51] This Anglo-French arrangement established the southern boundary of the future Solomon Islands nation.

East New Guinea's chartered companies, protectorates and crown colonies

Another BSIP boundary was that with New Guinea and its eastern islands. At various stages, Solomon Islands could easily have become part of a wider British protectorate including New Guinea and island Melanesia, although complicated negotiations between Queensland and Britain, and Britain and Germany, always precluded this outcome.[52] Sir Arthur Hamilton Gordon, the first resident Governor of Fiji and the first Western Pacific High Commissioner, in 1878 sent a special envoy on a naval ship to inspect Solomon Islands. Then, between 1879 and 1881, Gordon undertook protracted negotiations with the Colonial Office and the Admiralty on the relationship between the WPHC and the British Navy. The Admiralty was not interested in having the Commodore of the RNAS assume the duties of high commissioner, nor was the navy willing to continue carrying civilian WPHC officials on its ships. In November 1884, when south-east New Guinea was annexed as a British protectorate, an attempt was made to include Solomon Islands under the Port Moresby administration.

The final decisions about the future of protectorates in the Pacific were made at the Berlin Conference of 1884–85—called between Germany, France and Britain—and at the 1887 Australasian Colonial Conference. The three European nations pursued different approaches to colonisation. The Germans, for instance, continued to use chartered companies as agents of colonialism. In 1884, German New Guinea was proclaimed as a *Schutzgebiet* (commercial protectorate) and the Neu Guinea Kompagnie was established to settle the north-eastern mainland. The company, although an economic failure, continued to operate until

---

51 Bennett 1987, 176–217.
52 Scarr 1967, 136.

1899, when the German Government took control.⁵³ British colonialism had begun in the same way, with the formation in 1600 of the British East India Company—a chartered company that traded in India and South-East Asia and then expanded its operations to include China. Gradually extended from a trading company to be the government of India, the company remained powerful until the British Crown took over its monopolies in the early nineteenth century. British companies with the powers of governments continued to be established—such as the British North Borneo Company in 1881 and others in Africa, such as the British South Africa Company, formed in 1888, which received a royal charter the next year. However, a commercial company style of development was considered unsuitable for New Guinea and island Melanesia and, by the 1880s, the British chartered company concept was in decline, replaced with formal protectorate or Crown colony status. Britain disapproved of Germany's 1884–85 claims of sovereignty in the Pacific, which in British legal theory represented protection, not sovereignty, but it enabled the Germans to apply their system of criminal law throughout the German Empire, which was a distinct advantage. The French concept of territories incorporated into mainland France was different again, but their application of domestic law was simpler than the British system.⁵⁴ It took until 1890 for the British legal distinctions between sovereignty, annexations and protectorates to become fixed.

The British New Guinea Protectorate (1884–88) was the largest territory partly controlled by the WPHC. In 1883, Queensland audaciously attempted to annex south-eastern New Guinea on behalf of Britain, which refused to recognise the move. Then, in November 1884, pressed by the Australasian colonies, Britain proclaimed a protectorate over a similar area of south-east New Guinea. At the same time, in a planned move, Germany made a claim over north-east New Guinea. Britain then offered British New Guinea to Queensland on condition that there would be no expenses for Britain. Queensland had a new government, which refused the offer.⁵⁵ If either of these 1883–84 moves had succeeded, Queensland would have extended into south-east New Guinea and the neighbouring Pacific Islands.

---

53   Moore 2003, 143.
54   Johnston 1973, 201–04.
55   Joyce 1971, 99; Moore 1984.

There were three main officials in early British New Guinea. Major-General Sir Peter Scratchley was appointed as Administrator and WPHC Deputy Commissioner in 1884, although he was based in Port Moresby only for a few months in 1885, where he died from malaria. His replacement was the Honourable John Douglas, a former Premier of Queensland (1877–79), then Government Resident and Police Magistrate on Thursday Island in Torres Strait, where he also held an appointment as WPHC Deputy Commissioner. Once British New Guinea became a Crown colony, Douglas returned to his previous position. It was unusual situation. The Administrator of the British New Guinea Protectorate was always a WPHC deputy commissioner, but owed more allegiance to the colonies of Queensland, New South Wales and Victoria than to the High Commissioner in Suva.

The other important early British representative in New Guinea and Solomon Islands was Hugh H. Romilly. Romilly joined the WPHC staff in 1879 at the age of 23—appointed as a magistrate and private secretary to Gordon. Romilly was one of the first WPHC officials to travel widely on naval ships. Gordon's replacement, Sir William Des Voeux, sent Romilly into Melanesia and New Guinea in 1881 as a roving deputy commissioner based on HMS *Cormorant* and HMS *Beagle*. He returned to Melanesia again in 1883, this time on the Fiji labour trade vessel *Meg Merillies*. Romilly was also based in Port Moresby in 1883 but lacked power or independent transport, and in 1884 created a farce when he misinterpreted his instructions, mistakenly proclaiming the protectorate before RNAS Commodore James Elphinstone Erskine arrived to make the official proclamation. Romilly acted as Administrator after Scratchley's death, then in 1886 went to London to supervise the New Guinea exhibits at the Colonial and Indian Exhibition. Despite his experience and talents, he felt underappreciated and, after a short period as British Consul in the New Hebrides (1887–90), he resigned. Like many ambitious young Englishmen, he went to Africa.[56]

---

56   He joined a prospecting party to Mashonaland—now a region in northern Zimbabwe. Romilly 1887; Scarr 1967, 130–36, 259.

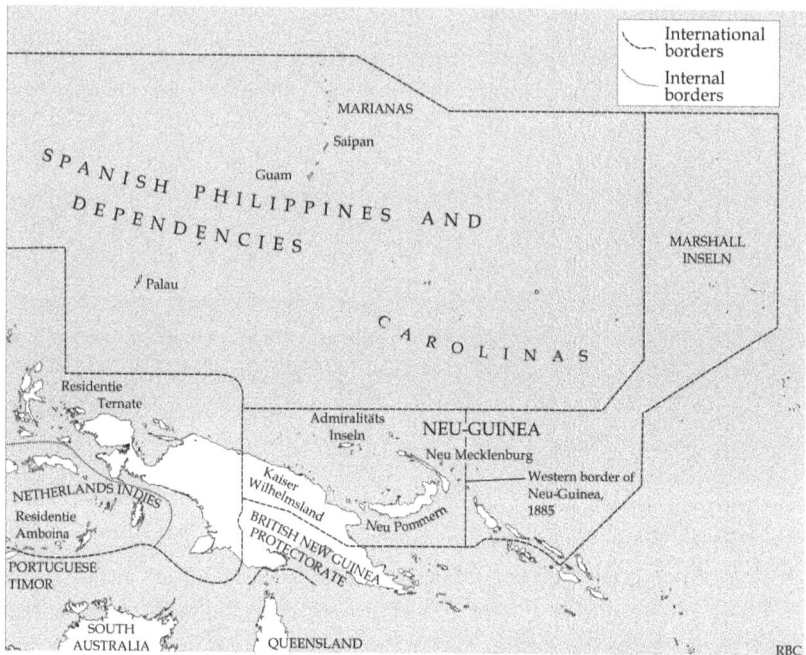

Map 1.2 European Pacific administrative boundaries, 1886
Source: Cartography by Robert Cribb.

Dr William MacGregor, Chief Medical Officer of Fiji, became Administrator of British New Guinea in 1887; its status was upgraded to Crown colony when he arrived in Port Moresby in September 1888. Sir John Thurston had been considered for the position, but instead was promoted to acting and then substantive Governor of Fiji and High Commissioner (1885–97).[57] Although Queensland had refused to take responsibility for British New Guinea, the colony was granted an 'uncertain and anomalous'[58] power of supervision over the territory. The Lieutenant-Governor of British New Guinea Crown colony was under the supervision of the Governor of Queensland, who was always consulted on important issues. Incongruously, while introducing legislation for the White Australia Policy in 1901—which deported Solomon Islander and New Hebridean labourers—Australia negotiated with Britain between 1901 and 1906 to transfer control of British New Guinea to Australia. There was no

---

57 Scarr 1980.
58 Joyce 1971, 104.

mention of any possible transfer of the BSIP to Australia, which could have been accomplished at the same time, although there was interest shown in gaining control of the New Hebrides.[59]

Proclaiming the British Solomon Islands Protectorate

Unique in the Pacific because of its size and complexity, the BSIP remained part of the WPHC for almost its entire existence. Senior staff in the protectorate were always deputy commissioners; from 1953, the BSIP became the headquarters for the WPHC.[60] Colonial plans for Solomon Islands were always made as part of a much wider package of British decisions. Two years after Britain and Germany divided eastern New Guinea between them, they agreed that the Marshall and Caroline islands would become German and the Gilbert Islands and Ellice Islands would be British. In the Solomon Archipelago—its north already part of German New Guinea—they agreed that the German New Guinea border would be extended south to between Isabel and Malaita. The remainder of the Solomon Archipelago as well as the Santa Cruz Group and surrounding southern islands became a British sphere of influence. In the early 1890s, echoing similar plans from almost a decade earlier, lieutenant-governor Sir William MacGregor and Queensland premier Sir Samuel Griffith proposed attaching the central and southern Solomon Islands and possibly the New Hebrides to British New Guinea. Thurston did not support this concept and, after a visit to the Solomons in December 1894, he recommended to the Colonial Office that a separate resident deputy commissioner be appointed for Solomon Islands and the Santa Cruz Group.

London refused, because there seemed to be no prospect of a BSIP administration becoming financially self-supporting. Thurston remained worried about ungoverned European settlements in the territories under his control, especially after the Queensland labour trade, which premier Griffith had signalled in 1885 would end in 1890, was revived in 1892. The Fiji and Queensland labour trades were only loosely governed—by the RNAS, by limited British, Queensland and Fijian legislation and

---

59   Bolton 2000, 246–50.
60   Scarr 1967, 23–35.

by ineffectual government agents on the labour trade ships. Thurston also needed to support the Anglican's Melanesian Mission, which was making progress in Solomon Islands. British rights in Solomon Islands were unassailable, whereas the New Hebrides would always be shared with France. A permanent British base in the Solomon Archipelago was the best long-term solution.

An 1890 amendment to the *Foreign Jurisdiction Act* enabled Britain to exercise jurisdiction over places acquired by treaty, grant, usage, sufferance and other lawful means in the same manner as territory acquired by cession or conquest. The 15 March 1893 order in council covered the whole Pacific, not just the Western Pacific, and British authority was extended to cover indigenous inhabitants and foreign subjects who had allegiance to the British Crown. By 1895, Britain had fallen into line with German and French interpretations of jurisdiction within protectorates. The consent of foreigners to the rule of law within the territory was assumed and the indigenous peoples were presumed to have given up their local jurisdiction to British authority. Ross Johnston put it neatly: 'A jurisdictional empire was possible and without great military or financial involvement.'[61] By the time protectorates were proclaimed over the Gilbert and Ellice islands in 1892[62] and over Solomon Islands and the Santa Cruz Group in 1893, the system had evolved into a more workable model.

The 1893 Pacific Order in Council was subject to the provisions of the *Pacific Islanders Protection Acts* of 1872 and 1875, the *British Settlement Act* of 1887 and the 1890 amendment to the *Foreign Jurisdiction Act*. The first three of these Acts empowered Britain to legislate for subjects who were resident outside her dominions, in the Pacific Islands or in any British settlement. Edward Wolfers suggests:

> [T]he British Solomon Islands Protectorate came under the Foreign Jurisdiction Act only to the extent that it did not conflict with the Pacific Islanders Protection Acts. For that reason, the British Solomon Islands Protectorate seemed to be differently constituted, to have restrictions placed on the jurisdiction of its government, that did not apply in the other British protectorates in Africa and Asia. Elsewhere, while it was clear that the Foreign Jurisdiction Act was specifically intended to grant extraterritorial jurisdiction to the government over British subjects who were

---

61 ibid., 263.
62 Macdonald 1982.

abroad, the Act was so broadly framed that it could be applied to anyone at all. Only in the Pacific did its application seem to be restricted, and especially in the Solomons.[63]

Fiji and British New Guinea had already become Crown colonies, followed by the Gilbert and Ellice Islands. The New Hebrides continued to be shared with France in a unique condominium. When the BSIP was proclaimed in 1893, it did not include the same set of islands that make up the nation today. In April 1886, German New Guinea was extended to include Buka, Bougainville and some small Polynesian outliers, the islands of the Shortland and Treasury Groups (except Mono), Isabel and Choiseul, Ontong Java (Lord Howe) and Nukumanu (Tasman) islands. The Marshall Islands in Micronesia were also included in German territory (see Map 1.2).[64] The 1893 order in council had declared a British protectorate over the New Georgia Group and Mono Island in the north-west, the central Solomon Islands and the southern part of the modern nation-state—the Santa Cruz and Reef groups and surrounding smaller islands and atolls. Next, the Berlin Convention of 14 November 1899, ratified in 1900, led to Germany renouncing its claims over the northern islands of the Solomon Archipelago, except for Bougainville and Buka, along with the small outliers to the east.[65]

Although there was no clear source of future income, the immediate justification for the proclamation of the BSIP was to control the trade in firearms and labour. To comply with the specifications requiring acceptance by indigenous leaders, a RNAS expedition was dispatched from Sydney, comprising HMS *Curaçoa* under Captain Gibson and HMS *Goldfinch* under Lieutenant-Commander Floyd. The ships visited Solomon Islands in June and July 1893. They landed about 30 times, and at each stop the commanders hoisted the Union Jack, ordered a *feu de joie* (the required celebratory rifle salute) and read a proclamation. The first was read out on Mono Island in the Treasury Group on 11 June. In most cases, handwritten copies of the proclamations were either handed to local leaders or buried in bottles. On 28 June 1893, HMS *Curaçoa* visited Port Purvis at the southern entrance to Mboli Passage in the Gela Group. The ship sailed through the passage, landing at Siota, the Melanesian Mission headquarters. Captain Gibson met with local bigman Joseph

---

63   Wolfers 1971, 8–9.
64   Moore 1984.
65   Richards 2012, 88–89.

Havousi, explaining that they had come to hoist the British flag and declare a protectorate. Reverend Comins accompanied the ship to Malaita and other islands, helping to explain the process at each stop. At Makira, two events were combined, as 'commodore justice' was also dispensed through bombardment in retaliation for the death of a crew member of the *Helena*, a Queensland labour trade vessel.[66] While Westerners had come to accept hoisting pieces of coloured cloth up poles as an assertion of authority, this meant nothing to Solomon Islanders. At Langalanga Lagoon on Malaita, the local bigman refused to touch the proclamation or gifts, supposedly fearing that alignment with the British would make the inland descent groups think the lagoon people were preparing for war and cease trade.[67] At Roviana Lagoon, New Georgia, the people immediately ripped up the flag to make loincloths.[68]

Some islands were not visited in 1893 or were not officially visited and included in the protectorate until 1897 and 1898. Rennell and Bellona islands, Sikaiana (Stewart) Islands, the Santa Cruz Group (including Temotu [Trevannion] Island), the Reef and Duff (Wilson) islands, Tikopia, Anuta (Cherry) and Fataka (Mitre) islands were all late additions. To correct geographic errors in an 1898 proclamation another was made in 1899 and in the same year Germany handed over its section of the island chain from the Shortland Islands south to Isabel. The borders of the BSIP and the current boundaries of the nation-state of Solomon Islands were finally established.[69]

---

66 Lawrence 2014, 169–72.
67 Western Pacific High Commission Archives [hereinafter WPHCA], 8 III 22 (1), Australian Station, Solomon Islands, 1893, H.W.S. Gibson, HMS *Curaçoa*, to Commander in Chief, 13 July 1893.
68 In 1966, one of the original Union Jack flags used for the proclamation was lodged with the Solomon Islands Museum collection. The flag came from Pileni in the Reef Islands and was thought to have been unfurled at Nukapu, where Bishop Patterson was killed. On 15 July 1970, a photograph appeared in the *British Solomon Islands Protectorate News Sheet* [hereinafter *BSIPNS*] of one of the original proclamations. The document had come into the possession of Spearline Wilson, the Commissioner for Lands, who took it with him to Sydney during World War II. He returned it to Solomon Islands after the war and it was held in the Treasury Department strongroom. This was probably the proclamation used at Gela. It still existed in 1971 but is now missing. *PIM*, September 1952; *BSIPNS*, October 1961, 21 April 1966; Wolfers 1971, 6.
69 Only two further changes have been made to the nation's territorial boundaries. As an independence gift, in 1975, Solomon Islands gave Polkington Reef (on the boundary between the two nations) to Papua New Guinea and, in January 1978, sovereign territory was extended to a 321-kilometre limit under the Fisheries Limits Ordinance. *Solomons News Drum*, 13 January 1977; Moore 2003, 196.

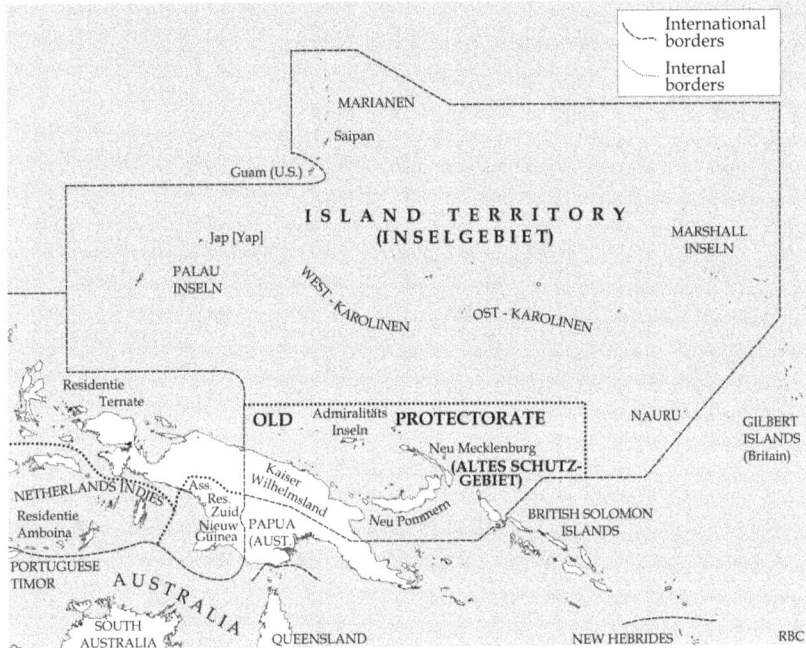

Map 1.3 European Pacific administrative boundaries, 1910
Source: Cartography by Robert Cribb.

This legal fiction of acceptance was enough to satisfy the Colonial Office that Solomon Islands was a genuine protectorate. The 1893 order in council that created the Solomons protectorate gave the High Commissioner, and through him the Resident Commissioner, the power to control prisons, immigration, lodgement of returns of imports and exports and taxation, to operate treaties and to legislate for peace, order and good government. Except for visits from the labour trade government agents and British naval ships, there was no on-the-ground presence until 1896–97.

****

Governors of Crown colonies were appointed by the monarch on the recommendation of the Secretary of State for the Colonies. In the 1910s and 1920s, plantation interests unsuccessfully lobbied the High Commissioner and the Secretary of State for the Colonies to have the BSIP turned into a Crown colony, which would have allowed more autonomy.[70] The planters also suggested an island confederation, with the

---

70 WPHCA, 1184/1925, Deputation to High Commissioner of Representatives of Residents, 29 September 1925, transcript, 2.

WPHC territories separated from Fiji. They objected to being 'dragged behind the chariot of Fiji'.[71] However, protectorate status was maintained even after WPHC headquarters was transferred from Suva to Honiara in 1953. At that time, the High Commissioner and his administration absorbed the duties of the BSIP Resident Commissioner and his staff, whose positions became defunct.

After the Pacific War, the emphasis changed because Solomon Islands required extensive rehabilitation and reconstruction. Although the High Commissioner proposed that the BSIP be developed as a 'native territory', the Secretary of State for the Colonies refused, asserting that to do so would interfere with economic rehabilitation. Britain maintained its protectorate concept, seeing its position as one of trusteeship for the 'native peoples' while continuing to believe that the inhabitants were not ready for political participation. The plan was to eventually take over control of the existing mission-based health and education sectors and to develop local government as a stepping-stone towards long-term district and national government. Shifting the High Commissioner and the administration of the WPHC from Suva to Honiara altered the dynamics of government. Although it would also have been a good time to change the status of the protectorate to that of a Crown colony, this did not occur. It was a strange situation. The High Commissioner was resident in a protectorate which he governed, along with half a condominium, the Crown Colony of Gilbert and Ellice Islands, and Pitcairn Island. Once more, the British proved to be versatile in their arrangements. Part of the explanation for British reticence may have been that inhabitants of Crown colonies were entitled to British passports, which gave them easy access to the United Kingdom. It was empire-wide policy that indigenous inhabitants of protectorates had no such rights.

The BSIP Advisory Council began in 1921. In 1950, the number of non-official representative members was increased, although all were chosen by the Resident Commissioner (and later the High Commissioner). Honiara grew quickly: new administrative buildings were constructed and new educational institutions began. This all befitted Honiara's role as the new urban centre of the WPHC. The BSIP Legislative Council was established in 1960, renamed the Governing Council in 1970. It had 26 members: 17 were elected, three were ex-officio appointees given seats because of their status or position and up to six public service members were

---

71   *Planters' Gazette*, 2 April 1921, 4; 5 February 1922, [editorial].

appointed by the High Commissioner. In 1974, the Governing Council was replaced with the Legislative Assembly, with 24 elected members and three ex-officio members, operating under a ministerial system with a chief minister. The BSIP became self-governing in 1976, with a 38-seat Legislative Assembly.

In 1973, the High Commissioner ceased acting for the Anglo-French condominium in the New Hebrides, which left the BSIP and the Gilbert and Ellice Islands as the only large WPHC territories. The High Commission was abolished in January 1976.[72] Rather bizarrely, in 1974, the High Commissioner was redesignated as Governor of the BSIP and the BSIP Chief Secretary became the Deputy Governor. The governors of the Crown Colony of Gilbert and Ellice Islands and the BSIP reported directly to the Secretary of State for the Colonies in London.[73] The constitution of the sovereign democratic nation of Solomon Islands came into force at independence on 7 July 1978, ending the last British protectorate. The strange legal meanderings that had created the BSIP were at an end.

---

72   A few residual functions, such as referral to the Fiji Court of Appeal, outlasted the WPHC.
73   The Crown Colony of the Gilbert and Ellice Islands was split in two in 1975 in preparation for independence as two separate nations. The Crown Colony of Gilbert Islands retained the position of governor, while the smaller Crown Colony of Ellice Islands was administered by a Queen's commissioner until independence. McIntyre 2012.

2

A 'very arduous task': Charles, Arthur and Frank

> In January last [1915] Mr. C.M. Woodford, C.M.G., the Resident Commissioner, retired from the service on a well earned pension. Mr. Woodford had been for many years associated with the Solomon Islands, and, from the establishment of the British Protectorate, successfully carried out the very arduous task of developing and establishing the Government. In the early days this was no easy matter, and lately the work incidental to controlling a new and rapidly progressing Protectorate was beset with many difficulties, which by tact and ability he was able to overcome.
>
> — British Solomon Islands Protectorate *Annual Report*, 1914–15[1]

Choosing Tulagi

Charles Woodford retired in 1915 at the age of 63. The slim young man of the 1880s and 1890s had become more thickset, with greying hair, and the beard of his youth had been replaced with a neat moustache. He had lobbied for and received the position of Resident Commissioner, created a town and established a colonial administration and a plantation economy. The 1914–15 BSIP *Annual Report*, prepared by his temporary replacement, Frank Barnett, concluded with an understatement that 'some years must elapse before complete control of the natives can be brought about'.[2] The protectorate was well established, although on some islands, such as populous Malaita, little progress had been made.

---

1   British Solomon Islands Protectorate *Annual Reports* [hereinafter BSIP *AR*] 1914–15, 7.
2   ibid.

Woodford arrived in Solomon Islands in May 1896 at age 44, aboard HMS *Pylades*, to take up the new position of short-term acting Deputy Commissioner for the incipient British protectorate. He toured the islands, mounted a punitive expedition on Guadalcanal to avenge the deaths of Austrian Baron von Norbeck and members of his expedition and established a temporary headquarters at Nielsen's trading station on Gavutu, 5 kilometres from Tulagi.[3] Woodford had known Nielsen since his first visits as a naturalist in the 1880s and had always enjoyed his hospitality. His initial official report said that there were 48 Europeans in the protectorate, four of them missionaries, and 21 trading vessels.[4] In the days before airplanes, the primary consideration for a settlement was a sheltered port: Tulagi and Gavutu harbours were suitable and central. Tulagi is well positioned for shipboard travel in the Solomons: 25 kilometres from the east coast of Guadalcanal (the largest island in the protectorate), close to Malaita (the most populous island) and central in the archipelago. Its soils are poor, mainly red clay, except for fertile pockets in small valleys. The island was uninhabited, used only for gardening and hunting.

Having been ordered specifically not to establish a permanent headquarters, Woodford seems to have passed off his purchase of Tulagi as a temporary measure.[5] After considering Uki Island between Makira and Ulawa islands, and the Marau Sound area of Guadalcanal, where he had spent time in the 1880s, Woodford purchased Tulagi as the site for the protectorate's administrative headquarters. The presence nearby of missionaries and traders, and the proximity of sheltered Mboli Passage, which could be used as a shortcut to other islands, proved irresistible. The owners had earlier offered to sell Tulagi to Nielsen. With the trader as his broker, on 29 September 1896, Woodford purchased the island. He paid the neighbouring Gela Sule landowners £42 in gold sovereigns—today equal to about SI$67,700 (A$11,700). Tambokoro and his sons received £12, while the inhabitants of Matanibana, Haleta and Tugumata villages received £10 per village. Misleadingly, Woodford assured the villagers that their garden rights would not be disturbed.[6]

---

3   Lawrence 2014, 172–76; Lawrence (p. 105, Figure 16) identifies one of Woodford's photographs as being possibly of Lars Nielsen's house at Gavutu, although later photographs do not look similar
4   PMB, Woodford Papers and Photographs, 1021, H. Monckton, E.P. Monckton, C.M. Woodford, and F.M. Woodford, Correspondence, British Solomon Islands, 1909–28, C.M. Woodford to R.P. Brown Johnson, 27 March 1919; Woodford 1890; Tennent 1999; Lawrence 2014, 172–79.
5   Lawrence 2014, 172.
6   Colonial Office [hereinafter CO], 225/50, Microfilm 2329, Colonial Reports, Miscellaneous, No. 8. Western Pacific, RC C.M. Woodford, Report of the British Solomon Islands, March 1897, 22–24; CO, 225/50, HC Sir John B. Thurston to Colonial Office, 8 December 1896. See also Lawrence 2014, 179–80.

2. A 'VERY ARDUOUS TASK'

Plate 2.1 Tulagi viewed from Gavutu, 2007
Source: Clive Moore Collection.

Woodford left the protectorate in October 1896, and from Suva and Sydney again lobbied for a permanent appointment. His first official report provided confidence that the protectorate could pay its own way and impressed Joseph Chamberlain, the Secretary of State for the Colonies. There was confusion about the exact nature of Woodford's position. Initially, it was thought that funds were available for an ongoing appointment as Resident Commissioner, but the Colonial Office only confirmed a non-renewable, six-month appointment as acting Deputy Commissioner. Chaffing under his temporary position, Woodford complained bitterly to authorities in Suva and London, who extended his acting tenure to one year. His continuing appointment as Resident Commissioner—no longer Deputy Commissioner—was confirmed on 17 February 1897. The Colonial Office must have wondered at his zeal to rule the newest far-flung outpost of the British Empire. He was given a £1,200 grant-in-aid, plus his salary, on the understanding that the protectorate would become financially independent as soon as possible. His tasks were to supervise the labour trade, stop illegal sales of firearms, consolidate the boundaries, protect the people and ensure a prosperous future. Woodford had an 8.2-metre open whaleboat purpose-built in Sydney, was given

Martini-Henry rifles with aiming tubes and ammunition for his armed constabulary, purchased supplies and had a small amount of money left over to employ local labour.[7]

In March 1897, Woodford joined HMS *Rapid* in Suva Harbour. The ship took him to Gavutu, then to the Western Solomons to investigate the deaths of several traders. In May and June, he employed Gela villagers to cut a track across Tulagi, clear sites for the residency and police barracks, cut timber for the buildings and remove enough mangroves to erect a jetty. In early June, he had a hut constructed near the landing place and returned to Gavutu only on weekends. A photograph exists of this flimsy structure—the first temporary British building on Tulagi. From late June, Woodford plus five prisoners and three labourers lived permanently on Tulagi. Soon after, HMS *Torch* arrived from Fiji with the first members of Woodford's armed constabulary. They were eight Solomon Islanders who had engaged in the labour trade but had lived in Fiji for some time and spoke Fijian. Among other duties, they served as crew on Woodford's whaleboat.[8]

Constructing the settlement

Woodford worked with local villagers and his armed constabulary, burning off the felled timber. Next, they built a track up to the central ridge and levelled a site for the first residency. The temporary accommodation at Tulagi became overcrowded, which forced the party to once more commute from Gavutu. On 5 August, BP's ship *Titus* arrived with extra materials to complete the residency and a prison; the ship brought a carpenter from Australia for the task. A year later, Woodford recorded having the walls of his verandah lined with tongue-and-groove Oregon pine boards, which made the structure much cooler. In 1901, he described his house as 54 metres above sea level, with substantial stone and concrete steps leading down to the landing place.[9]

---

7   Lawrence 2014, 185–86.
8   As they were the first Solomon Islanders to be employed by the protectorate government, they are worth naming. George Homina (or Homiana), a man called Johnson, Jacky Govuna, Peter Suinga (or Suiga) and Harry Tongolia (from Savo) enlisted in Suva on 1 May 1897. Four days later, Johnny Kuria and Jimmy Uvi (from San Cristoval) enlisted and, on 15 May, William Buruku joined the group. They signed contracts to work for one year at £1 a month plus free lodging, rations, clothing and medicine. *Solomon Islands Police Force Newsletter*, September 1972, 2.
9   BSIP *AR* 1901–02, 18.

Plate 2.2 The first residency, built in 1898 on Tulagi's central ridge
Source: ANU Archives (ANUA), 481-337-125.

Plate 2.3 The first two homes of the Resident Commissioner

The 1898 residency is to the centre and the 1905 residency is on the right. Government coconut plantations are in the foreground. The photograph is probably from 1907.

Source: British Museum, George Rose's photographs in the Edge-Partington Photographic Collection.

Plate 2.4 The back of Woodford's second residency, built in 1905, showing the gardens
Source: ANUA, 481-337-102.

All the members of the armed constabulary were able to relocate to Tulagi on 16 August. The residency and the prison, plus a short coastal track, were almost complete by the time the carpenter left at the end of November. During late 1897 and early 1898, the tracks were expanded, bananas and sweet potato gardens were planted and a permanent water supply was created.[10] The residency was ready for use early in 1898 and the prison and the small police headquarters were completed in March—built partly from Australian blue gum and red gum timber, with an Oregon pine floor and leaf walls.[11] The permanent buildings were a useful advance from the early days. When Woodford brought prisoners back from Guadalcanal in September 1897, they worked on the roads and in the gardens during the day and had to be chained to house posts at night.[12]

Woodford's 1896 and 1897 reports convinced the Colonial Office that a financially self-sufficient administration could be achieved through taxation and development of an economy based on coconut plantations. A smallpox epidemic broke out in German New Guinea in 1898, which required implementing a strict quarantine regime in the protectorate. The next year, when the German Solomon Islands south of Bougainville

---

10   ibid., 1897–98, 12, 1901–02, 18.
11   ibid., 1897–98, 12, 1911, 23; Lawrence 2014, 179–80.
12   Boutilier 1984b, 47.

Strait were transferred to Britain, the Colonial Office was pressured to give a larger grant for the protectorate. This enabled the purchase of the 33-ton ketch-rigged yacht *Lahloo*. The protectorate administration had crept over the line to become permanent, through circumstances not all of its own making. The Colonial Office made noises about there being no guarantees for further finances and suggested that the Australian colonies should assist with payment, in the same way as they had originally promised to do (but reneged on) for British New Guinea. The protectorate moved ahead to encourage the development of copra plantations. The companies that dominated the industry in the early days of the protectorate were the Pacific Islands Company and, later, Levers' Pacific Plantations Limited.[13] Levers, a British manufacturing company founded in 1885, successfully promoted a new soap-making process using vegetable oils from coconut and oil palms, rather than from tallow (rendered animal fat). Solomon Islands became Levers' Pacific base for the production of copra—the smoke-dried kernel of coconuts—to turn into oil.

Plate 2.5 *Lahloo*, the first government yacht, anchored off Arundel Island
Source: ANUA, 481-337-119.

---

13   Scarr 1967, 263–70; Bennett 1987, 125–49.

Plate 2.6 Tulagi Harbour and Mulallie Creek
Source: NASI, WPHC Photograph Album.

Arthur William Mahaffy

Woodford's first assistant was Arthur William Mahaffy, a top-rate appointment for such an isolated position. Mahaffy's father, Reverend (later Sir) John P. Mahaffy, was a Classics scholar who served as provost of Trinity College, Dublin. In his younger years, he had taught Oscar Wilde. Born in Dublin in 1869, Arthur Mahaffy was educated at Marlborough Grammar School—one of England's oldest—and at Magdalen College, Oxford University, graduating with a Master of Arts degree in 1893. After a short appointment as a junior teacher at Magdalen, he spent four years in the Royal Munster Fusiliers, reaching the rank of second lieutenant. He then joined the Colonial Service and was posted to the WPHC, serving first for two years as a junior officer in the Gilbert and Ellice Islands Protectorates. His Solomon Islands appointment began in 1898, as a resident magistrate and assistant to Woodford.[14] During his first year, although based in Tulagi, he travelled extensively through the islands. Houses were constructed for Mahaffy at Tulagi and Gizo. He was also appointed a deputy commissioner of the WPHC.

---

14   Richards 2012, 87.

Mahaffy's background suited Woodford's plans. Posted permanently to Gizo in 1900, he was provided with a force of 25 members of the armed constabulary to suppress headhunting around New Georgia and Vella Lavella. Pacification—the establishment of authority over indigenous polities—was key to the development of copra plantations in the Western Solomons. Mahaffy served under Woodford for several years before he became the assistant to the High Commissioner in Suva in 1904. Between 1909 and 1914, he returned to the Gilbert and Ellice Islands Protectorates as Resident Commissioner.[15]

Infrastructure, health and welfare

General improvements continued to be made to Tulagi by draining swamps and planting coconut palms and root crops for food, plus other experimental tropical crops such as cocoa, rubber and coffee. Within two years, 24 hectares were under cultivation. By 1901, the cultivated area had increased to 40 hectares, including 30 hectares of coconut palms. Woodford continued to have swampy areas filled in. Two years later, 60 hectares were under cultivation, 54 under palms. Later photographs show that the coconut plantations continued to increase in size. The nuts were used for both food and producing copra. The town's inner foreshore eventually became a pleasant promenade and transport route, with Queenslander-style office buildings dotted along the shore and houses on nearby hillocks and the central ridge.[16]

Malaria was a constant problem that debilitated expatriates and Solomon Islanders alike. The infection is spread by parasites in the bloodstream introduced by bites from female Anopheles mosquitoes.[17] Although malaria does not usually kill adults, it results in anaemia and its effects generally cause victims to function at about 80 per cent of their full

---

15 Lawrence 2014, 198–206; Richards 2012, 87–110; Moore 2013, entry for Arthur Mahaffy. Mahaffy returned to England and in 1914 he was appointed as Administrator of Dominica, a British Crown colony in the Lesser Antilles in the Caribbean. He died in 1919. His extensive ethnographic collection was donated to the National Museum in Dublin.

16 PMB, Woodford Papers and Photographs, Staniforth Smith, 'New Guinea and the Solomons: Their Future Development', *Daily Mail* [Brisbane], 4 January 1905, [newspaper cutting], in Reel 2, Bundle 8, 9/23, enclosed in 8.3; BSIP *AR* 1897–98, 12–13, 1898–99, 14–15, 1899–1900, 13, 1900–01, 16, 1901–02, 18–19, 1902–03, 21.

17 Malarial infections can be carried for many years. The worst form, cerebral malaria, can cause death. Malaria often resurfaces in the body because of another infection. The spleen plays an important part in the body's fight against malaria, but it enlarges and can rupture.

strength. Influenced by an 1899 report of a malaria expedition to West Africa published by the Liverpool School of Tropical Medicine, Woodford realised that he had to eliminate swamps. As he commented:

> The stagnant water in the swamps on Tulagi formerly swarmed with the larvae of Culicidae (mosquitos). The drains were cut from above downwards, and it is no exaggeration to say that when the first of the effluent matter was allowed to escape it contained as much of mosquito larvae as of water.[18]

Throughout the 1910s and 1920s, Tulagi's swamps continued to be drained and its low-lying areas reclaimed. Woodford also destroyed larvae with kerosene. This eradicated most mosquito breeding places and made the island a much healthier place. In 1911, Woodford summed up the situation:

> All new arrivals must be prepared, sooner or later, to pass through a course of malarial fever, but the methods of combatting this disease are now so well known that with intelligent precautions its after-effects can be to a greater extent guarded against.[19]

Sanitation was also improved by building pit latrines and latrines on platforms over the sea, for use by indentured labourers, police and prisoners. Incinerators were established to destroy empty tins and refuse. The first hospital was built in 1913.

Woodford set to work to implement basic laws and regulations. The sale of arms and ammunition to Solomon Islanders was prohibited. Regulations were promulgated in 1897 to try to ensure that cholera, smallpox, measles and yellow fever (an acute viral disease spread by mosquitoes) were not introduced from German New Guinea. All vessels entering the protectorate from the north had to first proceed to Tulagi for inspection and, if necessary, quarantine. Licence fees and capitation taxes were levied and exports of tropical products such as copra, ivory nuts, bêche-de-mer and pearl shell, green snail and turtle shell, rattan cane, coffee and orchids were also taxed. Licence fees were lucrative: £3 per passenger from Sydney, £5 for each small boat brought in on a schooner or steamer, £10 for trading licences and substantial harbourage fees. 'Natives' were legally defined to stop cash borrowing and indebtedness, and land acquisition began to be regulated. During these early years, the first copper and gold prospectors tried their luck, without success.[20]

---

18 BSIP *AR* 1901–02, 18–19.
19 ibid., 1911, 31.
20 ibid., 1896, 1897–98, 188–99; Lawrence 2014, 180–84, 186, 193–95.

2. A 'VERY ARDUOUS TASK'

Plate 2.7 The scene from Tulagi ridge, looking towards Gavutu, in the mid-1910s
The hospital is on the left, with the path from the residency passing by.
Source: ANUA, 481-337-121.

Plate 2.8 Tulagi's first hospital, built in 1913
Note the magnificent woven wall.
Source: ANUA, 481-337-124.

Shipping

Ships, large and small, were the lifeblood of the protectorate. BP's ships carried most of the cargo and passengers. Regular shipping communication with Sydney was established in 1896 by BP steamers on a route that left Sydney for British New Guinea and returned via Tulagi and Port Vila in the New Hebrides. The first BP voyage to the Solomons was in 1894—an attempt to compete with a temporary steamer service introduced by G.J. Waterhouse and Company from Sydney.[21] It took until the early 1900s for the route to become profitable for BP, using *Titus*, a 760-ton steamer that could carry 40 passengers. Once Tulagi was established, *Titus* began calling there every two months on a route that included Norfolk Island, Port Vila and the Santa Cruz Group. After 1898, BP's ship *Ysabel* (524 tons) was also used on this route, stopping at the New Hebrides, the Banks and Santa Cruz groups and Lord Howe and Norfolk islands. Woodford was critical of these circuitous routes, which took three weeks. A direct trip from Sydney to Tulagi took only eight days, which would have allowed tropical produce to reach Australian markets.

Communications had improved by 1910. BP began running a direct steamer service from Sydney to Tulagi every six weeks, and their Gilbert and Ellice Islands steamer also called in for mail on its way to and from Australia. As the years progressed, BP's service extended north to Rabaul on a circuit around the Coral Sea, joining the Australian east coast to New Guinea and Solomon Islands. From 1905, Levers' steamer *Upolu* called every 11 weeks. It was replaced in 1910 with *Kulambangara*, which continued in service until 1916, after which Levers used BP's shipping service to and from Australia. Levers also operated two small steamers within the protectorate.[22] A BP steamer made a round trip from Australia to Tulagi every six weeks during the mid-1920s and another sailed from Australia via Rabaul, entering the protectorate from the north at the Shortland Islands before travelling to Tulagi and back to Australia. Although other shipping companies, such as the Union Steam Ship Company and the Australian United Steam Navigation Company, tried to break into the Western Pacific trade, they were never as successful as BP

---

21 Bennett 1987, 51.
22 BSIP *AR* 1902–03, 17, 1912–13, 8.

After 1898, around 50 major voyages called at Tulagi each year, with the number growing as the years progressed. The commercial steamer services allowed direct communication with Sydney and Brisbane around 20 times annually, and a dozen labour trade vessels from Queensland and Fiji called at Tulagi before discharging their human cargoes or commencing recruiting. All ships had to pay harbourage charges, and many made several trips a year. Labour ships had to pay an annual £100 licence fee and allow a medical check of all passengers and crew and a search for contraband.[23] Ships were boarded by Tulagi-based officials—usually the medical officer, who carried out the health checks, and Treasury staff, who dealt with customs and excise matters. Trader and labour recruiter J.E. Philp described the scene in the early 1910s:

> [T]he port … official came off in a whale boat pulling five oars—each rower wearing a blue lava-lava with a diamond pointed hem—a leather belt round the waist and a bright scarlet fez atop of his short crisp curly thatch with different styles of ear ornaments—from a stick or piece of bone—to a festoon of seeds—thrust through [each] ear lobe.[24]

The centrality of Tulagi had its disadvantages for yachts entering from the north or south of the protectorate. Novelist Jack London had to deal with this in July 1908 when his yacht, *Snark*, entered protectorate waters via the New Hebrides and on the way stopped at Santa Ana, Uki and Guadalcanal. His wife, Charmian, made light of the incident:

> Mr. Woodford was unfortunately absent when Jack sailed to Gubutu [Gavutu], and he had to deal with a deputy who very tersely demanded the penalty of five pounds for our breach of quarantine. Jack says it is cheap at the price when he considers the six hundred extra miles he would have had to sail if he had entered properly in the first place, beat back to see Port Mary and then covered the return trip to Pennduffryn [a plantation on the east coast of Guadalcanal, later known as Berande]. We are going to frame the receipt for the fine.[25]

---

23   Smith 1898, 7 February.
24   J.E. Philp in Herr and Rood 1978, 30. See also Dickinson 1927, 30.
25   London 1915a, 375.

Plate 2.9 BP's SS *Minindi* at the wharf, Makambo Island
Source: Noel Butlin Archives Centre (NBAC), N115-513-3.

The Australian colonial and Commonwealth governments subsidised BP to supply a shipping service to adjacent Pacific Islands, including carriage of mail.[26] This gave the company a virtual monopoly, which it exploited. BP became a major force in the Solomons economy as well as in maritime transport. From the late 1890s, the New South Wales and Queensland governments provided subsidies to run steamers from Sydney, Brisbane and Cooktown to British New Guinea, German New Guinea, Solomon Islands and the New Hebrides. The Australian Government took over the responsibility in 1901, contributing a large subsidy each year, along with additional funds provided by the Australian Papua and BSIP governments. The protectorate contributed £1,800 each year. This rose to £3,000 in the early 1930s and, along with the Australian subsidy, led to lower charges for freight and passengers.[27] BP became shippers, storekeepers, copra-buyers, bankers and insurance agents and ran copra plantations.

---

26 Buckley and Klugman 1981, 68–71. By 1926, this subsidy had increased to £3,000. BSIP *AR* 1926–27, 8.
27 BSIP *AR*, 1934, 12. This cost was partly offset by abatements in the costs of passages and freight.

Plate 2.10 BP's Makambo Island, showing the rail system that transported supplies to and from the wharf. Tulagi is in the background
Source: NBAC, N115-520.

Plate 2.11 Makambo Island from the beach, with the manager's house at the top
Source: NBAC, N115-520-2.

TULAGI

Plate 2.12 The main store area on Makambo Island
Source: NBAC, N115-520-4.

Plate 2.13 BP's SS *Mataram* sailing from Tulagi Harbour for Sydney
Source: Clive Moore Collection.

In February 1925, a new BP service began using the *Makambo*, which sailed out of Sydney, travelling first to Port Vila in the New Hebrides and then on to Peu on Vanikolo before proceeding to Tulagi.[28] Overseas steamers arrived, dealt with formal procedures, then headed north to Gizo and the Shortland Islands and into Australia's New Guinea Mandated Territory (former German New Guinea). Over a two-week period, the ships collected freight and delivered cargo to plantations, missions and trading stations. They travelled to Rabaul before returning to Tulagi and southern ports. W.R. Carpenter and Company (known as Carpenters) also operated an intermittent steamer service via New Guinea, using the *Inga* to call at Tulagi and Vanikolo on the way back to Australia. The other major overseas ships calling in were copra vessels owned by American, Norwegian, Swedish and Japanese companies. Internally in the protectorate, BP steamers called at various islands as they passed through, but in the early 1920s even on this route their holds were only half-full.

The government, planters, traders, labour recruiters and missions all had their own small interisland vessels. Woodford used the *Lahloo* on patrol and to communicate with his deputy, Mahaffy, who was based in Gizo in the north-west. The *Lahloo* was small enough to be propelled by sweep oars if the wind failed. Mahaffy's main task was to discourage the headhunting that blighted the Western Solomons and Isabel and stood in the way of developing commercial coconut plantations. Gizo and Faisi, in the Shortland Islands, were the first British bases beyond Tulagi, established in 1899 and 1906, respectively. Both later became official ports of entry.[29] The main BP vessel after 1905 was the *Malaita*, while Carpenters used the *Duranbah* in the 1910s.[30] International ships brought mail into the protectorate, which was distributed from Tulagi using smaller craft.[31]

---

28   Under different management, before 1923, this was known as San Cristoval Estates Limited.
29   Until 1899, the Shortland Islands had been included in the territory claimed within German New Guinea.
30   BSIP *AR*, 1924–25, 9–10, 1925–26, 9.
31   ibid., 1928, 9, 1929, 8.

Once official procedures were completed, the commercial steamers anchored at Gavutu or Makambo before setting off around the islands. The recruiting ships left to drop off returning islanders and search for new recruits. At the same time as the external labour trade was closing in the 1900s and early 1910s, labour recruiting began for the approximately 20 plantation companies operating within the protectorate, which drew local smaller vessels to Tulagi. However, once the various district headquarters were established, not all internal recruiting vessels called at Tulagi. British warships from the RNAS fleet continued to visit regularly and sometimes carried the Resident Commissioner to the more distant islands in his domain. During the 1920s, the ungainly steam yacht HMCS *Ranadi* became the main vessel used by resident commissioners. In later years, a series of small vessels served the districts, and the resident commissioners used the handsome HMCS *Tulagi*, the largest ship in the government fleet. Gavutu was crucial for replenishing fuel supplies for steamships; the coal from its store was placed into baskets and wheeled down to the wharf on a rail track.[32]

BP soon realised the potential of combining cargo transport with regular passenger and tourist trips around the South Seas. Ships in use in the 1920s and 1930s provided comfortable accommodation in two, three and four-berth cabins. The *Malaita* and *Mataram* were replaced with a series of successors, *Makambo*, *Minindi*, *Marsina* and *Malaita II*. Tourists could take a round trip, moving on to mission stations and copra plantations, or get off at Tulagi and pick the ship up again on its return voyage. Visitors commented favourably on Tulagi, finding its inhabitants friendly. Groups of female schoolteacher tourists in the 1930s briefly inflated the number of single women on the island by several hundred per cent, much to the delight of resident expatriate men. When passenger ships were in port there was usually a dance arranged on board to which the resident males flocked, some resplendent in their white tropical suits or 'Red Sea rig'.

---

32   Sinker 1900, 42–43; Horton 1965, 21–22.

Plate 2.14 A man in a canoe, from an early Burns Philp & Co. advertisement for tourism in Solomon Islands

Source: NBAC, N115-619, June 1934, Vol. 6, No. 3, p. 64.

Plate 2.15 A woman in a grass skirt, from an early Burns Philp & Co. advertisement for tourism in Solomon Islands
Source: NBAC, N115-619, December 1932, Vol. 5, No. 3, p. 64, inside front cover.

'Steamer day' was always a red-letter day that buzzed with activity. People from all over Solomon Islands timed their trips to Tulagi to coincide with the arrival of the steamers. Passengers, mail, fresh and frozen meat, fruit and vegetables arrived from Sydney, and protectorate residents boarded the ships, travelling to Australia for business, medical treatment, schooling or holidays. Inbound cargo was unloaded on the Makambo or Gavutu wharves, where it went through customs clearance and was stored, before transhipment into the holds of small vessels to be dispersed throughout the protectorate. Once released by the officials, the passengers and crew went ashore at either of the commercial bases in the harbour or landed on Tulagi, mixing with the local European and Chinese population. Most of the international shipping used Chinese crews from Hong Kong in the engine and boiler rooms;[33] these crew made a beeline for Chinatown to pass on news and relax. New arrivals took in the sights of the pretty island capital and the residents gossiped and assessed the 'new chum' passengers, particularly if they were likely to become long-term residents. Elkington's Hotel (1916–34), on the edge of the ridge above the main wharf, bustled with activity and the Tulagi Club (built in 1927 on the outer side of the island) swung into action. Tulagi's residents tried to answer any mail quickly so as to post letters for return on the same ship. The ships dropped off their cargo and passengers, travelled their allotted route and then passed through again on their way back to Sydney.

These services enabled the Solomons to join the tourist circuit. BP began publishing a travel magazine in 1911, *Picturesque Travel*, later renamed the *BP Magazine*, to market Pacific tourism. There were attempts in the 1930s to set up temporary tourist facilities when the steamers were in port.[34] The cabins were small and accommodation in Tulagi was primitive compared with that in Suva or Honolulu. It was what would now be called 'adventure tourism' and began to bring short-term visitors to Tulagi. BP and Solomon Islands expatriates called it 'round trip' tourism. Australians arrived on three-week round trips hoping to see 'real wild cannibals'.[35] During the Great Depression, some residents attempted to tap into the new market. Charles and Kathleen Bignell at Fulakora plantation on Isabel tried to diversify by advertising homestays that included riding, tennis, swimming and home comforts.[36] Islanders from the Gela Group

33 Hilder 1961, 36.
34 Douglas 1996; Douglas 2004.
35 Bernatzik 1935, 73.
36 *PIM*, 26 January 1932.

participated in early tourism by making souvenirs to sell to the visitors, and some traders brought artefacts to Tulagi to sell to tourists. In the early 1930s, when Ernie Palmer made a trip to isolated Sikaiana Atoll, he purchased rare loom weaving, mats and model outrigger canoes to sell to tourists back in Tulagi.[37] Although they were largely outsiders to this urban development, some Solomon Islanders slowly began to incorporate Tulagi, Gavutu and Makambo into their island world.

Tulagi operated during the decades-long transition from sail to steam power. The early transport system depended on sails. Until engines became more common, sailmakers and repairers were essential on Tulagi, with services provided mainly by a Welshman, Jack Ellis, who was born in Bangor in 1876. An ex-sailor who had lived in the Solomons since the 1900s, Ellis became a fixture on the island. After a short trading career in the Western Solomons, he settled at Sasape in the 1910s, remaining until the outbreak of the Pacific War. He lived in a loft above his workshop, next to his small jetty (see Maps 2.1 and 4.1), with his mate Jack Newman. The relationship was based on alcohol and storytelling. Ellis was well read and rather cynical about humanity, particularly government officers. When not dealing with sails, he worked in Richard C. (Dick) Laycock's store (next door) or acted as an agent for Chinese traders. As a former sailor, Newman had no fear of heights and took on the annual job of painting the radio transmitter masts.[38] Sailing ships—once the main means of transport in the protectorate—were gradually replaced with motorised vessels, which took away the two men's livelihoods. By the 1930s, with Newman dead, Ellis eked out a living doing odd jobs, and was respected as a gracious but garrulous old man. He had a white beard and moustache and always wore a khaki drill jacket and trousers, which he made himself. Ernie Palmer remembered him as a 'dirty old man' who used a peephole to watch naked Solomon Islander women off Ernie's ships, whom he lured to shower in his bath house.[39]

---

37 Struben 1963, 52.
38 His fee to the government was said to have been £5 a day and free hospital treatment for bites from wasps that lived on the masts.
39 Golden 1993, 85–87, 283; Struben 1963, 41–42.

While the age of sail ended, hulls and engines also required repairs, as did the propellers and drive shafts of boats if they ended up wedged on reefs—a common occurrence. Chinatown's tradesmen had a variety of skills and could fix many mechanical problems. On Tulagi, Carpenters had an engineering workshop and there was another small engineering business. BP's Makambo had a slipway and workshop, although the only full-scale engineering workshop belonged to Levers, at Gavutu. Once refrigeration was introduced in the 1920s, including large commercial freezers, there were even more engines to maintain and repair.[40]

Providing services

The Tulagi enclave developed into a service centre for the protectorate, providing postal and banking services, sailmaking and mechanical and engineering services. Today, we are inclined to take for granted that there is a global communication system and that letters sent from anywhere will arrive at the destination written on the envelope. As is clear from the Woodford quote that began this chapter, this was not always the case. In the 1880s and 1890s, it seemed as though Solomon Islands did not exist, or at least no mail system could find it.

Once Woodford arrived in 1896, letters and parcels were placed into canvas bags and given to the crew of steamers to post in Sydney. New South Wales stamps were used and a locked bag was arranged for government business. In 1903, the High Commissioner refused Woodford's request to overprint Fiji stamps. Three years later, Woodford had a hand-franking rubber stamp made that read 'British Solomon Islands Paid' and designed another with a round Tulagi postmark for all outgoing mail. Initially, the envelopes were accompanied by cash or his personal cheque for stamps obtained in Sydney.

Woodford was very happy with the postage system he introduced; he was a stamp collector and was delighted to be able to design and issue his own stamps. However, he was also aware that his administration could make £500–£600 a year from selling stamps. With permission from the Secretary of State for the Colonies, he had the first BSIP postage stamps

---

40 Ashby 1978, 69; Golden 1993, 88.

printed in Sydney by W.E. Smith and Company, using a lithographic process. The first design depicted a crewed Western District *tomoko* canoe in front of Tulagi, with coconut palms on each side. The first day of issue was 14 February 1907, with the Customs Department and resident magistrates as the postmasters. Woodford had some difficulties when imperfect pages of stamps were sold illegally to a stamp dealer in London, creating a lucrative illicit market. Almost all of these were retrieved, although some facsimiles were also manufactured in Europe. After 18 months, the unofficial stamps were replaced with a similar but simplified design, produced in London by Crown Agents Messrs Thomas De La Rue and Company Limited from line-engraved plates conforming to Universal Postal Union rules. Five years later, this design was replaced with another, showing the head of King George V. Tulagi became the main postal centre in Solomon Islands, linked to Gavutu, Gizo, Faisi, Aola on Guadalcanal, Auki on Malaita and eventually Kirakira on Makira and Vanikolo in the south.[41]

British currency circulated in the protectorate from the 1880s and 1890s. Solomon Islanders working in Queensland began using the Queensland Government Savings Bank in the 1880s. Those who worked in Queensland until the 1900s often had substantial sums saved in banks.[42] In the mid-1900s, Solomon Islanders engaging as labourers within the protectorate often asked to be paid in coins rather than goods, while those returning from Queensland and Fiji frequently brought several pounds sterling with them, and in some cases even bank deposit receipts (which they could never have redeemed). Many returned from overseas plantations with coins—often gold sovereigns—which they kept in bottles buried in the ground. Solomon Islanders did not trust paper money, preferring coins.[43]

By the 1910s, Commonwealth Bank of Australia money orders were available from BP and Carpenters and postal notes could be purchased at the post office.[44] The government discouraged cash advances to Solomon Islanders, who sometimes gained credit facilities through traders. They were protected by the 1896 Native Contracts' Regulation (No. 2) under which no civil action could be taken to recover debts from Solomon

---

41   Gisburn 1956, 22–46; PMB, Woodford Papers and Photographs, 1021, H. Monckton, E.P. Monckton, C.M. Woodford, and F.M. Woodford, Correspondence, British Solomon Islands, 1909–28, C.M. Woodford to A.J. Watkin, 24 May 1911, 22 October 1912.
42   Moore 2015.
43   Moore 1985, 182–83; CO, 225/50, RC C.M. Woodford, Report on the BSIP, March 1897, 15.
44   BSIP *AR*, 1926–27, 8, 1966, 64; BSIP *Blue Books* 1923–24, 108.

Islanders. One reason for this was that Solomon Islanders sometimes refused to recognise debts negotiated by a company when one company representative was replaced with another. Only mixed-race Solomon Islanders had any chance of accessing limited credit. District officers added running money order services to their duties, which enabled funds to be remitted throughout the world.[45] Before World War II, protectorate residents could transact banking long distance through Suva and Sydney or use the Commonwealth Bank of Australia Savings Bank branches at Tulagi and Faisi—both established in 1931.[46] Tulagi, Makambo and Gavutu were at the centre of most of these transactions. In 1918, the BSIP issued its own paper currency (with notes to the value of 5/-, 10/-, £1 and £5) to supplement the British currency and Australian Commonwealth bank notes and gold and silver coins already in circulation. After 1919, the local currency was used to pay labourers, and £4,154 of it was in circulation.[47]

Plate 2.16 Tulagi, with the port and customs office in the foreground
Source: NBAC, N115-4.

45 BSIP AR, 1922–23, 6.
46 ibid., 1931, 12.
47 ibid., 1917–18, 5, 1918–19, 4.

Plate 2.17 A trade store on Tulagi
Source: NBAC, N115-513-1.

Another logistical issue was printing. When commercial houses or the government wanted to have printing done, it had to be commissioned in Australia or Fiji or they had to ask the missions to help. The Catholic Mission established the first printing press in Solomon Islands at Rua Sura, Guadalcanal, in 1910, using a small, primitive machine. The Melanesian Mission press was transferred from Norfolk Island to Hautabu near Maravovo on Guadalcanal in 1912, into buildings formerly occupied by the Welchman Memorial Hospital. Once Mota was abandoned as the Melanesian Mission language of instruction, and all teaching swung over to English, more translations and printing were required. At this stage, the Melanesian Mission press began to accept private orders, the first of which was to print the rules of the Tulagi Club. All of these buildings were destroyed during the Japanese invasion in 1942. The Methodists also installed a printing press at Kokeqolo in Roviana Lagoon in about 1928.[48] The early exclusivity of the mission presses explains why the *Planters' Gazette* (1920–23) was published by Bloxham and Chambers Limited in Sydney.

---

48   Information from Martin Hadlow, Brisbane, 17 July 2016.

1915: Woodford departs

What was Charles Morris Woodford like to deal with? His first visits to the Solomons were as a young man in the 1880s and he retired in 1915, aged in his 60s. He remained handsome as he aged, although he became more thick set. There is a substantial archive of his papers and photographs that provides some guidance, and a recent biography by David Lawrence.[49] Woodford grew into the job of Resident Commissioner and was allowed, within limits imposed by the WPHC, to shape the protectorate between 1896 and 1915. In 1907, Walter H. Lucas, BP's 'island manager' in Sydney, prepared a set of character sketches of Solomon Islands identities. He described Woodford as friendly to BP:

> Provided you do not offend him and always remember that he is His Majesty's Representative, the rest should be plain sailing. He apparently has to be careful how he offends Lever Bros.[50]

Seventy years later, academic K.B. Jackson assessed Woodford in a similar style, suggesting that he had a 'finely tuned sense of his own importance' (which was undoubtedly true) as someone who had guided the beginnings of a substantial Pacific territory.[51] Ian Heath, his first biographer, described Woodford as 'the product and an example of the aggressive empire building of the mid- to late-Victorians, with its assumed racial and social superiority leavened with benevolent paternalism'.[52] He could also be quite brutal in the 'pacification' methods he used.

Woodford assumed that British civilisation was superior and its technology would win out over any Solomon Islander opposition. He was correct about the technology. Solomon Islanders soon realised that Europeans possessed superior weapons and seemingly unlimited resources. A social evolutionist, Woodford thought Solomon Islanders were a dying race and would decline in numbers to the point of extinction; his views were backed up by missionary and medical opinion from the time.[53] Heath compared Woodford with William MacGregor and Hubert Murray, the

---

49   Lawrence 2014; Lawrence et al. 2015.
50   Buckley and Klugman 1981, 169.
51   Jackson 1978, 165.
52   Heath 1974, 113.
53   Buxton 1925–26; Rivers 1922; Lambert 1934a; Lambert 1934b.

administrators of British New Guinea and Australian Papua, respectively, both in his methods and in his rationale. Lawrence correctly observed that the 'history of the Solomon Islands from 1896 to 1915 was fundamentally determined by Woodford'.[54] For good or for bad, Woodford created the foundations of the modern nation. He chose the development of copra plantations as the fundamental economic underpinning and encouraged large-scale land alienation and development. He was also determined to rely on local, not imported, labour, which stopped the Solomons from ending up like Fiji with its substantial Indo-Fijian communities. Where Woodford was not correct was in underestimating the ability of Solomon Islanders to cope with change, which has proved to be their strength. Their cultures were never static and have continued to adapt.[55]

Woodford's health suffered after many years in the Pacific. As he grew older, illnesses such as malaria took their toll. When Graham Officer visited Tulagi in 1901, he described 49-year-old Woodford as a

> lithe thin man with finely cut features, slight moustache, firmly compressed rather than limp, a short incisive way of speaking, very uncommunicative, but a man who is I think 'not of words but of actions'.[56]

As a collector of material culture items for a museum, Officer had much in common with Woodford. Officer described the latter as very generous, kind and engendering confidence with the advice he gave. Officer's colleague Professor Walter Baldwin Spencer, from the University of Melbourne, was less flattering, describing Woodford as 'a very unapproachable man. Very strict in his manner.'[57]

---

54 Lawrence 2014, 349.
55 Moore 2017.
56 Richards 2012, Graham Officer Diary, 29 January 1901, 137.
57 The comment by Spencer was added by Richards from another source. See also Officer, 23 February 1901, in Richards 2012, 145.

Plate 2.18 Charles Woodford, Deputy Commissioner, 1896, and Resident Commissioner, 1897–1915
Source: ANUA, 481-337-7b.

Used to living rough in his youth, Woodford managed to create a comfortable existence on Tulagi. The first residency was replaced in 1905 with a prefabricated house purchased in Sydney, which, judging from photographs, appears to have been much larger than the original.[58] Still far from grand, it was built further up the ridge than the first house. On one level, set on high stumps with verandahs in colonial Australian style, the house had a flagpole in the front. Once this new house was ready, the old residency was allocated to the Treasurer, until a new house was built for him on the same site in 1914.[59]

In the 1900s, the town had grown to around 20 European residents, with others living on Makambo, Gavutu and Bungana. These interrelated settlements developed the standard trappings of an isolated colonial outpost. J.E. Philp arrived in 1912. Writing in the mid-1920s, he described Tulagi as well established:

> The headquarters at Tulagi is beautifully placed—the foreshore and slopes being all planted with coconuts evenly spaced and of nearly equal growth. Neath their shelter along a curve of beach are situated the boat-houses and natives' quarters. While on the summit of the slope some 230 feet [70 metres] above the water level are the houses of the officials—each of attractive design, white painted—with red roofs—a striking note of colour in strong contrast with the vivid lush greenery of the verdure. Where the soil is bare—it stands out red—rich volcanic—with rock faces of a creamy grey tint, with deeper shades of scoriated masses.[60]

Perhaps Joseph Dickinson's comment about Tulagi a few years later was more candid. He noted that it was a beautiful spot but that once on shore 'your first rapture loses its enthusiasm in the sweltering heat, for the harbor side of this station is something fierce'.[61] The civil servants who made Tulagi their home in the 1910s had to learn to cope. Regardless of the numerous eulogies to its beauty and tranquillity, Tulagi was small, hot, humid and isolated.

---

58 ANU Archives [hereinafter ANUA], 481-337-125; BM, George Rose's photographs, Edge-Partington Photographic Collection.
59 The *Handbook of the British Solomon Islands Protectorate, with Returns up to 31st March 1911* [hereinafter *BSIP Handbook*] (1911, 23) gives the date as 1905, but official correspondence suggests it was in 1908. British Colonial Office 1925, 406–07; WPHCA, No. 2549 of 1917, A/Treasurer R.R. Pugh to A/RC J.C. Barley, 28 July 1917. I presume Woodford is correct and the later official is wrong.
60 Herr and Rood 1978, 30.
61 Dickinson 1927, 29.

Woodford's retirement after 29 years of association with Solomon Islands, and almost two decades after the government was first staffed, was a good time to assess Tulagi and the protectorate. He had reason to be pleased, having created a small town and a rudimentary administration over 900 islands. Viewed from the sea, the red-roofed bungalows perched high on the ridge stood out from the jungle green, with the Union Jack fluttering above the residency. White coral paths ran spider-web–like between the government offices, shops and houses.[62] A series of houses had been built to accommodate the government officials, but with no plan—merely in the best places, usually high on the ridge. The protectorate's administration was always strapped for finances. Officers eventually received suitable houses, although the time it took them to get comfortable accommodation was always an issue. One early building was the single officers' quarters, built in 1911, initially with four bedrooms and a large main room that served as a dining and living room, all surrounded by a verandah. It was later expanded and, by the 1930s, was 'a long rambling building … designed to accommodate the unmarried government officials'.[63] As these officers were often travelling, there was little furniture and a sense of impermanency. Each room contained a single bed with a mosquito net tucked in all the way around. In 1917, the acting Treasurer noted that the 'cheerless quarters … tend to strain any feelings of good fellowship and make men less inclined to club together for their mutual comfort'.[64] Most officials began life on Tulagi in the single officers' quarters. Early on, a house and store were also constructed for a Chinese storekeeper, although as Chinatown developed and large commercial companies were established, the concept of a government store became redundant.[65]

When the first Judicial Commissioner (later termed Chief Magistrate) was appointed in 1913, his house was opposite the residency. The first jailer and labour overseer were also appointed in 1913; they bunked in together in a house built for the superintendent of the Public Works Department, who did not arrive until the next year and was not granted his own house until 1916. The first Tulagi Hospital was constructed in 1913. It consisted of two wooden buildings on the ridge above the wharf, beside

---

62 Knibbs 1929, 22–23.
63 Lever 1988.
64 WPHCA, No. 2549 of 1917, R.R. Pugh (A/Treasurer) to A/RC J.C. Barley, 28 July 1917, High Commissioner's dispatch No. 259, 17 November 1917.
65 ibid.

the path to the residency.⁶⁶ Separate houses for the medical officer and the nurse were constructed close by. The wireless operator had a house next to the wireless station and transmission towers, all built in late 1915 on the outer coast. The Commandant of the Armed Constabulary occupied a house originally built at Auki on Malaita when the position was based there. It was rebuilt at Tulagi in 1914–15. The first Assistant Inspector of Labour, A. Hedley Abbott, a carpenter by trade, built his own house in 1912—wedged into a precipitous site with no space for a garden. A house for the accountant was constructed in 1914 and another for the Crown surveyor in 1916—occupied first by Stanley Knibbs and then by Spearline Wilson.⁶⁷ In 1915–16, quite large quarters were built for the government carpenters. After the cutting through the central ridge—usually known as 'The Cut'—was constructed in 1918, it enabled easier use of the outer coast, where the Tulagi Club, the wireless station and the second hospital were built. The houses for the doctors and nurses were beside the new hospital. Before The Cut, access to the outer coast was by climbing over the central ridge.

By the time Woodford left, World War I was under way. Germans in the protectorate were interned in a 'civilised' manner; all had to move to Mallialli near Tulagi and promise to stay there without any guards. Friends could drop by and they could get supplies from Tulagi, including alcohol. Eventually, the administration let them return to their homes.⁶⁸ Another change brought by World War I is discussed in Chapter 7: the arrival of a group of settlers and officials with military training.

Australia took over German New Guinea in 1914 on behalf of Britain—a control perpetuated from 1921 as a 'C Class' Mandated Territory of the League of Nations. While Australia had always been the main trading connection with the Solomons, and regarded the islands surrounding the Coral Sea as its natural area of hegemony, from 1914, there was a joint Australian–British border at Bougainville Strait.⁶⁹ Solomon Islands planters' hopes of accessing Bougainville labour were soon dashed when Australia maintained north Solomons labour for New Guinea's needs. Hopes for an amalgamation of the British Melanesian territories once more faded. Although initially copra prices were high,

---

66 Boutilier 1974, 11; ANUA, 481-337-124.
67 Boutilier 1974, 11.
68 Golden 1993, 291–92.
69 Moore 1997; Moore 2003, 181; van der Veur 1966, 39–41.

a lack of shipping meant copra was stockpiled until the United States began to take the surplus in 1916. In the meantime, the price of imported consumer goods rose by 60 to 100 per cent. After the war, copra prices rose again briefly, then fell away, and major import commodities such as rice and tobacco remained expensive. Overseas capital for investment was in limited supply. Overall, there was an economic slump between 1914 and about 1924. When several BSIP Government staff left to enlist in the war they were not replaced, which weakened government services.[70]

Woodford served the protectorate well, although ultimately he was a man of his times, with all the drawbacks of a fin-de-siècle English gentleman. He had experience of the local people and of working in the British colonial system. He knew that a modern economy had to be constructed. He chose coconut plantations as the main vehicle and the indigenous people as the labour force. When one looks at Fiji, Hawai`i or New Caledonia, where significant numbers of foreign labourers were introduced, the Solomons was saved from issues surrounding non-indigenous citizens—except for the Chinese business sector and the introduction by the British of Gilbert Islanders in the late 1950s and 1960s. Charles Woodford created the first urban settlement. When he left in 1915, he was able to look down from the residency and marvel at what had once been an unoccupied island but was now a minor Pacific administrative centre. However, there must have been many waiting for him to depart, since his presence had dominated for so long.

Images of Tulagi

Each chapter of this book includes photographs that mirror the text. Woodford took some of the first photographs of the Solomons in the 1880s and continued to take photographs until 1915. What may be a Woodford photograph, of the first hoisting of the British flag on Tulagi, was reproduced in the *Sydney Mail* in 1900.[71] Although initially it seemed that not many of his photographs had survived, in recent decades 450 have been located, and many are of Tulagi.[72] Woodford's papers also include

---

70   Bennett 1987, 198–201, 219.
71   PMB, Woodford Papers and Photographs, 1290, Reel 2, Bundle 16, 9/29, *Sydney Mail*, November 1900 [newspaper cutting].
72   Phone interview with Joan Presswell (granddaughter of Charles Woodford), Bundanoon, NSW, 14 September 2008. Lawrence 2014, 112–22.

photographs of Guadalcanal, New Georgia, Ontong Java and Sikaiana atolls and Rennell and Bellona islands—many identifiable as the work of Northcote Deck and Frank Barnett—taken from the 1900s.[73] Some of the most interesting photographs in Woodford's archives are several of a whale skeleton preserved in a shed—presumably a specimen collected by Woodford, Mahaffy or Thomas Edge-Partington (another early official) to sell to a museum. There are also three photographs of the ceremony used for porpoise hunting at ʽAoke Island in the north of Langalanga Lagoon, Malaita, taken by Barnett in 1909.[74]

During the final decades of the nineteenth century, cameras began to be used on some labour trade, missionary and naval vessels and by visiting professional photographers and others—usually wealthy amateurs. At least 2,000 photographs have survived from the early decades of the protectorate.[75] In 1892, Bishop H.H. Montgomery from Tasmania travelled on the *Southern Cross* to the Melanesian Mission's bases. He used equipment loaned by Tasmanian photographer John W. Beattie to take a series of photographs of the mission's activities. Beattie himself toured Solomon Islands in 1906 on the *Southern Cross*, publishing more than 400 images from the protectorate. In the mid-1890s, Austro-Hungarian Comte Rodolphe Festetics de Tolna visited Santa Cruz, Santa Ana, Choiseul, New Georgia and the Shortland Islands on his 76-ton yacht *Le Tolna*, taking more than 400 photographs.[76] Edge-Partington took around 250 photographs and had copies of more than 100 photographs taken in 1907 by Australian commercial photographer George Rose. Walter Lucas from BP also took a number of early photographs, and Robert Lever, the government entomologist, was an avid photographer in the 1930s. There were many other photographers, but only fragments of their collections have survived. Tulagi was never heavily represented in the photographic record of Solomon Islands. The settlement had no resident commercial photographer and no commercial photo-developer

---

73 Rennell and Bellona are atolls, although because of their size and elevation they are usually described as islands.
74 PMB, Woodford Papers and Photographs, 1290, Reel 1, Bundle 5, 10/3, 'Three photographs of a whale's skeleton housed in a shed', Reel 2, Bundle 15, 10/31/1–3, 'Ceremony of Invoking the Porpoise at Auki, Malaita' (photographs by F.J. Barnett, 1909).
75 Burt 2015; Lawrence 2014; Richards 2012; Hviding and Berg 2014; Thomas 2014; Wright 2013.
76 Woodford 1890; Rannie 1912, 206–17; Beattie 1909; Festetics de Tolna 1903; Lawrence 2014, 159–60.

until the 1920s, when a Japanese trader filled the role.[77] In the early years, Woodford was probably responsible for developing photographs for other residents and visitors.

Photographers found the local people and their material culture far more exotic and photogenic than the buildings and social life in the small colonial town. The settlement was contained at the south and centre of the island and eventually spread on to both sides, separated by the central ridge. It was impossible to photograph the whole urban area in one shot. Most offshore photographs are of Tulagi's sparsely settled wharf area and show only the government offices, Elkington's Hotel[78] and the houses on the ridge behind. The first moving pictures of Tulagi were taken by Martin and Osa Johnson in 1917. They filmed the front of the residency, the constabulary on parade, Chinatown and Makambo Island.[79]

The greatest concentration of buildings was in Chinatown and beyond, where Morris Hedstrom's, and later Carpenters', stores and wharf were located. In the 1910s, several Chinese-owned stores began selling direct to Solomon Islander labourers who passed through while engaging for or ending contracts on plantations. The Chinese who came to work in the BSIP as artisans were quick to begin trading ventures and a small Chinatown soon sprang up in a swampy area next to the administrative centre. From the 1920s, the hospital, the Tulagi Club, the wireless station and the police headquarters and barracks were on the outer coast of the island and well away from the harbour where ships anchored. The prison was at the south-eastern end, quite separate and facing into the harbour. There are photographs taken from the height of the ridge looking down over the government offices, the wharf and Chinatown, or looking down to the outer coast, which was more spread out and not possible to include in one shot. Photographers used the high ground to capture as wide a view as they could but seldom turned around to photograph the houses of the leading public servants.

---

77 Johnson 1945, 112; Muhlhauser 1924, 204. Another of the Japanese residents, Ito, was written about by MacQuarrie (1946, 66–84).
78 Moore 2013, entry for Elkington's Hotel.
79 Behlmer 2018, 205–10. They produced three Solomons-based motion pictures from the footage: *Among the Cannibals of the South Seas* (1918), *Headhunters of the South Seas* (1922) and *Tulagi and the Solomons* (1943). Available from: www.safarimuseum.com/.

TULAGI

Compared with Samarai's Campbell's Walk, Victoria Parade in Suva or the palace waterfront in Nukua`alofa, Tonga, Tulagi lacked an extensive coastal promenade. Even in later years, one-third of the island was undeveloped and the formed path never went all the way around. Tulagi did not offer a panoramic view like those available of Levuka, Fiji's early capital, or the Apia waterfront and harbour in Samoa. Typically, photographs show only parts of Tulagi, such as ships loading export staples at the Gavutu or Makambo wharves or views ashore from out in the harbour. Overseas ships usually did not berth at Tulagi wharf, which meant passengers used small vessels to cross from the commercial wharves. Neighbouring Gavutu and Makambo islands were much more picturesque shorelines for photographers wanting to depict investment opportunities or commercial or shipping potential.[80] Paradoxically, when the Pacific War reached Solomon Islands, Tulagi became a major target, not only for bombs, but also for photographs, providing aerial images of the full extent of and the demise of the settlement.

Merchant companies

Tulagi faced on to an extensive protected waterway over to Gela Pile, usually divided into Tulagi Harbour and Gavutu Harbour. Between Gela Sule and Gela Pile, Port Purvis and Mboli Passage provided easy travel to the Anglican headquarters at Siota. In 1902, William Lever, the prominent British soap manufacturer, invested in the Solomon Archipelago, purchasing the assets of the Pacific Islands Company Limited, which held concessions over 112,000 hectares of land. This was the beginning of Levers in the Solomons. George Fulton, who was sent to Sydney to manage the operation, made annual trips to the Solomons. In 1907, Levers paid £40,000 (today about A$5.8 million or SI$35 million) for Oscar Svensen's assets, including Gavutu Island, which became their central depot, and installed a team of local managers on their plantations. J.J. Huddy was an early long-staying Levers' Gavutu manager. He was succeeded by Major Frank R. Hewitt between 1925 and 1935, who eventually took over the Sydney position.[81] Late in the prewar years, Levers built a small trade store on Tulagi, presumably to compete with Carpenters and Chinatown. In 1929, Levers merged with a Dutch

---

80   Quanchi 1994; Quanchi 1995; Quanchi 1997; Quanchi 2004; Quanchi 2010a; Quanchi 2010b.
81   Bennett 1987, 127–29; Golden 1993, 422, 424; Dickinson 1927, 31.

margarine company, Margarine Unie, to form Unilever, the world's first modern multinational company. Similar in its prominence to the Colonial Sugar Refining Company Limited (CSR)—the Australian company that dominated the Fijian sugar industry—Levers was the largest and most influential company in Solomon Islands. For Solomon Islanders, '*Lifa*' was a synonym for 'plantation'.

Plate 2.19 The wharves at Levers' headquarters, Gavutu Island, 1907
Source: British Museum, George Rose's photographs in Edge-Partington Photographic Collection.

Plate 2.20 Levers' headquarters, Gavutu Island, 1914
Source: British Museum, Edge-Partington Photographic Collection.

Europe began to switch from animal fat to vegetable oil–based margarines early in the twentieth century. Then World War I altered the balance in the world market for natural oils. Before 1914, Germany was the world centre for crushing heavy organic materials such as copra. The product was sold in Europe for use in personal soaps and for margarine—the first food to be industrially manufactured, which soon rivalled butter. Much of the coconut and palm kernel oil refined in Germany went to the Netherlands to make margarine for the German and British markets. Once the war began, Pacific copra no longer went to Germany and Britain imported the product directly from Pacific territories or via Australia. During the war, glycerine—once a minor by-product of soap-making—became an important component in propellants and explosives and a major industrial product. Britain needed margarine and glycerine but did not want to set up its own crushing plants. The answer was the United States, which was slower than Europe to switch to margarine, but did so during World War I. The British made arrangements to sell Pacific copra there and buy glycerine in return. This meant that American shipping began to call in to the Solomons to collect copra. Levers had got in early and prospered.

The other two of the big-three merchant enterprises were Australian in origin: BP and Carpenters were products of Australian entrepreneurship. Burns Philp (South Seas) Company Limited and Morris Hedstrom and Company were Fiji-based, although BP's Fiji company was an offshoot of the Australian mother company. Levers was the first big company to invest in the protectorate, along with their main rival, BP, which began in shipping and diversified into retail trade and plantations. BP became plantation owners almost by accident as they had to take over mortgages from planters who had defaulted on loans. However, they were struggling to make a profit based only on shipping, even with government subsidies, and could only remain competitive if they diversified into copra production and trading. The first of these plantations were part of Shortland Islands Plantations Company. BP's primary vehicle became the Solomon Islands Development Company, which by the early 1920s had amassed 1,600 hectares of coconut plantations in the protectorate. A new commercial venture was floated in 1920, Burns Philp (South Sea) Company, with headquarters in Fiji. New copra storage depots were erected at Makambo, Gizo and Faisi in the Shortland Islands. About this time, the copra trade began to swing away from Australia towards the United States. With the Fiji-based BP company in ascendancy, the Australian BP company declined as the means for shipping BSIP copra, although the shareholders and directors of the Fiji company were largely the same as those in the parent company.[82] These big companies provided a range of commercial services and were avaricious and demanding of debtors. The local expatriates had slang names for them. Two of the nicknames were based on the company initials: BP was called 'Bloody Pirates'; Carpenters became 'WRC', which local wits said stood for 'Would Rob Christ'. Levers was known as 'The Octopus', and some said its acronym stood for 'Levers Poorly Paid Labourers'.

Gavutu had commodious houses for the Levers' manager and his offsiders, as well as many buildings for supporting staff and its commercial operations. Joseph Dickinson, who arrived in the Solomons in 1908, published *A Trader in the Savage Solomons* in 1927. His descriptions of Levers' Gavutu headquarters are a composite of his experiences during those years:

---

82   *Planters' Gazette*, No. 6, May 1922, 10–11; Buckley and Klugman 1981, 81–85; Buckley and Klugman 1983, 108–24.

> Gavutu was a self-contained station. It possessed a large well-equipped bungalow, a small hospital, a large general store, engine and repair shops, carpenter and boat-building gear, recreation grounds, produce sheds, a large concrete reservoir, and a staff of six white men.[83]

By the early 1930s, there was also a recreation club, electricity, a reticulated water supply fed from a reservoir and beautiful gardens of flowering trees and shrubs and large rainforest trees and coconut palms.[84]

At first, BP concentrated on merchant shipping; then, in 1906, they began a new trade store at Gizo, matching their existing store at Faisi in the Shortland Islands. Two years later, BP formed the Solomon Islands Development Company to manage their plantation assets, and also purchased small Makambo Island opposite Tulagi, establishing their local headquarters and completing the three-island centre of the Tulagi enclave.[85] Makambo, just a five-minute launch trip across the bay from Tulagi, had large retail and bulk stores, an insurance agency, quarters for European male employees, labour barracks and a substantial manager's house on the hill, plus gardens, a tennis court and pavilion. The wharf was smaller than the one at Gavutu.

Due to its position, Makambo appears in many photographs taken from Tulagi; Gavutu was further away.[86] Martin and Osa Johnson's mid-1910s film, and company photographs from the same period, shows Makambo to have developed into a substantial commercial base. Photographic and written evidence suggests that vessels either anchored offshore and used lighters to ferry cargo and passengers or used the Makambo or Gavutu wharves if they needed to berth. Although Levers' Pacific operations were based in the Solomons, BP and Carpenters were part of a wider Australian commercial outreach throughout the Pacific Islands. They dominated in the Australian Papua and New Guinea territories, with BP controlling the shipping routes. From a commercial viewpoint, their Solomons operations were not separate from those in New Guinea.

---

83   Dickinson 1927, 31.
84   Cameron 1923, 273–74; Dickinson 1927, 31; 'Fancy Dress Functions in the Solomons', *PIM*, 26 January 1932.
85   Golden 1993, 415–16; Bennett 1987, 129–30.
86   Golden 1993, 68–69, 416.

There were also several Chinese companies and some smaller Tulagi businesses. For instance, Dick Laycock arrived in the Solomons with his brother in about 1905. He began work as a boatbuilder at Aola and then opened a small store at Balusana, both on Guadalcanal. Laycock did well, married a Sydney woman named Violet and moved to Tulagi in about 1914, where he opened a store. He succeeded through building up a reputation for honest trading and was soon able to lease land on Tulagi, as well as establishing plantations on Isabel. Violet and their five children lived on Tulagi, although each child was born in Sydney. Typical of European women based in the protectorate, Violet preferred to give birth in Australia. Around 1921, Laycock sold out to Carpenters, moving to Isabel, while his wife returned to Sydney where their children were being educated. During the Great Depression, he became a goldminer on Guadalcanal, although he was still closely involved with his family. He also leased 1.2 hectares of land at Sasape, where he ran a small trading business.[87]

The image to grasp is of three long-term settlements that together made up the central islands of the Tulagi enclave. Tulagi—with its government headquarters, Chinatown and one large commercial company (Morris Hedstrom, taken over by Carpenters)—was at the centre, along with Makambo and Gavutu across the harbour. Bungana was more of an outlier, with an Anglican mission and school, not a commercial base, although, as Tulagi's lighthouse was situated there, it was always in the consciousness of all residents of the enclave and the protectorate. A fifth settlement was added in the early 1940s when the Anglican headquarters was moved from Siota to Taroaniara, on Gela Sule, but within sight of the capital. Diaries, such as those of J.E. Philp, show there was constant movement between the three main islands by canoes, boats, lighters and ships, just as today we would drive around a suburb or town completing our shopping and other business. Missionaries, traders and plantation owners and managers came and went constantly, and there were always Solomon Islanders in their crews.

---

87   ibid., 327–29.

As an example of the way the commercial web operated, the story of Charles and Kathleen Bignell is symbiotically interwoven with these large trading companies. Charles Bignell was born in 1892 in Dungog, a small rural town in New South Wales. He arrived in the Solomons in 1911 and worked for well-known trader Oscar Svensen, mainly on his ship *Minota*, which constantly visited Tulagi. He began his own trading station at the end of Mboli Passage before purchasing small Beki Island in Sandfly Passage. He picked up his supplies from Tulagi and Makambo and returned with produce to sell to BP. About this time, Levers gave up its early concentration on trading and began to buy plantations, leaving a gap in the market that was eagerly filled by Bignell and other small traders. Bignell began by using whaleboats and then purchased the cutter *Newfoundland* from Levers at Gavutu. He then returned to Sydney to have a 13.7-metre ship built and fitted with a secondhand auxiliary engine. The *Ravu*, capable of carrying 15 tons of cargo, arrived strapped to the deck of BP's *Moresby*. In his days with Svensen, Bignell had spent time on Isabel and always wanted to begin a coconut plantation there. His trading business prospered, which enabled him to employ an offsider, and in 1913, Bignell leased a 485-hectare block at Fulakora Point on the north-east of Isabel. This was the beginning of Fulakora plantation.

In 1914, he married Kathleen Freeman, the sister of his manager at Beki. Twenty-two years old and from Scotland, she had arrived at Tulagi with her mother on BP's *Minindi*. She was immediately smitten with the islands, although it took her a little longer to accept Bignell's proposal of marriage. The couple's first child, Margaret, was due to be born in early 1916. This required a trip to Australia on the *Minindi* to give birth. Six weeks later, Kathleen and Margaret returned to Tulagi on the same ship, then headed off to Fulakora. *Yield Not to the Wind*, a biography of the Bignells, published by Margaret in 1982, reveals the constant movements between Beki and Fulakora and the close commercial and transport relationships between this family and the Tulagi enclave. They prospered and, although the marriage was troubled, they were typical of many other trading and plantation families who constantly visited the capital and its commercial satellites. In 1919, Kathleen gave birth to a son, Charles Edward—the first white baby born in Tulagi Hospital.[88]

---

88 Clarence 1982.

Chinatown, 1910s–1920s

The collection of buildings on the narrow strip of coastal land around Tulagi's harbour became an embryonic town, with houses scattered along the shore and the ridges behind. Chinatown was part of this, but always separate, although it bordered on the businesses of Dick Laycock, Morris Hedstrom and, later, Carpenters. There were also some European businesses within Chinatown. The Chinese became a dominant although never fully welcome presence. Even though they were the traders who made middle-level commerce operate smoothly, many impediments were put in their way and a sneering racism permeated many European comments about the Chinese.

The first Chinese business in Solomon Islands was Huong Lee (Wangli)[89] Company of Levuka, Fiji. The company began a trading station at Star Harbour on Makira in 1877, with Canadian John Champion Macdonald as their agent. The venture was ill-fated, since by 1880, Macdonald seems to have absconded with Huong Lee's ship, *Star of Fiji*, and set up in competition on nearby Santa Ana with his brother William.[90] Huong Lee pursued Macdonald to the Solomons to recover his vessel, to no avail.[91] The first Asians to live permanently in the protectorate probably arrived in the 1890s and 1900s. In an early report, Woodford said about 10 Japanese and Filipinos were employed in the pearl-diving industry. Chinese first came to the protectorate from German New Guinea as cooks, carpenters and gardeners. Many stayed for only one six- or 12-month contract. Woodford's explanation of their transitory behaviour was that they 'become discontented as they find no opportunity here of satisfying their desire for sexual intercourse' and were also looking for a back door into Australia.[92] Once free of their initial contracts, a few continued to work as mechanics and carpenters in government service; most entered business.[93]

---

89 There are complex issues with Chinese nomenclature, as several English-language versions are used in the sources and different branches of the same modern family choose to spell the same names differently. I have followed the advice of my colleague Chi-Kong Lai, who provided the new wording.
90 Bennett 1987, 58; Golden 1993, 282, 353, 355–59.
91 Golden 1993, 356.
92 CO, 225/83 (1908), Western Pacific No. 13758, RC C.M. Woodford to HC Sir Everard Im Thurn, 13 February 1908.
93 BSIP *AR* 1934, 13.

Chinese workers who migrated overseas in the nineteenth and twentieth centuries arrived at their destinations in different ways. Some paid for their own passage, some used a credit-ticket system, which could involve debt bondage relating to their families at home or to themselves, and others came under contract or indenture. In 1908, BSIP plantation companies made moves (which came to nothing) to bring in Chinese indentured labourers. Their lack of success was partly a consequence of British colonial failures elsewhere. A move to import Chinese into the West Indies in the nineteenth century was unpopular, and antagonism from the Boers and the British public to Chinese labourers working in the Transvaal mines between 1904 and 1907 was one of the reasons for the toppling of the British Unionist Government in the 1906 general election. This anti-Chinese ripple flowed through into the British Pacific, where the Australian colonies established discriminatory policies against the Chinese in the second half of the nineteenth century. The new Australian Commonwealth Government also expressed an aversion to Asian migrants, legislating in 1901 to ban non-European immigration. This became known as the White Australia Policy. The Australian Government did not want any similar immigration into neighbouring colonies.[94] Although a large Chinese population lived at Rabaul and nearby Kokopo in the New Guinea Mandated Territory, there were virtually none in British New Guinea (the Australian Territory of Papua from 1906), where legislation had been introduced in 1889 to ban Chinese from the new goldfields. Ten years later, Queensland legislation restricting Chinese immigration was adopted in Australian Papua and the White Australia Policy continued the ban.[95] In 1910, the Colonial Office declined to allow Indian labour to be imported into Solomon Islands and, two years later, it refused similar plans to import Javanese labourers. During the 1910s and 1920s, Levers unsuccessfully advocated the use of Chinese labourers and BP considered but rejected a Sydney Chinese merchant's proposal to settle Chinese in the Solomons to grow bananas for the Sydney market. In 1931, Levers again advocated importing Indian labour.[96]

---

94 Price 1974; Rolls 1992; Markus 1994, 110–54.
95 Inglis 1974, 170–71. The exception was Luk Poy Wai (Lee Poy Wai) and two assistants, who were allowed in as tailors for Port Moresby's European community during the early decades of the twentieth century.
96 Buckley and Klugman 1981, 247–48, 277. There were exceptions in the Pacific. Chinese worked phosphate deposits on Nauru and Ocean Islands, and New Zealand—short of labour after the 1918 influenza pandemic—allowed Chinese immigration. Laracy 1974, 27–29; Willson et al. 1990, 78–107; CO, 225/92, Microfilm 2916, Western Pacific No. 3141 10/11: Labour in the Solomons, Joseph Meek, Chairman, Levers Pacific Plantations Ltd, to Secretary to HC, 8 November 1910; *PIM*, 18 December 1931; H.C.S., [Letter to editor], *PIM*, 26 January 1932.

Plate 2.21 Chinatown during the first half of the 1910s
Source: ANUA, 481-337.

Nevertheless, some Chinese were in the Solomons for the long term. The nucleus of the early Chinese settlers came south from Rabaul, where the Germans had encouraged Chinese immigration, and later, under Australian rule on behalf of the League of Nations, the strictures of the White Australia Policy did not apply. Although the Germans imported Chinese 'coolie' labourers into German New Guinea in the 1880s, the majority of these served out their indentures and returned to China. Most of the early Rabaul and Solomon Islands Chinese were Cantonese who came as free migrants to German New Guinea in the 1890s, 1900s and 1910s. The majority came from four counties—Kaiping, Taishan, Xinhui and Enping—in southern China's coastal Guangdong Province. Ah Tam (Ya Tan, also called A Tan or Lee Tam Tuk) from Huiyang district in Guangdong, an independent shipbuilder, trader and labour agent, arrived in Rabaul in the late 1870s or early 1880s. He worked initially for the Hernsheim Brothers[97] and was responsible for organising much of this early migration. The Chinese spoke the Szŭ Yap (Siyi) and Hakka (Kejia) dialects; Siyi became their lingua franca.[98] In 1900, there were about 30 Chinese living in the Bismarck Archipelago, working for the government and the missions as artisans, mainly as carpenters but also

---

97   Hernsheim 1983.
98   Willmott 2005; Willson 1989; Cahill 2012; Wu 1982, 51–53.

as cooks. Their next move was to become independent traders, collecting indigenous-produced copra and shell products and establishing a small fleet of trading vessels.

Albert Hahl, the Imperial Judge and later Deputy Governor and Governor (1896–1914) of German New Guinea, supported Chinese immigration through British Singapore. After some illegality at the start, the practice brought permanent Chinese settlers.[99] Their occupations between 1903 and 1914 are listed as merchants, traders, gardeners and artisans in all trades, including tailors and cooks, carpenters and engineers, seamen and labourers. When German New Guinea was taken over by Australia in 1914, there were 1,000 Chinese residents in Rabaul. In the 1920s and early 1930s, the Rabaul Chinese population was around 1,300, increasing after 1933 as Chinese residents brought their families to Rabaul to escape the Japanese invasion of coastal China, and again after 1937 when Chinese artisans were brought in to rebuild Rabaul after a volcanic eruption. The total figures are difficult to establish but officially there were 2,061 Chinese living in or around Rabaul in 1940.[100]

The Australian Government recognised the Chinese who had arrived in the mandated territory before January 1922 as permanent residents, although still foreign nationals. Those born there were not made British subjects.[101] In fact, Chinese born in Hong Kong Crown colony or Singapore—then part of the Straits Settlements Crown colony—were British subjects, even if the Australian administration never acknowledged this. The China-based wives and children of New Guinea Chinese were allowed only limited entry rights.[102] Nevertheless, these families became traders, manufacturers and agriculturalists. It was a small step for them to move into the protectorate and to Tulagi, from where they used their wholesale trade links with Rabaul. Once the steamers were travelling regularly between Rabaul and Tulagi, it was an easy trip, and Chinese trading schooners could easily island-hop their way south from Australian Bougainville.

---

99   Wu 1982, 20–43.
100 LNMTNG *AR* 1925–40: 1925, 1935, 1940.
101 This did not occur until 1957. The Menzies Government offered Australian citizenship to the New Guinea Chinese—a reaction to the communist takeover of China, which had left them stateless. Wu 1982, 75.
102 ibid., 27–40.

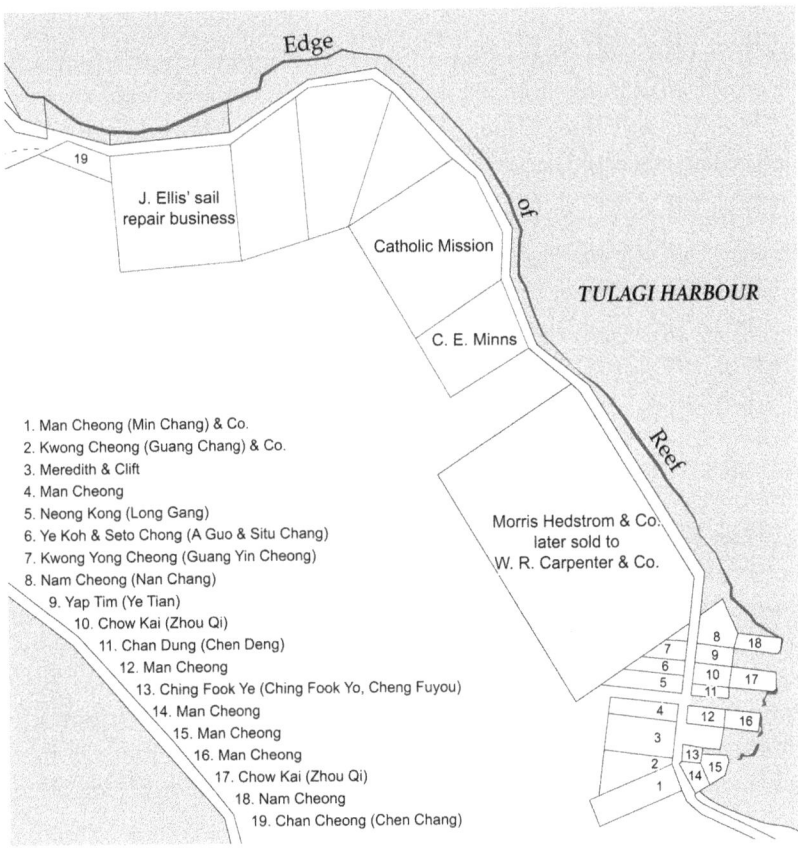

Map 2.1 Tulagi's commercial area, circa 1922
Source: Cartography by Vincent Verheyen.

The first Chinese, a tailor, arrived at Tulagi from Rabaul in 1912. Charles Woodford granted him permission to lease a small parcel of land on the edge of a swampy area next to the government offices, out of which grew 'a ramshackle collection of leaf huts and rickety jetties, straggling into the water at all angles'.[103] One of Woodford's photographs shows the beginning of Chinatown and its wharves. The Quan (Guan) family, originally from Kaiping County in Guangdong Province, were early settlers, and Quan Sung Wai (Guan Songwei) always claimed to have been the first Chinese permanent resident in the protectorate. Family history suggests he initially worked as a carpenter for two years, which must have been in the early 1910s. Another early Chinese was Quan Park Yee

---

103 Chaperlin 1930.

(Guan Baoyi), who arrived in 1926 via Canton and Australia. He worked on Tulagi as a tailor. Six of Quan Park Yee's half-brothers followed him to Solomon Islands. He founded the QQQ trade store, which still operates in Honiara's Chinatown today as QQQ Holdings Limited—the family well integrated into the Solomon Islands community.[104]

Ah Choi (A Cai) was another of the early residents of Tulagi's Chinatown, as were Lo King (Lu Jing) from Shun Dak, close to the city of Guangzhou, and James Wang (Wang Desheng), who came from Shanghai. The most common surnames among the early Chinese were Quan and Leong (Liang). The Quan family married into the Leong family, who were also from Kaiping County. Twenty-year-old Quan Hong (Guan Houyuan), a younger brother of Quan Park Yee, arrived from Kaiping in 1924. He adopted the Christian name Augustine and became an important community leader in Honiara's Chinatown in the mid-1940s. Ho Man (or Ho Nan, also called He Min) arrived in the mid to late 1920s as a cook on a steamer, and stayed on to become well known as a restaurateur, both on Tulagi and later in early Honiara. Johnny Chan Cheong (Chen Chang or Zhang) arrived about the same time, establishing his boat-repair business at Sasape on Tulagi and on Gizo. Another early settler who made a mark was Suete, whom locals called 'Sweetie'. He was related to the Quan family. The company he founded still operates today from premises at Point Cruz in central Honiara, trading as Sweetie Kwan Wing Leung Limited.[105]

By 1913, Ah Choi had applied for a land lease on Kokona Island in the Gela Group, and in 1914 Quan Sung Wai and Leong Tung (or Tong; Liang Dong) established a Tulagi-based business named Kwong Cheong (Guang Chang) Company. In the early 1920s, Quan Sung Wai was joined by his nephews Quan Hong (Guan Houyuan) and Quan Park. The other early Chinese companies in Tulagi were Kwong Yong Cheong (Guang Yin Chang) Company, founded by Ho Chi Tak (He Zhide), and another begun by the Yip Yuk (Ye Yun) family.[106] In a pattern typical of these early immigrants, Ho Chi Tak sponsored many of his relatives to come to Tulagi. These early Chinese settlers sold goods to the indentured labourers who passed through Tulagi and provided an alternative source

---

104 He references an article in the *Solomon Voice* (9 September 1992, 10), celebrating the company's 68 years in the islands.
105 Willmott 2005, 12–13.
106 ibid., 10; Information from Sir Henry Quan, Honiara, 31 January 2016.

of goods, with an Asian bias, to those traded by the large Australian or Fiji-based wholesale and retail companies. They also purchased schooners and cutters and went 'beach trading' around the protectorate.

While the labourers provided the bulk of their business, Chinese stores were beginning to provide the necessities of life for other residents as well, and Chinatown developed on 2 hectares of reclaimed mangrove swamp on the edge of the government centre.[107] In 1917, American visitor Osa Johnson did nearly all of her shopping at one of the Chinese stores, 'which had everything from fish and vegetables to dry-goods and hardware':

> The owner was a jovial old man who would rather talk pidgin English with me than sell me his goods. But, like all the others here, he was probably so lonely that he made the most of every visitor from abroad to catch up on the world he had practically abandoned. He prospered, despite the smallness of the community, and was said to make a real fortune from the traders, who were profligate with their money when they had it.[108]

The 1917–18 BSIP *Annual Report* recorded 61 Chinese in the protectorate.[109] These Chinese merchants had connections with Hong Kong, Singapore, Rabaul and Sydney. The first Chinese child was born on Tulagi in 1918, and the number of children slowly increased.[110] In 1920, Chinatown had 10 Chinese stores, with 13 Chinese schooners based in Tulagi and operating throughout the protectorate, purchasing copra, bêche-de-mer, turtle shell, trochus shell and green snail shell and selling cheap manufactured items and tinned and dried foods. Small-scale ship and mechanical repairs were available in Chinatown, which also functioned as a reliable source of tradesmen.[111] There were tailors, carpenters and cabinetmakers. If, for instance, a camphorwood chest was required to keep blankets and other woollen items safe from moths and silverfish, Chinatown was the place to go to purchase one or have one built. Other Chinese furniture could also be purchased there.

---

107 WPHCA, No. 1209 of 1921, A/RC R.B. Hill to HC WPHC, 4 April 1921.
108 Johnson 1945, 111–12.
109 BSIP *AR* 1917–18, 5.
110 WPHCA, 1918/1289, Dr N. Crichlow, Annual Medical Report, 1917, 2; CO, 225/232/64124, Annual Medical and Sanitary Report, 1927, 2.
111 Ashby 1978, 69.

Despite the usefulness of Chinatown, some expatriate residents were unhappy at its success and alarmed at the quick growth of the trading area. For a variety of reasons—many of them spurious—European settlers wanted to see an end to the growing Chinese commercial presence. In October 1920, 66 European residents (mainly plantation owners and managers, traders, employees of large companies and two missionaries) petitioned resident commissioner Charles Workman to halt the issuing of business and trading licences to Chinese immigrants, asking that existing licences be revoked. The reasons given were that the requested action would be good for Solomon Islanders and would maintain British authority. Chinese were not only luring the best qualified labourers away from other employers, the petitioners argued, but also were undermining European prestige and corrupting the minds of Islanders:

> [A]ssociation with the allurements and temptations offered by the Asiatic traders is proving to have a most depraving effect of the native mind, and discloses an increasing tendency to produce a diminution of that respect and esteem which the native has hitherto held for British rule.
>
> Social evils are rapidly developing from this close contact between the trader and the native labourer—contact which would and could not exist but for the prestige, power and authority conferred upon the Asiatic trader by the possession of the British license to trade.[112]

In his advice to the WPHC High Commissioner, Workman said there were only 55 Chinese in the protectorate, employing 47 Solomon Islanders—22 under indenture and 25 as casual labourers—out of 4,000 employed in the protectorate. The only Chinese store away from Tulagi was at Aola on Guadalcanal and that was situated beside the government station. The British Government had no official racial restrictions and some of the Chinese were from Hong Kong, which meant they were British subjects. There was an 8 pm curfew on Tulagi for Solomon Islanders, which also applied to Chinatown. Allegations of disorder and depravity in Chinatown were exaggerations. Insinuations about 'social evils' referred to Chinese women in Tulagi, of whom there were five—all married to Chinese storekeepers. Workman saw no reason for alarm and shone a light on the root of the irritation. The Chinese, despite their disadvantages, were the most popular merchants with Solomon Islanders.

---

112 WPHCA, 2905/1920, Petition to the Resident Commissioner.

Workman explained that 'the Chinese pay higher prices for produce and charge lower rates for goods and consequently are much more popular with the natives than are the European traders'.[113]

High commissioner Sir Cecil H. Rodwell was happy to maintain the existing Chinese trading licences, although he thought any further increases should be gradual. Rodwell investigated when he visited Tulagi in September 1920. He ruled that the number of trading licences issued to Chinese on Tulagi should be capped at 30 and no more were to be issued outside Tulagi, although the Aola licence was permitted to remain.[114]

Map 2.1, based on a government map from 1922, provides a detailed plan of the land leases in Chinatown and the names of the lessees. There were 18 registered blocks in Chinatown and one quite separate; Johnny Chan Cheong's Sasape slipway and boatbuilding business have been mentioned above. The Chinatown land was leased to 10 Chinese companies, partnerships and individuals. Man Cheong and Company held five blocks. The anomaly was a large block in the centre of Chinatown leased in the name of Owen G. Meredith, a planter on Isabel in the 1910s and 1920s, and one of the Clifts, either Geoff or Jack. The other interesting feature of the map is a substantial lease, bigger than Chinatown, abutting the area—that of Morris Hedstrom and Company, later owned by Carpenters. There were also other businesses operating in Sasape, further around the island. Chinatown was not an isolated commercial site; it was part of a larger trading area, with each section attracting customers to the other parts.[115]

Solomon Islanders at Tulagi

The introduction to this book makes clear that Tulagi was never a '*ples blong Solo*' ('a Solomon Islander town') in the way that Honiara has become. Yet, thousands of Solomon Islanders, mainly males, visited there and had some level of understanding of its functions. One of the hardest parts of writing this book has been gaining a view of the lives of Solomon Islanders on Tulagi and giving them a 'voice'.

---

113 ibid., RC C.R.M. Workman to HC Sir Cecil H. Rodwell, 25 October 1920.
114 ibid., No. 206, HC Rodwell to A/RC, 24 January 1921.
115 Golden 1993, 163–69, 339–40.

Plate 2.22 Solomon Islanders were constant visitors to the Tulagi enclave
This photograph shows Gela canoes off Levers' Gavutu Island headquarters.
Source: Clive Moore Collection.

Plate 2.23 Solomon Islanders on Tulagi wharf
Judging from their caps, they are likely prisoners being used to unload supplies.
Source: BM, Robert Lever Photographic Collection.

Plate 2.24 Prisoners maintaining a path on Tulagi, 1930s
Source: UQFL, Wilson Papers and Photographs.

It is unclear just what the population of the BSIP was when Woodford began his administration. In 1911, he estimated the figure was somewhere between 150,000 and 200,000, although he admitted that this was a 'mere guess'.[116] The extent to which Solomon Islanders were visitors to and residents of Tulagi is seldom recorded, but can be pieced together from multiple sources. Gela villagers were close by across the harbour. Right from the beginning of the Tulagi settlement, they brought fruit, vegetables, pigs and fish to trade, just as they had done with early passing ships, resident traders and missionaries. They also helped clear land for and build the initial settlement. Another group were the 30 to 40 members of the constabulary who were based on Tulagi, moving out on patrols to surrounding islands. Each day from 6.30 am to 8 am, they were paraded and trained using physical exercises and games and drilled in the use of firearms and bayonets. At six each evening, a detachment marched to the residency, accompanied by drummers and buglers, to lower the flag.[117] They patrolled the town area and performed sentry duty at the residency and around the wharf and offices. Smartly dressed in *sulus* (wrap-around tailored skirt-like men's apparel) with leather belts,

---

116 CO, 225/96, Microfilm 2920, Western Pacific Solomon Islands Western Pacific Confidential Dispatch, 30 June 1911, 26126 Recruitment of Indian Labour for Solomons; RC C.M. Woodford, 27 June 1911, Minute on the supply of native labour for employment in the British Solomon Islands, enclosure.
117 WPHCA, 1921/2682, Constabulary Annual Report, 1920, 3.

the armed constabulary were always the most permanent and prominent Solomon Islander presence on Tulagi. As will become clear in a later chapter, they were at times ill-disciplined and accused of poor behaviour.

From 1897, the government hired labourers to work on Tulagi. In 1915, at any one time, some 60 to 90 were employed to complete public works on the island. They were accommodated in two galvanised ripple-iron buildings on the island's outer limits, each holding 20 labourers, and in two leaf houses on the inner harbour side. In the early years, there were no recreational facilities, although work on an oval (the cricket ground) commenced in 1915.[118] Alongside this group of labourers were others hired to work for traders or the government. Over several decades, prisoners were the most constant source of labour on Tulagi, and were used to construct paths, keep the grass cut and to help unload supplies at the docks. In the mid-1930s, two dozen prisoners were lent for a day to the Bungana school to help build agricultural terraces.[119] Eustace Sandars, subinspector of the armed constabulary in the late 1920s, commented that: 'They [prisoners] maintained the golf course, roads, sanitation and a special gang of old trustees did all the house painting.'[120] There were usually 70 to 80 prisoners on the island.

Other labourers were hired on indentures or as casual appointments. Over many years, until the early 1930s, teams of indentured labourers, mainly from Malaita, worked to fill in swamps to make Tulagi into a 'first class township'.[121] Other Malaitans worked as stevedores. When Charles Weetman arrived in 1937, he watched the labourers at work:

> The first job on tying up at the Makambo wharf was the engagement of a native crew to handle cargo while the ship was in the Solomon Island waters. Under the direction of one white man and an efficient 'boss boy,' this was soon fixed, and the unloading began, the natives working the winches, loading the slings of goods in the ship's holds and discharging them either on to the wharf to be man-handled into the big storage sheds or into cargo boats to be ferried by the ship's launches across to the Tulagi landing stage. The ship's officers kept a watchful eye over the work.

---

118 WPHCA, 1916/1236, Dr N. Critchlow, Annual Medical Report, 1916, 3.
119 Cross 1979, 26.
120 PMB, Sandars, Papers on the Solomon Islands, 16.
121 WPHCA, No. 1739 of 1932, RC F.N. Ashley to HC WPHC, 9 April 1932.

> It was an interesting introduction to the world of natives, this spectacle of 'civilised' work being carried out expertly by seemingly uncivilized, barefooted, half-naked, chocolate-coloured gabbling men, with thick mops of hair ranging from jet black through all shades to decided blonde, depending upon the stage to which their peroxiding had progressed.[122]

Steamer day also brought other Solomon Islanders to Tulagi. Ketches, schooners and motor launches from all over the Solomons converged on the port, each with its own local crew. This human traffic enabled information about new arrivals and circumstances in the Tulagi enclave to be communicated throughout the islands.[123]

Once Woodford declared Tulagi the only port of entry for the protectorate, a constant stream of labourers began to pass through the town. Between 1898 and 1904, 5,085 labourers left for Queensland. Another 1,900 labourers left for Fiji between 1896 and 1910, with 1,493 of them leaving in 1904 alone, after the Queensland labour trade ended. The protectorate government attempted to seize all arms being smuggled in and to ensure that the returning labourers returned via the same passages from whence they came. A substantial correspondence was generated by Woodford as he supervised the returning labourers. At the same time, European and Chinese businesses tried to get the returning labourers to spend their remaining cash in their stores. Also passing through Tulagi were several thousand returnees from Queensland, until 1908, and lesser but still substantial numbers from Fiji until early 1915.[124]

Although most of the labourers from Queensland and Fiji purchased their goods while overseas, over decades, tens of thousands of pounds in wages passed to the local traders in return for 'trade goods'—a remarkably lucrative process for the merchant companies. After 1914, Levers and BP had stores at their labour transit depots at Gavutu and Makambo, while Morris Hedstrom, Carpenters and BP had direct access to the labourers signing off on Tulagi, as did the Chinese stores.[125]

---

122 Weetman 1937, 33. Foreigners often assume that peroxide is responsible for the blond hair of some Solomon Islanders. In fact, this is the result of a rare genetic characteristic, although sun, salt water and occasionally lime do augment nature.
123 Weetman 1937, 33; Fowler 1959, 225.
124 CO, 2915, 225/91, Western Pacific 18136: Solomons Draft Labour Legislation, 72, Return of Immigrants introduced into the colony of Fiji from the Solomon Islands since 1890, with number repatriated and the total number of deaths in Fiji; Price with Baker 1976, 111; Siegel 1985; Moore 2000a.
125 Bennett 1993, 148.

During the mass deportation of labourers from Queensland in the 1900s[126] and at the end of the external labour trade from Fiji in the 1910s, the scene would have been much as J.E. Philp described at Makambo in 1912:

> We then went across in steamer's boat (native rowers) to Makambo—Burns, Philp and Coy's establishment. About 80 natives (natives of Guadalcanar) from Fiji are here waiting return to their island home or may be engaged again at their option—men, women and children—the latter being very quaint—one pretty little half-caste (about 6 or 7 years) Samoan girl taking my fancy, as, I was told, she had done everyone else's. There was a babel of voices as they prepared their meals—cooking at fires along the beach in front of the sheds where they are quartered—much laughing and some singing—happy and careless of tomorrow …
>
> At 7 a.m. shifted abreast B.P's store and took in returned boys with all their possessions of new finery, boxes, etc.—the spending of three years' accumulated wages. Every boy invests the major sum of his capital in goods which he distributes lavishly on return to his village—and at the same time bedecks himself in new lava lava, belt, pouch, knife, pipe etc. …
>
> Tonight the steamer left with a number of recruits for Guadalcanal. These have just returned from a term in Fiji, and their goods and chattels were of a varied description. I noticed some Fijian food bowls—also a Kava bowl amongst them—and a good many had invested in umbrellas.[127]

Oscar Svensen negotiated a deal with BP to arrange the return home from Australia of around 4,000 Solomon Islanders who were deported under the 1901 legislation that formed the White Australia Policy. By 1908, he had made £9,000 (today about A$1 million or SI$6 million) from this venture.[128]

---

126 Moore 2000a.
127 Herr and Rood 1978, 30, 31, 70.
128 Bennett 1981, 181, 183.

Plate 2.25 Inspection of an armed constabulary guard of honour, Tulagi Club, 1930s

The drummer in the front row is `Abaeata (Abaeatha) Anifelo from east Kwaio, Malaita, who later became a headman and then Federal Council leader during Maasina Rule. He was the son of Basiana, who was executed for his role in the 1927 attack on William Bell, Kenneth Lillies and their police.
Source: BM, Robert Lever Collection.

Labour and plantations

Complete protectorate labour records for the 1900s have not survived. The plantation industry took off in 1905 when larger-scale capital began to enter the protectorate, encouraged by access to cheap land. By March 1911, there were 3,960 labourers employed within the protectorate and the head of a one-man labour department had been appointed. Between 1913 and 1940, 54,110 indentured labour contracts were issued in the protectorate, probably involving around 40,000 individuals—all males. Many labourers enlisted more than once.[129] Like those in Queensland and Fiji, the protectorate's indenture contracts were based on English *Masters and Servants Act* contracts. The first protectorate labour regulation was issued in 1897. In these early years, the BSIP had to compete with Queensland and Fiji for labour, and local contracts were for two years. Labourers were transported to and from the workplace by plantation-

---

129 Shlomowitz and Bedford 1988; Frazer 1990, 192–93.

owned or privately contracted labour recruiting vessels. Protectorate employers obtained a licence from the government, officials had the right to inspect all plantations and employers were required to submit reports every three months. The regulations were revised in 1915 to provide heavier fines for labourers who defaulted on their indenture contracts and, as usual in the indenture system, strikes and organised protests were forbidden.

Labour conditions on Tulagi were under constant official observation and were much better than those in the far-flung islands of the protectorate. Early BSIP plantations had unsavoury reputations. Clearing land for coconut plantations was labour-intensive and strenuous. The overseers were brutal and physical violence was a normal part of employment. Conditions did not start to improve until regular government inspections began in the 1920s. The labourers passing through Tulagi, Makambo and Gavutu were often youths or young men following in the footsteps of their uncles and fathers who had worked in Queensland and Fiji.[130] The majority were from Malaita. Photographs from this period show men cutting down huge rainforest trees and clearing hectare after hectare of land. Adolescent workers were easier to obtain than mature men, who were too aware of the poor conditions, having perhaps earned better wages in Queensland. Protectorate wages were low. In Queensland, the basic wage for Pacific Islander indentured labour was £6 a year. In Fiji, it was £3 a year for much of the time, rising to £6. Time-expired labourers could demand much higher wages in Queensland—up to £23 a year in the 1900s.[131] In the BSIP, about 10 per cent of the labour force was paid 10 to 15 shillings a week, although the majority received only 2/6- a week (£6 a year).[132] When the tax on tobacco doubled in 1906, the insult was compounded, effectively reducing the purchasing rate of their wages. However, youths and men often served multiple contracts away from home. The average time spent away on a plantation was six years.[133]

---

130 Bennett 1987, 150–91; Bennett 1993.
131 Moore 1985, 172–74.
132 Bennett 1993, 135; Bennett 1987, 160–61.
133 Bennett 1987, 160–64.

2. A 'VERY ARDUOUS TASK'

Plate 2.26 This photograph shows labourers typical of those who passed through Tulagi
Source: Clive Moore Collection.

The costs of labour recruiting varied enormously over the decades, with recruiting expenses per labourer escalating from £6 to £8 in 1911 and to £20 in 1920. The components were the costs of the recruiting process, the 'beach bonus' (an advance payment in cash or goods given to the tribe or kin) and the wage. Labourers would have carefully considered the changing beach bonus and wage, plus taxation, and the proportions that were paid in cash and in kind. Initially, until 1922, the basic pay rate was £6 per year along with a beach bonus of several pounds, paid in tobacco, axes, knives and cloth, but not cash. The beach bonus varied between £1 and £12. Malaitans on two-year contracts received the highest bonus, valued at £1 to £3 (1909–13), £3 to £5 (1915–16) and £8 to £12 (1921–23). In 1923, the beach bonus was fixed at £6, out of a total wage that had increased to £12, and, in compensation, recruiting ships could carry their own trade stores. A head tax was introduced gradually in the early 1920s—of £1 a year for all able-bodied males aged between 16 and 60—but was later much reduced. In 1922, the BSIP Advisory Council recommended the bonus be limited to £7.

Some of these changes came after the 1922 Labour Commission, headed by K.J. Allardyce, which had a brief to investigate the beach bonuses. The 1923 regulation forbade payment of passage masters and beach bonuses, although up to one-quarter of the total wage for a two-year contract could be supplied in advance.[134] In 1935, during the Great Depression, the minimum labourer's wage was reduced to £6 a year, with a consequent decrease in any initial bonus from £6 to £3.[135]

The government argued that a head tax was necessary to fund the protectorate. However, given that it was set at a low rate and was costly to collect, it was mainly to ensure recruits could be signed on from heavily populated islands such as Malaita, where there was virtually no other way to earn an income. Taxation did not expand the labour supply; about 6,000 labourers were part of the labour force each year in the 1910s and none of the later policies adopted increased the number. Planters objected to the increased wage and continued to charge 100 per cent (or higher) mark-ups on all trade goods. 'Passage masters'—indigenous bigmen who controlled enlistment at the various island passages and bays—acted as mediators between the demands of the recruiters and the interests of their kin, gathering prestige and wealth in the process, just as they had since the 1870s. The 1923 regulation reduced the influence of passage masters, who lost their bargaining power over the beach bonuses. They had always levied each recruit a portion of the goods given as the beach bonus and were also rewarded by recruiters with 10 shillings to £1 per enlisted man. Recruiting ships began to carry Solomon Islander assistant recruiters—usually coastal Malaitans—and this, along with the spread of Pijin, caused the complete eclipse of passage masters by the 1930s. Recruits also began to demand that larger portions of their beach bonus be given to them directly as cash—the equivalent of up to one-quarter of their wages for two years. About one-tenth of an individual's wages ended up as tax in some form and one wage might have been used to pay the head taxes for several men.[136]

---

134 *Planters' Gazette*, 6, May 1922, 12–13; *Western Pacific High Commission Gazette (Supplement)* [hereinafter *WPHCG (S)*], King's Regulation No. 15 of 1921, No. 7 of 1923.
135 *Planters' Gazette*, 7, 8 December 1922, 1; Shlomowitz and Bedford 1988, 67.
136 Bennett 1987, 164; Bennett 1993, 148.

Table 2.1 Indentured labour in Solomon Islands, 1913–40

District/island	1913–19	1920–29	1930–40	Total 1913–40	Percentage 1913–40
Central	100	350	200	650	1.20
Choiseul	424	319	25	768	1.41
Guadalcanal	1,874	3,831	2,627	8,332	15.30
Isabel	226	284	159	669	1.23
Makira	1,064	1,223	926	3,213	5.93
Malaita	10,476	15,707	10,413	36,596	67.63
Rennell and Bellona	n.d.	n.d.	n.d.	n.d.	n.d.
Temotu	815	1,490	499	2,804	5.18
Western	n.d.	n.d.	n.d.	n.d.	n.d.
Other islands	268	588	222	1,078	1.99
Total	15,247	23,792	15,071	54,110	

n.d. = no data

Source: Shlomowitz and Bedford (1988).

Although planters wanted more labourers, subsistence production was easy enough for most Solomon Islanders, so special circumstances were needed to encourage participation in wage labour away from home. The statistics in Table 2.1 provide some idea of who was passing through Tulagi, Makambo and Gavutu. Malaitans (68 per cent) were the largest group, although men from Guadalcanal (15 per cent) were also important. These two islands dominated recruiting before the Pacific War, along with lesser numbers from two other significant areas, Makira (San Cristobal) (6 per cent) and Eastern Outer Islands, now Temotu Province (5 per cent).[137] The heaviest labour recruiting was during the 1920s and early 1930s, when 4,000 men from Malaita (about 10 per cent of the island's population) were away on plantations in any year. Guadalcanal had 7 per cent away each year between the two world wars. This must have affected societies, as the figure was well above what was considered safe for Pacific cultures to remain strong and resilient. The majority passed through Tulagi.

---

137 Bennett 1993, 139.

As labour was the crucial element for developing the protectorate and was central to the original need to create the WPHC, Tulagi officials must have constantly discussed the labour supply, recruiting practices, taxation and working conditions. In 1929, the High Commissioner in Suva established a board to inquire into labour conditions. A teenage labourer over 14 years of age could perform light duties, although they were not fully eligible for adult work (or adult wages) until the age of 16. A contract system was used, with two years the maximum length. Minimum adult wages were fixed at 20/- per month and 10/- per month for light work. Labourers were usually recruited from their homes by professional licensed recruiters who operated licensed vessels. There were 6,115 labourers employed in the protectorate in 1927 and 6,016 in 1928. In 1929, there were 5,171 labourers employed throughout the BSIP, with a further 2,005 recruited during 1929. The numbers then increased slightly in 1930 (5,363), before beginning to decline further during the Great Depression.

During the late 1920s, labourer death rates averaged 60 per 1,000, with pneumonia and dysentery the greatest causes of mortality.[138] Employers were required by law to feed, clothe and house the labourers at fixed minimum standards, to provide medical care and to repatriate them at the completion of their contracts. If dependants accompanied labourers, the employers had similar obligations towards them. The hours of work were controlled by regulation and a 'task-work' system was used: 5.5 tasks completed one week's work. On 'time-work', the labourer could be asked to work nine hours a day, while on task-work, the jobs were to be completed in six hours.[139] Working as a plantation labourer involved only muscle power, with no prior training needed. There was also a labour elite—men who worked as wharf labourers in the Tulagi enclave, at Gizo and at Faisi. Malaitans from Langalanga and Lau lagoons dominated these jobs at Tulagi, Makambo and Gavutu. Others could be found as crews on trading, recruiting and plantation ships and working as domestic servants.

Tulagi became the main place at which labour was engaged, particularly after 1914, when a government officer had to be present when indentures were signed. Many of the Solomon Islander labourers passing through Tulagi had never left their home islands before and would have been shy teenage bushmen, often travelling with *wantoks* (kin or speakers of the same language). They would have marvelled at the delights of Chinatown,

---

138 BSIP *AR* 1931, 7.
139 ibid., 1929, 4, 12, 1930, 14–15.

while watching the strange white men and the Chinese who congregated in the small settlement. Others were more sophisticated travellers who already knew the streets of Levuka, Lautoka and Suva in Fiji or Mackay and Bundaberg in Queensland, long before they explored Tulagi. They interacted with the canoe-borne visitors from the Gela Group who traded produce to residents of Tulagi and the neighbouring commercial islands, and with the few hundred Solomon Islanders resident in the Tulagi enclave. The picture that emerges is of a large Solomon Islander presence on Tulagi, with only a small core of regulars and the bulk of the individuals changing constantly.

The Great Depression brought a severe downturn in the economy. Indenture contracts protected workers to some extent but also ensured that labour was available for a contracted period. The head tax also forced men to work to obtain cash. Employers reduced costs and used the labourers to produce local foods rather than rely on expensive imports. Indenture contracts were still considered cheaper than a free labour market. Although recruiting continued, the workforce in the 1930s was reduced to half the 5,000 to 6,000 labourers employed each year in the 1920s. Planters experimented with 'partnership' and 'profit-sharing' schemes, paying experienced labourers by the bag and providing them with land to produce their own food or letting local villagers cut their own copra and then use company-run driers and sell the product to the plantations. This system was first introduced by Fred Campbell, in 1933, on Makira. When the wages of labourers halved in 1934, there were boycotts of enlistment in some areas. Only the steamer gangs who serviced ships in the Tulagi enclave still maintained a reasonable wage—of around 3 shillings a day.

During the first half of the twentieth century, the Solomon Islands plantation economy required local labourers, many thousands of whom passed through the Tulagi enclave at the start and end of their indentures. There was a lot of money to be made from selling items to labourers. Young Solomon Islander labourers had their first experience of urban life. They wandered the streets of Chinatown, congregated around the wharves, walked through The Cut to the hospital and gazed in wonder at the houses on the ridge. If we calculate that labourers received on average £12 per year (in bonus and wage), and we know that after the early 1920s most passed through the Tulagi enclave, even if they had already distributed one-quarter of their wages for personal use or recompense to their elders from their beach bonus, around £18 was paid out on about 38,000 two-year contracts between the early 1920s and the early 1940s (a total of approximately £684,000). Let us presume that the profit margin on goods sold to the labourers was 100 per cent (it was probably higher); the profits would have been at least £300,000 to £400,000, and much more if we could calculate back to the 1900s. If we calculate an equivalent figure in modern currency, £300,000 in 1930 would be worth around A$107.8 million or SI$645.4 million today.

****

A town planning committee was established in 1933 to supervise urban development in Tulagi.[140] Tulagi had become a significant British–Australian and Chinese port and township—smaller than but comparable with others in the Pacific. During these early years of the twentieth century, Samarai—once the administrative and commercial hub of eastern Papua—like Tulagi, was also limited by its geographic size. Rabaul boomed, although the town was destroyed in 1937 by a volcanic eruption and then rebuilt. Port Moresby, on the central coast of Australian Papua, had consolidated. Small Port Vila on Efate in the New Hebrides struggled along with its dual British and French administration.

Planters and their staff and missionaries all frequented Tulagi, passing through on their way to and from the Solomons. Government services, particularly medical facilities, made Tulagi crucial to expatriate life in the protectorate. Officials emanating from Tulagi made and enforced rules, travelling through the islands but always retreating to the comfort of Tulagi. The indigenous trade networks incorporated European settlements of all sizes; mission bases, plantations with trade stores and small government stations were all part of these networks. The Tulagi enclave was the largest and most central of these foreign bases. While established indigenous trade items and circuits continued, adaptations were made to trade with foreigners. The focus of this new trade and power slowly shifted to the Tulagi enclave between the 1900s and the early 1940s.

---

140 WPHCA, No. 1739 of 1933, RC F.N. Ashley to WPHC, 9 April 1932.

Plate 2.27 Two constables from the armed constabulary, Tulagi
Source: BM, Robert Lever Collection.

TULAGI

Plate 2.28 Solomon Islanders manning a large rowing boat in Tulagi Harbour, 1930s

Source: BM, Robert Lever Collection.

3

Administration: Pop, Spearline and the poodle

> Tulagi was a pearl—very small—the walk around at a leisurely pace only takes two hours. It was triangular in shape. The apex to the triangle being where the gaol was on the southern end of the island and a ridge of hill running from the back of the gaol right through the centre of the island. All the houses were similar, built of wood and on high piles with red corrugated iron roofs. Each house had several 400 gallon water tanks attached to it. We had to rely entirely on rain water for our drinking and washing water. These houses had good verandahs and a dining room and one or two bedrooms according to the status of the officer occupying them.
>
> — Eustace Sandars, BSIP official[1]

Viewed from its harbour, Tulagi—strewn with white coral paths and gardens—was picturesque and rather beautiful. Wilfred Fowler joined the government staff there in about 1928. After waking on his first morning at the single officers' quarters, he shuffled out to the verandah:

> I was entranced by what I saw and went down the steps into the garden. There were hibiscus bushes with scarlet, white and apricot coloured flowers. Frangipani trees with funereal cream-and-white blooms gave off a cloying scent. On a tree at the end of the garden a purple orchid was in full flower. Then I noticed the *poinciana regia* [sic], the flame tree, at the edge of the path outside, a gorgeous medley of red and yellow. Down the slope

---

[1] PMB, Sandars, Papers on the Solomon Islands, 11.

below the house, three hornbills, with black wings and white tails, flew laboriously with raucous staccato cries and whirring wings to a clump of trees. Further away a flock of cockatoos frightened by something screeched noisily. I walked around the garden. At the top of a coconut palm two red parrots clung upside down pecking at flowers. A crimson pygmy parrot perched on one of the hibiscus bushes; it flew off to the end of the garden and then a remarkable butterfly appeared. Its colouring was of rare beauty, but I marvelled at its size. It must have measured seven or eight inches across its open wings.[2]

One of Woodford's legacies was the rapid spread of Japanese clover (*Kummerowia striata*), a vivid-green mat-like plant used as grass in most gardens on the island (and now used throughout the Solomons), which he inadvertently introduced with cargo from Asia. District officer Hector MacQuarrie, who arrived in Tulagi in 1924, fresh from a spell as aide-de-camp to Governor of Fiji and Western Pacific High Commissioner, Sir Cecil Rodwell, described the lush beauty of the Japanese clover and the pretty 'white-painted bungalows, with their wide verandahs rising from intensely green lawns adorned with palms and coloured shrubs'.[3]

In the years between Woodford's departure in 1915 and 1939, when war began in Europe, parts of the settlement altered. The prison was moved temporarily to the outer coast while new administration buildings were constructed on higher ground on the sheltered harbour side,[4] and the hospital was moved to a healthier, breezier area at the southern end of the outer coast. The impressive cutting through the central ridge was completed in 1918 with the aid of prisoners and indentured labourers. It enabled use of large areas of flat land on the outer coast and provided easy access to both sides of the settlement without an arduous climb. The hospital, wireless station, the Tulagi Club and the police headquarters and barracks were on the outer side, facing towards volcanic Savo Island and Guadalcanal. The residents of the main government houses on the ridge had a bridge over The Cut for easy access along the central ridge.[5]

---

2   Fowler 1959, 6.
3   MacQuarrie 1946, 21–22; Laracy 2013, 243–56.
4   BSIP *AR* 1917–18, 4, 1918–19, 3.
5   PMB, Woodford Papers and Photographs, Photo 58/7–72, 92.

Plate 3.1 A tinted photograph of Tulagi, viewed from the harbour, circa 1935

The 'Top Office' is on the right halfway up the ridge. The third residency is at the top of the ridge in the centre. The large Lands Department office is on the shore and the canoe shed is on the far left.

Source: NASI, ACOM Collection.

Tulagi's early plantation of coconut palms was reduced in size as the settlement grew and required more land. On the harbour side of the island, the government wharf (a small affair compared with Levers' and BP's wharves) was flanked by the administrative buildings, looking out over Tulagi Harbour. The only exception was the 'Top Office'—sited halfway between the residency and the wharf. It was shared by the Resident Commissioner, the Government Secretary and the Judicial Commissioner.[6] The government area was called 'No. 1'. Ramshackle Chinatown marked the start of 'No. 2', the commercial sector, with the remaining business area spreading up the coast to Sasape.[7] There were no roads and no vehicles other than a few bicycles and wheelbarrows, although there was a track around the island and connecting tracks joined the government buildings on both sides. The first horse arrived in the late 1920s and was owned by Stanley (Monty) Masterman, the labour inspector. The second was owned by Jack Barley while he was acting Resident Commissioner in the 1930s.[8] Everyone else walked or rode a bicycle.

6   Lawrence (2014, p. 199, Figure 31) is a sketch of Woodford's office on Tulagi.
7   Knibbs 1929, 264–65.
8   Sandars 1971.

All houses and offices were clad with timber weatherboards painted white, had galvanised ripple-iron roofs painted red and were set on concrete stumps (some short, but others were 1.7 metres high). The houses were surrounded by tropical flowers and hedges formed by red and purple bougainvillea, Brazilian cherry trees (with their tart red fruit), bright hibiscus and crotons. Caladiums ('elephant ears') grew profusely and indigenous ground and tree orchids also adorned gardens. Just as still occurs in modern Solomon Islands, residents competed to have the best floral displays.[9] There was a large European store and three hotels (each of very different character), with an iceworks adjacent to the expanding Chinatown, which consisted of a closely packed street of shops with houses at the rear and several rickety wharves.[10] Across the harbour, the commercial establishments on Gavutu (Levers) and Makambo (BP) also grew in size.

The Cut through the central ridge was the only major infrastructure development. An idea mooted in the 1930s, to build a causeway from Tulagi to Gela Sule, was too costly when compared with the possible benefits and, anyway, there was no spare money during the Depression.[11] Tulagi, despite its poor soils and swamps, was to remain the small, peaceful, pleasant capital of the protectorate—until the Pacific War intervened.

Resident commissioners

No local decision was certain to be implemented. The Government of the BSIP was answerable to the WPHC and ultimately to the Colonial Office in London, which was staffed with veteran administrators of the empire. From 1921, there was also the small Advisory Council, which met a few times each year on Tulagi, offering advice to the Resident Commissioner.

---

9   Knibbs 1929, 112–13.
10 Fryer Library, University of Queensland [hereinafter UQFL], Wilson Papers and Photographs. I have based this description on one written in 1972 by A.H. Wilson, who was on the staff of the Lands Department from 1919 to 1945.
11 WPHCA, No. 1679 of 1922, WPHC Minute Papers No. 1301 of 1918, S.C.G. Knibbs to RC C.R.M. Workman, 19 April 1918, Workman to HC WPHC, 10 May 1922, No. 2898 of 1920, Workman to HC WPHC, 16 October 1920, No. 3732 of 1933, A.H. Wilson to RC F.N. Ashley, 29 September 1933, Ashley to HC WPHC, 9 October 1933.

Just as the WPHC high commissioners had varied backgrounds, so too did the BSIP resident commissioners. Although Woodford had significant on-the-ground experience in the Solomons from his younger years, most of the other resident commissioners did not. There were transfers back and forth between Fiji, the Solomons and the Gilbert and Ellice Islands, and later transfers to and from colonial administrations in Africa and Asia. Between 1897 and the Pacific War, there were six substantive appointments as resident commissioner or military governor (during the war) and more than 30 acting appointments covering interregnums between permanent appointments or periods when the Resident Commissioner was on leave.

Table 3.1 Deputy commissioner, resident commissioners and military governors, 1896–1948

> No appointments, 1893–96
> **Charles Morris Woodford** (b. 1852 – d. 1937)
>   Deputy Commissioner, 1896–97
>   Resident Commissioner, 1897–1915
> **Charles Rufus Marshall Workman** (b. 1874 – d. 1942)
>   Resident Commissioner, 1917–21
> **Richard Rutledge Kane** (b. 1877 – d. 1958)
>   Resident Commissioner, 1921 – 13 October 1928
> **Francis Noel Ashley** (b. 1884 – d. 1976)
>   Resident Commissioner, May 1929 – 1939
> **William Sydney Marchant** (b. 1894 – d. 1953)
>   Resident Commissioner, 1940 – 5 October 1942
>   Military Governor, 5 October 1942 – April 1943
> **Owen Cyril Noel** (b. 1898 – d. ?)
>   Military Governor, 31 August 1943 – 31 March 1946
>   Resident Commissioner, 1 April 1946 – 10 October 1948

Sources: This table was drawn largely from information collected by David Akin (2015) and Judith Bennett (1987).

After Woodford retired in 1915, his temporary replacement was 56-year-old Frank Barnett, who had been Government Secretary from 1908 to 1914 and then Treasurer and Collector of Customs from 1914 to 1915. Barnett was born in Geelong, Victoria, in 1859, the son of Alfred A. Barnett. He served as acting Resident Commissioner during Woodford's absences, and again from 1915 to 1917. He died in Wellington, New Zealand, on 15 July 1917.[12] Based on a reading of his correspondence,

---

12 Archives New Zealand, Last Will and Probate of Frederic Joshua Barnett, Ref. AAOM 6029 Box 322; *Evening Post* [Wellington], 16 July 1917.

Barnett was officious and often unreasonable, more interested in the administrative rituals of the British Empire than in the practicalities of running the protectorate. Malaita's first resident magistrate, Thomas Edge-Partington, and William R. Bell, head of the Labour Department and later district officer on Malaita, both detested Barnett because of his high-handed ways. Their correspondence with him was often insubordinate and barely civil.

Resident commissioner Charles R.M. Workman arrived in mid-1917 as Woodford's permanent replacement, transferred from the Crown Colony of Gilbert and Ellice Islands. The 43-year-old Workman was confirmed as Resident Commissioner in 1918 and remained in Tulagi until 1921. Educated at Leys School in Cambridge and Christ Church College in Oxford, Workman was called to the Bar in 1900 and then joined the Colonial Service. He oversaw the Australian expedition that took possession of Nauru in World War I.[13] Workman considered shifting the protectorate's headquarters to other sites: to nearby Port Purvis on Gela Sule, Point Cruz on Guadalcanal (today's Honiara), Thousand Ships Bay (Tanabuli Harbour) on Isabel, Bina Harbour on Malaita, Russell Islands and Lingutu in Marovo Lagoon, New Georgia. However, the government had expended considerable amounts of money on buildings on Tulagi (16 residences and 24 other buildings), as well as the wharf and had reclaimed land and drained swamps. Commercial companies had sunk money into wharves and buildings on Gavutu, Makambo and Tulagi. No move was made and, instead, Workman had The Cut built through the central ridge—his main legacy to Tulagi.

---

13 From 1921 to 1931, he was Colonial Secretary of the Gambia. He was awarded a CBE in 1927.

Plate 3.2 The cutting through the central ridge was constructed in 1918 using prisoners and indentured labourers
A light rail line was used to remove the soil and rocks.
Source: ANUA, 481-337-92.

Plate 3.3 The completed cutting, showing the bridge over the top
Source: UQFL, Wilson Papers and Photographs.

Plate 3.4 The bridge over the cutting enabled easy contact between all residents on the ridge
Source: PMB, AU PMB PHOTO 58-70 (ANUA 481-337-70).

A.H. ('Spearline') Wilson from the Department of Lands and Surveys described Workman as 'the usual cultured English Gentleman, who in my opinion would have been just as well employed in the diplomatic service or as a politician'.[14] In 1921, Workman was replaced with Richard Rutledge Kane, who spent a short period as Government Secretary before transfer to the top position. Kane's salary in 1921 was £1,000. He served until October 1928, although he remained in Tulagi until early 1929, taking his final leave before retiring. Wilson's assessment of Kane was acidic, and he was not alone in holding a negative opinion:

> Transferred from Fiji service in 1921, and came with a reputation of being a strict and ruthless disciplinarian but did not continue along those lines. Like his predecessor, displayed no great interest in the matter of native land ownership and its problems, the key to success in a backward country just emerging from the stone age. Gradually became 'One of the Boys' and was very popular with them. Retired rather under a cloud in 1928.[15]

---

14   UQFL, A.H. Wilson, 1972, Notes for James Boutilier.
15   ibid.

Kane, a Protestant Irishman and proud of it, seems to have been the oddest of the Tulagi resident commissioners. Eustace Sandars (a long-serving protectorate official) said Kane was such a nuisance in Fiji that he was promoted to the Solomons to move him on.[16] He had a reputation for heavy drinking and was capable of public brawling. Historian James Boutilier mentions (but does not name) a resident commissioner who supposedly seduced the wife of one of his district officers. This was probably Kane, although the story could also be a malicious creation, based on the testimony of his contemporary Hector MacQuarrie. Even after historian Hugh Laracy's investigation into MacQuarrie's detailed accusations against Kane, the evidence was not conclusive. However, there is another similar tale told by Ernie Palmer, which indicates that the illicit affair might have been true, and actually quite public. On one occasion when his mistress arrived at Tulagi at the same time as an official guest, Kane—decked out in his white uniform and feathered hat—went forward to greet her and help her off the small boat. The locals tittered at the spectacle, at which Kane turned around and said, 'Gentleman, you can find fault with my morals—but not with my manners'.[17] Kane was also accused of having affairs with indigenous women, which was not acceptable within the Colonial Service or contemporary mortality.

After Kane, the position was held in an acting capacity, first by A.W. Seymore and then by long-serving government secretary Captain Norman S.B. Kidson, then Jack Charles Barley and Ralph B. Hill, until the arrival of Francis Noel Ashley in late 1929. Hill was another early appointment, serving as District Magistrate at Gizo (1909–12) and as a district officer on Malaita (May to June 1915), Guadalcanal (1920–23 and 1924–25) and Isabel (1927–29). He was also acting Resident Commissioner from late 1923 until October 1924 while Kane was on leave.[18]

Ashley was the first of several resident commissioners with experience in British Africa. He was educated at Westminster School in London and had spent his working life in Nigeria, where he was appointed as a Resident. He was 45 years old when appointed to the BSIP on a salary of £1,200

---

16   PMB, Sandars, Papers on the Solomon Islands, 9.
17   Boutilier 1984a, 48; MacQuarrie 1946, 9–10; Laracy 2013, 243–56; Akin 2013, 362–63, n. 59; Struben 1963, 42.
18   Bennett 1987, 211, 398, 399, 401.

a year.[19] Ashley had been a captain during World War I. According to Wilson, Ashley was the first resident commissioner interested in local land tenure systems.[20] While in some ways Ashley was a welcome change and broadened administrative perspectives, Dr Sylvester Lambert, an American from the Rockefeller Foundation's yaws and hookworm eradication campaign, said Ashley seemed inclined to think that because they had a similar skin colour, Solomon Islanders were the same as Africans. As is obvious below, based on his treatment of Wilson and his destruction of confidential papers, Ashley was not beyond reproach. Wilson detested him and called him a 'poodle'.[21] There is collaboration from Lambert, who described Ashley and his wife as 'strange people'. Lambert noted that when Ashley returned from leave in 1933, there was a negative reaction:

> Great disappointment to the service here, who all have their tails down since this man came back. Great blow to administrative affairs and all hold him in contempt—and this is not too strong a term. Not trusted, judgment poor. As one man says 'Because he is such a damn fool Fiji thinks we are all damn fools and everything we propose, no matter how good, is looked at askance' …
>
> If he has a difference with an official he may refuse to speak to him for a long interval. For instance, Johnson the Treasurer differed with him and refused to follow a certain course on account of Colonial Regulations. He would not speak to him and called for Blake on the phone and say 'Major Blake, would you please ask Mr. Johnson so and so'. Possibly Johnson answered the phone originally. At about that time Johnson went on leave. Another question about finance arose and Blake, the acting, refused to do a certain thing against Regulations. Mr. Ashley says 'I order you to'. Blake says 'please look at Colonial Regulation No. 2, I refuse to'. Next day he called up, Blake answered. He said 'may I speak to Mr. Dix'. 'Mr. Dix, will you please ask Major Blake so and so'.[22]

Ashley remained until 1939, replaced with 41-year-old William S. Marchant OBE, who served until 1943, during the Pacific War. He held a wartime appointment as Military Governor, as did Owen Cyril Noel, who succeeded him. Noel had been a district commissioner in Uganda, and Marchant had also transferred from the British African service,

---

19 PMB, Sandars, Papers on the Solomon Islands, 20; Lambert 1946, 344; *Pacific Islands Year Book* [hereinafter *PIYB*] 1935–36, 129.
20 UQFL, Wilson, 1972, Notes for James Boutilier.
21 UQFL, Wilson Papers and Photographs, A.H. Wilson to F.A.G. Wilson, 9 November 1939.
22 Akin 2009, Notes from Lambert, 21 May 1933.

where he served as a deputy provincial commissioner in Zanzibar from 1935 to 1937, followed by a similar position in Tanganyika until 1939. Marchant's BSIP salary was £1,400 a year. Although well liked, he came to the protectorate on the cusp of war and had little chance to implement anything other than the evacuation in 1941–42. He was responsible for establishing the government in exile on Malaita, which was moved to Honiara once the Americans took control. In 1943, he returned to Africa to serve as Chief Native Commissioner in Kenya until he retired in 1947.[23]

Tulagi was not known for excessive pomp and ceremony, although important visitors were always received at the residency and all new protectorate employees were greeted by the Resident Commissioner at the 'Top Office' or the residency. Fowler described his experience in the 1930s when he had his interview with the Resident Commissioner:

> The Residency stood on a hillock at the highest point of the island. A grassy bank sloped down to a bed of bronze-leafed cannas, showy plants with large scarlet blooms which made a gaudy display in the bright morning sun. I climbed the cement steps to the house … [The Resident Commissioner] was a good-looking dark-haired man, slightly above average height, compactly built and with an unmistakable air of authority …
>
> Prints of officers in the Peninsular campaign hung around the room and there were some team groups. A hide cricket-bag lay on the floor against a wall; a bag of golf clubs stood in a corner with two tennis-rackets in an outsize press.[24]

Tulagi's public servants

The British colonial and oversees civil services evolved over centuries as the empire expanded. In 1899, a major review instituted by Joseph Chamberlain, the new Secretary of State for the Colonies, provided support as Britain moved into an era of accelerated colonial expansion. The BSIP administration began in this new phase, when the Colonial Service was becoming increasingly professional and the number of new territories required a large increase in staff. Woodford and Mahaffy were products of the old era, but over the next few decades, most of the BSIP

---

23 UQFL, Wilson, 1972, Notes for James Boutilier; *PIYB* 1942, 129.
24 Fowler 1959, 7. The peninsular campaign probably refers to the Crimean campaign of the 1850s.

public servants were part of the new system. Training courses began in the mid-1920s, initially at the Imperial Institute in London and then at Oxford, Cambridge, Trinity College, Dublin, and, later, the London School of Economics. Another change was the introduction of the Dominion Selection Scheme in the late 1920s, which began to recruit public servants from Australia, New Zealand and Canada. The third change was the Warren Fisher Committee report of 1930, which led to the separation of colonial and dominion affairs and regularisation of appointment processes, leaving less space for patronage. Colonial Office staff began to be seconded to positions as assistant district officers and district officers, and district staff could move to Colonial Office jobs. Another recommendation was unification of each territory's public service into one Colonial Service, which facilitated the movement of officers between territories.[25]

Colonial officials were expected to conduct themselves with dignity and to follow a complex set of rules drawn up in a handbook that was used throughout the empire. Confidential reports on senior public servants were regularly forwarded to London; they were expected to remain neutral and not express opinions in public. Those who breached the code received a reprimand and could be demoted, transferred, pensioned off or dismissed. Senior headquarters officers were often transferred between British territories. Most of the regular officers came from Britain, where they undertook a three-term course at one of the aforementioned universities. The Colonial Office then chose in which part of the empire they would serve. If it was the WPHC, they signed a contract to serve in the Crown Colony of Fiji, the Gilbert and Ellice Islands Protectorates (later one Crown colony) or the BSIP.

From its humble one-person beginnings in 1896, the staff of the BSIP central administration had risen to 38 by 1926.

In the 1925–26 financial year, revenue was £71,430 and expenditure was £60,330 (roughly equivalent to A$5.7 million and A$4.8 million today, respectively). Ten years later, during the middle years of the Great Depression, revenue had fallen to £58,465 and expenditure was £49,224.[26] In 1935, basic salaries (without bonuses or extra allowances) varied from the Resident Commissioner's £1,200 a year, down to £290 for

---

25   Kirk-Greene 1999, 15–32; Burton 2010.
26   BSIP *Blue Books* 1925–26, 16, 1935–36, 16.

the third-level clerk in the Treasury and £160 for a nurse at the hospital.[27] Quite a few BSIP headquarters staff worked for many years on Tulagi. Some Tulagi-based positions involved little travel, whereas others—for instance, lands and surveys staff—were required to complete tasks in the districts for a month or six weeks at a time. The district officer positions (paid at £500–£600 per year in 1935) suited staff who were physically fit, adventurous and capable of interacting constantly with Solomon Islanders. District officers had to pass exams, be familiar with one local language (always Pijin) and to understand local customs. There were different levels of appointment. New staff usually began as cadets and climbed the career ladder to become assistant and then full district officers. A surveyor might eventually become Commissioner for Lands (paid at £700 a year in 1935). The most competent district officers often filled in for senior deskbound positions on Tulagi when the incumbents were absent or positions were vacant, and some Tulagi-based officers took over district posts for short periods, mainly when there was a shortage of district officers. Given that there were very few staff, it was often a matter of 'mucking in' to ensure key posts were covered.

Table 3.2 The Tulagi civil service establishment, 1925–26

Position	Salary
Resident Commissioner's Department	
Resident Commissioner	£1,000*
Government Secretary	£475*
Clerks (2)	£270*
Treasury, Customs and Postal Department	
Treasurer and Collector of Customs	£500*
Accountant	£300*
First Clerk and Boarding Officer	£350*
Second Clerk and Boarding Officer	£220*
Third Clerk and Boarding Officer	£200*
Postmaster	£260*
Storekeeper	£200*
Port and Marine Department	
Lights Attendant (joined with Foreman of Public Works)	£15

---

27   *PIYB* 1935–36, 129–30.

3. ADMINISTRATION

Position	Salary
Native Labour Department	
Chief Inspector	£350*
Assistant Inspector	£280*
Legal and District Administration	
Chief Magistrate and Legal Adviser	£500*
District Officers (5)	£500*
District Officer (1)	£450*
Assistant District Officer	£340*
Police and Prisons Department	
Commandant of the Armed Constabulary and Superintendent of Prisons	£400*
Subinspector	£260*
Jailer	£210*
Medical Department	
Senior Medical Officer	£700**
District Medical Officer	£650***
District Medical Officer	£500*
Sister in Charge	£150****
Nurse	£120*
Dispenser and Clerk	£210*
Lands and Surveys Department	
Crown Surveyor	£600*****
Surveyor	£400*
Surveyor	£400*
Surveyor	£200*
Public Works Department	
Foreman (also Lights Attendant)	£270*
Wireless Station	
Engineer-Operator	£400*
Assistant Operator	£260*

* All received a bonus of 15 per cent, plus £22/10/- and a £50 local allowance.
** On a five-year contract, plus a £50 local allowance.
*** Received a £50 local allowance.
**** Received rations, a temporary bonus of 30 per cent, a £50 local allowance and a £12 uniform allowance.
***** Received the same as *, plus £50 as Superintendent of Public Works.
Source: BSIP *Blue Books* (1925–26: 38).

Plate 3.5 The Treasury and Customs House, Tulagi, 1930s
Source: BM, Sir Ronald Garvey Photographic Collection.

It was possible to begin as a cadet officer and rise to the level of resident commissioner. Jack Barley, who arrived in Tulagi as a 25-year-old cadet in 1912, served as temporary Resident Commissioner several times between 1921 and 1932. Born in Eton in Buckinghamshire on 4 December 1887, Barley had a degree from St John's College, Oxford University. He was also a champion cricketer.[28] His request to enlist in World War I was refused and instead Barley became a mainstay of the BSIP administration. After a period as a district officer at Gizo (1912–13 and 1915), he served at Marovo Lagoon (1913–15) and Ontong Java (1915–16). Between 1919 and 1921, he was the District Officer for Eastern Solomon Islands. His first posting as acting Resident Commissioner was at the age of 34, between Workman's and Kane's appointments. He resumed his substantive position on Makira until 1923, serving as acting Resident Commissioner again in 1928 and 1929. He worked on Tulagi as Francis Ashley's assistant when he arrived in 1929 and replaced Ashley for several months in 1932 when the Resident Commissioner was on leave. Barley continued to work on Tulagi in various positions, which, with leave periods, explains the gaps in his district career path, and he also spent some time based in Fiji. He was the District Officer for Malaita in 1930–32 and briefly in 1933,[29]

---

28   'Jack Barley', in Wikipedia (available from: en.wikipedia.org/wiki/Jack_Barley). His degree had a first in 'Greats' (*Literae Humaniores*, the undergraduate course focused on Classics).
29   Bennett 1987, 398, 399, 402, 403, 404; Akin 2015; Akin 2013, 362–63, n. 59.

before he married and was appointed Resident Commissioner for the Crown Colony of Gilbert and Ellice Islands.[30] Dr Sylvester Lambert's comment about Barley is apt: '[T]o most of the natives in the group Barley is the Government.' Lambert also believed Barley should have been Kane's permanent replacement.[31]

Barley's attitudes to Solomon Islanders were unusual, in more than one way. Just before he left the islands in 1933, he provided the following assessment of the attitudes of Europeans towards Solomon Islanders:

> Speaking with over 21 years' experience of conditions in the British Solomon Islands, I regret to state that my considered opinion is that—with the exception of the Missionaries—scarcely 10 percent of the European settlers in the Protectorate regard the native otherwise than a 'necessary evil' in the economic life of the community or as being entitled to any sort of sympathetic attention or interest outside his sphere of utility as a customer or labourer. He is almost universally looked down upon as belonging to a somewhat unclean and definitely inferior order of creation, as one who does not know the meaning of gratitude, loyalty or affection, and who will invariably mistake kindness for weakness and immediately take advantage of any person rash enough to trust him and treat him as a fellow human being. My personal experience of the native of the Solomon Islands has always been diametrically opposite to this.[32]

While this seems laudable, Barley made ethnographic errors, had a light-hearted attitude to learning local languages and there is the ethical issue of his sexual relationships with local women, discussed in Chapter 5.

Another good example of the life of a cadet officer who became a district officer in the late 1930s and early 1940s is provided in the personal file of Michael J. Forster. Born in 1916, he was 20 years old when he first arrived in the protectorate. He received his fares out (travel was at half-salary and costs had to be refunded if the cadet stayed for less than three years), an annual salary of £350, a special annual loading of £25 to compensate

---

30 Akin 2013, 69–70.
31 Akin 2009, Notes from Lambert, 21 May 1933. Lambert was part of the Rockefeller Foundation assisted medical campaign to prevent yaws. See also Lambert 1946, 344; Lambert 1934a; Lambert 1934b.
32 WPHCA, 1064/33, J.C. Barley, Memo (n.d., c. March 1933) encl., quoted in Bennett 1987, 179. Interestingly, Akin (2013: 65) stressed Barley's strong opposition to the government granting serious positions or power to local leaders.

for 'the less favourable living conditions' and a yearly local allowance of £50 while resident in the BSIP. By the end of three years, providing he received good reports and passed examinations in a local language, the colonial and financial regulations, general orders, local legislation and the 1893 order in council, Forster would be eligible for a full appointment. The Colonial Office advised new officers to stay unmarried while cadets. The salary was not considered sufficient to maintain a couple unless they had private means. Government officers received free medical attention, as did the wives and children of officers with salaries of less than £400 a year. Accommodation in partly furnished quarters was rent-free, in strict accordance with rank. Salaries were paid locally, in English, Australian or BSIP currency—the last pegged to the Australian exchange rate. Taxation was in accordance with local regulations. Initially appointed to the Customs Department, Forster's accommodation was in the single officers' quarters next to the Tulagi Club.

Forster's employment conditions included a return leave fare to England, although officers hired in Australia or New Zealand received their leave fare only as far as their place of recruitment. If they wished to travel to Britain, they could apply for a supplementary grant of £90, plus £15 for their wife and the first two children. Leave accumulated at a rate of four days for each month of service and was due every two years. Under certain circumstances, officers could obtain special leave on half-pay. They could receive sick leave for up to 28 days a year, with extra short periods of local leave, without impinging on biannual leave allowances.[33]

In 1940, Forster failed his law examination and spent his spare time over the next few months swatting up on contracts, torts, summary jurisdiction, indictable offences and the order in council. He sat again in 1941 and passed. Presumably, he had family obligations in England, because in 1941, he attempted to remit half of his salary home. He was refused permission as it was considered he would not have enough left on which to live.[34] Posted to Malaita between August and December 1940, Forster was then seconded to Fiji, returning to Tulagi in August 1941. Forster's next appointment was as the District Officer for Kirakira in the Eastern Solomons, from November 1941 until 1943. He continued

---

33   National Archives of Solomon Islands [hereinafter NASI], BSIP/III F58/68, Conditions of Service for Michael J. Forster, 31 August 1938.
34   ibid., Government Secretary to M.J. Forster, 5 November 1940, 16 January 1941; Noel Butlin Archives Centre [hereinafter NBAC], Burns Philp & Co. Archives, Sydney to Government Secretary, 4 April 1941.

to run the administration there during the Japanese occupation of the islands to the north.³⁵ His postwar Malaita years are well covered in a book by David Akin. In 1950, Forster transferred to the Malaya civil service.³⁶ Local people remember Forster warmly: he was willing to eat food with them (very rare for a European at this time), spoke Pijin well and participated in bride-wealth exchanges.³⁷

By the time of Forster's appointment, there was a complex civil service regime on Tulagi, but it had not always been so. In the beginning, all administration was in the hands of the Resident Commissioner. Soon, however, Woodford gained the services of Arthur Mahaffy (see Chapter 2), who was based in the BSIP between 1898 and 1904. The price of copra fluctuated but provided the basis of the protectorate's economy, which enabled the expansion of the administration. When Woodford retired in 1915, his salary was £1,050 per year.³⁸ There were 14 staff in the central administration within various departments (medical, native labour, lands and surveys, public works, the armed constabulary and prisons, and treasury and customs). And there were several outstations, each with at least one government officer: Gizo (which opened in 1904), Shortland Islands (1906), Malaita (1909), Marovo Lagoon (1913), Guadalcanal (1914) and Ontong Java (from 1915 to 1916). Once the Western Solomons was 'under control' (Mahaffy's main task), the next need for 'pacification' was on Malaita, from a new base established at Auki (`Aoke) at the northern end of Langalanga Lagoon. Between 1912 and 1915, the BSIP armed constabulary's headquarters was based at Auki, to aid initial 'pacification', after which the Commandant was transferred back to Tulagi. The Tulagi police barracks had accommodation for 36 men, extra housing for two married men, a guardroom, office and store.³⁹ In 1916, the armed constabulary consisted of the commandant, one subinspector and 62 Solomon Islander police of all ranks.⁴⁰ From 1923, Savo, Tulagi and the rest of the Gela Group were administered by a district officer based on Tulagi—usually a conjoint appointment held by the commandant.

---

35 Bennett 1987, 403, 404.
36 NASI, BSIP/III F58/68, Treasurer BSIP to Accountant-General, Kuala Lumpur, Malaya, 8 November 1950.
37 Akin 2013, 76.
38 British Colonial Office 1925, 406; BSIP *AR* 1914–15, 7.
39 CO, MP 21141 WPHC MP No. 1814/1916 (1916), Report on the Work of the Police in the Protectorate (with special reference to Malaita), 23 June 1916, G21150 WPHC MP No. 500/1917 (1917), Commander F. Campbell's Annual Report on the Police and Constabulary for the year 1916.
40 CO, MP 21141 WPHC MP No. 1814/1916 (1916), Report on the Work of the Police in the Protectorate (with special reference to Malaita), 23 June 1916.

Beneath the resident commissioners there was a strictly ordered hierarchy of officials—their salary levels, the size of their houses and their positions on the ridge all signs of their relative importance. In 1923, there were 24 headquarters staff and six officers in the district stations. The most senior Tulagi headquarters staff under the Resident Commissioner were the Government Secretary, the Judicial Commissioner, the head of Treasury and Collector of Customs, the medical officers, the Commandant of the Armed Constabulary, the Commissioner for Lands and Government Surveys, the Superintendent of Public Works and the Chief Inspector of Labour. Table 3.2 outlines the government salaries during 1925–26, but not the cost of providing furnished living quarters and other allowances.

Various officers held the government secretary position, some of them for many years (for instance, Barnett and Kidson). They also doubled as acting resident commissioners when the incumbents were absent or when there was an interregnum. The Judicial Commissioner (the title changed to chief magistrate in the early 1920s) was equal in rank. There were six judicial commissioners or chief magistrates before the Pacific War. The first was appointed in 1913—26-year-old Isaac Grainger Bates, who remained until 1923. He was replaced between 1924 and 1928 with the less-than-competent N.W.P. De Heveningham, on a salary of £500 per year. The next was R.C. Higginson, a temporary appointment brought in from Fiji in early 1928 at the time of the trial of the Kwaio Malaitans accused of involvement in the death of district officer William Bell's party at Sinalagu.[41] Next came P.C. Hubbard, who began as a cadet in 1928 and then took over the position in 1930, after Higginson. Hubbard stayed for four years; the post was left vacant from 1934 to 1937 during the Depression, when it was filled for only a year by D.R. McDonald. The last prewar incumbent was Ragnar Hyne, former Chief Justice of Tonga (in 1936), who arrived in 1938, although he had held a temporary appointment on Tulagi in 1930. Born in 1893, Hyne held a University of Queensland arts degree and was called to the Queensland Bar in 1924.[42] As with many government positions today, individuals were

---

41 Keesing and Corris 1980, 193.
42 Hyne was later Chief Justice and Chief Judicial Officer for the WPHC, followed by terms as acting Chief Justice and later Senior Puisne Judge of Cyprus (1953–58). He was knighted and died in 1966. *Sydney Morning Herald*, 6 October 1966.

initially appointed in acting capacities or were owed leave and did not take up appointments until months after they began to appear on the payroll. The WPHC also shuffled staff about its territories.[43]

There were not always unanimity and friendship between the staff, as is clear below in relation to Spearline Wilson's promotion in 1939. They all had different motivations: some drank too much or were womanisers, while others were quiet Christian family men who disapproved of disreputable behaviour. In 1927, young anthropologist Ian Hogbin told Professor Alfred R. Radcliffe-Brown: 'Apparently from conversation everyone hates everyone else and regards him as incompetent. In most cases they are probably right.'[44] Hogbin was correct. Not everyone was enamoured of the skills of the senior administrators and, as the Tulagi correspondent of the *Pacific Islands Monthly* commented in October 1931:

> [T]he younger fry of the service are beginning to show the strain and are frankly amazed that at least half of their number have not been long ago given 'extensive leave'.[45]

Some officials stayed for only short periods or transferred around the protectorate, making their way up the hierarchy. These people had little long-term impact on Tulagi, although they would have travelled in and out constantly. William Bell was one whose name is remembered. He was based on Tulagi from 1911 to 1915 while head of the Labour Department, although his position involved extensive travel. Born in 1876, Bell was educated in government primary schools in rural Gippsland, Victoria. In 1899, he enlisted in the 2nd Victorian Mounted Rifles in the Boer War in South Africa. After the war, he was working with his uncles on their farm at harvest time when a pitchfork entered his right hand and a doctor had to remove a portion of his palm and two fingers. He was very conscious of the injury and in his early years wore a glove and shook hands with his left hand. 'Buster' or 'Will' Bell then decided to go to Fiji to work for a trading company as an accountant. In 1904–05, he joined the crew of a labour recruiting vessel for the same company and then secured an appointment as a government agent on the schooner

---

43   Boutilier 1984b, 44; BSIP *Blue Books* 1929–30, 36; UQFL, Wilson Papers and Photographs, J.A. Wilson 29 June 1930 to Mary [surname unknown].
44   University of Sydney Archives, A.P. Elkin Papers, Box 159, File 4/1/49, H.I.P. Hogbin to A.R. Radcliffe-Brown, 31 July 1927, H.I.P. Hogbin to A.R. Radcliffe-Brown, 31 July 1927. My thanks to Geoffrey Gray, Adelaide, for providing this reference.
45   *PIM*, 23 October 1931.

Clansman. He made several labour recruiting voyages to the Solomons between 1905 and 1911. Two of his shipboard journals have survived, which show him to have been an upholder of regulations. He came to respect the tough and straightforward Malaitans who were the core of the labour force. When Solomons labour recruiting to Fiji ended in 1911, Bell applied for and received the position as head of the Labour Department. He was accommodated in the single officers' quarters in Tulagi for four years before he was allocated his own house. When several officers left to enlist in World War I, he was promoted to District Officer for Malaita, from November 1915 until his death in 1927, which is discussed in Chapter 4.[46]

Five long-staying public servants formed the backbone of the Tulagi administration from the 1910s to the 1940s: Spearline Wilson (30 years), Dr Nathaniel Crichlow (28 years),[47] Frederick E. ('Pop') Johnson and Stanley G.C. Knibbs (27 years each) and Arthur E. Osborne (25 years). Osborne oversaw the radio station from its construction in late 1915 until 1940. He married a nurse from the hospital and became a permanent fixture on the island. Although he was in poor health in his final years, along with his assistant, Robert S. Taylor, Osborne was responsible for Tulagi's radio communications with the outside world. Between them, the two men managed to keep the increasingly antiquated equipment operational.[48]

Plate 3.6 Pop Johnson, Treasurer, Collector of Customs and Registrar of Shipping, 1919–42
During the war, he was in charge of the BSIP office in Sydney. He retired in 1946.
Source: Suzanne Ellis Collection.

---

46   Keesing and Corris 1980, 45–49.
47   Crichlow's career is summarised in the section on the Medical Department later in the chapter.
48   *WPHCG (S)*, 5 April 1940, 214, Minutes of the Advisory Council [hereinafter MAC], 27 November 1939, 214.

Pop Johnson, born Frederick England in Wandsworth, Surrey, on 18 March 1878, changed his name to Frederick England Johnson before he enlisted in the British Army in 1896 and served in the Boer War. We know that his father was a policeman who died in 1905 and his mother was Mary Ann England.[49] Pop returned to England from Africa in 1903, paid his way out of the army and left for Australia the next year, before travelling to the New Hebrides, where he worked for the Kerr brothers as supercargo on their ships and managed copra and coffee plantations. In 1908, he transferred to the WPHC administration, first as Inspector of Labour and then as acting Commandant of Police. In 1911, he married 18-year-old Agnes Wilhelmina Watt Cronstedt, one of 11 children of Ester (née Ellis), from England, and Axel Frederik Auguste Cronstedt, a Swedish trader resident at various times on Tongoa, Aneityum and Efate islands. Johnson's next move was to apply for the Treasurer's position on Tulagi, which he held along with the positions of Collector of Customs and Registrar of Shipping from 1919 until he was evacuated in 1942. Johnson also acted as Resident Commissioner for periods during 1938, 1939 and 1941. He oversaw the BSIP office in Sydney during the war years, retiring in 1946.[50] Johnson never took acting positions in the districts and remained based on Tulagi, because of his centrality to the administration and possibly also because of his higher rank and pay scale. In 1925, he earned £500 per year, which rose to £650 in 1935 and £900 by 1942.[51]

Johnson qualified as an accountant, was exacting and could be overly officious, even supposedly questioning Jack Lotze (his daughter's fiancé) to see whether he had paid duty on her engagement ring. From 1927, he was a government member of the BSIP Advisory Council.[52] He was a constant pipe smoker, and he and his wife, Agnes, were fixtures on Tulagi. His attention to financial details kept the government budget balanced. His family's nickname for him in his old age was

---

49 Mary Ann England, Sworn statement, London, 2 September 1919, in the possession of her great-granddaughter Suzanne Ellis, Toowoomba, Queensland, May 2016.
50 Golden 1993, 95–96.
51 His family holds correspondence from 1922 and 1925 about his pay and pension. WPHCA, 2789/1922, confidential 1208/22, A/RC C.C. Francis to HC WPHC, 11 September 1922, F.E. Johnson to Burns Philp & Co. Ltd, 1426/25, 6 April 1925; *PIYB* 1935–36, 129, 1942, 314.
52 *PIM*, 23 June 1932; ISC award document, 3 June 1932, in the possession of Suzanne Ellis, Toowoomba, Queensland, May 2016.

'Frugal Fred', which applied to his own finances, but also, it would seem, to those of the BSIP. He received an Imperial Service Order in 1932 for his lengthy public service.[53]

Stanley Knibbs, educated at Sydney Grammar School, arrived in Solomon Islands via Fiji, having previously worked as a field engineer for CSR. He was one of four children of Sir George Handley Knibbs, who trained as a surveyor, but was better known as an Australian scientist, the first Commonwealth statistician and first director of the Commonwealth Institute of Science and Industry (predecessor of the CSIRO).[54] Knibbs's deputy, Spearline Wilson, generously described him as probably 'the best brain that ever went to the Solomon Islands'.[55] Knibbs held a series of posts relating to land alienation and infrastructure development: Crown Surveyor (1913–24), Commissioner for Lands and Crown Surveyor (1924–39), Registrar of Land Titles (1919–39) and Chairman of the Mining Board (1927–39). In 1918, when the public works head retired, Knibbs was requested to keep an eye on the portfolio, but instead became the 'permanent' acting Superintendent of Public Works (1918–39). Although he refused to relinquish his public works position, it was always a problem and retarded the amount of work that could be accomplished in the lands and surveys portfolio. Perhaps the extra £50 it gained him in his salary had a bearing on his decision. Surveying always meant long periods in the districts. Knibbs also acted as District Officer for Shortland Islands for a few months in 1917 when the BSIP was short-staffed during World War I. He was forced to retire in 1939 due to ill-health brought on by alcoholism, making way for his long-serving deputy, who had carried the department for several years as Knibbs declined. Knibbs died in Sydney in 1941.[56]

---

53   Golden 1993, 95–97. The ISO was replaced with the Order of the British Empire. *PIM*, 23 June 1932.
54   Bambrick 1983.
55   UQFL, Wilson Papers and Photographs, Wilson, 1972, Notes for James Boutilier. The CSIRO is the Commonwealth Scientific and Industrial Research Organisation, an independent Australian Government agency responsible for scientific research.
56   Bennett 1987, 397; UQFL, Wilson Papers and Photographs, A.H. Wilson to F.A.G. Wilson, 23 June, 27 September 1939; *Sydney Morning Herald*, 8 February 1941, 20.

Plate 3.7 Spearline Wilson worked in the Lands Department from 1919 to 1942

He was Commissioner for Lands from 1939 to 1942, before being transferred to the Sydney office during the war. He returned as lands commissioner from 1944 to 1946, this time in Honiara.
Source: UQFL, Wilson Papers and Photographs.

All through the 1930s, Knibbs was bitter and distrustful of Spearline Wilson and seems to have had resident commissioner Ashley as his ally. There was palpable ill-feeling between Knibbs and Wilson. As Wilson wrote to his wife in 1939:

> But what do you think of Dear Stanley? And his attempt to stop any promotion for me? He did the same thing once before, about 1931. He is just about as dirty, despicable, and contemptible as it is possible to be. I know for a long time he had resented the fact that I have always been able to carry on the job when he was too drunk to do it, and I expect the rest of it is an attempt to curry favour with Ashley by joining him in his hate. I am afraid I would be far from polite if I were to encounter him this morning. However, as things stand at present, the attempt seems to have got Knibbs and Ashley nowhere.[57]

---

57 UQFL, Wilson Papers and Photographs, A.H. Wilson to F.A.G. Wilson, 23 June, 27 September 1939.

Against Ashley's advice, high commissioner Sir Harry Luke, who closely observed Wilson's work during a 1939 visit, recommended Wilson's appointment to Knibbs's old position.[58] Wilson, disgusted by the behaviour of Knibbs and Ashley, named Pop Johnson and M.J. Forster as two senior officials. Johnson put in a good word for Wilson with Luke. When Ashley left, he destroyed a confidential report on Wilson by Knibbs.[59] The reason for the animosity is not entirely clear. Wilson had a 'run in' with Ashley in 1933, when the latter pronounced Tulagi to be malaria-free. Wilson, who lived closer to the jungle areas on the ridge than did most officers, regularly found Anopheles mosquitoes and their larvae, which he took to Dr Harry B. Hetherington, the Resident Medical Officer. Ashley reacted with anger: 'You are an enemy of mine. I have reported that I have cleared the island of Malaria. I don't want to hear any more of this. They aren't here.'[60] To be fair to Ashley, Sylvester Lambert described Wilson as 'Bolshevik and erratic, hard to manage'.[61] While this only means he had Australian Labor Party sympathies, it indicates that he was politically to the left of Ashley and Lambert. He may also have had a difficult personality.

Like Knibbs, Wilson was appointed to the central BSIP staff after a term as field engineer for the CSR in Fiji. He served in World War I and then moved to the Solomons. Born in 1890, he worked in the BSIP from 1919 to 1942, first as a surveyor in the Lands and Surveys Department (1919–24) and then as Crown Surveyor (1924–39). Spearline[62] (even his wife called him this) held the position of Commissioner for Lands until 1942, although he never broke the unsatisfactory nexus between the Lands and Surveys and Public Works departments. In charge of the logistics of Tulagi's wartime evacuation, Wilson was himself evacuated to Sydney in 1942, where he assisted Johnson to run the BSIP office. Wilson also did some secret war-related work as he was knowledgeable about all parts the archipelago. Fifty-four years old, he returned to the Solomons in 1944, this time to Honiara, to reestablish the Lands and Surveys Department.

---

58   UQFL, Wilson, 1946, Lands and Public Works Department: A Brief History.
59   UQFL, Wilson Papers and Photographs, A.H. Wilson to F.A.G. Wilson, 27 September 1939, Frank Rupert Hewitt (from Levers) to A.H. Wilson, 23 November 1939.
60   Akin 2009, Notes from Lambert, 24 May 1933.
61   ibid.
62   Named for the boundary of surveyed land.

He also served as acting Government Secretary for a short period. In ill-health—largely because of his injuries from World War I—Wilson retired at the end of 1946.[63]

When he received his 1939 appointment, Wilson detailed his salary to his wife, giving us a window into personal finances:

> The increase in salary is only £50 to start with, but rises for the next four years at £25 per year to £700. Salary of the post is £600 to £700 up by £25. But there is also the local allowance of £50 per year, which however is not paid when I am on leave. Boiled down, the increase will be £150 at the end of 4 years. But that will make a difference of almost £100 to my pension at the end of that time. Of course, if the unexpected happens, and this long talked of reorganisation ever does eventuate, I would be on a much better salary, as the salary of the reorganised post goes up to £900. But I think that is quite dead now.[64]

Other officials

Tulagi's senior officials were the administrative and social elite of the BSIP, and their wives were the most senior women in European society. Other officers stayed for lesser but still substantial periods. The Commandant of the Armed Constabulary in the second half of the 1920s was Captain Ernest Nelson Turner, a tall overweight man with a loud voice, who always dressed in a khaki uniform. Born in Bristol, England, and known as 'Ernest Nelson', he seems to have been unpopular, leaving in 1928, not long after helping resident commissioner Kane lead the punitive expedition to Malaita on HMCS *Ranadi* and HMAS *Adelaide* in late 1927.[65] Eustace Sandars, Turner's new subinspector and temporary replacement, arrived in 1928. He became a long-serving district officer, remaining until 1942. At various times between 1923 and 1942, Turner and Sandars both held conjoint appointments as District Officer for Savo, Tulagi, the Gela Group and the Russell Islands.[66]

---

63 UQFL, Wilson Papers and Photographs, A.H. Wilson to F.A.G. Wilson, 12 December 1946.
64 ibid., A.H. Wilson to F.A.G. Wilson, 9 November 1939.
65 *BSIPNS*, 14 February 1968 (Father D.J. Moore reminiscence).
66 Bennett 1987, 400.

Despite the Great Depression, during the 1930s, the BSIP Government began to appoint a broader range of staff. Robert A. Lever served as Government Entomologist from 1930 to 1937, and in 1939 the BSIP seconded William C. Groves as the first BSIP Education Officer. He had worked for the Australian administration in New Guinea between 1922 and 1926 and then lectured at Melbourne Teachers' Training College. Groves lived on Tulagi with his wife and children, completing the first major report into education.[67]

Missionaries seldom entered the administration. One who did was A. Hedley Abbott. He left the South Seas Evangelical Mission (SSEM) in 1913 and became secretary, consecutively, to Woodford, Barnett and Barley. Once Workman became Resident Commissioner, Abbott transferred to be Assistant Inspector of Labour. He was not a newcomer to the Solomons, as he had arrived with the first group from the Solomon Islands Branch of the Queensland Kanaka Mission in 1904.[68] Trained as a carpenter in Ballarat, Victoria, he was a practical man, who taught himself navigation so that he could captain the mission's vessels, *Daphne* and *Evangel*. Abbott played a significant part in the establishment of the mission on Malaita and Guadalcanal. He did not remain with the government and joined the Malayta Company (the commercial arm of the mission) as its plantation inspector. He and his wife returned to Australia in 1920.[69]

Other midranking officers served long periods of employment. Monty Masterman joined the BSIP administration in 1923 as Assistant Inspector of Labour and was promoted to the inspector's position between 1924 and 1942. In 1925, he served a few months as Isabel's District Officer and filled the same position on Malaita for two months after the death of William Bell in 1927.[70] In 1935, his salary was £400 a year.[71] Masterman enlisted in World War II, taking part in the Normandy landing, and then returned to the BSIP administration after the war, until 1952.[72] Tom Russell, a senior postwar officer, noted Masterman 'had two negative

---

67   Boutilier 1978; Groves 1940; Cross 1979 31–37; *PIM*, 23 April 1932.
68   Queensland Kanaka Mission 1903–04, 8–9
69   Golden 1993 401–02. He became an ordained minister and later in life became Australian Secretary of the British and Foreign Bible Society. *Cairns Post*, 25 June 1940, 3 (available from: trove.nla.gov.au/newspaper/article/42264000).
70   Golden 1993, 412; Bennett 1987, 399, 402.
71   *PIYB* 1935–36, 130.
72   NASI, BSIP P1/iii, 58122, Part 1, S.G. Masterman; Akin 2013, 254, 255, 288–89, 290, 300, 302, 303, 305, 306, 428, ns 74–75.

attributes, however. He had no political antennae and was about the worst Pidgin English speaker in the service.'[73] He seems never to have been very competent and was brutal in his treatment of Solomon Islanders, so was not the right person to oversee labour. In 1935, he was reprimanded for losing his temper and striking a prisoner while acting jailer. His personal file shows that he applied for promotion often. He also wanted to leave the public service but was constrained by lack of personal finances.[74] However, in 1937, Masterman was appointed acting Government Secretary—the second highest administrative position. Perhaps this indicates that the administration was 'scraping the barrel', as the next year Ashley told Masterman that there was 'little evidence of fitness for promotion, even were a suitable vacancy available'.[75] Cumulatively, his BSIP service equalled that of the prewar long-stayers.[76]

There were also many lesser government employees (and their wives) who did not stay long: clerks, postmasters, storekeepers, hospital staff and crews on government ships.[77] There were tensions between them all, based on education, experience, competence, origins, tenures and personalities. Some of the most senior public servants were Australians, who, despite their skills and long tenures, would always have been looked down on by those with Oxford and Cambridge degrees and English or Irish middle-class or elite backgrounds.

The Armed Constabulary and Prisons Department

In the initial years, the armed constabulary consisted of about 30 men, each armed with a Martini-Henry rifle, with the majority stationed at Gizo to control headhunting in the north-western islands. They were called '*solodia*', the Pijin term for members of the armed constabulary. The establishment increased quickly: the 1918–19 annual report recorded

---

73 Russell 2003, 57.
74 NASI, BSIP 1/P1 iii, M 58/22/1, RC F.N. Ashley to S.G. Masterman, 21 November 1935.
75 Akin 2013, 288, 428, n. 74.
76 ibid., 288–89.
77 Golden (1993: 409–13) provides a partial list of other government employees. Bennett (1987: 397–404) provides a list of all district officers until World War II. These two lists, plus an unpublished list by David Akin of BSIP staff on Malaita, give a good outline of the entire public service before 1942, all of whom lived on or constantly passed through Tulagi.

it as comprising 92 men.[78] Recruitment was always an issue, as the men did not like the mobility necessary in the force. Most of the police were first, second or third-class constables, with wages ranging from £12 to £18 a year. Lance-corporals, of whom there were 10, earned £24, the three corporals were paid £27 and two sergeants received £36. The sergeant-major earned £48 a year. Many of the men served their two years and refused to reengage, preferring to become plantation labourers for less pay. Policing was dangerous and confronting work. Most of the police came from Malaita, Guadalcanal or Gela. The first commandant, Fred Campbell, found Malaitans to be the best *solodia*, although few of them wanted to join the constabulary. They were drilled in a squad using infantry training methods and, by Campbell's time, were armed with old, unreliable Lee Enfield .303 rifles.[79]

In 1922, there were 152 members of the BSIP Armed Constabulary, with the non-commissioned officers sent to Fiji for training.[80] District police remained under the command of district officers. The Armed Constabulary and Prisons Department of the 1920s was administered by the commandant—a pattern that continued into the Honiara years. The commandant was assisted by a subinspector and a jailer. By 1929, the armed constabulary personnel consisted of two sergeant-majors and 141 other ranks, and there were 11 warders attached to the prison at Tulagi. The Tulagi headquarters on the outer coast was the training centre for all police in the BSIP. Spearline Wilson remembered Sandars, the subinspector who arrived in 1928, as a 'typical English Gentleman, always correct in every detail. Well respected but not always liked'.[81] Stephen Sipolo was one of the sergeant-majors; the quarter-master was Heman Ioi and the head warder was Ba`etalua—'a huge very black skinned man'.[82]

---

78   BSIP *AR* 1918–19, 3.
79   WPHCA, G21141 MP No. 1814/1916 (1916), Report on the Work of the Police in the Protectorate (with special reference to Malaita), 23 June 1916.
80   Boutilier 1984b, 45.
81   UQFL, Wilson, 1972, Notes for James Boutilier.
82   PMB, Sandars, Papers on the Solomon Islands, 4–6.

3. ADMINISTRATION

Plate 3.8 The armed constabulary barracks and offices, Tulagi
Source: ANUA, 481-337-64.

Plate 3.9 The armed constabulary on their daily parade
Source: UQFL, Wilson Papers and Photographs.

167

Plate 3.10 Inspection of an armed constabulary guard of honour, Tulagi
Source: BM, Robert Lever Photographic Collection.

In 1935, during the Great Depression, the establishment was reduced to the commandant, one subinspector, 112 constables and two sergeant-majors. The next year, as a cost-saving exercise, there was no subinspector. There were also 15 warders at Tulagi prison and one warder at each of the district prisons.[83] Police in the early days wore khaki *sulus* with a cummerbund covered by a leather belt—the latter obtained as surplus from the Manchester police force. Sergeant-majors wore a white cummerbund, sergeants wore black cummerbunds, corporals wore blue and ordinary constables sported red cummerbunds. There were also several boy buglers and drummers based at Tulagi and in the districts. Sandars' memoir mentions Baura, a teenager from Malaita, as an early Tulagi bugler and 'Abaeata (Abaeatha) Anifelo, son of Basiana, a Kwaio leader,

83 BSIP *AR*, 1927, 9–10, 1929, 10, 1935, 13–14, 1936, 16.

was another.[84] For police transport, the government used small launches attached to the Labour Department and the district headquarters, as well as the dispatch boat *Belama*, until it was wrecked in 1921.[85]

The commandant or the subinspector also served as Crown prosecutors in the local court, with murder trials forming most of the work; they were held before the Judicial Commissioner and four assessors. In cases were the person was found guilty of murder, the matter was referred to the Supreme Court of Appeal in Fiji. All court materials were forwarded to Suva via Sydney, for review. A guilty verdict, which carried the death sentence, could take three months to finalise. A description from the 1930s gives some idea of conditions at the armed constabulary depot on the outer coast:

> The blaring of bugles, more or less in tune, and the spasmodic rattle of a drum lured us around a bluff and to the head-quarters of the police force. A soldierly Englishman, of the very-correct school, showed us around the 'barracks'—the armoury where the rifles were neatly racked, each police 'boy' being allotted his own weapon and being responsible for keeping it in perfect condition; the sleeping-quarters where the comfortable beds comprised a few boards nailed to two battens of different widths, the higher batten being at the head of the 'bed' to give a slope towards the foot; the 'common-room' and eating house and the cookhouse, all perfectly tidy and clean; the pet parrot, which, unlike the police 'boys' who answered all calls on the 'toot', uncompromisingly refused to do its trick of dancing, despite the continued cajoling by the commanding officer; the native carving of turtles, crocodiles, and other creatures decorated the buildings; and the batch of recruits being put through their rifle-drill on the edge of the ground.[86]

Prisoners were held on Tulagi from 1896, before there was a prison, and by 1898, there were 21 prisoners, most of them from Gela and Guadalcanal;[87] Gizo prison was established soon after. The usual policy was that prisoners on long sentences were not kept locally. Prisoners from the south and central Solomons were sent to Gizo, while those from the north were sent to Tulagi—making escape more difficult. Occasionally,

---

84 PMB, Sandars, Papers on the Solomon Islands, 4–6; Keesing 1980.
85 BSIP *AR* 1921–22, 6.
86 Weetman 1937, 35.
87 BSIP *AR* 1898–99, 16.

prisoners did manage to leave a little too readily, such as one Isabel man in 1905 who had been on Tulagi for barely an hour when he swam for the mainland and had to be recaptured. Tulagi prison and the jailer's house were surrounded by a 3-metre–high galvanised ripple-iron and mesh fence. During 1903–05, there were 42 prisoners at Tulagi and Gizo—the majority sentenced for adultery, assault and theft. Five were sentenced for murder, one of whom was executed. In 1905, Tulagi prison received its first European prisoner, who had shot a Guadalcanal man. He had to pay compensation, plus serve a sentence.[88]

Plate 3.11 An armed constabulary canoe in the canoe shed on Tulagi, 1930s
Source: BM, Robert Lever Photographic Collection.

---

88   ibid., 1903–05, 33–34.

Plate 3.12 Tulagi Prison, 1930s
Source: Clive Moore Collection.

The first substantial prison consisted of two buildings, one with concrete walls and floor and a galvanised ripple-iron roof, containing 10 cells. The second building had a concrete floor, a ripple-iron roof and wooden walls. The prison remained on the foreshore of the inner coast, although the 1918–19 annual report recorded that after the buildings were moved to higher ground, the health of the inmates improved.[89] Further improvements made in the early 1920s meant Tulagi was able to house around 100 prisoners.[90] At the time, Tulagi and Gizo prisons were accommodating around 80 prisoners, including two Europeans and two Chinese. Eustace Sandars described the new prison in 1928, which was run by Bill Hynam, whom he described as a 'spit and polish merchant':

> The prison on the southern end of Tulagi was a beautifully kept place with white wood houses with their little red roofs and barbed wire stockade surrounding the whole. All the stone work was done in white, it really was a show … One quite extraordinary thing was that they used to fly a blue ensign at the masthead there, I never was able to discover why.[91]

---

89 ibid., 1918–19, 3.
90 WPHCA, 1916/1236, Dr N. Crichlow, Annual Medical Report, 1916, 10; Knibbs 1929, 264–65.
91 PMB, Sandars, Papers on the Solomon Islands, 10. The Blue Ensign is the British naval flag.

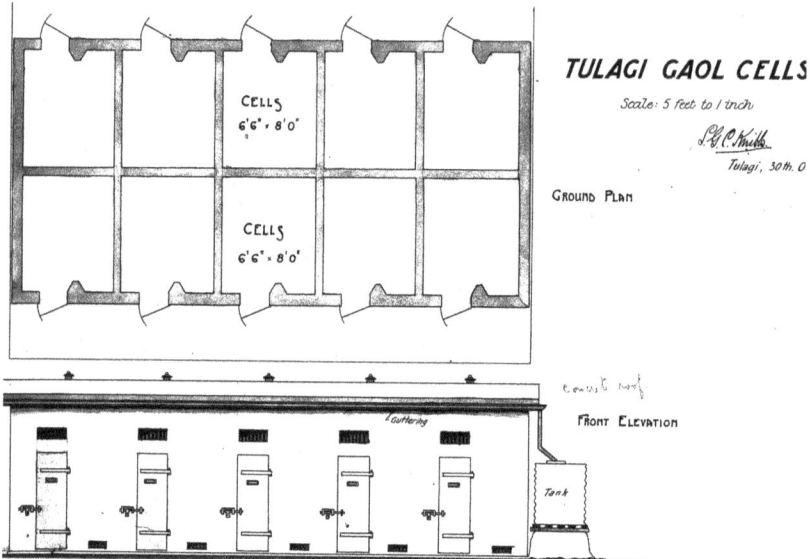

Figure 3.1 Tulagi's new prison, 1919
Source: Annika Korsgaard, from a BSIP plan partly redrawn by Vincent Verheyen.

One of the early constructions was gallows erected 1.6 kilometres from the prison; later these were transferred to Bangi Island, just off Tulagi. It seems the first execution took place in 1903, when Pogula of Visali on Guadalcanal was hanged for the murder of Momo.[92] In 1920, there were 82 prisoners on Tulagi, with others on shorter sentences at the six district outstations, where temporary lockups were used.[93] By 1931, Tulagi's prison comprised one cell for Europeans, four other cells and four associated wards, together containing enough space for 94 prisoners. District prisons were built from local materials and, as with Tulagi prison, they were surrounded by high fences or barbed wire stockades.[94]

---

92   Boutilier 1984b, 47.
93   BSIP *AR* 1919–20, 3.
94   ibid., 1931, 14, 1933, 14.

Plate 3.13 The wireless station, built in 1915 on a flat area on the outer coast of Tulagi
The Tulagi Club and golf course were alongside.
Source: Clive Moore Collection.

The wireless station

Letters sent by ship were slow to arrive. Establishing a wireless network was crucial to improving communications in the Pacific, advancing shipping, trade and security. British and Australian discussions in the 1900s led to government control of the new media and the WPHC passed a regulation ensuring that all wireless transmissions were licensed, preventing independent commercial development.[95] Ships began to carry wireless telegraphy equipment, which meant that when they docked at Pacific ports, residents gained up-to-date information on world affairs. With Europe unstable and on the edge of war, Britain was concerned to advance wireless technology in its territories. In May 1914, Cecil Monckton, the WPHC's Superintendent of Telegraphs and Telephones, arrived from Fiji to find a suitable site on Tulagi. He chose the only large piece of flat land on the island—a swampy area on the outer coast. In July, Marconi Wireless Company won the tender to supply the service: a 5-kilowatt station costing £4,742. Installation was slowed by World War I, with the

---

95 PMB, Woodford Papers and Photographs, 1290, Reel 4, Bundle 20, Conference on Wireless Telegraphy in the Pacific, Melbourne, 1909.

equipment and engineers not arriving until 1915. The wireless station connected the BSIP to the world via two 55-metre masts made from welded tubular steel bases with wooden tops. Full transmission began in January 1916, with the wireless available for public messages later that year. Arthur E. Osborne, the technician in charge, was designated Engineer and Chief Wireless Operator. In fact, the government had been gazumped by a year when Cyril Buchanan, assistant manager for Levers at Gavutu, and another man, Fitzpatrick, applied independently for wireless licences. The WPHC prevaricated over their applications, finally granting Buchanan his licence on 27 July 1914, after which he set up a limited range experimental wireless station. Once World War I began, private licences were withdrawn.[96]

Between 1916 and 1921, Radio Tulagi sent 4,679 messages and received 4,261. By 1936, the annual traffic had increased to 1,314 outgoing messages and 905 received messages during the year, earning the Treasury £159.[97] Initially, Radio Tulagi carried all government and commercial messages by Morse code. Signals could be sent to and received from as far away as New Zealand and Australia, although atmospheric conditions often made communication difficult, even with Fiji. Osborne was joined by Arnold Cookson in 1922, who was supposed to take over the senior position at the station, but it proved to be beyond his abilities.[98] The Tulagi system was soon joined by others in the BSIP. In 1922, Levers, Malayta Company, the SSEM and the Methodist Mission all sought licences to operate wireless transmitters.[99] In August the next year, the Methodist Mission installed a Marconi telephony/telegraphy system at Kokeqolo in Roviana Lagoon, New Georgia, enabling fast communication between Tulagi and the Western District. The Methodist service could use Morse code or voice transmission, forwarding telegrams and other cable traffic to Tulagi to be relayed to the outside world. A year later, San Cristoval Estates Limited, a major timber company on Vanikolo in the south of the BSIP, installed its own Morse code radio communications. In the early 1930s, the Catholic Mission also developed its wireless communications, based at Visale on Guadalcanal. Planters and missionaries who could

---

96 Information from Martin Hadlow, Brisbane, 15 January 2017. Hadlow 2015; Hadlow 2016, 76–79.
97 Hadlow 2016, 143.
98 BSIP *AR* 1923, 55–56; PMB, Sandars, Papers on the Solomon Islands, 12; Hadlow 2016, 87.
99 The SSEM and the Malayta Company did not proceed with installing wireless technology until 1934. Hadlow 2016, 133.

not afford expensive wireless systems installed 2-volt pedal-powered wireless sets, perfected by the Amalgamated Wireless (Australasia) (AWA) Ltd, for use in the Australian 'outback'. All that was needed was a strong set of legs (usually belonging to a servant) to pedal furiously, thus creating the necessary electricity. Until the mid-1930s, Osborne at Radio Tulagi attempted to keep the wireless system under government control. By then it was clear that costs had decreased and technology had changed so much that wireless communication was widespread. The BSIP had become 'wireless literate', although officials still doubted whether Solomon Islanders were capable of learning Morse code. Interestingly, the Methodists had no qualms about training Solomon Islanders to send and receive Morse code and to operate their telegraphy/telephony wireless system.[100]

In 1929, after 14 years of service, the original Tulagi equipment was malfunctioning and needed to be replaced, before it became technically redundant in 1935. The next year, the equipment was even more antiquated and one of the masts was broken. The problem was partly solved in 1932 when Robert S. Taylor, Osborne's new deputy, managed to construct a short-wave transmitter for £20. Taylor, who had considerable technical expertise, had joined the BSIP administration after World War I. The improvised system he created meant that messages could be transmitted to London via Rabaul with what was considered astounding speed: 17 hours to London and a 4.5-hour reply time.[101] Unfortunately, his equipment did not work for shore-to-ship communications, which still required medium-wave transmissions via the Marconi system. Taylor persevered and managed to build a new radio capable of sending signals for 1,200 to 1,600 kilometres, which used only a fraction of the power required by the old Marconi system. He managed to save the BSIP £5,000, for a while at least. Two years later, the communication battle had moved on to establishing wireless links with the district offices. By 1937, with the Great Depression biting hard, the government was planning to install a radio at Auki on Malaita, and the network had been extended to include Gold Development Limited at Berande on Guadalcanal. Although Taylor continued to try to manufacture his own transmitters to equip all district stations, in 1938, the government purchased two wireless telephone sets from AWA Ltd—one for Tulagi and one for Auki—with another budgeted

---

100 BSIP *AR* 1914–15, 7, 1921–22, 4, 1922–23, 4, 1925–26, 9; Hadlow 2016, 105, 107–15, 133.
101 Hadlow 2016, 135.

to go to Gizo. These made a large difference to the ability of Tulagi staff to communicate quickly with the districts.[102] In 1939, as war approached, there were 65 licence-holders for wireless receivers in the BSIP, showing the rapidity with which radio transmission advanced.

In 1938, Radio Tulagi began experimenting with broadcasting at 10.15 am every Monday, providing London and local produce prices and shipping movements. The next year, this was broadened to include service messages and news, until war was declared. Having watched the Methodist success in the Western Solomons, Osborne began to plan to train Solomon Islanders as wireless operators.

The Medical Department

One large advantage of establishing a government was that it brought permanent Western medical care to the BSIP. Before that, the missions were the only source of medical treatment and doctors were rare. Isolated settlers dealt with their own ailments using home medical guidebooks.[103] Even small scratches could become infected and turn into major health disasters.

The first medical doctors in the archipelago travelled on whaling and naval ships. British and French whaling ships were required by law to carry surgeons, although the same was not the case for American whaling ships.[104] The first permanent doctor based in the BSIP was Henry Palmer Welchman, an Anglican missionary in the Solomons for 13 years from 1888. He worked on Isabel (1890, 1893–1901) and at Siota in the Gela Group (1896–1900).[105] After Welchman departed, the next doctor was John Northcote Deck, who visited in 1908 and returned permanently the next year as resident head of the SSEM, until 1928. Northcote's brother Norman, a dentist, was based in the Solomons from 1913 until 1948.[106]

---

102 *WPHCG (S)*, 11 February 1930, MAC, 6 November 1929, 15–16, MAC, 30 December 1930, 20 October 1930, 143, 29 January 1932, MAC, 11 November 1931, 16, 17 December 1932, MAC, 1 November 1932, 120, 28 March 1935, MAC, 7 May 1935, 95; 18 February 1936, MAC, 4 November 1935, 16, 25 November 1936, MAC, 12 June 1936, 86, 19 August 1938, MAC, 20 October 1936, 18, 19 August 1938, MAC, 4 April 1938, 122.
103 One readily available was James (1949), first published in the 1930s for use in Solomon Islands and other areas of Melanesia.
104 Watters with Koestenbauer 2011, 25, 34–78.
105 Moore 2013, entry for Henry Palmer Welchman.
106 Braga 2004; Moore 2013, entries for John Northcote Deck and Norman Deck.

In 1911, the Anglican Melanesian Mission built a hospital at Hautabu near Maravovo on Guadalcanal, which was run by Dr Russell Marshall. Named the Welchman Memorial Hospital, it was short-lived, closing in 1916 when Marshall married the matron and both went off to war—never returning to the BSIP. In 1918, Levers employed Dr Sakurai, of Japanese origin.[107]

At various times, the SSEM, the Methodists, the Seventh-day Adventists and the Vanikolo Kauri Timber Company also employed medical officers. Dr Lucy Holt-MacCrimmon was based at Su`u, Malaita, during the second half of the 1920s, at her husband's timber lease, which had connections with the SSEM and its commercial arm, the Malayta Company. She received a government stipend to extend her services to the surrounding villages. Later, she was based on Vanikolo (or Vanikoro). The Methodist mission at Kokeqolo, Roviana Lagoon, established a hospital in 1927, with Dr Edward Sayers in charge. The next year they opened another, at Sasamungga on the Choiseul coast, under Dr Clifford James. Both were subsidised by the BSIP administration. Dr Dorothy Mills-Parker began work at the Seventh-day Adventist's Kwalibesi Hospital in Lau Lagoon, Malaita, in 1934. The Melanesian Mission tried again in 1928, this time with Dr Lysander Montague Maybury and his wife, Florence Edna Johnson-Kaine, (a nurse) at the Hospital of the Epiphany at Fauaabu in Coleridge Bay, west Malaita, which included the BSIP's first Hansen's disease (leprosy) colony from 1929.[108] Dr John Gunther became health officer for Levers in 1935;[109] and in the same year, Dr C.A. Courteney replaced Holt-MacCrimmon on Vanikolo. This small team of expatriate doctors was soon joined by Fijian and Solomon Islander native medical practitioners trained at the Fiji Medical College in Suva.[110] All were in communication with the Tulagi Hospital.

---

107 Boutilier 1974, 18.
108 Detailed documentation on Fauaabu is held by Helen Barrett MBE, CSI, Brisbane, with a copy now in the author's possession. The orderlies were John Patterson Nana, Frederick Fafele, Simon Peter Nwasina, Thomas Tosia (short term), Joe Qai (short term) and Ereryn Tharetona (also a teacher).
109 Later better known as Deputy Administrator of the Territory of Papua New Guinea and first Vice-Chancellor of the University of Papua New Guinea.
110 Boutilier 1974.

Malaria was a serious problem faced by all residents of the islands, and blackwater fever (malarial hemoglobinuria, a complication of malaria) was also common during the 1920s. However, the main issue dealt with by medical authorities were dysentery outbreaks among labourers and prisoners. There were outbreaks during the drier months (July to October) of 1914 and 1915. For instance, in 1914, out of 172 recorded deaths, 101 were from dysentery (58.7 per cent). In 1915, 71 deaths from dysentery were reported out of a total of 119 deaths (59.6 per cent). Tulagi Hospital treated 131 cases of all types in 1915, with 21 deaths—20 of them from a dysentery outbreak, the origin of which was traced to the prison. The figures for 1916 and 1917 were lower.

Accommodation for labourers on Tulagi was inadequate and their sanitation arrangements and drinking water were substandard. Their water supply came from two 1,500-litre tanks and there was only one toilet—built over the sea near their barracks. Most of their work was on the other side of the island, where there were no facilities, which meant, as the annual medical report quaintly described, they 'stooled everywhere'. Eventually, pit latrines were built for use by the labourers.[111] Neither was there any easily accessible drinking water on some parts of the island, which meant labourers drank from springs that were considered unsafe. Other major medical problems among the labourers were tuberculosis, bronchitis, pneumonia, pleurisy, influenza and colds. Yaws (*Treponema pallidum pertenue*) affected about 50 per cent of the population in the Solomons, causing many deaths among children and, in its tertiary phase, possibly also insanity. No attempt was made to bring the disease under control until the 1920s and 1930s.[112] Gonorrhoea became common on some islands during the early twentieth century, although syphilis was rare. Neither seems to have been an indigenous disease; both were introduced by labourers who had worked in Fiji and Queensland and by traders and fishermen.[113] The explanation for the lack of syphilis is that, where yaws is predominant, immunity is created and syphilis is seldom found. Nurses were excused from treating male venereal disease patients, who were sent to the male doctors.[114]

---

111 CO, 225/232/64124, Annual Medical and Sanitary Report, 1927, 2.
112 WPHCA, 1916/1236, Dr N. Crichlow, Annual Medical Report, 1915, 1918/1289, Crichlow, Annual Medical Report, 1918, 18; Mitjà and Marks 2016.
113 Bennett 1974, 138–41; Bowe 1899; Buxton 1925–26, 438–39; Pirie 1972.
114 Boutilier 1984a, 188.

3. ADMINISTRATION

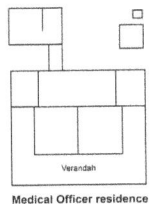

Plan of proposed Hospital Tulagi

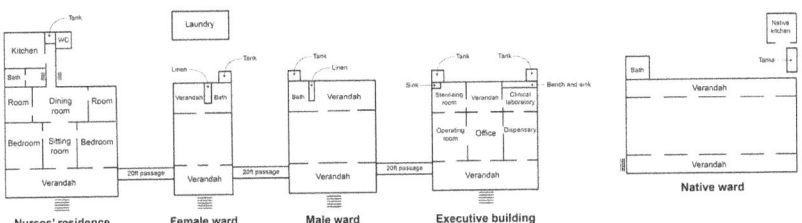

Figure 3.2 The new Tulagi Hospital, 1914
Source: From a BSIP plan redrawn by Vincent Verheyen.

Tulagi's first temporary hospital was constructed in 1913–14, with 18 beds for Solomon Islander males, a small ward for women and a four-bed ward for a 'better class' of Solomon Islanders and Asians. It had an interesting feature: an ornate woven exterior wall—the first government-sponsored public art. This building was replaced in 1915 with a new, more spacious hospital complex, built on the outer coast. The new hospital had residences for the medical officer and the nurses, quarters for the orderlies, a female European ward (four beds), a male European ward (six beds), a 'native' ward (20 beds) and a main building with an office, operating theatre and dispensary. During the 1920s, the medical establishment usually consisted of two doctors and two nurses, an engineer-navigator for the department's ship *Hygenia*, a sanitary officer on Tulagi and a squad of several labourers assisted by prisoners on Tulagi, plus about 40 local staff. There was a small isolation ward in the first hospital, with a similar facility added to the second hospital in 1920–21. There was no X-ray equipment or laboratory. In 1929–30, the executive council supported

179

installing X-ray equipment. Despite the offer of part-private funding, the decision was not supported by the WPHC or the Secretary of State for the Colonies.[115]

The first government doctor was S.C.M. Davies, who was appointed at Tulagi in 1913 and transferred to Fiji at the end of 1914. Dr Nathaniel Crichlow arrived in November 1914, equipped with bachelor's degrees in medicine and surgery from the University of Edinburgh. The first nurse was Edith Elizabeth Elliot, who arrived in March 1915 and had experience in West Africa.[116] As the years progressed, the BSIP managed to maintain two medical doctors on its staff—one based at Tulagi Hospital and one travelling through the districts. There was often also a third doctor. Once the new doctor J.E. O'Sullivan arrived in July 1915, Crichlow became the travelling medical officer. Dr O'Sullivan and his wife were not well received. In 1917, Workman asked for O'Sullivan to be removed because '[o]fficially he is distasteful to the European community' and he had the 'qualities inherent in an Irish peasant'. The truth was that Mrs O'Sullivan was a Sinn Fein supporter and both expressed pro-German sympathies at the time of World War I.[117] The O'Sullivans departed in November 1918, after which Crichlow and Sakurai (on secondment from Levers) shared the task.

It was always difficult to recruit and hold on to nursing staff. Elliot left in February 1918 to marry Jack Svensen, son of early trader Theodor Svensen. Her place was taken by sister Beavan in April, who was assisted by nurse Rushton, who arrived in July. Beavan resigned to marry A.E. Osborne, the wireless technician. The nursing staff always had a high turnover. Nurse Corfield arrived in May 1919 and had left by Christmas. The next was sister Bosden, in 1920.[118] They were poorly paid.

Crichlow—of Chinese and Scottish descent, from the West Indies—was the second-longest serving member of the prewar administration. Officially, he was the District Medical Officer until 1927, when the position became Travelling Medical Officer, although in the early years he was often also acting Senior Medical Officer on Tulagi. Once Gizo and Faisi had been declared ports of entry, it was considered useful to

---

115 Boutilier 1974, 12; WPHCA, 1236/1916, Annual Medical Report 1915, Minutes of the Advisory Council, 20 October 1930, 144; Hermant and Cilento 1928–29, 26–30; Pirie 1972.
116 Boutilier 1984a, 188.
117 Boutilier 1974, 15.
118 WPHCA, 1921/1207, Dr N. Crichlow, Annual Medical Report, 1920, 8.

have a medical doctor based in the north-west; the position was allocated to Crichlow, who became District Officer for Shortland Islands between 1915 and 1917, and again in 1923 and 1933.[119] He was transferred back to Tulagi during the Spanish influenza pandemic in 1919–20. Appointed conjoint Medical and District Officer for Gizo (1925) and for Kirakira (1925–26), he also worked in Santa Cruz (for a few weeks in 1929, half of 1937 and a few months in 1940). Crichlow was acting Senior Medical Officer on Tulagi when Hetherington was on leave in 1934. None of the other medical doctors took on district duties. Crichlow's willingness to do so is probably an indication of his peripatetic existence in the BSIP. He continued as permanent Travelling Medical Officer until 1942. Crichlow's travels on the *Hygenia*, a 15-metre diesel launch, and its replacement, *Hygenia II*, made him known throughout the BSIP.[120] Unmarried, he was a pleasant, clever man, whose only failing was deafness, which meant he could not use a stethoscope. One source also implies that he may have had relationships with local women.[121]

Plate 3.14 The 'native' ward, Tulagi Hospital, 1930s
Source: ANUA, 481-337-68.

---

119 Bennett 1987, 397; WPHCA, 1919/552, Annual Medical Report, 1918, 2.
120 The ship was wrecked and replaced with *Hygenia II*, although most accounts do not differentiate between the two.
121 UQFL, Wilson Papers and Photographs, F.A.G. Wilson to Mary, 21 May 1926; Akin 2009, Notes from Lambert, 23 May 1933.

Plate 3.15 Jessie Watt worked as a nurse at Tulagi Hospital in 1923, before she married Spearline Wilson

Source: UQFL, Wilson Papers and Photographs.

Plate 3.16 Dr Nathaniel Crichlow in old age
He worked at Tulagi Hospital and as a travelling medical officer between 1914 and 1942.
Source: Clive Moore Collection.

Table 3.3 contains the admission statistics for Tulagi Hospital for the years 1914–21. The rapid increase in patients over the period 1919–21 relates to the worldwide Spanish influenza pandemic, which spread throughout the BSIP. In 1922, the hospital was described as well equipped, with separate wards for Europeans (10 beds), Asians (four beds) and Solomon Islanders (30 beds). The hospital staff consisted of the new Senior Medical Officer, Dr Andrew G. Carment, a delightful elderly Scott; Crichlow, by then the Travelling Medical Officer; two European female nurses, E.G. Ralph and E.L. Low; and Solomon Islander orderlies and servants. Training was available for small numbers of 'dressers' from the districts, who were schooled at Tulagi Hospital for periods of three months, after which they were supplied with simple drugs and dressings and returned to their villages.[122]

Table 3.3 Tulagi Hospital admissions, 1914–21

Year	Europeans		Solomon Islanders		Outpatients
	Admissions	Deaths	Admissions	Deaths	
1914	0	0	60	24	n.a.
1915	0	0	185	24	n.a.
1916	13	1	167	1	n.a.
1917	14	3	180	17	5,195
1918	21	3	177	16	3,042
1919	35	3	485	27	4,436
1920	54	1	345	23	7,394
1921	52	5	529	19	6,207

n.a. = not available
Sources: BSIP *Handbook* (1923: 29); Annual Medical Reports, 1915–21, SINA, BSIP.

Because Tulagi was the main port of entry, any diseases introduced from outside the BSIP were usually observed there first. As soon as it broke out in Australia and New Zealand in late 1918, the Spanish influenza pandemic was expected in the Solomons. Although the BSIP Government declared influenza an infectious disease and introduced strict quarantine, the pandemic reached the archipelago in March 1919 aboard BP's *Marsina* out of Sydney. Within two days, almost everyone on Tulagi had

---

122 BSIP *AR* 1917–18, 4–5, 1923, 29, 63; WPHCA, 2034/15 to 391/15, No. 800 of 1914, Dr S.C.M. Davies to RC C.M. Woodford, 16 February 1914, Woodford to HC, 3 April 1914, 2954 of 1926, Dr N. Crichlow to Government Secretary, 27 May 1926.

influenza, but the ship had already departed. The disease spread to most islands in the BSIP—its effects exacerbated by concurrent bronchitis and pneumonia. On some islands, the effect was limited to scattered pockets, although on Malaita and other large islands the disease spread throughout. It is likely that thousands died, although it could have been even worse.[123] Prompt treatment lessened the number of deaths on Tulagi; in 1919, 225 cases were treated, with only eight deaths. The highest death rate was on Malaita, where some villages were decimated. On Tulagi, the armed constabulary barracks was converted into a hospital ward. Former nurses Elliot and Beavan returned to the hospital to help manage the pandemic. In May, BP's *Minindi* arrived with 10,000 doses of vaccine, which slowly restored normality, although in November and December, there was a second round of infections. All government employees were vaccinated. Only 7,500 doses were used because the smaller plantation companies were unwilling to pay for the vaccine for their labourers.[124] From March to May 1920, the pandemic struck again. Labour recruiting stopped for two months and the government inoculated new indentured labourers with the vaccine. Tulagi Hospital was strained, having to deal with 399 inpatients during the year, as well as thousands of outpatients—mainly labourers passing through the capital. The disease continued to affect the BSIP until 1923.[125]

There were times when there were no European patients in the hospital, although the general ward for Solomon Islanders was often full. During epidemics, the European nurses were told to stay out of the 'native' ward and leave all treatments to the orderlies. The isolation ward was converted into an Asiatic ward in 1926. Although this ward was unfurnished, the Chinese still had to pay the same hospital fees as Europeans.[126] Carment departed, replaced with a less pleasant, alcoholic Irishman, Dr C.R. Pattison, who was soon asked to resign. He had been based in Lautoka, Fiji, where he had caused problems and was given the Tulagi posting as his last chance.[127]

---

123 Boutilier 1974, 7–8.
124 WPHCA, 1920/2491, BSIP Annual Medical Report, 1919.
125 BSIP *AR* 1903–05, 33–34, 1918–19, 3, 1919–20, 4.
126 WPHCA, 2954 of 1926 to RC R.R. Kane, 15 October 1926, Dr N. Crichlow to Government Secretary, 27 May 1926; UQFL, Wilson Papers and Photographs, J.A. Watt to Mary, 28 September 1924.
127 Boutilier 1974, 15; UQFL, Wilson Papers and Photographs, F.A.G. Wilson to Mary, 20 and 21 March 1926. His wife, a nurse, stayed and joined the Methodist Mission.

Late in 1928, Dr Hetherington, the new Senior Medical Officer, chaired a medical committee to give advice on further expansion of the medical facilities. A quarantine station was established on an adjacent small island and four new isolation rooms for infectious cases were built at Tulagi Hospital. Provision was made to construct a 'public lunatic asylum' in 1928 and government records show that a small mental health facility existed at the hospital from about 1933, with seven males and one female admitted in that year.[128] Outside assistance with health came through the 1928–31 Rockefeller Foundation yaws and hookworm eradication campaign—the largest medical campaign undertaken in the BSIP up to that time.[129]

Tulagi Hospital had a sister-in-charge (a matron) and one or two nurses and, at various stages, there was also a pharmacist. R.W. Stone arrived at Tulagi in July 1927 as clerk and dispenser in the Medical Department. He died from pneumonia following an acute malarial infection in September. He was replaced with Xavier Herbert—later an outstanding Australian novelist—who worked at the pharmacy between February and May 1928 and who was attracted to Tulagi because his stepsister was acting matron at the hospital. Herbert was ill for much of his stay and contemptuous of the pompous colonial world he found there. He detested resident commissioner Kane and was very happy to leave. Interestingly, he had a small role in the plight of the Kwaio prisoners imprisoned after the murder of William Bell and his tax-collecting party, and his short stay influenced the beginning of *Capricornia*, his first novel, published in 1938.[130] Herbert was replaced in 1929 with Francis (Frank) T. Stackpool on a six-month temporary contract that became permanent.[131]

Nurse Jessie Watt worked at the hospital in 1923, employed at £120 a year plus annual uniform and other allowances totalling another £62.[132] After working in Shanghai and Manila, she found Tulagi quite charming:

---

128 McElwaine and Horne 1930, 140.
129 BSIP *AR* 1928, 5; BSIP *Blue Books* 1933–34, 120; Bradbury and Traub 2016; Mitjà and Marks 2016.
130 De Groen 1998, 65 68.
131 BSIP *AR* 1923, 63, 1928, 5; WPHCA, No. 2954 of 1926, RC C.M. Woodford to HC WPHC, 21 February, 3 April 1914, Dr S.C.M. Davies to Woodford, 16 February 1914, No. 800 of 1914, Dr N. Crichlow to Government Secretary, 27 May 1926, WPCH to RC R.R. Kane, 15 October 1926, 4/IV 222/1934, RC No. 530, 13 December 1933, 259/1934, RC, No. 21, 5 January 1934; Keesing and Corris 1980, 206, 209; *BSIP AR* 1923, 63; Bennett 1987, 397, 404.
132 UQFL, Wilson Papers and Photographs, Burns Philp and Company Island Agencies to J.A. Watt, 27 May 1925.

> The pay is good, the people nice & it won't be hot till November. We have two nice tennis courts here at the Hospital, & our garden slopes right down to the beach, which is fringed with palm trees. It is so beautiful …
>
> There is a soft rain falling (tropical rain) & the tide is low & one can see the tops of the coral reefs just beneath the water, & all green & silver shadings in the streaks. Very pretty indeed & it feeds my soul just as much as 'white hyacanths' [sic]. We are just a tiny island in the midst of tiny islands. I can count seven from where I sit—all palm covered & coral reefed. The real South Sea Islands effect. Also, two black boys in red lavas out in the shallow water spearing fish for their Kai-Kai (Dinner). They are hospital orderlies, 'John', & 'Harry' …
>
> I love it and so far have been very, very happy. It is not nearly so hot as the Philippines & is far prettier, & we have the dearest little home all to ourselves.[133]

Although her descriptions of patient care are paternalistic by modern standards, there is also a sense of fondness. One of her patients was Marfee, an elderly man who had worked in Queensland and had been in the hospital for about a year. She described him as a 'character', who pronounced that he could 'Savee white man too much'. Marfee was remarkably grubby. Watt ordered an orderly to scrub him with hot water and Lysol and shave his beard. The improvement was so great that Marfee announced that '*the man he stop long bed before, he die-finish* [I am a different man to the previous one in this bed, who died]'.[134]

Malaria was always rife, even though the authorities had filled in or drained most of the swamps. A medical report in 1927 criticised Tulagi and particularly Chinatown, which was constructed on a reclaimed mangrove swamp, in which mosquitoes bred:

> There is a great deal of scrub & weedy ground. Close behind the town is bush & this bush clothes the sides of the hills which shut the town in. I had the opportunity of examining some twenty of the inhabitants. All had enlarged spleens. Some of them were tremendously enlarged.

---

133 ibid., J.A. Watt to Mary, 18 June 1923.
134 ibid.

> Through cleaning of the scrubby & weedy ground in the Town, clearing of the bush behind it & cleaning of the drains of grass etc. And construction of new drains, and lastly regular inspection and filing where necessary—all these are required to render this important portion of Tulagi reasonably free of malaria.[135]

Foreign residents regularly took quinine, had screened sections in their homes and used mosquito nets over their beds. Some ensured that their staff took quinine as a prophylactic. Subinspector Sandars described the regular doses:

> Everyone took his five grains of quinine each evening and my little police force used to parade at six o'clock and be given their dose of quinine and a drink of water. One had to watch them pretty carefully to see that they actually swallowed it because they liked it no better than anybody else. I was fairly lucky, I never suffered really badly from malaria as did some others. I was meticulous about taking my quinine and always used to see that my housestaff took theirs too.[136]

Quinine had disadvantages: common side effects were headaches, ringing in the ears, eye problems and sweating. There was also the possibility of more severe side effects, and users could become prone to sunburn, headaches, temporary deafness and nausea. However, for the majority, it was the standard malaria prophylactic or cure. Long-term residents frequently forwent their daily doses, instead using large doses to control the fever whenever it struck. After some years—just as still occurs with Solomon Islanders—early Europeans and Chinese residents gained a degree of tolerance and managed to function well enough, despite occasional bouts of fever and being constantly below optimum health. Atebrin (quinacrine) became available in Tulagi in 1934 and was substituted for quinine, although it turned the skin a bright bronze to yellow colour. This was known as the 'mark of the Solomons'.[137]

Tulagi Hospital was a godsend, but it was isolated and primitive compared with 1920s and 1930s metropolitan standards. For instance, in 1927, Kathleen Bignell, a planter's wife from Isabel, was bitten by a centipede. She failed to respond to treatment and was evacuated to Tulagi Hospital,

---

135 WPHCA, No. 2010 of 1927, Dr H.B. Hetherington, Report of Malaria Control Measures, Tulagi, 7 March 1927, in RC to HC WPHC, 8 August 1917.
136 PMB, Sandars, Papers on the Solomon Islands, 12.
137 Keays 1995, 66; UQFL, Wilson Papers and Photographs, J.A. Wilson to Mary, 17 July 1934.

where she made no progress. The next move was to Fairlight Hospital at Manly, Sydney, where for a while there was a possibility that her leg would have to be amputated. Some years later, her husband Charles grazed his ankle while diving for trochus shell. The wound turned into a septic ulcer and he was evacuated to Australia for five months, before the infection was cleared up. He walked with a limp for the rest of his life.[138]

The hospital also acted as a nursing home for the older foreign residents of the BSIP. For several months in the early 1930s, Philip Palmer senior was a patient there when he had a leg ulcer and anaemia. His bill of £377 was never paid and his estranged sons Ernie and Philip never visited him. Left to the charity of Dick Laycock and Geoff Clift, he returned to his plantation and died horribly in 1939.[139]

Dental problems were usually dealt with by deadening the pain with oil of cloves, aspirin and patent medicines. There was only one dentist resident in the Solomons, Norman Deck from the SSEM (1913–48), who was infamous for only treating SSEM patients. Often the only local possibility was extraction with clean pliers—an operation Charles Bignell once performed on himself.[140] While there were dentists intermittently at Tulagi Hospital, when there were not, the options were to travel to Rabaul, Suva, Brisbane or Sydney. Dental problems were a constant issue for many expatriates. Some of the stories now seem amusing but would not have been to the individuals involved. Dick Horton had one screwed-in tooth that fell out while he was crossing a river. It was eventually retrieved and Eroni Leauli, a Fijian native medical practitioner, stuck it back in using gutta-percha (a rigid natural latex). Intended as a temporary solution, this repair lasted five years. Obtaining new false teeth was extremely difficult. At one stage, the Anglican bishop was capsized out of a small boat while going ashore across a reef at Alanguala, Makira. In the mayhem, he lost his false teeth. There was no way to replace them until a dentist employed by another denomination passed through Tulagi and made him a new set. His parting words to the bishop were: 'You might preach Anglican doctrine, Bishop, but never forget that you're doing it with Methodist teeth.'[141]

---

138 Clarence 1982, 80–81.
139 Golden 1993, 337.
140 Watson 1991, 56.
141 Knox-Mawer 1986, 71, 85.

The Lands and Surveys Department

Tulagi's officials controlled all land matters in the BSIP. Understanding the large variety of customary land tenure systems was the key to economic development. Large-scale land alienation had followed the proclamation of the BSIP and there was always a nagging doubt that this was not legal in the circumstances of a protectorate. Regardless, the land alienation continued. Although resident commissioner Woodford wanted sufficient land to be transferred into the hands of expatriate plantation developers, it was a balancing act. He also needed to curb land speculation and to safeguard indigenous land rights. It was some years before he could convince the British Government that the BSIP had long-term financial prospects. One of the ways Woodford did this was to declare 'unoccupied lands' to be the property of the Crown. Immediately he arrived, Woodford issued the September 1896 land regulation, which declared that all previous land 'contracts' were regarded as provisional until investigated by BSIP officers. The regulation stipulated improvement clauses for land acquired as trading stations and for agricultural purposes, which enabled legal negotiation of leases with Solomon Islanders.

Until 1912, it was possible to purchase freehold land directly from Solomon Islanders and land declared as 'waste' could be leased for up to 999 years with a certificate of occupation. However, the basis of the legal right of the BSIP Government to claim control over 'unoccupied' land was not entirely clear. Initially, the Colonial Office gave an opinion that the BSIP Government had no right to declare any land in the protectorate to be the property of the Crown and that the 'vacant' land provision of the 1896 regulation was invalid. This was soon superseded by an 1899 Law Office ruling that it was legal to declare land Crown land if the inhabitants were 'practically savages without any proper conceptions of ownership of land'. These two opinions were at cross-purposes and the solution was to issue certificates of occupation on land 'neither owned, cultivated nor occupied by any native or non-native person'.[142] Today, we understand that all land and the surrounding reefs and sea have indigenous owners.

---

142 Quoted in Heath 1981, 64.

Plate 3.17 The Tulagi waterfront with the Lands Department building in the foreground
Source: Clive Moore Collection.

Plate 3.18 Government offices on the Tulagi waterfront
The Labour Department building is in the foreground.
Source: ANUA, 481-337-77a.

Plate 3.19 The Post Office, Tulagi
Source: ANUA, 181-337-77a.

Maintaining indigenous rights to land was a consistent theme in Fiji, British New Guinea and BSIP land policy, although in practice, there was considerable variation in implementation. Woodford's attitude was a marked swing away from the situation in Fiji, where Britain had assumed rights to all non-alienated land upon cession in 1874, with indigenous land rights protected by the Governor. The *Native Lands Ordinance, 1880* made Fijian land inalienable. In the Solomons, land policy was closer to the situation in British New Guinea (later Australian Papua), where the government controlled all land matters and the indigenous people were guaranteed rights to their customary lands, but with large areas of 'waste' lands declared and made available for sale or lease. By 1910, the Government of Australian Papua had declared more than 400,000 hectares to be Crown land available for sale to investors.[143] Despite the 1896 BSIP regulation, until the creation of the Lands Commission in the early 1920s, no attempt was made to investigate pre-protectorate land sales or the rapid acquisition of land in the 1900s and 1910s. Foreigners were able to gain control of 'native land' reasonably easily. This trend in the 1890s–1910s encouraging European enterprise, combined with shallow rhetoric supporting 'native rights', was to provide the marker of land policy in the BSIP. Nevertheless, the government only ever claimed rights to 'unoccupied' land and never made a claim to the underlying title of all land.[144]

---

143 Lawrence 2014, 248–49.
144 Heath 1981, 64.

The 1896 and 1900–04 Solomons (Waste Lands) Regulations provided the basic legislative framework enabling alienation of 162,000 hectares (about 5 per cent of the BSIP) between 1900 and 1914, most of which was accessible coastal land used for coconut plantations. This land was obtained by foreign companies, with no thought of indigenous rights or participation in development, other than as a labour force. Woodford believed that Solomon Islanders attached little importance to land and were more interested in productive crops planted on the land (a concept closer to usufruct in European law). He did not understand that even if land was unoccupied it was still owned or that Melanesian custom seldom allowed permanent alienation. Added to this was the complexity of land tenure systems, which differed from island to island.[145] He also believed that the people were dying out and that it was in the best interests of the government to buy and control the land. The government paid a standard price of 2 shillings an acre and, for a 10 per cent commission, it would broker leases. The intention was to allow the government greater control over land, to stop inflation and to create revenue.

Solomon Islanders were not in a position to comprehend the huge hectarage that had passed into foreign hands and had no understanding of the British land tenure concepts involved, nor that their actions in marking papers and accepting gifts had permanently separated them from their customary lands. Eventually, the strength of protests by Solomon Islanders—particularly in the New Georgia Group, on the Guadalcanal Plains and on the west coast of Malaita—brought about the Phillips Lands Commission.

During the 1900s and the first half of the 1910s, Woodford negotiated with the WPHC for his administration to be able to purchase land directly, which could then be sold to developers at a reasonable price. In 1911, it was agreed that all nongovernment land purchases should be banned.[146] The 1914 Land Regulation enabled leases to be issued for 10 to 99 years, including a forfeiture clause. With minor amendments, this regulation remained in force until 1959. The Resident Commissioner could authorise land to be leased to 'non-natives' for cultivation, grazing and building purposes, if the consent of the owners was obtained and if the land was not under cultivation or required for the future support

---

145 Lawrence 2014, 245–49. See also Heath 1979, for a detailed analysis of land tenure, and Heath 1981.
146 Allan 1957, 37.

of the landowners. This replaced the long-term interests in land created by the government under the 1900–04 regulations. The new regulation also halted the previous system that allowed 999-year leases, although occasionally after 1914 owners of freehold were allowed to obtain a lease in perpetuity. In 1918, the government introduced regulations to enable the compulsory registration of land title deeds and established a land registry office in Tulagi. No provision was made for investigation of the validity of deeds lodged with the registrar. Copies of all entries in the register of land claims held in Suva were transferred to Tulagi.[147]

The staff of the Department of Lands and Surveys were crucial to the economic development of the BSIP. To administer land matters, Woodford created the Tulagi-based position of Government Surveyor in 1911, which was held by G.R. Turner until his resignation the next year. The Lands and Surveys Department began in 1912, with the appointment of the Commissioner for Lands, who was also the Crown Surveyor. Another surveyor arrived in 1919. The rent for cultivation leases was 3 pence per acre for the first five years, 6 pence per acre for the second five years, 3 shillings per acre from the 11th to the 20th years and 6 shillings per acre from the 21st to the 33rd years. At the expiry of the 20-year or 33-year period, the rent was reassessed at a rate not exceeding 5 per cent of the unimproved value of the land. A condition of cultivation leases was that one-tenth of the area leased had to be cultivated within five years. However, some aspects of the old system continued, and nongovernment Europeans sometimes dealt directly with Solomon Islanders in land matters, although when the agreement was ratified, the government became the owner and renter of the land. Slowly, Solomon Islanders were beginning to understand the nature of land sales and leases, and that district officers were willing to investigate their claims that foreigners had gained control of some land by fraud.[148] All of this meant that Tulagi was the central source of all government land policy and practice.

Stanley Knibbs, mentioned earlier, arrived on 22 May 1913 as the first Commissioner for Lands and Crown Surveyor. In 1918, the department expanded, with the appointment of Felix F. King to the position of Government Surveyor. Like Turner, King resigned quickly after making only a few surveys, replaced with Spearline Wilson on 3 May 1919, who

---

147 BSIP *AR* 1971, 23; Allan 1957, 41.
148 Allan 1957, 42.

succeeded Knibbs in 1939. Knibbs and Wilson made an effective team (at least in their early years), although they seem to have been surrounded by incompetent junior appointments in lands and public works and often had no support staff, not even clerical assistance.

The next addition to the Tulagi department was Harry W. Sando, appointed as temporary Government Surveyor on 1 October 1924, but forced to resign due to ill health. Then came Edward C. Chester—seemingly well qualified, with American degrees in surveying and engineering. He proved inept and was permitted to resign. The next to occupy the position was E.L. Leembruggen from Fiji, but he, too, was not up to the task and, even with on-the-job training from Wilson, could not carry out even basic surveying duties. To solve the ongoing difficulty, the administration decided to train survey office clerk N.L. Nevison, who had been a surveyor's assistant in Canada and Australia, to be a surveyor. He qualified and became the Government Surveyor on 27 June 1929, but was retrenched the next year because of the Depression. All of this severely limited the amount of surveying possible. Surveying remained combined with public works, but the latter always dominated, which led to constant neglect of the surveying section of the portfolio.[149]

The much-needed Lands Commission operated between 1919 and 1924. Although it investigated only 55 claims out of 300 European titles, it was a check on the rapacious land-grabbing that had occurred. The commission added a little to the patchy understanding of the nature of and variation in customary land tenure. There were two commissioners, both based on Tulagi, who travelled around the BSIP. The first was Captain G.G. Alexander, a legal officer from Fiji, who left the Solomons when he was appointed Junior Puisine Judge in Tanganyika, Africa. Alexander's investigations were rushed and unsatisfactory. The life of the commission was extended and Frederick Beaumont (Monty) Phillips, a young barrister from Melbourne, was appointed. Phillips was thorough and made it his practice to hold his hearings on the lands in question, which revealed numerous discrepancies. His success was even more remarkable when one realises he had a damaged leg and was short in stature. Monty Phillips sailed his own yacht—designed for a one-legged sailor—and (rather oddly) used musical instruments to provide showmanship when adjudicating land disputes. Not bluffed by the large companies making

---

149 UQFL, Wilson, 1946, Lands and Public Works Department: A Brief History, 1–2.

many of the claims, he halved one 106,569-hectare Levers' lease in the Western Solomons. Phillips's success in the BSIP led to his appointment to the New Guinea Mandated Territory as a magistrate.[150]

Rather than quelling indigenous discontent, the Phillips Lands Commission (as it became known) drew attention to the inequity of the land alienation.[151] In the 1920s and early 1930s, the Lands Department concentrated on surveys connected with the Lands Commission's findings. The 1930s and 1940s brought little change in land policy and administration, although Levers' numerous certificates of occupation were replaced with leases. The Australian Navy began preparing large-scale surveys and coastal traverses of Guadalcanal, Shortlands and Banika (the smaller of the two main Russell Islands, on which Yandina is situated)—all areas of plantation development. The Lands Commission occupied most of the time of the Lands Department staff (Knibbs was seconded as Deputy Commissioner), slowing routine surveys. Even so, by 1930, approximately half of the alienated land in the BSIP had been surveyed.[152] This commission was central to business on Tulagi over several years, and staff and ships were seconded to assist.

During the 1930s, Knibbs and Wilson performed clerical as well as surveying duties. Most of their jobs revolved around public works, and once small-scale mining began in the BSIP, surveying new mining leases took up the rest of their available time. As Wilson gently phrased it:

> The Head of the combined departments had lost heart and interest, and had given way to a weakness which gradually increased until it culminated in his retirement during the visit of Sir Harry Luke to the Protectorate in 1939.[153]

The only other European officer in the department was Jimmy Mutch, the Foreman of Public Works, who, like Knibbs, was an alcoholic. This left Wilson virtually alone to carry out most duties. Temporary respite came when C.E. Spencer was appointed as clerk between late 1937 and late 1941. Again, Wilson phrased his opinions carefully and mysteriously: 'Spencer was found to be suffering from a malady which precluded his

---

150 He later became a judge there, then Chief Judge, and was knighted in 1956. Quinlivan 1988.
151 Files on the individual cases investigated are held in Solomon Islands National Archives and, although there was a brief overall final report, no copy can now be located.
152 BSIP *AR* 1930, 14; UQFL, Wilson, 1946, Lands and Public Works Department: A Brief History, 3; Allan 1957, 43–47.
153 Wilson, 1946, Lands and Public Works Department: A Brief History, 2.

confirmation in the Colonial Service, which influenced his subsequent actions, and resulted in his decision to resign.'[154] Could this be code for relations with indigenous women, homosexuality or alcoholism? Once Wilson took over from Knibbs in 1939, World War II had begun in Europe and rigid economies were in place.

∗∗∗∗

This chapter has outlined key areas of the administration on Tulagi. The small number of Tulagi-based officials were at the core of the BSIP's elite. Certainly, that was how they regarded themselves. They paid little attention to the Chinese, who were the major group of foreign residents. The 1920s was an important decade for consolidation. Tulagi became a permanent home for government and commercial employees, both on the island and on Makambo and Gavutu. Marriages occurred, children were born and life rolled on at the Pacific outpost. The next chapter looks at other aspects of life in Tulagi in the 1920s.

---

154 ibid., 3.

4

Chinatown, the club, hotels and the 'black hole'

> The harbour is now bounded on the Tulagi side with many buildings, starting with a hotel ... then many government offices which some visitors from Australia described as b ... little Kiosks. Then beyond the government station comes an ice factory, and engineering shops. Then comes the great reclamation which I was congratulated upon after starting to dry up that swamp upon which some hundreds of Chinamen now live. They have quite good buildings including about a dozen stores, some bakeries, a laundry and a restaurant where first class meals are reputed to be sold. Next comes an extensive set of buildings the property of W.R. Carpenter & Co. on Laycock's old lease. They are in keen competition with B.P.s, still on Makembo [sic]. Further on are several blocks leased to Jack Newman and others, running right up to where the narrow passage separates Tulagi from the mainland.
>
> — Ralph B. Hill, 1915[1]

This chapter returns to the 1920s and its events and institutions. The first section discusses the role of hotels and the Tulagi Club in creating a settled urban community. The second section extends earlier discussion of the Chinese community and its importance to Tulagi. This is followed by an outline of the events around the 1927 killings on Malaita, which led to a massive and destructive government response. The chapter ends with the arrival of the first seaplanes, beginning a change to air transport, which

---

1 PMB, Woodford Papers and Photographs, 151, Reel 2, Bundle 10, 2/26, Ralph B. Hill to C.M. Woodford, 22 January 1915.

eventually meant that Tulagi, regardless of the wartime damage, could not be the permanent capital of the BSIP. The planes were also a harbinger of the centrality of aircraft in the Pacific War.

Photographs and maps help us to judge the rapid development of Tulagi during the 1920s and 1930s. At the beginning of the 1920s, there were only about 30 Europeans—most of whom were members of the administration—plus growing numbers of Chinese. The Resident Commissioner, Government Secretary, Treasurer and Commissioner for Lands lived on one side of the bridge over The Cut, with the Judicial Commissioner, the Commandant of the Armed Constabulary and the Inspector of Labour on the other. The big changes on Tulagi seem to have come during the middle years of the 1920s. The commercial area grew rapidly and there was a telephone system connecting the government offices, as well as some businesses and private houses. Chinatown had many shops, jetties and houses, and Morris Hedstrom and then Carpenters also had their store, offices, staff houses and wharf there.[2] Further around the coast, at Sasape, Johnny Chan Cheong (Chen Chang) operated a slipway and boatbuilding yard. Jack Ellis had his home and sailmaking shed nearby. The prison was situated at Point Tulagi at the entrance to the harbour on the south-eastern end of the island. A row of dilapidated concrete cells is all that remains today.

All the trappings of the British Empire were paraded when dignitaries visited. When high commissioner Sir Eyre Hutson arrived in 1927, Union Jacks, the BSIP flag and that of the Crown Colony of Gilbert and Ellice Islands were either flying or draped decoratively about. The European men were decked out in tropical whites and wore pith helmets (sola topees). Their wives wore light tropical dresses, observing the decorum of the day with hats and gloves. The armed constabulary paraded bare-chested in their tight-fitting *sulus*. Tulagi was a pretty British tropical town, picturesque and garden-like with its profusion of luxurious tropical plants. The hotels and the Tulagi Club were the centres of social life.

---

2   After the war, he was manager of the British Solomon Islands Trading Corporation in Honiara.

Hotels and the Tulagi Club

> Tulagi Club
> The Club was built delightfully beneath the palm trees tall.
> There is a table in the billiard room and trophies on the wall.
> There is a reading room and card room and bathrooms and a bar.
> And all shines with electric light as brilliant as a star.
> A lovely place is our Club, for when the day is through,
> We can talk Tulagi scandal as only men can do.
> And none can overhear us, the tale need not be true.
> We are all good fellows in our Club, we laugh and chat and smoke
> Over lots of tasty yarns and many a pungent joke.
> We've a tennis court, a golf course, a swimming bath and lots
> Of really jolly company to share a round of pots.
> Yes! We're all good fellows in the Club, but alas it may be told
> That the beer tastes all the better and the stoutest heart's more bold
> When the latest scandal's mentioned and the latest stories told.
> We rush like rabbits to our Club for twice a day at least,
> For a bit of spicy talk is like a noble feast.
> It's like turtle soup and roast beef and cream and caviar
> For us to hear where Mrs 'This' and Mr 'So-and-so' are,
> Oh! Yes, we're noble fellows, but it sometimes seems to me
> If we read some healthy books and drank a bit more tea,
> A really truly decent place Tulagi Club might be.
> Yes! After all our Club card room and our after dinner joke
> Do not make up for the loss of friends and really decent folk.
> But there's but one trick to chat old Time, and that's to follow youth,
> And tell one better every time regardless of the truth.
> For a long and lonely life we live when all is said,
> So let us tell our scandal, then toddle off to bed.
> The Club's A1, but Oh! I wish I had a home instead.
>
> — Kathleen Bignell[3]

Before hotels were built, alcohol could be obtained wholesale and retail from different stores. While we do not know exact consumption figures for the Tulagi enclave, taking the 1926–27 BSIP *Annual Report* as a guide, that year the protectorate imported £8,554 worth of alcohol: £3,135 of the value in spirits, £1,135 in wine and £4,287 in beer. Most would have been consumed by the protectorate's European and Chinese residents and visitors, and in today's dollars, the value is close to A$664,700 or

---

3   Clarence 1982, 44.

SI$3,324,000.[4] This would have included clandestine sales to Solomon Islanders, but nothing approaching the huge total. The total foreign population of the BSIP was no more than 500, about 150 of whom lived in the Tulagi enclave. Some of the expatriates were teetotallers or were not big drinkers. One-third of Tulagi's foreigners were Chinese—seldom big consumers of alcohol. The missionaries and expatriate women (there were no more than 100 in the BSIP) were probably not excessive drinkers or did not drink alcohol at all.[5] A small number of Tulagi residents and visitors did a lot of drinking and the businesses provided the alcohol for the rest of the protectorate. If the steamer from Sydney was late, supplies ran low and on occasions were totally exhausted. When the steamer arrived, there was a gathering of schooners, cutters and launches at Tulagi, Makambo and Gavutu, with the BSIP residents intent on replenishing their supplies of alcohol and other commodities.

Plate 4.1 Tulagi in the 1930s, showing Elkington's Hotel on the left on the top of the ridge
Source: NBAC, N115-513-4.

---

4   McArthur 1961, 9.
5   BSIP *AR* 1926–27, 6; Golden 1993, 433.

Plate 4.2 Elkington's Hotel, Tulagi
Source: PMB, AU PMB PHOTO 58-73 (ANUA 481-337-73).

Finding lodgings for visitors was always a problem. For all its delights, the club did not provide accommodation. Elkington's Hotel, the first on Tulagi, was built in 1916 on the edge of the ridge on the harbour side. It was the earliest centre of social life on the island, providing excellent meals and rooms. Photographs show the hotel building raised on short concrete stumps and with wide verandahs. There were 10 guest rooms around a central dining room with a bar and parlour. If there were too many guests, they were allocated mattresses in an annex.[6] The building was often insufferably hot as the site was sheltered from breezes. The proprietors, Thomas H.G. and May Elisabeth Ann Elkington, had installed carbide lights in the main parts of the hotel, enabling bright if dangerous illumination. Tom was born in Lincolnshire, England, in 1861 and arrived in Brisbane in late December 1886. A few months earlier, May Elisabeth Ann Bathe, born in Derby, England, in 1881, landed in Brisbane with her parents and a sister. The Bathes became tin miners in north Queensland and Tom and May married in Mt Romeo, near Cooktown, on 30 January 1907. Tom was also a miner in north Queensland. The couple moved to Samarai soon after they married and their son, Thomas junior, was born there on 17 November 1908. Their initial capital came from a large win at the races, which enabled them to have a prefabricated building sent to Samarai, where it became the core of their Cosmopolitan Hotel. In about

---

6   Golden 1993, 91–94; Cameron 1923, 271; Ashby 1978, 69.

1912, they moved to the BSIP and, by 1916, had applied for a land lease for a hotel. May decorated the hotel with her own paintings and artefacts from the islands and was the proud owner of one of the protectorate's few pianos, a Brinsmead. When she was not playing to entertain patrons, the instrument was stored in an asbestos cabinet to keep out humidity.[7] Wilfred Fowler describes a trip to the hotel:

> I leaned against the bar with my foot on the rail and gazed round the place while I waited for Tom. Island trophies were displayed on the walls. Clubs, shields, spears and stone-head axes hung in profusion, and there were crescent-shaped body ornaments worked from gold-lipped shells, arm-rings made from clam shells and chief's insignia in intricately fretted turtle shell. Tom took my order in silence. He wore a striped cotton shirt with a plain neckband. His face was shrivelled and lined and his hair and moustache were quite white. He had been more than forty years in New Guinea and South Pacific islands.[8]

Despite Tom Elkington's taciturn demeanour, the hotel was the main early social centre. Sometimes people hired it out for private functions, such as in 1922, when Charles and Kathleen Bignell of Fulakora plantation on Isabel held a party for 40 guests—all of the leading Europeans from the Tulagi enclave and nearby plantations.[9]

The hotel had a monopoly during the 1910s and 1920s. In these early years, its patrons had a reputation for hard drinking and womanising (although few women were available), which made it off limits for more 'respectable folk'. As Fowler recorded:

> There were tales of fabulous spending at Elkington's Hotel. Traders and recruiters off schooners used to come ashore in the 'twenties and buy up the entire stock of liquor. The copra slump had brought an end to spectacular extravagance but not too hard drinking.[10]

---

7   Pop and Agnes Johnson also had a piano at Tulagi. In the 1900s, George O'Neil and his wife had a pianola at Gozoruru, Isabel, although the climate quickly took its toll on the rolls and the piano. The Edge-Partingtons had a piano at Auki on Malaita in the 1910s; they left the protectorate in 1915. Golden 1993, 314; BM, Thomas Edge-Partington Photographic Collection, Album 5, MMDscn1076. See also Boutilier 1984a, 189.
8   Fowler 1959, 210.
9   Golden 1993, 323–25; *Planters' Gazette*, 8, December 1922, 22.
10 Fowler 1959, 157–58.

Fowler suggests that, in his later years, Tom Elkington 'cultivated an air of rectitude' and would not let his patrons 'go beyond the limits he allowed in his hotel'.[11] May died in 1927 and Tom in 1930, after which the hotel was managed by their son, Tom junior, and then Bill Fyfe and his wife, before it was sold to J.A. ('Johno') Johnstone and John Mather.[12] No attempt was made to replace the hotel after a fire destroyed it in 1934. The next building on the site was a Catholic church. By the time it burnt down, Elkington's Hotel had competitors in Chinatown: one Chinese hotel and Sterling's Hotel, two licensed Chinese restaurants, which seem to have doubled as bars, the Tulagi Club and Mrs Boyle's boarding house. BP had a hotel licence for its branch store on Tulagi. In 1936, acting resident commissioner Kidson wrote that 'no hotel will be built at Tulagi for many years to come'.[13] He did not know how right he was.

Bobby Sterling, owner of one of the two hotels in Chinatown, moved to the Solomons in 1915 at age 20 and worked as a trader, planter and recruiter. A short, wiry man, he is rumoured to have made enough money from gambling sessions to open his small hotel, which became a haunt for less reputable Europeans, including those no longer welcome at Elkington's Hotel. Colloquially known as the 'Blood House' (because of the number of fights that occurred there),[14] it was not much bigger than the surrounding Chinese stores. There was a kitchen and bar, a room containing three iron beds and a verandah at the front. Fowler also visited Sterling's establishment:

> A babel of noise rose from the fog of tobacco smoke which hung over the bar. The night was sultry and men stood drinking, hairy chested and bare to the waist, wiping away sweat with the trade towels they carried. The lamps, flickering as flying insects got caught in the flames, cast a poor light on the whiskey advertisements and prints of undressed girls displayed in a calamitous attempt to enliven the place.[15]

---

11 ibid.
12 UQFL, Wilson, 1972, Notes for James Boutilier; Golden 1993, 93; WPHCA, No. 2785 of 1936, A/RC N.S.B. Kidson to HC WPHC, 22 August 1936, J.M. Wall to Kidson, 11 August 1936.
13 NASI, BSIP, A/RC N.S.B. Kidson to HC WPHC, 22 August 1936.
14 Golden 1993, 179.
15 Fowler 1959, 207–09.

Fowler described some of the staff and patrons. Behind the bar was Charlie Koenig, a 'tall, big-boned man with a hard humourless face'.[16] Charley Shatz, a sailmaker, was 'a small man wearing a sleeveless vest and white drill trousers', with white stubble showing on his bony chin.[17] Drunken Peter Cullen, in filthy clothes, stood 'swaying, wild-eyed and ill-looking, mouthing with incoherent anxiety'.[18] A small American, bearded and with tawny sun-bleached hair and a body tanned leathery brick red, wore only a pair of tight-fitting shorts. He was sailing his yacht single-handed around the world and had perfected the art of always getting someone else to pay for his drinks.[19] Some of Sterling's patrons, it is said, became such a nuisance that resident commissioner Ashley ordered them deported. After Bobby Sterling died from cancer in Sydney in 1931, the hotel continued to operate under his name, with new ownership, until the Japanese occupation. Sam Doo (Du) ran the other Chinatown hotel, known under his name, which also had a good Chinese restaurant. As with Elkington's and Sterling's establishments, Sam Doo's Hotel carried his name long after he left Tulagi.

Mrs Boyle's boarding house provided accommodation for those wanting a less alcoholic stay. Other visitors to Tulagi were fortunate enough to be invited into the homes of the government officers, the company managers or other staff. For instance, in the 1930s, anthropologist Ian Hogbin always stayed with Spearline and Jessie Wilson when he passed through Tulagi.[20] Important visitors were usually invited to stay with the Resident Commissioner.

---

16 ibid., 207.
17 ibid.
18 ibid., 209.
19 ibid., 208.
20 UQFL, Wilson Papers and Photographs, Ian Hogbin to A.H. Wilson 10 December 1934.

Plate 4.3 The Tulagi Club, 1920s
Source: NBAC, N115-520-7.

Plate 4.4 The Tulagi Club, 1930s. Shutters and sides have been added to enclose the verandah
Source: UQFL, Wilson Papers and Photographs.

In 1925, resident commissioner Kane raised the need for a 'Europeans only' club, proposing that the government pay £1,000 towards building expenses. This was authorised a year later, with the Tulagi Club paying £25 rent each year to use the premises. Kane estimated that the club would be visited regularly by 65 members: 43 headquarters civil servants and their wives, 10 'country' or outstation officials and perhaps a dozen or so commercial or plantation-based individuals and their wives. Once the club opened in 1927, management was taken over by BP, presumably using their existing Tulagi liquor licence. Casual guests were welcome and government officers could join automatically, but other residents in the islands had to be nominated and only after they had been in the protectorate for six months. The vetting process was strict and membership fees varied. Protectorate officers each paid £3/3/- a year and their wives paid £1/1/-, which included their children. Rates for residents from outside Tulagi varied according to how far away they lived. Although it had no accommodation, the Tulagi Club was the premier social centre. Its recreational facilities and the bar and reading room were the drawcards. The bar was small—just a servery hatch where a Chinese barman dispensed the drinks. Members then retreated to the verandahs to drink. Chits were signed and bills arrived monthly. It became a venerable institution and it was considered a high honour to be invited to play golf or tennis with the current Resident Commissioner, who was president of the club's committee.[21] The club held an annual sports competition between government and nongovernment employees. Competitions between 'the government' and 'the rest' were played out in a 'Five Events Cup', with rival 12-man teams competing in golf, cricket, tennis, billiards and swimming in the shark-proof enclosure. Dick Gaskell junior was a sportsman of repute and, in the 1930s, always headed 'the rest'. The competition was intense and expatriates came from all over the Solomons to compete. It ended with a 'Five Events Dinner' at the club, which always commenced formally but degenerated into a 'sixth event'—a beer swilling competition.[22]

---

21 Golden 1993, 407; Tulagi Club 1934.
22 Brown 2007, 11.

4. CHINATOWN, THE CLUB, HOTELS AND THE 'BLACK HOLE'

Plate 4.5 The Tulagi cricket ground, 1935
Source: Annika Korsgaard Collection.

Plate 4.6 The Tulagi cricket ground, 2 April 1939
Source: Martin Clemens Collection, courtesy of Alexandra Clemens.

In Kathleen Bignell's poetic assessment at the start of this section, the club was a hotbed of gossip—and men, not women, were the ones doing the drinking and gossiping. Eustace Sandars described his first trip to the club in 1928 (he later became its secretary):

> The Club ... was full of people, almost all the government servants who lived on Tulagi were there with their wives, and being steamer time, many of the outside plantation people were in Tulagi and they all came along to have a chat and a drink. The Club was the centre of all social life in Tulagi and many very pleasant hours I spent there. In the evening we generally used to play snooker. Everybody on Tulagi seemed to own a dog. There were dogs of all sorts sizes and descriptions and they all came along to the Club with their masters. Most of them lay down in the cool under the club until about six o'clock and then they all started, most of them wanted to fight each other.[23]

Fowler also left us a description of life at the club, including an evening of dancing:

> We walked in couples down the graded coral-metalled paths to the golf-course. We could hear the dance music as we walked across the course to the Club. Coconut-palm fronds fixed along the verandah, a crudely fashioned archway of foliage over the entrance and sprays of purple bougainvillea displayed in corners of the building and tied against the wall, all failed in their purpose. They were not decorative—they merely gave the Club a raffish and untidy appearance. Kelsey and Hardy left us as soon as we arrived, but the rest of the men danced in turn with the women on the Club verandah.
>
> There were twice as many men as women at the dance and the women, warm and moist in the still close night, danced heroically time after time to the gramophone music. The sweating, animated crowd grew boisterous as the night advanced. The Club boys brought us drinks to the table outside, where we sat watching the incoming tide washing over the coral shark-barrier at the bathing-pool.[24]

Dick Horton, a district officer who arrived on Tulagi in August 1937, found the community friendly. He noted that 'life was somewhat circumscribed by the local conditions and any new arrival was a heaven-

---

23 PMB, Sandars, Papers on the Solomon Islands, 7.
24 Fowler 1959, 184–85.

sent gift for dissection and discussion'.[25] Much of this took place on the golf course or at the Tulagi Club—the social centre in the evenings and weekends. Along with billiards and table tennis tables, there were reading and dining areas, with comfortable wide verandahs on which to relax. The King George V cricket ground and the tennis courts were next to the club and a nine-hole golf course had been laboriously constructed from nearby swamp land. Unusual hazards included the wireless towers, coconut crabs that stole golf balls and a ninth hole beside the sea, into which many balls disappeared. Sandars described the course as

> something very strange to me being sand browns and not greens. It was kept in beautiful order and provided you kept straight there was no problem but, once off the line there were crab holes down which a ball went and that was the end of them until the crab had eaten them and spewed them up again being quite worthless both for him and for you.[26]

Tulagi's men, particularly if single, spent a great amount of time at the club, and visitors usually ended up there being entertained with tall tales of crocodiles and sharks, big fish that got away, dangerous sea voyages, the problems of living with malaria and, of course, the 'natives'. Women also included the club in their social circuit, usually in the afternoons for a swim, a game of tennis or to read the overseas newspapers.[27] In 1933, Jessie Wilson described the small procession needed if she wished to descend from her house on the ridge to visit the club:

> I think I've told you that we are on a hill about 400 feet [120 metres] above sea level, although we are nearly within stones throw of the beach & to get the pram down the Hill on to the flat road it has to be carried by two boys & another walks behind to carry Ann & then I come along with Michael by the hand. So you see it is quite a complicated business to get a game of tennis & golf. One boy then pushes Ann around about the club & another plays with Michael on the beach. The other one came back to cook the dinner & 'Mother' plays at something till 6 pm, & then begins to round up the family. Of course when 'Father' is at home he can stay on the hill & mind the family.[28]

---

25 Horton 1965, 14.
26 PMB, Sandars, Papers on the Solomon Islands, 7.
27 WPHCA, No. 282 of 1925, RC R.R. Kane to HC WPHC, 16 January, 14 July 1925, No. 1568 of 1929 (next to No. 2276 of 1929), J.C. Barley to HC WPHC, 16 May 1929, No. 2276 of 1926, Tulagi Club 1934, Foreword to Rules of the Tulagi Club, RC to HC WPHC, 25 October 1926.
28 UQFL, Wilson Papers and Photographs, F.A.G. Wilson to Mary, 14 February 1932.

Plate 4.7 A tennis court, next to the Tulagi Club
Source: UQFL, Wilson Papers and Photographs.

Plate 4.8 The Tulagi golf course and the Tulagi Club
Source: UQFL, Wilson Papers and Photographs.

Plate 4.9 The two wireless station masts and the golf course, 1930s
Source: BM, Robert Lever Photographic Collection.

Chinatown: Flourishing despite prejudice, 1920s and 1930s

While the European residents may have seen the Tulagi Club or Elkington's Hotel as the social centres of Tulagi, for Solomon Islander residents and visitors, Chinatown was central and welcoming. Chinese merchants learnt not to hurry Solomon Islanders deliberating over purchases. They went 'eye shopping' or made small purchases; they could lounge about, get something to eat and maybe purchase some forbidden alcohol. Chinatown consisted of a two-sided row of shops. The settlement abutted the coast and buildings on the outer side had several wharves, which enabled the Chinese trading schooners to tie up close by. Dr Hetherington was worried about the prevalence of malaria, and in 1927 focused his attention on Chinatown:

> Chinatown will require special attention of its own for the control of malaria. Built practically in a swamp, the water in its drains flows slowly back and forth with the tide, the ground between drains is marshy and sodden. There are many depressions & crab-holes with water either fresh, brackish or frankly salt.[29]

---

29 WPHCA, No. 2010 of 1927, Dr H.B. Hetherington, Report of Malaria Control Measures, Tulagi, 7 March 1927, enclosed in RC to WPHC, 8 August 1927.

Typical of Chinatowns in the Pacific, the wooden shops fronted the street, with the homes at the rear. There were shady front verandahs with crisscrossed wooden batons, with the eves, walls and railings painted in blue, red or green. There was one difference from most other Chinatowns, in that quite substantial buildings were built on the wharves to cope with the swampy land, expanding the living and shopping areas. Solomon Islanders saw Chinatown as the social and economic core of Tulagi and they felt comfortable there, just as they did later in Gizo's or Honiara's Chinatowns. The Chinese also employed Solomon Islanders. The oldest shops in Gizo's and Honiara's Chinatowns today are quite similar in style to those once found on Tulagi.

One of Tulagi's early restaurants was begun in 1925 by Alois Akun, representing a Rabaul company owned by the Chan (Chen) family. Alois (a contraction of Aloysius) Akun may have been a relative of one of the three Chan brothers who arrived in Rabaul in 1894, 1897 and 1902, respectively, originally from Taishan County, with the first two arriving via Singapore.[30] His name matches that of the youngest Rabaul Chan brother, who had been given a good European education. In 1902, Rabaul's Aloysius Chan became the first Christian Chinese in the town, and over the following decades, he established one of the largest wholesale businesses in east New Guinea. Tulagi's Alois Akun also became prominent in business. He was allowed to open stores in Gizo and the Shortlands. The reason seems to have been an attempt by the government to provide some competition with BP, which was placing an exorbitant mark-up on its goods, both to Solomon Islanders and to local planters.[31]

---

30 Chan Tai-hei (aka Chan Lock, aka Paul Ah Lock), Chan Tai-fun (aka Cahn Chai, aka John Achai) and Chan Tai-yok (aka Chan Kun, aka Ah Kun, aka Alois Akun). Cahill 2012, 24–25; Wu 1982, 53–56.
31 Bennett 1987, 208; WPHCA, 2564/1926, Paper 3 of the Special Meeting of the Advisory Council, 30 June 1926.

Plate 4.10 Chinatown in the 1930s, with BP's Makambo Island in the background
Source: UQFL, Wilson Papers and Photographs.

Plate 4.11 The main street of Chinatown, 1938
Source: NASI, BSIP Photographic Collection.

Quan Hong, who arrived at Tulagi as a carpenter in October 1924, was granted a licence to trade at Gizo in 1927, where he began a partnership with other Chinese from Tulagi.[32] The Yip (Ye) family from Kaiping County were other early arrivals. In 1926, Yip Yuk brought out his two teenage nephews, Yip Sing (Ye Xing) and Yip Choy (Ye Cai), to work for him. Like Alois Akun, Leong Ben moved from Rabaul to Tulagi, where he became a boat builder and repairer. A mechanic, Chan Wing (Chen Rong), arrived in Tulagi in the 1930s to establish his own ship-repair business.[33] Today, this family runs the Honiara Hotel, Wing's supermarket and the Chan Wing shipping company, all based in Honiara.

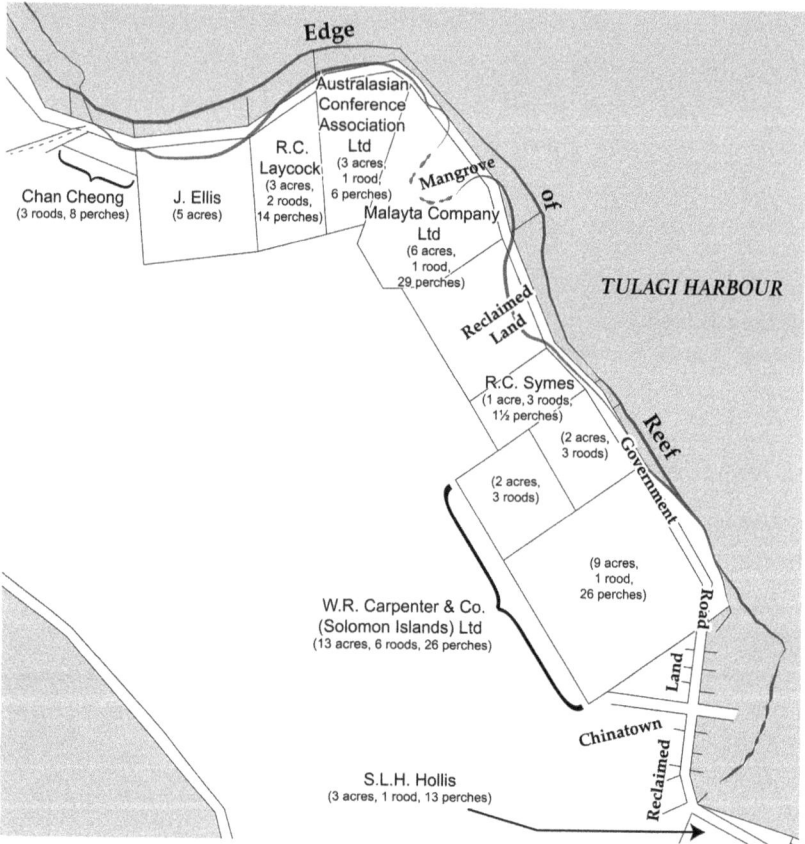

Map 4.1 'No. 2', the commercial area on Tulagi, circa 1934
Source: Cartography by Vincent Verheyen.

---

32 'QQQ's Milestone Celebration: A History in its Own Making', *Solomon Star*, 8 February 2016.
33 Willmott (2005, 12–13) provides details on the origins and approximate years of arrival of these settlers.

4. CHINATOWN, THE CLUB, HOTELS AND THE 'BLACK HOLE'

Chinatown (Map 4.1) was part of what became 'No. 2', the extensive commercial area on Tulagi. During the late 1920s and early 1930s, the area spread to cover all the coastal land between the Hollis Brothers' iceworks and Chan Cheong's slipway at Sasape. Carpenters held the largest piece of land, of more than 5 hectares adjoining Chinatown. Next to them were R.C. Symes, the Malayta Company Limited (the commercial arm of the SSEM), the Australasian Conference Association Limited (the commercial arm of the Seventh-day Adventist Church) and Dick Laycock's store, then Ellis's sail repair business and Chan Cheong's slipway business.

During the 1920s, Tulagi's Chinatown grew to such an extent that it was surveyed and, in 1929, had a street plan imposed.[34] In June that year, Mr Lin, the Chinese Consul-General to Australia, visited Tulagi and helped negotiate the long-term residence of 10 Chinese families. Tulagi's Chinese community maintained its Rabaul and Guangdong links, and also developed strong connections with the Australian Chinese business community. Several Tulagi men were shareholders in a joint-stock company that produced the *Chinese Times*, a newspaper published in Melbourne between 1902 and 1922, which was later moved to Sydney as the media organ of the Guomindang (Kuomintang).[35] While the Chinese experienced discrimination in the protectorate, their overseas links enabled them to be part of a much wider Chinese diaspora.

There are many good photographs of Chinatown, which show its extent and complexity. Using a late 1930s photograph and imposing on it the 1922 land leases detailed in Chapter 2 (Map 2.1) gives some idea of the possible sites in Chinatown.

---

34 BSIP *AR* 1929, 12; Knibbs 1929, 264.
35 The Tulagi shareholders were Long Kock (Guo Long), Joe Youm (Ren), Long Sun, Hoe (Hao) Chen, Leong Lum (Liang Lin) and Tomo Moo (Tumu Mu). The final name is not clear; it could also be Jono Mao (or Moo or Mu). Information from Mei-Fen Kuo, 19 November 2015. There is a photograph and story in the *Chinese Times* (Sydney), dated 25 June 1920. The sources are in the Archives of the Chinese Nationalist Party of Australasia (Sydney). The reference number is 523-01-297.

Plate 4.12 Chinatown in the 1930s, with identification of the leases added from Map 2.1 (1922)

Code: 1. Man Cheong (Min Chang) & Co.; 2. Kwong Cheong (Guang Chang) & Co.; 3. Meredith & Clift; 4. Man Cheong; 5. Neong Kong (Long Gang); 6. Ye Koh & Seto Chong (A. Guo & Situ Chang); 7. Kwong Yong Cheong (Kwong Ying Cheong); 8. Nam Cheong (Nan Chang); 9. Yam Tim (Ye Tian); 10. Chow Kai (Zhou Qi); 11. Chan Dung (Chen Deng); 12. Man Cheong; 13. Ching Fook Ye (Ching Fook Yo); 14. Man Cheong (Min Chang); 15. Man Cheong; 16. Man Cheong; 17. Chow Kai (Zhou Qi); 18. Nam Cheong (Nan Chang).

Source: Annika Korsgaard Collection; cartography and numbering by Vincent Verheyen.

The BSIP's Chinese community grew quickly—from 55 in 1920, to 90 in 1925, 164 in 1931 and 193 in 1933.[36] Chinese numbers then dropped slightly, to 180 by 1941. The Crown Colony of Hong Kong Government did not issue passports and they were difficult to obtain in China, which is usually given as the reason the Solomons' numbers declined, although, in comparison, the Rabaul Chinese community increased in size during the mid to late 1930s. The majority of Solomons Chinese lived on Tulagi.[37] Chinatown was replete with trade stores and eating places. Saturdays became the regular market day on the nearby shore, where swarms of Gela canoes brought produce to sell.[38] Chinatown was exotic, and Fowler had a good eye for detail:

> We walked down the slope to the waterside path, past the offices and the wharf, and then on for a quarter of a mile to a cluster of flimsy wooden shacks with coral jetties leading off to deep water. This was where the Chinese lived—hard working traders in piece goods, cheap lamps, fish hooks, jews' harps, beads, pipes and gaudy-labelled low-grade tinned food. Their schooners lay at the

---

36 Laracy 1974, 29; NASI, BSIP 14/6, RC C.M. Woodford to Resident Magistrate T.W. Edge-Partington, 24 December 1911, BSIP 14/60, District Officer W.R. Bell to Resident Commissioner, 12 June 1927.
37 McArthur 1961, 9.
38 Knibbs 1929, 274; Godfrey 1928, 6.

end of the jetties, discharging trochus shell and copra or loading with trade goods. High-pitched chatter, sibilant exclamations and the clatter of counters disclosed a session of fantan in one of the sheds we passed.[39]

Smart Chinese traders turned on their gramophones to attract customers to buy their enticing wares, as Stanley Knibbs described:

> Clocks that grind out a tune every hour instead of striking, electric torches with enormous lenses suggestive of correspondingly large powers of illumination, accordions adorned with gaudy tinsel of every colour, loin-cloths of startling hue and design.[40]

The traders also let off firecrackers and in the evenings lit their premises with colourful paraffin lamps. European residents shopped in Chinatown and, if comparisons with Rabaul's Chinatown are valid, Chinese-style women's matching pants suits and silk pyjamas were easily available and cheap, as were rattan and wooden furniture—all imported from Asia. Basic work clothes for men were also sold there.[41]

Many of the Chinese were single men, but there was a core of married couples with a few children.[42] Eugen Paravicini visited Tulagi in the late 1920s, staying with Carpenters' manager on the far side of Chinatown. His description of Chinatown is not flattering as he failed to realise the control the administration placed on Chinese migration and allocation of space. They were only allowed to use the Chinatown site because it was an unwanted low-lying area:

> At the beach of Tulagi, the Chinese erected dirty corrugated iron huts. One can see that the Chinese prefer confined settlements, even far from home while the dwellings of the Europeans are spread over a big area. The Chinese quarter looks sad: broken boxes, bits of jute sacks, broken glass and petroleum cans are all over the place, creating plenty of little puddles, an ideal breeding place for mosquito larvae. No wonder that Tulagi has a reputation for being the source for malaria. Out in the sea natives and Chinese live in stilted huts which are poorly mended with corrugated iron and therefore look quite neglected.[43]

---

39 Fowler 1959, 206–07.
40 Knibbs 1929, 275, see also 339–40.
41 Keays 1995, 59–61.
42 BSIP *AR* 1927, 10, 1934, 13.
43 Paravicini 1931, 43.

Chinese traders—deliberately discouraged by government policy from establishing permanent stores outside Tulagi—managed to trade from vessels around the coast, collecting copra and trochus shell. Photographs show seven jetties in Chinatown—an indication of the network of Chinese traders that existed and the centrality of the Chinese community to commerce.

Restrictions were eased during the late 1920s and 1930s, allowing Chinese to set up stores at Midoru on Isabel, at Gizo and the Shortlands in the north, Aola on Guadalcanal and on Malaita. Johnny Chan Cheong expanded his Tulagi and Gizo-based operations to Isabel. Yee Poy (Yi Bo) used his base in the Shortlands to trade locally for trochus shell and copra, extending his operations to include Choiseul. A partnership between Akun, Quan and Chow (Zhou) operated from Gizo. This was eventually replaced with Quan Chow (Guan Zhou) Company, trading throughout the Western and Central districts. In 1917, Leong Tong (Liang Dong), on behalf of Man Cheong and Company of Tulagi, applied for land for a trade store on Malaita, which was refused. The same Chinese company tried again in 1920, through Ay Choy (A Cai) representing Kwong Chong and Company, an associated company. They were refused again. Finally, in October 1927, Malaita's district officer William Bell recommended that Chinese traders be allowed to establish trade stores at Su`u on the south-west coast and at `Ataa on the north-east coast, but not at Auki.[44] In 1934, Quan Chow Company leased the former Mala Development Company chain of trade stores around Malaita, then owned by Messrs McLeod, Bolton and Company. These Chinese companies used Tulagi's Chinatown stores and the big companies (Carpenters, BP and Levers) to obtain wholesale supplies. Kwong Chong Company's success was only possible because of the economic downturn in the 1930s, which caused European-owned trading companies to withdraw from the outer districts.

---

44   NASI, BSIP 14/48, DO W.R. Bell to RC C.R.M. Workman, 22 March 1920, 14/14 Workman to Bell, 27 February 1920, 14/60, Bell to Workman, 12 June 1927, 14/25, Government Secretary to Bell, 5 October 1927.

Plate 4.13 Solomon Islands leaf houses and a substantial Chinese house built over the water in Chinatown
Source: NASI, BSIP Photographic Collection.

Plate 4.14 Solomon Islands leaf houses built over the water in Chinatown, and a Chinese trading vessel
Source: Clive Moore Collection.

The big British and Australian merchant firms continued to oppose the Chinese, wanting to limit the size of Chinatown and stop any development of Chinese stores in other parts of the protectorate. They were assisted in 1925 by an eight-man deputation (of planters, traders and Reverend John Goldie) to the High Commissioner, attempting once more to place controls on the Chinese. This time, the stress was on the 'degeneracy of native morals'—mainly through gambling and the dangers from opium consumption—and the lower standard of produce collected by the Chinese. The Chinese were accused of overflowing Tulagi's Chinatown and inculcating the protectorate with 'Asiatic national ideals'. The petition complained that the Chinese were providing 'rest houses' (shelters for Solomon Islanders visiting Tulagi), which encouraged loitering and vagrancy. The petition alleged that the Chinese were breaching the curfew imposed on Solomon Islanders and Chinatown, and that the gambling they encouraged could lead to assaults on European women:

> [A] number of attempted assaults on European women resident at Tulagi have taken place during the last two or three years. We are of the opinion ... that these are encouraged by the fact that natives are, by the facilities afforded, encouraged to leave their quarters for the purpose of gambling, and to remain away from them until a late hour. It is a very simple matter for natives to leave the gambling dens during the night and to make their way into European houses.[45]

One Chinese was accused of consuming £40 (about A$3,200 in today's money) worth of opium a month, and others were said to live in local villages with their Solomon Islander wives. The petition topped it all off with the ludicrous accusation that the majority of the Chinese were members of the 'Kuo Min Tang', which the petitioners erroneously claimed was 'essentially the Communist Party of the Chinese Republic'. Finally, the petition requested that the Chinese be limited to contract work as 'mechanics, tradesmen, [and] domestic servants'.[46] Their request was denied.

---

45 WPHCA, 1184/1925, Deputation to High Commissioner of Representatives of Residents, 29 September 1925, transcript, and Annexure C, read by H. Chaperlin.
46 ibid.

Plate 4.15 A branch of Jiang Jieshi's (Chiang Kai-shek's) Chinese Nationalist Party, the Guomindang (Kuomintang or KMT) operated on Tulagi from 1925. The building dates from about 1927
Source: Queensland Museum, EH15349 2.

The Resident Commissioner had total control over all entries without a passport. A 1922 regulation required all new arrivals to have at least £50 in cash, to ensure they did not become a burden on the government. Employers also had to post a bond to cover the repatriation costs of all workers brought into the protectorate and, in 1928, a new regulation levied a bond of not less than £20 on jobless immigrants. While there was no mention of the Chinese, the intent was obvious.[47] Restrictions became harsher in 1929, and in 1930 Chinese traders were limited to the exact localities stated on their trading licences. Djienbien Young (Dianbin Yang), a Chinese consular officer from Sydney, arrived in Tulagi in March 1931. He registered diplomatic complaints about the discriminatory restrictions, much to the annoyance of resident commissioner Ashley. However, when Sir Murchison Fletcher became High Commissioner in 1930 (earlier in his career he had been posted to Hong Kong) and the Depression began to bite, circumstances changed. Fletcher believed that a Chinese presence could be an advantage. Most restraints on the Chinese were lifted in 1933, although they were still forbidden to obtain freehold land.[48]

---

47 Willmott 2005, 17.
48 ibid., 16–17.

The smaller European companies did not want to face Chinese competition, but the major companies—although they raised the usual complaints about the corrupting influence of the Chinese on the local people through gambling, alcohol and other vices—could survive without being beholden to the Chinese middlemen. The big companies also made use of the itinerant Chinese trading vessels, buying village-sourced copra and trochus shell from them, and selling them wholesale goods. The latter was an attempt to lessen Chinese imports directly from Sydney, Rabaul and Hong Kong and thus bind them into local European commercial networks.[49] In 1930, an article in the *Pacific Islands Monthly* accused the Chinese of falsifying the weights of 'native' copra by adding water to swell the dried coconut flesh and lamented that the Chinese had been allowed to prosper beyond their rightful place as labourers and domestic servants.[50]

In 1931, five European traders on Isabel protested to the Resident Commissioner about the introduction of Chinese trade stores on the island. Two years later, Harold C. Corry of Ivatu plantation on Guadalcanal, wrote to the WPHC High Commissioner complaining about extra trading licences recently granted to the Chinese. He claimed that they were inconstant in their purchases of copra and ivory nuts, were governed by the markets and that their real reason for being floating traders was to sell inferior Asian merchandise to labourers. The implication was that European traders did not react to markets or sell inferior goods—both unlikely. Once more there is a reference to these goods being cheaper than similar products sold by European traders or on plantations, which made the Chinese traders more competitive. Corry's only solution, during the hardship years of the Depression, was

> in self-defence to buy Chinese and Japanese goods from Hong Kong when I could have obtained goods of British origin though at an enhanced cost. The quality of the British goods gives better value for the money but the natives prefer to take the cheaper article.[51]

---

49 Willson et al. 1990, 98–99; Moore 2008; Laracy 1974; Bennett 1987, 152, 206, 208–09, 216, 224–25, 230, 236, 232–38, 249, 250, 252, 253, 254, 256, 268, 269, 271, 288, 319, 330; Willmott 2005, 19.
50 Chaperlin 1930.
51 WPHCA, 3223/33, H.C. Corry to HC, 8 September 1933.

Corry's gripe was discussed in Suva and, interestingly, Anglican Bishop Walter Baddeley supported the Chinese, saying that they 'gave the natives a squarer deal than the European trader'.[52] One of the solutions was to encourage Solomon Islanders to become traders, cutting out the need for European or Chinese middlemen. However, even after a reduction in the licence fees for Solomon Islander traders, this did not work. The acting Resident Commissioner reported to Suva that, as of December 1932, there were only 12 store licences and 61 hawker licences issued to Solomon Islanders, the former in only two districts. The response supported the Chinese:

> The average Solomon Island native had little aptitude for business and practically no sense of economic values and cannot face the competition of European and Asiatic traders. Further the physical nature of the islands renders trading for a native storekeeper's position an unenviable and unprofitable one. In conclusion the Acting Resident Commissioner considered that native interests in the Protectorate would best be served by unrestricted Chinese trading for many years to come.[53]

The Chinese were restricted again in 1936 when the government began to think once more about fostering indigenous entrepreneurs. By the mid-1930s, there were about 30 Chinese in business at Gizo and another 100 at Tulagi; a few more Chinese women had joined the Tulagi community. There are indications that there was also a mixed-race community on Tulagi, with part-Chinese and part–Solomon Islander children.[54]

A branch of Jiang Jieshi's (Chiang Kai-shek's) Chinese Nationalist Party, the Guomindang (Kuomintang), operated a community hall with a room at the rear that provided accommodation for new arrivals and served as a home for any destitute Chinese. The Guomindang was active at Tulagi from about 1925—initially led by Quan Park.[55] Tulagi's Guomindang building seems to have been constructed in about 1927 and expanded in

---

52 WPHCA, 99/33, 2592/31, Precis, Trading by Natives in the British Solomon Islands Protectorate.
53 ibid.
54 Weetman 1937, 34. Bishop Steward denied this in June 1926, telling the Advisory Council that there were no Chinese mixed-race children in the protectorate. WPHCA, 2564/1926, Paper No. 3 of the Special Meeting of the Advisory Council, 30 June 1926.
55 Willmott 2005, 17–18.

the 1930s by adding two side wings.⁵⁶ Europeans seldom understood the dual purpose of the Guomindang branch, which was political and social, acting as a community centre.

Chinese continued to work for the administration, usually as tradesmen, and there were a few Europeans who worked with or for the Chinese, based in Chinatown or assisting their business negotiations. C.E. Minns, who 'floated' around the protectorate from the 1920s, working on ships and managing plantations, spent his final years in poor health on Tulagi, where he was in and out of hospital. He held a lease on a piece of coastal land at Sasape, worked as a boot repairer in Chinatown and died in 1934.⁵⁷ Arthur L. Threlfall was another 'floater', a rough 'knockabout' type from Sydney. He had managed a store at Marau Sound, Guadalcanal, where he had a reputation for mistreating the local people. Threlfall married Isobel (Bella), the part–Solomon Islander daughter of a local settler named Bill Dumphy.⁵⁸ They moved to Tulagi in the 1930s. Threlfall had different jobs, including managing stevedores and working behind the bar in Sterling's Hotel.⁵⁹ Though fluent in Pijin, many of the Chinese wrote English poorly and relied on friendly Europeans to help them arrange business deals and negotiate with Western suppliers, often for a fee.

Although always marginalised, the Chinese were central to the retail trade in the protectorate. Europeans appreciated their trade skills, cursed their entrepreneurial flair and patronised their stores. Solomon Islanders availed themselves of the cheap goods in the Chinese trade stores and probably thought little of their Asian languages and customs, which were

---

56 I have two photographs of the building, one held by the Queensland Museum and one from the collection of Mei-Fen Kuo. The Kuomintang records in Sydney indicate that eight BSIP Chinese joined the party in Sydney in 1921. Their chairman was Ceng Chang-yan (曾昌言) and the secretary was Zhang Huan-ting (張煥廷). The Solomon Islands Kuomintang branch was officially launched in August 1923 by Yee Wah (余) as a sub-branch of the Rabaul Kuomintang, which was established in 1922. In 1931, Tulagi's Kuomintang became a branch of the Australasian Kuomintang in Sydney. The next year, the Chinese names listed as executive members of the Tulagi Kuomintang were Feng Nan (馮南), Guan Fei-yan (關非炎), Johnny Chan Cheong (陳章), Augustine Quan Hong (關洪) and Zou Gui (鄒). By 1933, the anti-Chinese restrictions had affected the Kuomintang but Huang Long-cai (黃隆才—possibly this was James Wang [Wang Desheng] [的中文名字叫]) and He Chi de (何池德) helped to maintain the association. The executive members of the Kuomintang in 1933 were Huang Long-cai (黃隆才), Situ Chuang-guo (司徒創國), Liang Yi-chi (梁意池), He Chi-de (何池德) and Chen Deng (陳登). I am indebted to Mei-Fen Kuo for this information on the Kuomintang in Tulagi. I have included her use of Chinese characters in the hope that it will aid future research into the Solomon Islands Chinese community. Kuo and Brett 2013.
57 Golden 1993, 114.
58 Bill Dumphy died in 1922. *Planters' Gazette*, 6 May 1922, 9.
59 ibid., 156.

just as alien as those of the Europeans. The early decades of the Chinese presence began the ambivalent relationship that still exists today between Solomon Islanders and Asian businesses.[60] White residents on Tulagi were outnumbered by the Chinese, although if we add in Gavutu, Makambo, Bungana and Taroaniara, the balance is more even. Commerce was always dominated by the big British and Australian companies. Nevertheless, some of the Chinese companies were also substantial and prosperous, and some residents were unhappy about the level of Chinese dominance.

The Kwaio massacre: Imprisonment, disease and death

Incidents that occurred elsewhere in the protectorate also involved Tulagi as the centre of authority. One such event was the murder of district officer William R. Bell, cadet officer Kenneth C. Lillies and 13 police at Gwee`abe in Sinalagu Harbour at 11 am on 4 October 1927 during a tax-collecting patrol in the Kwaio area of east Malaita. Bell and Lillies arrived on the small government boat *Auki*, meeting up with the armed constabulary, who came overland from Auki. The police knew that trouble was brewing but pugnacious Bell, although he was amply warned, decided he could bluff the Kwaio. It was not in his nature to show fear or retreat and there were three other ships nearby, which would have reassured him. There was personal animosity between Bell and some of the east Kwaio bigmen, partly because several of their kin had been arrested and hanged for murder. By demanding that they turn in their guns without compensation (a Malaita-wide policy), Bell had further humiliated them.[61] At the time of the attack, F.A.H. Bonnard was close by on the motorised recruiting schooner *Wheatsheaf*, pastors G. Peacock and John D. Anderson from the Seventh-day Adventist Mission were in the harbour on the *Advent Herald* and a labour recruiting schooner, *Ruana*, was working nearby. What followed was the most notable violent event in the prewar BSIP—both the attack and the vicious official retribution. It was also the most dramatic and traumatic event associated with the Tulagi enclave before the Pacific War.[62]

60 Willmott 2005; Moore 2008.
61 Akin 2013, 46.
62 The incident is described best in Keesing and Corris 1980.

Plate 4.16 Malaita's district officer William Bell, who was assassinated in 1927
Source: Clive Moore Collection.

Plate 4.17 *Auki*, district officer William Bell's ship
Source: BM, Sir Ronald Garvey Photographic Collection.

Men led by Basiana, primarily from three kin groups from inland of Sinalagu, mounted the attack. Their motivations were mixed and largely related to the ban on guns, taxation and the steady creep of government intrusion. Sacrifices were made to fighting ancestors to assist in the attack and there was a great deal of planning and discussion.[63] *Auki* was anchored close offshore. Tax collecting began on Monday and the attack occurred the next day. On Tuesday morning, the two missionaries and Bonnard came to talk to Bell about leasing land in the harbour. Peacock and Anderson returned to their ship to prepare medical injections to give to people who had assembled on board. Bonnard, aware of the impending trouble, shifted his schooner further away. Bell and Lillies were sitting at their tables while the police were positioned inside the tax house to try to diffuse the tense situation. Men lined up to pay their taxes in the clearing by the beach.

About 200 men from inland groups appeared, bringing down a few old guns to surrender, which explains the presence of some weapons. They were clearly angry, shouting out, which caused concern among the armed constabulary, but not from Bell. The constabulary's 14 modern repeating rifles should have been more than a match for a few old single-shot rifles, and Bell and Lillies had revolvers. Basiana joined the line twice, the first

---

63 ibid., 108–25.

time paying his taxes. On the next round, he caved in Bell's skull with a rifle barrel consecrated to his ancestors that he had concealed in a bag. Lillies received a glancing blow from a machete, but was able to retreat into the tax house and began shooting with his revolver. He killed two men with one shot before he was killed by a shot through his chest.

The police seriously wounded about half a dozen Kwaio and several others received superficial wounds. For a group armed mainly with old weapons coming up against repeating rifles and revolvers, the Kwaio inflicted considerable damage. The tax house was demolished during the fracas. The armed constabulary who were killed were mainly from north Malaita. Bonnard heard the noise of the attack and moved his ship closer to shore to pick up any survivors.[64] One of Bell's police swam to the *Wheatsheaf* but died soon after. Four police, all badly wounded, swam to the *Auki*. Bonnard sent his engineer in a dingy to start the *Auki*'s engine, bringing the government craft to the *Wheatsheaf*. In a state of shock, Bonnard then sailed both ships across to the *Advent Herald*, which was anchored at the mouth of the harbour. They all attempted to treat the wounded. Then the boson from the *Auki* and eight Christian Kwaio went ashore to collect the bodies of Bell, Lillies and the police. Bonnard used the *Auki* to tow the *Wheatsheaf* to the SSEM base on nearby Ngongosila Island, where the surviving police were given medical assistance and Bell and Lillies and the dead police were buried.[65] The crew of *Ruana* also helped with the burials. Bonnard then sailed for Tulagi with the wounded police on board. Eighteen hours later, *Auki* and *Wheatsheaf* arrived at Tulagi, where Bonnard broke the news of the killings to the residents. Tulagi, Makambo and Gavutu were in turmoil. Talk of retaliation began immediately. The news reached the world via Radio Tulagi and was widely reported in the Australian newspapers. BP also sent wireless messages to Australia to reassure people who had relatives in the Solomons that the report of a 'native uprising' was exaggerated.[66]

When news of the attack reached Tulagi, resident commissioner Kane was touring the Eastern District, which left government secretary Norman Kidson in command. There was no evidence that the attack was more than an isolated incident, and indeed Bell could have faced a similar attack anytime during his years on Malaita, given his belligerent style

---

64 ibid., 83–147.
65 ibid., 148–49.
66 Hadlow 2016, 129; Golden 1993, 100.

of administration. Tulagi's residents nevertheless convinced themselves that the incident could be the beginning of a wider Malaitan uprising and demanded severe and sudden retribution. Kidson was weak and acquiesced. He was a 'pen-pusher', with little feeling for the subtleties of life in the protectorate. Believing the rumour that the incident was part of an uprising, Kidson sent off a string of cablegrams. He managed to alarm the High Commissioner in Suva, who contacted the Colonial Office to request the admiralty to send assistance.

Kane returned to Tulagi on 10 October, by which time plans were irreversible. An Australian warship was on its way. He supported Kidson's actions, realising that the mood at Tulagi favoured mounting a local retaliatory expedition supported by a naval force. The news of the attack spread quickly among protectorate expatriates, many of whom made their way to the town with offers of assistance. The harbour was soon full of small ketches, schooners and motorboats, their owners spoiling for a fight with the Malaitans. The Europeans believed that, with the assistance of the armed constabulary, bolstered by former members called back into service, they were more than a match for the Kwaio. Chinatown and the big commercial houses did a good trade, buoyed by the sudden influx of residents. BP and Levers pledged to provide coal and supplies to the retaliatory force that was gathering.[67]

Meetings were held to choose the participants for the counterattack. Dozens volunteered and 28 were chosen. The special constables—ostensibly recruited to assist the naval personnel—were also imbued with a spirit of pure vengeance. Bell was well known: he had spent several years based on Tulagi before moving to Auki in 1915. Although the general feeling on Tulagi favoured retribution, even the most gung-ho must have begun to have doubts when they heard of the carnage that resulted in Kwaio and later when Kwaio prisoners began to die during their incarceration. The initial attack and the subsequent retaliation and massacre (mostly of innocents), then the unfortunate Kwaio deaths while in captivity and the executions and imprisonments were the main topics of conversation on Tulagi during late 1927 and early 1928.

The two main civilian players were Edward Geoffrey (Geoff) Clift and Charles V. Widdy. Clift, a 42-year-old planter, took charge. He had been in the Solomons since 1908 and had military experience from World

---

67   Keesing and Corris 1980, 154.

War I.[68] A member of the BSIP Advisory Council, Clift was held in high regard and Kidson willingly chartered him one of the main government vessels, *Hygenia*, to collect a volunteer force of planters and traders to go to Tulagi. Clift, from an Australian pastoral family based at Breeza Plain inland from Tamworth, NSW, was a tough bushman; although endearingly he had a speech impediment that turned initial 'fs' in words into 'ts'.[69] Widdy began his Solomons career as an overseer at Levers' West Bay plantation in 1923. Three years later, he became Levers' plantation inspector for the Western Solomons, and in 1927 he was manager at Banika plantation, Russell Islands (Cape Marsh). Next, he became Levers' manager at Gavutu. Widdy was notorious among Solomon Islanders for his violent approach to dealing with labourers.[70]

When Roger Keesing and Peter Corris published *Lightning Meets the West Wind* in 1980 (the only extensive account of these events), few details were known about the special constables. Like me, those authors failed to locate the original list of names in the BSIP records. Keesing and Corris concluded that the majority were plantation owners, managers and staff, some were ex-military men, and by and large they were not young men. With the assistance of Keesing and Corris's book, Graeme Golden's *The Early European Settlers of the Solomon Islands*, supplemented by Judith Bennett's *Wealth of the Solomons*, Margaret Clarence's *Yield Not to the Wind* and a newspaper article in the Sydney *Sun* newspaper,[71] it is possible to flesh out the origins of some of the punitive expedition's participants. Kessing and Corris were largely correct, although they underestimated the connections to the Tulagi enclave. Once the *Hygenia* was chartered, Clift set off to Guadalcanal and the Western Solomons to recruit members for the expedition. Syd ('Pansy') Elder was the master and chief engineer of the *Hygenia*. Elder had arrived in the Solomons as a young man in 1919, after serving in World War I. By 1927, he would have been aged in his 30s. He drank heavily and his local crew often had to run the ship until he sobered up. Despite his early involvement, his name is not among those of the 28 special constables recorded by Charles and Kathleen Bignell.[72] F.A.H. Bonnard may have joined the group, if he is the 'J. Banard' in the *Sun*'s list. He was traumatised by the attack at Sinalagu and his trip back

---

68   ibid., 163.
69   Struben 1963, 15.
70   ibid., 427; Keesing and Corris 1980, 150.
71   *Sun* [Sydney], 10 November 1927, 14.
72   Golden 1993, 98; Clarence 1982, 59.

to Tulagi with the maimed, bleeding police. Bonnard had to recount his story many times on his first night on Tulagi and seems likely to have participated in the retribution.[73]

There are several men who have been identified as among the special constables whose names do not appear among the 27 in the *Sun*'s list. Johno Johnstone was one of these. His name first appears in about 1920 as an employee on the Malayta Company's plantation at Aola, Guadalcanal, and later at Talina in the Russell Islands, in 1923. In the early 1930s, he and John Mather purchased Elkington's Hotel. Later in the same decade, he became a gold prospector at Gold Ridge on Guadalcanal. In 1941, he worked for Hollis Brothers on Tulagi, the owners of the icemaking plant and cold store, which was a branch of the New South Wales Fresh Food and Ice Company.[74] In his Tulagi days, he ran a butchery in tandem with the iceworks—a useful combination. After the Pacific War, he did the same thing in Honiara. In 1927, he would have been aged in his 20s or 30s and presumably had local knowledge useful for the expedition.[75]

Fred Campbell is also said to have participated in the attack. Campbell had been a NSW police officer, reaching the rank of inspector before he moved to the Solomons as commandant of the armed constabulary in 1912, followed by work as a district officer and then planter on Makira. A member of the BSIP Advisory Council, he would have been a useful participant; however, his name is not on the Bignells' or the *Sun*'s lists.[76] There is also doubt about John Edward (Bill) Adams, whom Golden lists as a special constable. He was probably a relative of the Clifts and, as he arrived in the Solomons in about 1919, there is the possibility that he also had a military background. An engineer, he was in partnership with A.W. Stirling in a small engineering business on Tulagi. In the 1930s, he became a Tulagi-based labour recruiter.[77] There is a photograph of him with John McElhone (Jack) Clift and Johno Johnstone, supposedly taken of them on Malaita as special constables,[78] yet he is not included in the

---

73 Golden 1993, 100.
74 UQFL, Wilson Papers and Photographs, A.H. Wilson, Manuscript notes: general, and A.H. Wilson to F.A.G. Wilson, 1 January 1941.
75 After the Pacific War, he moved to Honiara and, in the 1950s, was manager of the Honiara butchery for Ken Hay, on the site of the present-day Mendana Hotel. Moore (2013: entry for Kenneth Houston Dalrymple-Hay). The family surname is Dalrymple-Hay, although he seems to have called himself Ken Hay.
76 Information from Christopher Chevalier, October 2016.
77 Golden 1993, 114.
78 ibid., 115.

Bignells' or the *Sun*'s lists. Nor is Bobby Sterling on the *Sun* list. He is supposed to have done well out of being a member of the expedition, making a good profit from gambling while on Malaita.[79] Perhaps these men were on Malaita, but not officially as special constables.

There is more certainty about C.E. Minns and Anton Olsen, who was mentioned earlier in the chapter. Anton Daniel Olsen was born in Norway in 1885, making him 42 years old in 1927. He left home at 15 and was a seaman on the four-masted wooden sailing ship *Susquehanna*, which was wrecked off New Caledonia in 1905. The surviving crew drifted to the Solomons in lifeboats. Olsen's boat was rescued by trader Oscar Svensen and Olsen and two others on board decided to stay in the Solomons. Olsen became master of Levers' trading vessel *Lindsay*, working in the outer islands, mainly around Ontong Java, Sikaiana and Santa Cruz. *Lindsay* was wrecked in 1907, after which Olsen took command of another Levers' vessel, *Jessie*. He married an Australian woman and leased land at Tenamba on Guadalcanal to begin a coconut plantation. A cyclone wrecked his plantation in 1916, after which he took up gold prospecting on Guadalcanal in partnership with Geoff Clift, while also working as an occasional labour recruiter.[80]

L.J. Hanscombe was another participant. He was well known to the Bignells as he was best man at their wedding in 1914, and we know he was their neighbour between 1928 and 1936 when he was manager of Hivo plantation on Isabel.[81] The Bignells' list also contains the names R. Cambridge, A. Dickes, R. Gaskell, R. Harper, C. King and F. King, J. Svensen, W.F. Wilmott and G. White. Rolfe Cambridge managed Aruligo plantation on Guadalcanal between 1930 and 1932, which was owned by Jack Clift and then sold to the Malayta Company in 1931.[82] R. Harper (not on the *Sun*'s list) is presumably Richard (Dick) Harper, who arrived in the Solomons in 1922 after serving in World War I. Until the Pacific War, he had a lease on Mandoliana plantation, on a small island of that name off Gela Pile. He also worked as a trader and labour recruiter.[83] Richard Luke Jack (Dick) Gaskell, son of Richard and Edith Gaskell, was born in 1915 on Tete Island in Sandfly Passage in the Gela Group. His father was a boatbuilder, planter, trader and labour recruiter

---

79 ibid., 179.
80 ibid., 141.
81 ibid., 312, 331.
82 ibid., 122, 167.
83 ibid., 66, 101–02, 184.

who first came to the BSIP in 1906 to build Makambo wharf for BP.[84] G. White is probably Charles Havelock Gordon White, who was involved in the yaws and hookworm eradication campaigns of the late 1920s and early 1930s.[85] Between 1923 and 1936, W.F. (Bill) Wilmot held the lease on the small Malavare plantation on New Georgia. He would have known Jack Clift on nearby Seghe plantation.[86] Jack Svensen was a son of Theodor Svensen, a leading early trader and planter, and a business partner of his better-known brother, Oscar. In 1918, Jack was manager of Lavoro plantation on Guadalcanal; in the 1920s, he negotiated a lease over isolated Kokomuruki Island on the Weather Coast of Guadalcanal. He was married to Edith Elliot, the first nurse at Tulagi Hospital.[87] C. King may be Charles King, a subinspector of police who worked for the administration on Malaita for two years after the Bell massacre, although it is odd that such a person would be a special constable.[88] Alan W. Dickes had been a clerk in the Lands and Surveys Department and then became the Tulagi postmaster.[89]

The *Sun* lists Monty Masterman as a special constable. He was the Inspector of Labour and features largely in this book. It would have been entirely in character for him to have participated. A name that appears to be B. Filiers in the *Sun*'s list is presumably F.B. Filose, clerk to the Resident Commissioner in 1925, acting District Officer for Aola (1925–26) and for Kirakira, Eastern Solomons (1927–28), and District Officer for Malaita (1928–29), Santa Cruz (1929–31) and Isabel (1932–33).[90] Another name has recently come to light, Ian Troup, who appears on the *Sun*'s list as J. Troup. He was born in Aboyne, Scotland, in 1894 and joined the Gordon Highlanders 52nd Highland Regiment in 1914, fought on the Somme, was twice decorated (with MC and DC medals for bravery) and promoted to corporal. After the war, he returned to Scotland and worked in his father's butcher's shop in Aboyne, before taking up a similar job in Hong Kong. He left for Australia in 1923 and worked as a stockman in New South Wales before moving to the Solomons, where he also worked with cattle, presumably on one of the bigger coconut plantations where cattle

---

84 ibid., 88–89.
85 Bennett 1987, 277. See Chapter 7, this volume.
86 Golden 1993, 196.
87 ibid., 153–54.
88 Bennett 1987, 276, 357; Information from David Akin, 23 December 2016; NASI, BSIP 14/61, Malaita Annual Report 1929, DO J.C. Barley to Government Secretary, 17 January 1930.
89 Golden 1993, 362; BSIP *Blue Books* 1927–28, 38.
90 Bennett 1987, 399, 401, 402, 403, 404.

were used to keep the undergrowth down. He suffered trauma from the events on Malaita and returned to Australia in December 1927 after his time as a special constable. His military training and possible plantation connections with the Clifts would have made him useful.[91]

I have been unable to locate any information about other special constables listed by the Bignells or the *Sun* and, as some of the newspaper names cannot be deciphered, we may never know.[92] R. Bruce, S.A. Halliday, T. Ferry and F. King appear on the Bignells' and *Sun*'s lists; none of them appears on the civil establishment as BSIP government employees.[93] J. West, on the Bignells' list, is possibly J.C. West, listed in 1935 as a recruiter on Guadalcanal. S. Fitton and R. Seddon are on the Bignells' list, as is E. Cunningham, who may be D. Cunningham, manager of Malayta Company's Manaba plantation, West Malaita, from 1920 to 1923.

And while we can try to understand something of those who participated, we will never know who else considered participating but could not or who refused outright to have anything to do with the foolish venture. There are two illustrative examples. Charles Bignell did not volunteer, although he would have if his wife had not been sick.[94] One of the most eligible who refused was Ernie Palmer, born in South Africa in 1904, who spent his young years in England and accompanied his father and brother Philip to the Solomons in 1919. Their father, Philip Sydney Palmer, developed a plantation on San Jorge Island, just off the Isabel coast, but was so harsh and bad tempered that the boys ran away. Geoff Clift took them into his care and Ernie became an island trader and labour recruiter—one of the best. In 1927, he was 23 years old, had a strong Clift connection and would have been very suitable, but he scorned the expedition.[95]

Apart from Clift and Widdy, the special constables were not leading figures in the protectorate. The Clift family and Levers' connections were strong and one suspects that the special constables were men whom the Clifts and Widdy knew well. While they were competent bushmen and seamen, none of them had much idea of how difficult the Malaitan terrain could be. The special constables were sworn in, issued with .303 rifles

---

91 I am indebted to Lyn Innes for this information on her father, December 2018.
92 Clarence 1982, 59.
93 BSIP *Blue Books* 1925–26, 39, 1927–28, 38, 1928–29, 38–39. See also Golden 1993, 430.
94 BSIP *Blue Books* 1925–26, 63.
95 Golden 1993, 103.

and underwent training on Tulagi. Some had prior military experience and most would have been able to use and maintain guns competently enough. They were paid £1 per day with an extra 5 shillings a day ration allowance. Kane armed his ship, the 300-ton *Ranadi*, with a Lewis automatic light machine gun, added a detachment of 25 members of the armed constabulary and then sent the ship off to Aola, Guadalcanal, to pick up district officer C.E.J. Wilson, who had a reputation for toughness. *Ranadi* then patrolled the east coast of Malaita. Wilson reported that the people were in a state of anxiety, expecting some sort of retribution.[96]

Kidson's request to Suva was passed to the British Admiralty and on to the Australian Naval Board in Melbourne, then forwarded to the Minister for Defence. The advice back to the admiralty was that Australia could immediately ready HMAS *Adelaide*, a 5,650-ton Town-class light cruiser constructed at the end of World War I, powered by coal and oil. Under the charge of Captain G.H. Harrison, the ship left Sydney on the evening of 10 October, carrying extra ammunition, tents, ground sheets, large numbers of Mills bombs (grenades) and food supplies.

Calling in the navy was anachronistic, which made the Australian Government uncomfortable, although its small fleet of ships was at the beck and call of Britain and the 'uprising' was on Australia's doorstep. The general feeling in Australia was that Solomon Islanders needed to be shown who was boss. The final decision rested with Stanley Bruce, who had been Prime Minister since February 1923. He had served in World War I and belonged to the liberal-conservative National Party.[97] Bruce assured the parliament that *Adelaide* would remain under Australian control. William Bell's brother, Lieutenant-Colonel George John Bell, was a member of the House of Representatives—something that Bruce pointed out. The Australian newspapers were roundly supportive, with one noting that *Adelaide*'s captain had experience with 'native outbreaks' and would 'put the Fuzzy Wuzzy in his place'.[98]

---

96   Keesing and Corris 1980, 154–55.
97   Radi 1979.
98   ibid., 154.

Plate 4.18 HMAS *Adelaide* and HMAS *Sydney* in Tulagi Harbour
HMAS *Sydney* was not part of the 1927 Malaita expedition.
Source: BM, Sir Ronald Garvey Photographic Collection.

Plate 4.19 The government ships *Ranadi* and *Hygenia* at Tulagi wharf, late 1920s
Source: BM, Sir Ronald Garvey Photographic Collection.

4. CHINATOWN, THE CLUB, HOTELS AND THE 'BLACK HOLE'

Initially, HMAS *Adelaide* steamed at 20 knots, slowed to 16 knots on 12 October and arrived at Tulagi on 14 October. An officer and 17 sailors were sent ashore to bolster local law enforcement. The ship then proceeded to Malaita. Australia also dispatched the 9,700-ton naval collier HMAS *Biloela* as the supply ship, commanded by P.B. Hugo. *Biloela*'s full speed was 11 knots. The ship left Sydney three days after HMAS *Adelaide* and did not arrive at Malaita until seven days after the cruiser. As the cruiser made its way down the coast, the Kwaio Malaitans heard the deep vibrations from its engines long before the warship's 140-metre bulk loomed into sight around Cape Aracides (Darongongora) on the border between the Fataleka and Kwara`ae language areas. HMAS *Adelaide* anchored off the Kwaio shore while the land operation was carried out. A platoon of sailors was landed on 17 October.[99] Resident commissioner Kane was on board, although after the first night he transferred to *Ranadi* and left for Auki, where 3,500 Malaitans had visited the station, with hundreds volunteering to avenge the deaths.[100] *Ranadi* returned to Sinalagu carrying the special constables, plus Kane, Wilson and Captain E.N. Turner, the Commandant of the Armed Constabulary.[101]

The special constables came equipped with too much luggage, their own staff and an ample supply of rum and whisky—hence their description as the 'whisky army'. They seemed to believe they had a right to attack all Kwaio, without any proof of their involvement in the original deaths. Perhaps Kane, Turner or Wilson had quietly told them that there would be no repercussions if they exterminated innocent Kwaio. Widdy later said they had been told they could 'shoot any native on sight'.[102]

An initial camp was established near the beach, with an advance camp (Base B Camp) several hours' march inland at about 1,000 metres above sea level and, finally, Base A Camp at Gounaile, Basiana's village high in the mountains.[103] There were about 50 naval ratings and 50 permanent and temporary members of the armed constabulary, 28 special constables and 211 north Malaitan carriers (some of whom were ex-police) at Base B Camp.[104] The expedition had three Lewis machine guns, plenty of

---

99   Swindon 1994.
100 Akin 2013, 47.
101 Keesing and Corris 1980, 158–59.
102 Akin 2013, 382, n. 27.
103 These names were provided by H.R. Wilmot, the leading telegraphist on HMAS *Biloela*. Information from his son Jeff Wilmott, Tallarook, Victoria, November 2010.
104 Akin 2013, 47.

ammunition and a wireless transmitter. Although the Europeans were ineffectual in the rugged mountainous terrain, the north Malaitan police and volunteers were efficient and ruthless, avenging the deaths of their own people among Bell's police. They ranged far and wide, returning at night to Base B Camp. Women and girls were gang-raped, many were shot, children and old people were murdered and prisoners executed and mutilated. Gardens were sprayed with defoliants donated by Levers, pigs were killed and houses were destroyed. The retaliatory force roamed north to Uru Harbour, south into the 'Oloburi area and into west Kwaio— far from where the attack occurred. Keesing and Corris estimated that around 60 people were shot and others—some children—died from exposure while hiding from the attackers. The Kwaio estimate of the number of deaths is far higher. Ancestral shrines and sacred men's houses were desecrated, which the Kwaio believe caused their angry ancestors to kill more descendants later, through illness and mishap. A woman gang-raped by the police was taken to Tulagi, and after she became pregnant hanged herself in shame.[105]

Plate 4.20 Labourers being fed during the expedition to Kwaio, Malaita
Source: Jeff Willmot Collection.

---

105 ibid., 48; Keesing and Corris 1980, 166–68.

Plate 4.21 A member of the 1927 expedition shaking hands with a Kwaio man
Source: Jeff Willmot Collection.

HMAS *Adelaide* began its return journey to Australia on 23 November. Captain Harrison did not turn his ship's guns on the Kwaio and, once he realised there was no general uprising, he began to doubt the usefulness of the cruiser's presence. This was the last time the British used a naval ship to attack Pacific Islanders. The naval presence was similar in style to the nineteenth-century expeditions that had regularly bombarded Malaita and other islands, indiscriminately destroying villages, although in this case *Adelaide* served only as the means of transport. The big difference was the high death rate inflicted by the police, the north Malaitan volunteers and the special constables. The special constables were not needed, they were disruptive and caused trouble. Although they were official representatives of the protectorate government, they were there to wreak vengeance, operating beyond the edge of legality.

One hundred and ninety-eight Kwaio men were taken to Tulagi prison. An astonishing 173 were hospitalised for dysentery during their time on Tulagi and 30 men died (28 in 1928 and two in 1929). Rather unconvincingly, the government tried to explain that some of the deaths were from old age and senility. While a few of the prisoners were elderly, that raises questions of why such vulnerable men were in prison, initially not charged with any offence, and what role they could have played in the attack. Perfunctory trials eventually proceeded. Basiana and four others had turned themselves in to stop further killing of innocents. They were among the 11 charged with murder, six of whom (including Basiana) were executed. Seventy-one were tried for offences less than murder, of whom 51 were acquitted. Six were imprisoned for life, eight for 20 years, two for 12 years and one for three years. Their wives and families either fled further inland or took shelter in the SSEM villages along the coast or at the Seventh-day Adventist Mission base at Uru. There was little food left in their gardens and few materials available to rebuild houses.[106]

Reports of the indiscriminate killings soon leaked out. Kane had even recommended that, as a final punishment, all of the Kwaio should be rounded up and moved to Isabel, with the hope that intermixing with the Isabel people would genetically soften their aggression. Wilson and Kane tried to defend themselves and, in the end, the Tulagi administration closed ranks around the perpetrators.[107] The upshot was an official investigation by Lieutenant-Colonel Sir Harry Moorhouse, the retired Lieutenant-Governor of Nigeria (1921–25). He concluded that 'practically the whole of the adult males of the Sinarango tribe had been rounded up and lodged in gaol in Tulagi'.[108] The deaths while in detention were defended in his report. There had been outbreaks of dysentery among the police who had taken part in the attack. Moorhouse concluded that the exposure to the disease had occurred on Malaita and was transferred to Tulagi. He also assured the British Government that as soon as the outbreak was evident, emergency procedures were introduced to try to isolate the disease and stop its spread. He said the old men who died 'suffered from increasing feebleness and finally died from failure of the circulation'. The report exonerated the administration and denied accusations of callous neglect or that the term 'The Black Hole of Tulagi' (used in an Australian newspaper article) was at all appropriate.[109] Moorhouse's report questioned whether the implementation of taxation during the early 1920s was responsible for the Kwaio attack. He felt that Bell had taken a reasonable, gradual approach and that local circumstances were also involved.

---

106 Moorhouse 1929, 14; Keesing and Corris 1980, 184–86.
107 Keesing and Corris 1980, 180–81.
108 Moorhouse 1929, 10.
109 ibid., 18.

Plate 4.22 Prisoners on Tulagi
The Kwaio Malaitans would have looked like this. The guard, a member of the armed constabulary, is on the left.
Source: BM, Sir Ronald Garvey Photographic Collection.

The Kwaio massacre and its aftermath were the largest and most severe random punishment ever meted out by British authorities in the Pacific. It was central to activities on Tulagi over several months in 1927 and 1928, and Kwaio people have never forgotten or forgiven the excesses.[110] The strength of the reprisal also signalled to all Malaitans and Solomon Islanders more generally that, if they had not already realised, the British administration was too strong to resist by direct means.

****

Such extreme dramas were rare. However, other events began to shape the fate of Tulagi. Aviation was the crucial transport change that eventually made Tulagi obsolete. The first aircraft to visit the protectorate, a De Havilland DH50A seaplane belonging to the Royal Australian Air Force (RAAF), flown by Group-Captain Williams, arrived at Tulagi on 31 October 1926. The seaplane was on an aerial survey of Papua and New Guinea, Solomon Islands, the New Hebrides, New Caledonia, Fiji and Samoa. Arriving from the north, it landed first at Shortland Islands, visited Gizo and a few weeks later landed at Tulagi. At each stop, the local

---

110 Akin 1999.

people were astonished. At Tulagi, the crew decided to obtain some new engine parts before travelling south and these were shipped in on the *Mataram*. Locals inspected the plane thoroughly while it was beached at Makambo. The crew shelved plans to fly further south due to poor weather and flew back north on 23 November.[111]

The next plane to arrive was an old seaplane with an Anzani engine, imported to Tulagi by ship in the 1930s by Monty Masterman, the Inspector of Labour. After much tinkering, it flew for the first and last time, or rather skated along the water, before settling nearby at Bungana Island forever. Masterman could not swim and hacked off one of the floats to buoy himself until a Chinese trading vessel rescued him.[112] We can be fairly certain that when he tried to join the Aeronautical Inspection Directorate of the British Air Ministry and the Auxiliary Air Force in 1936, he failed to mention this inglorious aerial escapade.[113] Masterman and his flying machine must have caused a great deal of mirth.

The next two chapters concentrate on the 1930s and examine the type of colonial society that developed on Tulagi in its final years as the capital. Public servants developed an efficient administration and interacted, not always harmoniously. Eccentricity, alcoholism and petty hatreds abounded. Fears of racial and sexual relations with the 'natives' surfaced, similar to those present in New Guinea, the New Hebrides and Fiji at the time.

---

111 Knibbs 1929, 269–70; BSIP 1926–27, 3; *Solomons News Drum*, 1 October 1976. A set of stamps was issued in 1976 to celebrate the first flight.
112 Sandars 1971; Russell 2003, 56.
113 NASI, BSIP 1/P1/M58/22/1, S.G. Masterman to Secretary of State, 8 December 1936.

5

Mildewed elegance, houses and servants

> Spearline is away again about 200 miles away at a place that is never visited by anyone—he is doing a survey for a mission & will be 6 weeks away. We are not so nervous this time. We all sleep in one room (my niece, my son & myself) & so feel more courageous! My 6 shooter & a police man on the beat add to our satisfaction.
>
> — Jessie Wilson, Tulagi, 18 August 1930[1]

Mildewed elegance

Tulagi, like most of Solomon Islands, is often unmercifully hot, with the temperature reaching the high 30s Celsius in the middle of the day. Rainfall is also high and the humidity is as debilitating as the heat. From March to September or October is called the *Ara*—the south-east season when there are good breezes during the day. By nightfall the wind usually dies, although sometimes wind continues to blow. In the north-east season that follows—the *Komburu*, from November to February—humidity remains high and the evenings are hot. These months can be marked by windless days, but at the end of the year storms and cyclones are common and seas are rough and dangerous.

---

1 UQFL, Wilson Papers and Photographs, J.A. Wilson to Mary, 18 August 1930.

Some descriptions of early Tulagi give an impression of tropical elegance, while others describe a down-at-heel mildewed stub of the British Raj. Anthropologist Ian Hogbin passed through Tulagi regularly in the late 1920s and early 1930s. He was surprised at the level of sartorial elegance required. He said Tulagi was

> quite one of the places one reads of as an out-post-of-the-British-Empire. Yet strange to say the fashions are quite Bond Street. All wear bow ties, starched shirts and walking sticks.[2]

Xavier Herbert was also resident about this time. Commenting on his short stay in 1928, Herbert was scathing about the pomp and pretension of British life:

> You had to wear white clothes, and you always wore a coat—you couldn't go coatless—and you carried a walking stick and it was like a uniform, and you had to do that. So too the topee, the white suit and the walking stick.[3]

When American filmmakers Martin and Osa Johnson passed through Tulagi 10 years earlier, they were not impressed by the seedy elegance. The following description is of the Resident Commissioner—possibly Woodford's temporary replacement, Frank Barnett, already a long-term resident:

> His white suit had shrunk noticeably and, although the shorts were severely creased, their colour was on the jaundiced side and they were considerably the worse for wear. The coat was short at the sleeves and looked as though the house-boy had stopped pressing after he finished the lapels. His white helmet was scuffed, but freshly whitened. He wore brown brogues, highly polished, and heavy brown socks that had obviously been mended several times. His starched collar and polka-dotted tie, done into a fixed knot, and his neatly cropped moustache were thoroughly respectable. And his Malacca cane, with a beautiful tortoise-shell handle, was the official touch.[4]

---

2 University of Sydney Archives, A.P. Elkin Papers, Box 159, File 4/1/49, H.I.P. Hogbin to A.R. Radcliffe-Brown, 31 July 1927.
3 Keesing and Corris 1980, 208.
4 Johnson 1945, 106.

Dick Horton arrived in 1937 wearing his newly purchased (ex-Suez) white suit and pith helmet. He was met by Peter Colley, secretary to resident commissioner Ashley. Colley was decked out in a sports shirt, shorts, long socks and tennis shoes, with a small towel around his neck to wipe away perspiration and flies. Horton said that he never needed his white suit again, which indicates either a relaxation in dress standards over a decade or perhaps that Herbert and Johnson were exaggerating (as the Johnsons so often did). If we rely on photographs from the 1920s and 1930s, they show a preponderance of men in light-weight white suits, and pith helmets continued to be used. Red Sea or Gulf Rig—a British dress code for semiformal evening events in regions of high heat and humidity— remained in vogue at the residency. Males wore black formal trousers, a white starched shirt and a black bow tie, but with a cummerbund in compensation for being allowed to remove their coats. Female guests wore long evening dresses, strangely but sensibly augmented with mosquito-proof leggings. After dinner, the ladies retired and the men gathered to drink port. British etiquette is that port circulates clockwise, always received with the right hand and passed to the left. You poured a glass for your neighbour on your right then passed on the decanter.[5] This was the style at the residency. Makambo, Gavutu and Taroaniara also had small European populations who observed a similar social hierarchy and the same standards of dress and etiquette.

Houses and social construction of space

Colonial Pacific historical writing is inclined to be very male oriented, since expatriate males far outnumbered females and gender has not been high on research agendas related to the colonial Pacific. Very little has been written about expatriate women living and working in the Pacific colonial environment, let alone in urban areas, although in the 1970s and 1980s, there was a spate of analysis of moral panic, sexuality, gender and empire, which continued into the 2000s.[6] The few important sources on

---
5   Horton 1965, 5. This was still the custom at Government House in Honiara in the 1950s. Information from Alan Lindley, Adelaide, August 2010.
6   Inglis 1974; Inglis 1982; Nelson 1982; Cowling 1984; Hoe 1984; Knapman 1986; Hyam 1990; Bulbeck 1992; Bullbeck 1993; Keays 1995; Sturma 2002; O'Brien 2006.

the role of expatriate women in colonial Solomon Islands—particularly those by James Boutilier, Judith Bennett, Hugh and Eugénie Laracy and Graeme Golden—have been useful as background. I have also been able to tap into the lives of expatriate women in colonial Papua New Guinea to augment deficiencies in the Solomons material.

Domestic space tells us a great deal about social processes. Over time, houses are modified, expanded, renovated and rebuilt. Wooden houses in the tropics need constant maintenance: they rot, termites devour them and they need constant painting to preserve the wood. Houses have material forms, but their uses are socially constructed. Different occupants put different amounts of effort into maintenance and style, and gardens are an extension of the personalities of the occupants. Among the markers of Tulagi status were the size of one's house, its contents and its position—and the beauty of the garden. All houses had a tropical ambiance, with wide verandahs.

Plate 5.1 The second residency in the 1910s
Source: PMB, AU PMB PHOTO 58-175 (ANUA 481-337-175).

Plate 5.2 Florrie Woodford at the back gate of the residency
Source: ANUA, 481-337-073.

Plate 5.3 Florrie and Charles Woodford having tea on the residency verandah in the 1910s

The cane chairs are typical of Pacific and Australian tropical furniture in the twentieth century. They are using a silver teapot and fine china, while their pet parrot watches.

Source: PMB, AU PMB PHOTO 56-216 (ANUA 481-1C-216).

The houses were all Queenslander-style—an adaptation of Indian colonial architecture.[7] In southern Melanesia, there were more substantial houses, but in the Solomons all were made from timber, sometimes with split-bamboo plaited feature walls.[8] The best Tulagi houses were commodious but never grand. Life in 'Queenslanders' was lived on the verandahs and people often slept there as well, using the bedrooms only for dressing and storage. There was no reticulated water supply up on Tulagi's residential ridge and each house had several water tanks. The toilet was usually a pan in a small outhouse, which was changed once a week. By 1927, water-flushed toilets that emptied into the sea had been installed at the Tulagi Club and the single officers' quarters, and there was one house with its own septic tank.[9] Showers usually ran off water tanks or, if primitive, consisted of a kerosene tin with holes punched in the base, suspended on pulleys. Small galvanised iron bath tubs and kerosene heaters were available for those who required a hint of luxury.

Houses were often hot, particularly in areas such as the verandahs, which had unlined galvanised ripple-iron roofs. There were no *punkahs* (fans) swinging from the ceilings with a small boy to pull the cord, as in India. During heavy rain, which was common, the noise on the iron roofs was deafening. Electricity came very late to the settlement, so for many years there were not even primitive electric fans. The best houses were high on the central ridge, where they caught the breezes. The residency was central and dominant. In the 1930s, the home of the Treasurer was close by, with the Judicial Commissioner further down the ridge on the other side of The Cut. The doctors and nurses and the Commandant lived close to their respective workplaces on the outer side of the island, but still on the ridge. The disadvantage of living on the ridge, of course, was that one had to walk up and down steep paths to gain access, although the view over the harbour (and for the medical staff and commandant, over to Savo and Guadalcanal) made it all worthwhile. There were two ways across the island: 'up and over' and, starting in late 1918, via The Cut. Even after The Cut was open, people still sometimes took the scenic route across the ridge. Charles Weetman did this in 1937:

---

7   Bell 1984.
8   Lagarde 2016.
9   CO, 225/232/64124, Annual Medical and Sanitary Report, 1927, 2.

5. MILDEWED ELEGANCE, HOUSES AND SERVANTS

> We climbed one of the steep paths that led through flowering shrubs and palms across the ridge, past the bungalows whose verandahs were so wide that there seemed to be little 'house' left; past the Commissioner's residence, where a police 'boy', clad in brown lap-lap, scarlet cummerbund, and white belt, and armed with a rifle with fixed bayonet, marched up and down on guard; down-hill again past the golf-links, where a notice, alongside one tee, attracted our attention by the unusual wording, 'Wait until the 6th *brown* and 7th tee are clear'; and on to the path that runs along the shore at the opposite side of the island, a distance in all of about a quarter of a mile.[10]

Houses were perched on concrete posts to allow air flow underneath to keep them cool; they were kept safe from termites by placing tin lids on top of the posts and were designed to be as earthquake-proof as possible. Solomon Islands lies in one of the world's most active seismic areas. Earthquakes of widely varying severity occur throughout the islands and there are several volcanoes. As a consequence, tsunamis occur, which leave coastal areas uninhabitable for long periods, and reefs can be raised several metres out of the water by tectonic movements. On 3 October 1931, a severe earthquake was felt all through the central and eastern islands, with the tremors continuing spasmodically for a month. On Makira, a tsunami following the initial earthquake destroyed 18 villages and killed 48 people. On Santa Catalina (Owa Riki) Island, the quake badly damaged the reef. Christians thought Judgement Day had come while others decided that their ancestral spirits were angry.[11] Jessie Wilson recorded:

> It was quite a bad one … There must have been many casualties. As it is, most of those who lost their lives were the victims of the tidal wave which in some places went 2 miles inland. There are a few broken legs etc. in hospital (not whites) & about 20 natives dead. We were terrified & my husband was away on a job on another island. I gathered Ann out of her cot & ran shrieking to find Michael who was by this time out of the house—carried by the cook. After it passed we came in again & were no sooner settled than another 'quake' came … Really for 10 days we had tremors every now & then but not enough to make us leave the house. You can imagine the noise which goes on with the rattling of everything that can rattle in the house & the falling of everything that can fall. Brass trays, bottles, lamps etc. make a lot of noise.[12]

---

10 Weetman 1937, 35.
11 Tedder 2008, 76; BSIP *AR* 1931, 20.
12 UQFL, Wilson Papers and Photographs, J.A. Wilson, 20 October 1931.

At Tulagi, the bottom of the harbour rose by around 3 metres. Stores had their stock damaged, Carpenters' wharf was damaged and left in shallow water, preventing ships from berthing, and the decking on BP's wharf at Makambo subsided.[13]

The Resident Commissioner's home had progressed from a shack on the beach to a pleasant, substantial structure with a guard house and flagpole. It was a public reception area as well as a private residence. The other houses were smaller. Spearline and Jessie Wilson's house was medium in size, commensurate with his position (as Government Surveyor). There was one large bedroom (6.7 metres by 3.6 metres) and two smaller bedrooms for their children. It was positioned on the ridge above Chinatown. All the rooms had polished floors and were screened against mosquitoes.[14] Often the front verandahs of Tulagi's houses were completely screened or had a section enclosed as a mosquito-proof room. Kitchens were semidetached at the rear, to limit the risk from fires. After 20 years, the Wilsons took over Knibbs's house, which was bigger and in a more central position on the ridge, just above the offices on the shore. Designated for the Commissioner for Lands, the house was painted white inside and out, with the usual red galvanised ripple-iron roof. It had deep verandahs with dark-green shutters and was furnished with cream-painted and lacquered cane chairs. The internal floors were polished and there were also polished wooden tables. Curtains on the windows of the two large central rooms and floor mats in the formal rooms and on the verandahs completed the pleasant tropical style. Beds were decked out with nets. The Wilsons imported curtain materials from Australia and had them made up in Chinatown. The servants kept the brass knickknacks polished and everything clean and tidy.[15]

---

13   *PIM*, 23 November 1931.
14   UQFL, Wilson Papers and Photographs, J.A. Wilson to Mary, February 1925[?].
15   ibid., J.A. Wilson to Mary, 14 December 1933.

Plate 5.4 Spearline and Jessie Wilson's home, with the wireless station and the golf course in the background
Source: UQFL, Wilson Papers and Photographs.

Plate 5.5 Spearline and Jessie Wilson's home in the centre, with a neighbouring house to the right
Source: UQFL, Wilson Papers and Photographs.

Residents had furniture shipped in from Australia or purchased items from the big companies or the Chinese merchants. Utility items such as small tables, shelves and cupboards were sometimes made from packing cases, particularly boxes that once held cans of kerosene. Borers attacked rattan, cane and other furniture; these were killed by dunking the items in salt water or soaking them with linseed oil. Timber floors were polished in a very Pacific way. The grease-cutting properties of bush limes were used and floors were re-oiled and polished using the flesh of young coconuts.[16] Woodford, Johnson and Wilson family photographs show comfortable casual furniture very similar to that found on Queensland verandahs in the same period: cane and canvas chairs, including 'squatters' chairs with leg extensions. Colourful talking parrots were kept on verandahs, in cages or using the method still common in Solomons villages today—a wooden 'lock' on the bird's leg attached to a tough vine cord. I have located no photographs of living room interiors at Tulagi, but there are some from the government station on Malaita during the first half of the 1910s, which we can safely presume was similar in style. Silver services, fine bone china and family photographs in ornate frames all made their way to the Solomons. Photographs from the Bignells' Fulakora plantation on Isabel from the 1930s show polished floors and gracious furniture and a combination of Solomons shields, turtle shells, cane and ornately carved furniture, the last made by the talented Kathleen Bignell.[17]

Plate 5.6 Pop and Agnes Johnson's home, 1930s
Source: Suzanne Ellis Collection.

---

16 The same methods were used in Papua New Guinea. Keays 1995, 53–54.
17 Clarence 1982, 34, 85. At Auki, the Edge-Partingtons had brought with them formal furniture, silver items and heavy framed photographs. The contents of the best Tulagi enclave houses would have been similar. Photographs taken by Thomas Edge-Partington are held by the British Museum.

Plate 5.7 The manager's house on Gavutu in 1907, showing canvas sheeting on one side that could be let down to shield the verandah from rain

Source: BM, George Rose's photographs in the Thomas Edge-Partington Photographic Collection.

A variety of photographs from the Solomons show that concrete stumps were the preferred foundations for buildings, presumably to combat attacks from termites, although Woodford's first residency was on high wooden stumps. One crucial consideration in house design was the risk of cyclones; houses needed to be able to be closed against strong winds and driving rain. The Tulagi houses for which details remain were all government-owned, which limited the alterations occupants could make to the fabric of the building and required the Treasury to authorise any changes. In the New Hebrides, sections of verandahs were enclosed for bedrooms and offices and verandahs were insulated to lower the level of heat radiating from exposed iron roofs. Louvres were added to reduce the glare from the water, to keep out the rain and to circulate the breeze.[18] Photographs of early Tulagi houses show little sign of louvres, rollup wooden blinds or plantation shutters capable of being tilted to deflect light and rain. Light metal mesh mosquito screens and pushout wooden shutters seem to have been the main mechanisms of protection. In the 1930s, these were used at Pop and Agnes Johnson's home, although an early photograph shows open verandahs on three sides with no shutters.[19] A photograph of one large house on Gavutu shows a screened verandah and canvas sheeting that could be let down on one of the outside walls to give protection from heavy rain. Another photograph, from Makambo, shows heavy shutters on the verandah and windows.[20] The houses were well designed for the tropics and were altered over the years to improve living standards.

Domestic ingenuity

Many women were uneasy about being colonial wives, dealing with servants and living the life of an isolated white 'misis'. As well, life on Tulagi required domestic ingenuity. Although there were no dangerous wild animals, smaller varieties still tested the residents. Flying foxes (fruit bats) lived in huge colonies, hanging upside down in trees and issuing forth at night to raid all kinds of fruit. Possums were everywhere and unless households took care to close off access, they moved into roof cavities, keeping the humans awake at night with their strange hissing calls, and all too often urinating down the walls. One the great challenges was dealing with vermin and insects. Rats were common and were caught with traps or poisoned. Frogs, lizards, snakes and centipedes were also plentiful and invaded the houses. Lizards, particularly small geckoes, became almost domestic pets. People kept cats and dogs for company and to keep wild creatures at bay.

---

18 Rodman 2001, 209.
19 Pop and Agnes Johnson family photos, in Suzanne Ellis Collection; Johnson 1945, 49.
20 SINA, BSIP Photographs, bungalow on Gavutu; NBAC, N115–520.

5. MILDEWED ELEGANCE, HOUSES AND SERVANTS

Plate 5.8 Spearline and Jessie Wilson and their Irish setter
Source: UQFL, Wilson Papers and Photographs.

Plate 5.9 This living room is in the district officer's house at Auki, Malaita, in the 1910s, during the tenancy of Thomas and Mary Edge-Partington

The furnishings show pictures and other accoutrements from England. The table legs are sitting in bowls that would have contained water to stop ants and cockroaches climbing up. No interior photographs from Tulagi houses have survived. Tulagi living rooms would have been similar to this one at Auki.

Source: BM, Thomas Edge-Partington Photographic Collection.

Dry foods such as rice and flour were difficult to keep fresh in the high humidity. Residents learnt to sift the weevils out of flour and rice and to inspect slices of bread to dislodge them. Cockroach infestations of houses and boats were another domestic hazard, battled against with poison baits and out-and-out domestic warfare. Boats were often home to a particular small variety by the thousands, scurrying about like a liquid plague that flowed from every crack and crevice. Large cockroaches lived in houses and, when pursued, withdrew to safety between loose boards and cracks in floors and joints. Their feral comrades flew in for visits from the surrounding undergrowth. Toilets were favourite cockroach breeding grounds. Cockroaches might crawl out of one's clothing at the most inopportune times and, if you forgot to pour water into the containers in which each bedpost sat, you might wake itching with cockroach bites. Before sipping a bedside glass of water, one checked first for swimming cockroaches.[21] Book covers were varnished to make them less palatable

---

21 This is based on my personal experience and descriptions by R.H. Standley, headmaster of All Hallows' Senior School at Pawa on Uki Island in the late 1950s and the first half of the 1960s. Standley 1981, 7–8.

to cockroaches. Ants abounded, too, and were controlled with poison powder or (like the beds) by sitting the legs of kitchen and dining room furniture in containers of water. Before gauze and wire mesh screens arrived, residents had to live with the incessant mosquitoes and other flying insects.

Cupboards and drawers had to be aired regularly and cloth items put out in the sun to kill off mould and insects. Keeping food fresh was difficult. People preserved vegetables and fruits in bottles. Refrigeration was a luxury before World War II. The lucky few had their own Hallstrom 'Icy Ball', a refrigeration device patented in 1923 that consisted of two large metal balls joined by a pipe and a large insulated box. The machine was cheap to run since it used about one cup of kerosene a day. One ball contained pressurised ammonia and the gas escaped through a valve to cool the contents of the box. The cycle lasted 24 hours, then the ammonia was reheated and performed the process again. The disadvantages were that the devices were apt to explode and, although useful for cooling drinks, they did not keep meat fresh for long.[22] By the late 1930s, the wealthier residents possessed safer Electrolux 'ice machines' (kerosene-fuelled refrigerators), which cost about £50.[23] Other residents made do with 'Coolgardie safes' (an Australian invention)[24] and regular supplies from the iceworks, stored in an insulated box. Lighting depended on kerosene lamps, candles and torches and, from the 1940s, Coleman and Aladdin kerosene pressure lamps. Another household accoutrement that sometimes exploded was carbide lighting, which, provided residents were willing to take the risk, gave out a bright flame. People cooked on wood-burning stoves. All of these domestic devices made life in the Pacific Islands comfortable, with a great improvement once electricity arrived.

---

22 Horton 1965, 19; 'Ice-Chests for the Islands', *PIM*, 23 April 1932.
23 UQFL, Wilson Papers and Photographs, A.H. Wilson to J.A. Wilson, 9 November 1939; Watson 1991, 54.
24 'Coolgardie safes' were invented in the Western Australian mining town of Coolgardie in the 1890s. They were made from wire mesh on a wooden frame and were covered with hessian (made from woven jute or sisal fibres, which was called burlap in Canada and the United States), with a galvanised iron tray on top filled with water. The water dripped on to the hessian sides; breezes evaporated the water and cooled the contents. A metal tray at the base collected excess water. The life of perishable foods was extended by using the safes. They were usually placed on verandahs to catch the breeze. A simpler version, with a wooden frame and wire mesh sides, was also used in Australia, and is still used in many houses in Solomon Islands. The safe relies on a breeze to keep its contents cool and the wire keeps flies away from the food.

Plate 5.10 BP's Makambo Island, 1930s
Source: NBAC, N115-520-2.

Plate 5.11 A staff cottage on Makambo Island
Source: NBAC, N115-520-3b.

Living costs were high, particularly for imported foods. At the beginning of the 1930s, 1 pound (450 grams) of fresh meat cost 1/5- and the best joints cost 2/3- for the same amount. Ice cost 1/6- for a large block, bread was 9 pence per 2-pound (900-gram) loaf and eggs cost 3 pence each.[25] Residents clung to using imported foods—tinned, bottled, dried and frozen. Wives and servants learned how to make delectable meals using variations of recipes based on tinned fish and 'bully beef'. They became connoisseurs of different brands and swapped recipes using curry powder, chillies, ginger root, turmeric and coconut milk as the bases for new delicacies.

Residents received food parcels from home containing luxury items such as honey, cheese, peanut butter, Vegemite and sweet biscuits. When imported supplies ran out, people were left with plenty of local food choices. The main requirement was a willingness to adapt to local foodstuffs and to learn how to use them. Once this was done, tropical banquets could be prepared. Servants scraped the flesh from halved coconut kernels using the point of a machete clasped between the legs or with a serrated piece of metal attached to a stool. The shredded coconut fell into a container below and water was added to make a creamy fluid to use in cooking.[26] The fragrant water from green coconuts became a standard drink, as did the juice of bush limes in water, tempered with a little sugar. The meat supply arrived mostly in cans or frozen, brought in on the steamers from Sydney. There were a few cattle on Tulagi and large herds on the nearby Guadalcanal plantations, which occasionally put fresh beef on the menu. Most residents kept fowls for a ready supply of eggs and meat.[27] Marine life abounded and house staff needed little urging to take the afternoon off and go fishing to provide the evening meal. Usually fish and crustaceans were speared: *bonito* (tuna or kingfish) and rock cod were the favourites, although many varieties of reef fish, crabs, lobsters and prawns were available. *Soup-soup* was the name given to fish or *kumara* (sweet potato) soups cooked with plenty of juice from desiccated coconut added to the water. In the final analysis, the hankering for non-local cuisine was mere habit since excellent local foods were available.

---

25   BSIP *AR* 1931, 11, 1934, 13.
26   The grating sounds of this process are still common around most Solomon Islands homes in the late afternoon.
27   UQFL, Wilson Papers and Photographs, A.H. Wilson to J.A. Wilson, 6 October 1939.

Plate 5.12 Fish were always on the menu
Source: BM, Robert Lever Photographic Collection.

An enormous range of tropical fruit grew in house gardens: Cavendish bananas and local cooking (plantain) and sweet (lady finger) bananas, pineapples, pawpaws, citrus fruits (bush limes, oranges, grapefruits and mandarins), star fruits (carambola), custard apples, Brazilian cherries, avocadoes, passionfruit and granadillas, soursops and mangoes.[28] Residents also grew European vegetables (especially cabbages, tomatoes, cucumbers, beans and pumpkins) and Chinese green vegetables. Woodford was proud of his tomato patch and photographs show that he had a substantial garden, which was tended by two prisoners.[29]

28 Henderson and Hancock 1988; Knibbs 1929, 107–11.
29 There are photographs of Woodford's vegetable garden and of pumpkins grown on Tulagi. PMB, Photo 38, 81, 105–07.

Plate 5.13 These cattle are on Tulagi. Most plantations also had herds that were used to keep down vegetation around coconut palms, and for food
Source: NASI, WPHC Photograph Album.

Small bush mushrooms were also on the menu, for those who could differentiate them from poisonous fungi. Residents also learnt to use and appreciate local produce, which they both grew and acquired from around the Gela Group. Even today, foreign residents in the Solomons take a while to adapt to using the very nutritious 'slippery cabbage'—the leaves of *Abelmoschus manihot* (an edible hibiscus plant)—which is like spinach. Taro, yams and sweet potatoes soon replaced English potatoes and grated coconut kernels became the major subtle flavour in meals, replacing milk and cream. The eggs of megapodes (bush turkeys) made huge omelettes.[30] *Ngali* (Canarium) nuts—an almond-like delicacy produced from large trees—were harvested locally and also brought in from surrounding villages. The Wilsons' correspondence mentions sending bottles of these nuts to their children at school in Sydney. Cushions, pillows and the occasional mattress were stuffed with the fluffy contents of seed pods from tall kapok trees. Coconut fibre was the more usual stuffing for mattresses.

People on Tulagi spent their spare time in domesticity, sport, drinking or enjoying the natural beauty of the surroundings. Reading was a standard pastime, as were playing cards, listening to gramophones and radios, playing musical instruments, singing and games such as charades. Women knitted, embroidered, crocheted and made and repaired clothes. Starting

---

30   UQFL, Wilson Papers and Photographs, A.H. Wilson to J.A. Wilson, 12 December 1945. See also Dickinson 1927, 166.

in the mid-1920s, many residents listened to radios, mainly in the early mornings or evenings when atmospheric conditions were best. The wireless radio system opened new avenues for communication, domestic pleasure and relaxation. Once telephonic 'listening-in' sets became available, a world of news, music and entertainment reached Solomon Islands. Australian commercial and government (the Australian Broadcasting Commission, or ABC) broadcasts began in the 1920s and 1930s. Solomon Islands residents could receive medium-wave signals from stations on the NSW and Queensland coasts. They also listened to shortwave through the AWA Ltd broadcasts (from 1931) from Sydney and the British Broadcasting Commission (BBC) through the Empire Service (from 1932). Broadcasts from the US mainland and Hawai`i were also audible. 'Listening-in', as it was known, became a favourite local pastime. The first 'listening-in' licence was issued to Fred Campbell at Waimamura plantation on Makira in 1925 and the second to Major William V. Jardine Blake, the accountant in the BSIP Treasury and Customs Department on Tulagi. Those with radios invited their friends to visit and 'listen-in'. Owners of private wireless sets had to pay a government licence fee, but they gained a new medium of entertainment that linked them to the outside world. Tall coconut palms were useful for stringing up antennas.[31]

Using and supervising gardens formed another enjoyable pastime. Spaces under large trees in gardens were often cooler than the houses and were used as social places to serve tea or gin and tonics, or to while away the hours listening to music on a gramophone. House and garden servants did most of the work of clearing land and carrying water, but there was still room for planning and imposing personal touches. Spearline Wilson wrote to his daughter at school in Australia in 1939, after he had taken over Knibbs's job and house. It was much larger than his old house and more comfortable:

> I am sorry you don't like Mr. Knibbs' house. It is really quite nice. Much nicer now that I am living in it. I cut some of the trees down that were smothering the house and attracting mosquitoes, and later on I will make a nice garden. At present I have a garden in six boxes up on a stand. I have some nice lettuce, radishes, and tomatoes, but the weather is very dry, and it is hard work to make things grow. Eric and my new boy Bennie have to carry water every afternoon for the garden. Next year I am going to have a big rose garden.[32]

---

31 My thanks to Martin Hadlow, Brisbane, 11 February 2017, for this information.
32 UQFL, Wilson Papers and Photographs, A.H. Wilson to F.A.G. Wilson, 6 October 1939.

Domestic and social life on Tulagi

Woodford was cited earlier saying that on his first trip to the archipelago in 1886 there were two other foreigners living ashore. His memory of 30-plus years earlier was faulty; although the number was small, it was closer to a dozen.[33] When he arrived a decade later as Deputy Commissioner, there were 50 Europeans living in the new protectorate—almost all of them men. By 1919, there were 349 expatriates, of whom only 95 were women, most of them wives of plantation managers or missionaries, although some missionaries were single. Only six European women lived on Tulagi in 1914, the wives of administrative staff whose status varied according to their husband's position.[34] Few European women on Tulagi worked in paid positions, the exceptions being May Elkington at the hotel, Mrs Boyle at her boarding house and the nurses at the hospital. They contrasted starkly with missionary or plantation wives, who usually assisted in running those enterprises and often ran them single-handed for months at a time. Tulagi's women ran their households and entertained for their own pleasure and to advance their husbands' careers.

Tulagi was a town 'born modern' in the sense that it did not really begin in any substantial way until the 1900s and 1910s. There was no sense of a nineteenth-century past, no rough beginning in dirt-floor and thatched-roof shanties as had existed at Levuka in Fiji or Port Moresby in British New Guinea. Tulagi was built to regulation standards, except for structures in Chinatown or out of sight in the Sasape fringe settlement, where standards were lower. The other 'modern' aspect was the residents. Most were born in the late nineteenth or early twentieth centuries, a period when the family structure was reorganised to be more 'modern', based on the nuclear family. The best houses had labour-saving devices—such as they were at the time: stoves, sewing machines and refrigeration[35]— and political rights for women were being discussed.[36] A great leveller on Tulagi was that, regardless of rank and aside from a few who owned bicycles or horses, everyone had to walk. Just like anyone else, the Resident Commissioner trudged up and down the ridge tracks.

---

33 Bennett (1987, 59) suggests seven in 1870, four in 1875, six in 1880, 10 in 1885 and 14 in 1890.
34 WPHCA, No. 800 of 1914, RC C.M. Woodford to HC WPHC, 3 April 1914.
35 Reiger 1985.
36 On Empire Day in 1914, the pork pies were festooned on top with 'Votes for Women' picked out in green peas. *SCL*, November 1914, 168–70.

While the resident commissioners expected to receive respect, vestiges of the British upper class were few. This was in contrast to Suva, where the High Commissioner was a vice-regal governor, usually a knight, and 'calling' was limited to the first and third Thursdays of each month.[37] The etiquette of leaving a calling card at the residency in hopes of being invited to visit existed in the early days on Tulagi, but this custom had been abandoned by the 1930s. Most of Tulagi's resident commissioners were single and lived a bachelor's existence. If they had wives, they were mostly 'grass widows' living overseas and their children attended school in Australia or Britain. Woodford's wife, Florrie, and their children visited Tulagi regularly, although she chose to live in Sydney most of the time, rather than face Tulagi's heat and humidity and diseases such as malaria. This was also usual practice in Australian Papua, where lieutenant-governor Sir Hubert Murray's wives (he married twice) and family did the same, seldom visiting Port Moresby. Joseph Dickinson described Florrie Woodford as 'charming … and gracious to the few scattered settlers in the group, but a very natural lady amongst the native women and children'.[38] Kate Barnett, who was married to Woodford's deputy, Frank Barnett, had several children. Their two sons were born in New Zealand and Frank moved to Wellington in the final months of his life—an indication that his family maintained links there.[39]

Agnes Johnson, married to treasurer Pop Johnson, was a perfect fit for Pacific urban life. Born in the New Hebrides, she married Pop in 1911 and the couple moved to Tulagi in 1919. Two of their daughters were born in the New Hebrides and one in Sydney, and all three attended school in Sydney, where the family had a house in the suburb of Lindfield. Agnes lived both on Tulagi and in Sydney, and Pop usually spent his holidays in Sydney with his family. The children visited Tulagi regularly. Although it was expensive to maintain two households, it was the best way of keeping a family together and the children educated, while the breadwinner worked in the Solomons.

---

37 Boutilier 1984a, 189; Knapman 1986, 108; Scarr 1984, 79; Knox-Mawer 1986, 33–40.
38 Dickinson 1927, 98.
39 Archives New Zealand, Frederic Joshua Barnett, Last Will and Testament and Probate Documents, Ref. AAOM 6029, Box 322, 1917.

It was not easy to maintain a household, particularly at the lower end of the salary scale. Table 3.2 illustrates the range of government salaries in 1925–26, from the Resident Commissioner on £1,000 to a hospital nurse on £120. In 1925, a delegation of senior public servants met with the High Commissioner to request higher salaries. Judicial commissioner N.W.P. De Heveningham provided a breakdown of his expenses (Table 5.1). As one of the highest-paid officials, his salary, bonus and allowance came to £647. He claimed his living expenses were £586, leaving him only £61 for all other expenses and savings.

Table 5.1 The Judicial Commissioner's living expenses, 1925

Item	Cost (£)
House servants (x 2) at 30/- a month	36
House servants' food and clothing	48
Kerosene	15
Groceries, wine, beer, etc.	150
Food (from Chinese restaurant)	100
Ice	13
Family allowance	200
Widows and Orphans Fund	24
Total	586
Salary, bonus and allowance	647
Balance	61

Source: Colonial Office, 225/209, Meeting with Representatives of Protectorate Civil Servants, 29 September 1925.

De Heveningham's justification of his alcohol bill was that the 'Colonial Office says that a little alcohol is beneficial in the tropics'.

Managing servants

Dealing with domestic servants was a necessary part of life on Tulagi. Every European and Chinese household had Solomon Islander servants, and most had four or five.[40] *Haus-bois* (teenage or adult male servants), not house girls, were the usual Tulagi domestic servants, even though there

---

40 Rodman 2001, 210; Boutilier 1984a, 179, 188–90; Collinson 1926, 21–22.

were fears expressed over having adult Solomon Islander males as part of the household.⁴¹ There is some evidence of Chinese domestic servants in early decades and the Tulagi Club had a Chinese barman in the 1930s.

Prisoners crossed the line between controlled unfree labour and domestic labour; they were part of the regular labour force on Tulagi and were allowed access to houses, gardens and surrounding paths. They did most of the maintenance, including house painting, and worked loading and unloading supplies at the government wharf. One story about Woodford is that he had a convicted murderer on his permanent garden staff.⁴² Even the single officers had a servant each to do their washing. Eustace Sandars was faced with the need for servants when he arrived in 1928:

> Having taken over Turner's house I found myself with a servant problem on my hands but was fortunate in obtaining the services of one Kanda, a native of Ysabel, as a cook, a very excellent cook too. Captain Swanson brought me a Polynesian piccininny [sic] named Tubo. He was even lighter skinned than I am. His main aim and object seemed to be to sleep under the kitchen table all day and go fishing at night. He wasn't a very useful member of the staff for some months. Tubo was a delightful fellow and he remained with me for the whole of my time in the Solomons some 20 years. Later he married a very nice girl from his home island of Sikiana [Sikaiana] some 150 miles to the north of Malaita.⁴³

Sandars also mentions his servant Willie Hoeler, part-Polynesian and part-German, who was well-educated, read cookbooks and loved cooking. Hoeler was capable of making out a grocery order to be filled in Sydney, which needed calculation six weeks ahead to cover three months of supplies—no small feat for anyone. Like Tubo, Hoeler stayed with Sandars for the rest of his time in the protectorate.⁴⁴

---

41   Rodman (2001) suggests that female servants were the norm in the colonial New Hebrides, which was not the case in Solomon Islands or Papua New Guinea. Keays 1995, 71–73.
42   Richards 2012, Diary of Graham Officer, Melbourne Museum, 28 January 1901, 137.
43   Captain Ernest Nelson Turner was the police commander. PMB, Sandars, Papers on the Solomon Islands, 10–11.
44   ibid., 20.

Plate 5.14 Jessie Wilson at the beach with a house servant and one of her children
Source: UQFL, Wilson Papers and Photographs.

White women and girls had some freedom in moving around Tulagi, although there were always servants available to accompany them. The Wilsons had Jessie's teenage niece Edna Campbell staying with them for several months during 1930. Her diary shows an innocent domestic and social life, with freedom to wander along the beaches collecting shells, swimming, visiting Chinatown and socialising with the various leading families on Tulagi, Makambo and Gavutu. Swimming was only undertaken in the shark-proof enclosure at the Tulagi Club—for good reasons. In 1924, Edna's aunt, Jessie, described a scene that must have been typical over decades:

> We've all just rushed down to the water to see a cheeky big shark that came right up close. Everybody including about 40 natives always rush down to see a 'crocodile' or shark or any of the sea creatures that inhabit the waters here.[45]

---

45 UQFL, Wilson Papers and Photographs, J.A. Watt to Mary, 3 September 1924.

The lives of European women on Tulagi revolved around supervising servants, doing personal washing, baking cakes, biscuits and bread, sewing and mending, knitting, doing 'fancy work' and reading. Some women enjoyed making their own clothes, while others had to do so to save money. Many households had Singer treadle sewing machines, although sewing and washing services were also available in Chinatown. Women soon learnt to stop wearing wool undergarments. Heavy corsets and tight dresses were likewise abandoned as unsuitable for the climate. Looser, lighter garments were much more sensible apparel. Photographs from the 1920s and 1930s show women in stylish light dresses.

Residents lent each other books, newspapers and magazines. A number of the men were highly educated and some had read Greek and Latin at university. Many of the women, depending on their level of education, had studied both languages at private schools or at least Latin at government schools. A great variety of English-language books was available, and they were passed from house to house. Jessie Wilson recorded reading Countess Margaret Asquith's autobiography, a two-volume life of Christ and a book on life after death—all lent to her by Captain Turner, who was just back from England in 1933. A few years earlier, A.A. Milne's *Winnie-the-Pooh* (1926) had done the rounds. Resident commissioner Ashley claimed friendship with Milne from when they were at school together. Milne's *Peace with Honour* (1934) also circulated, as did Francis Ratcliffe's *Flying Fox and Drifting Sand: The Adventures of a Biologist in Australia* (1938). Gerald Elliot of Taronne pastoral station, at Lomead in Queensland, who was mentioned in the latter book, had a brother who worked as a plantation manager at Russell Islands. Many Europeans in the Solomons escaped everyday life through reading and, if books were unavailable, mail-order catalogues or almost anything printed would do. Jack McLaren, a long-term resident from the 1920s, read everything he could find, including a copy of Immanuel Kant's *Critique of Pure Reason*.[46]

Wealthier residents subscribed, while others had periodicals sent in batches by friends and relatives. Newspapers and magazines arrived months after they were published but were nonetheless welcome. They were read and then passed on to neighbours or were made available at the club. The main British periodicals consumed were the *Weekly Times*, *Tattler*, *Punch* and the *Illustrated London News*. Australians favoured Sunday papers and weekly

---

46 McLaren 1923, 77.

and monthly digests such as the *Bulletin*, *Sydney Mail*, *The Queenslander*, *Pacific Islands Monthly* (from 1930 on) and the *Australian Women's Weekly* (from 1933).[47] Mail-order catalogues were also circulated, as this was the main way to purchase new clothes and domestic equipment. Women swapped pattern books, which were used as templates for making clothes. There was a sense that Tulagi was clinging to the fringe of another world through periodic literature and mail-order catalogues.[48]

Due to the heat, people typically changed clothes two or three times a day, which increased the amount of washing for households.[49] Clothes were washed in cast concrete or galvanised iron tubs set against the back wall of the house or tucked away underneath. Sheets and large items were boiled in 'coppers' (open vats set in brick furnaces) or in half of a 44-gallon drum. When the water was hot, a lather was created by agitating a cake of soap kept in a meshed container with a handle. The equipment was completed by having a flat concrete surface on which to knead washing, plus a furrowed board on which to soap and scrub dirty garments. Wringers were used to remove excess water. The clean clothes, towels and sheets were pegged on metal clothes lines supported by timber props. Ironing was done with flat irons heated on the wood stove. Not everyone had an ironing board and those without spread a blanket on the kitchen table to create a suitable surface. Women usually washed their own underwear rather than give the task to servants, and it was probably safer to deal with fragile items oneself.

Visitors, male and female, came for morning or afternoon tea, and often stayed for lunch or dinner. Rainy days, of which there were many, meant staying at home. Small card parties and dinner parties were constant events. People often danced on the verandahs to music from wind-up gramophones after dinner. As Edna Campbell recorded in her diary:

> Monday 14 July 1930: Mrs Knibbs & Miss Croan called in the morning … I went down to Chinatown in the afternoon & purchased a present for Uncle's birthday. Still windy. We all received invitations to attend a dance at the Residency on the 23rd inst.

---

47   Sandars, PMB, Papers on the Solomon Islands, 173.
48   UQFL, Wilson Papers and Photographs, J.A. Wilson to Mary, 1933, 8 January 1937; Boutilier 1984a, 189.
49   Keays 1995, 64–65; CO, 225/209, Revision of Salaries, 14 April 1926.

> Tuesday 15 July 1930: It rained in the morning. I did some washing. A very windy day. Major Blake, Mr Masterman & Mr Lotze came for dinner at night.
>
> Wednesday 16 1930: I did some ironing & Aunty made a cake. Mrs Hewitt came for lunch. Uncle & I played singles tennis in the afternoon. Still windy.
>
> Thursday 17 July 1930: Aunty, Mike & I went to Mrs Hewitts in the Gavutu launch for the day. Uncle & Mr Masterman came over about 4 p.m. Still windy & rained during the night.[50]

Surviving evidence is silent on where the servants lived. The main houses were of average size with no space upstairs for servants' quarters, and this would not have aided privacy. The stumps were sometimes too low to allow accommodation underneath or the underfloor space could only be part-used. They most likely lived in separate servants' quarters nearby, in small houses made from local materials. Servants kept the households functioning and were wonderful support, if occasionally frustrating. Finding and training servants were always issues. Soon after she married, Jessie Wilson complained to a friend back in Australia—and although a little entertaining storytelling was involved, there is a core of truth here. We can also unpack some of her ingrained racist and condescending views about Solomon Islanders, which were typical of other expatriates:

> I've had a bit of trouble breaking in house boys. First I had 'Gideon' and 'Luke'—I forget what state of efficiency their namesakes reached in the bible, but these two nearly drove me crazy. They didn't 'savvy' anything at all, & actually made jelly out of Lux instead of jelly crystals & boiled Spearline's best silk shirt & got tar into the copper amongst the boiling clothes. So Spearline boxed their ears & swore at them & has given us two of his survey boys. They are making a much better fist of things. One of them Johnnie Aliang is the son of a chief & has been the Theodolyte [sic] bearer for Spearline. He owns a sewing machine, a mouth organ & a pair of trousers (shorts).

---

50   UQFL, Wilson Papers and Photographs, Diary of Edna Campbell.

> … The other boy is only 14 & named 'Aloysius'. He's a bit mad I think, but willing, & Johnnie Aliang being the son of a chief is priveledged [sic] to spank him & that saves me doing it. Then we have 'Malamu' who does the washing & ironing & is a good old thing & irons beautifully. He saw me washing some of my own things one day & said to me: 'Me Savvy clothes belong Missus Too much'. So Missus was glad to hear it. They each get 5/- per week & rice and tobacco.[51]

Regardless of the dramatisation, the account is revealing of Europeans' infantilising attitudes towards Solomon Islanders. It also illustrates the difficulties involved in teaching villagers to operate in European domestic surroundings.

In 1925, the minimum pay rate for adult domestic servants was £1 a month, although the average rate was 30/-, and well-trained servants received £2. Knibbs paid his staff monthly: his laundry-boy received £2, the cook-boy 25/- and a younger boy who assisted received 20/-. Food and clothing were also provided, at an estimated cost of £18 a year for each servant.[52] The Wilsons employed five male servants. They were bare chested, dressed in *lap-laps* with coloured cummerbunds and white belts.[53] Europeans discouraged or often outright forbade Solomon Islanders from wearing clothes above the waist.

Religious divisions among the servants occasionally caused issues. In 1936, two of the Wilsons' servants were Catholics, one was a Methodist from the Western Solomons and one '*belonged wicked*' (worshipped his ancestors). The Methodist came to Jessie Wilson asking to leave because one of the Catholics had accused him of being lazy. The conflict was resolved, but Jessie said she made a mental note to try to employ servants from only one denomination in future.[54] Once more, Jessie Wilson is revealing in her simplistic understanding, as there may well have been other reasons for the dispute.

---

51 ibid., J.A. Wilson to Mary, February 1925[?].
52 CO, 225/209, Meeting with Representatives of Protectorate Civil Servants, 29 September 1925.
53 UQFL, Wilson Papers and Photographs, Photograph 54.
54 ibid., J.A. Wilson to Mary, 14 February 1932.

Plate 5.15 The Wilson family servants with Michael James Wilson and Andrea Gordon Wilson
Source: UQFL, Wilson Papers and Photographs.

By 1932, Jessie Wilson's cook had been with the family for seven years and was an excellent employee. Jessie does not seem to have worried about male servants washing her undergarments. Two years later, however, the Wilson household experienced some staffing changes:

> I'm glad your domestic affairs are so good. Mine have never been so bad. My old cook—who was with me all my married life & was in the house 3 years before that, has at last gone home to stay. He said he was very tired & who can blame him! & my house boy who was here 8 years has gone to be a policeman & so I'm left with 3 raw recruits who at first don't know the difference between a spoon and a shovel & cant even light a stove & they look so sad & forlorn that I know they want to go home but they cant for 2 years. When I told them they look at me with their great big brown eyes & I just cant help seeing their point of view & agreeing that really all this fuss about spoons and table linen is very silly.
>
> Even my wash-boy who has had a little experience & should know better, puts starch in the handkerchiefs & pillow slips & leaves it out of the table napkins & the brute boiled a pair of my silk stockings. He says he has never washed 'calico' belong missus

before. His last master was a bachelor. Of course they wont be any good really for about 2 years & it takes about 6 months to get them to wash themselves properly with soap, & to keep their hair short & clean. I just seem to be turning into a cross old woman & just at present I work really hard—but of course I get many a laugh out of it too![55]

Jessie makes mention of Spearline 'boxing' a servant's ears. Corporal punishment was often meted out to Islanders in Papua New Guinea and Solomon Islands plantation and domestic labour settings. They might be beaten with a strap or cane or luxuries were docked from their rations. Castor oil was a standard purgative: expatriate adults used it on themselves and their children. It also seems to have been administered to servants as a purgative and sometimes as a punishment.[56]

For many Europeans, this was their first experience having multiple servants and some gloried in showing off their stylish domestic assistants. The higher a European's status and income, the more servants they had and the better their servants were expected to dress. In 1927, at Levers' manager's house on Gavutu, American visitor Caroline Mytinger described the following:

> [T]wo Malaitan house-boys, spotless in blue-bordered sarongs (called *lap-lap* here), with even the monogram of the house appliquéd on the opening flap, were shimmering noiselessly about serving tea like a couple of Jeeveses. There was not a hair out of place in the perfectly round black ball of their coiffures, and each had a red hibiscus blossom stuck in the very top centre of his mop. Their hands were clean and beautiful. Their fingers were the long tapering bony spatulates of the aesthete … The finger-nails were unusually long, though cut to the end of the finger, and they were a pale-lilac colour (because there was no pigment under the nail). And these delicate hands were handling the fragile china with the elegance of a Ming poet.[57]

At the same time as observing the perfect servants, Mytinger was told that 'Malaitamen were insolent, untrustworthy, filthy, stupid, lazy, cunning, ungrateful'.[58]

---

55 ibid., 13 November 1936.
56 Keays 1995, 266–70.
57 Mytinger 1943, 26.
58 ibid.

The pattern of discrete and well-groomed house servants was duplicated on Tulagi and Makambo. At one Tulagi house in the 1920s: 'Two little boys waited at table. They wore scarlet loin-cloths, which contrasted pleasantly with the beautiful bronze of their skins.'[59] The emphasis in descriptions was often on how quickly the 'savages' had been transformed into compliant servants. There is also a clear appreciation of physical beauty, often bordering of eroticism, such as this description of a 'boat-boy' by Lieutenant G.H.P. Muhlhauser, author of the *haus-boi* description above:

> In fact it is extraordinary what progress the natives have made. For instance we went over to Makambo in a launch which was run single-handed by a native clad in a loin-cloth and a necklace, with a comb in his mop of woolly hair. His muscular body was a joy to see. He ran the engine, steered, and made fast or cast off all by himself, yet a few years ago he must have been a pure savage, who had never seen or imagined such a devilish thing as an engine, or had any idea of mechanics.[60]

Mentions of acts of violence against servants are hard to find, although they plainly occurred. Spearline Wilson boxing the ears of his staff is proof enough. The most substantial account by a Solomon Islander of life on Tulagi is by Jonathan Fifi`i, later a Maasina Rule leader and parliamentarian. Born in 1921, he moved from the Kwaio bush to a Seventh-day Adventist village and then worked as a house servant for sister H.M. Cleaver, a hospital nurse and later matron who had arrived in Tulagi in 1929. Fifi`i was just a child when he began work in 1930. His memory of Tulagi does much to balance the syrupy views of the Europeans. Although he continued to work for Cleaver, his early years were difficult. His job was to polish the floors with coconut kernel, to polish household items and to carry food and serve at the table. He had no experience of working for Europeans and, although he tried his best, it was not good enough. As he described: 'She used to beat me—whip me with a broom. Sometimes she'd slap me.'[61] The worst occasion was when Cleaver threw a hot boiled egg at him, scalding him badly:

---

59   Muhlhauser 1924, 204.
60   ibid., 203. See also Boutilier (1984a, 191), who provides a similar appreciative comment of physiques, by a woman.
61   Fifi`i 1989, 32.

> I'll always remember the day when I brought her a three-minute boiled egg from the kitchen and served it. I served her egg from the right side, instead of the left. She picked up the boiling egg and threw it into my face. The boiling egg exploded, just under my eye.
>
> My face was badly hurt, where that egg had exploded under the eye. I still have a scar there under my eye to remind me. My face was split open and swollen. I went to the hospital in tears—Sister Cleaver must have been too ashamed of what she had done to take me to the hospital herself.[62]

Dr Hetherington examined Fifi`i and patched him up, advising him to go back to work rather than quit. Hetherington then went to Cleaver and arranged for her to pay Fifi`i 15 shillings in compensation, which was about three months' wages. We do not know what Hetherington said, but the size of the compensation payment is an indication of the severity with which he regarded the matter, and Cleaver changed her manner of behaviour:

> After she had injured me, Sister Cleaver felt sorry for me, and treated me much more nicely. She ordered two schoolbooks for me. One was called 'Primer' and the other was called 'Cat'. That had stories about a cat. I taught myself to read with those books. She would drill me: 'train', 'engine', 'top'. She helped me to learn to read. I can still remember that. She taught me to speak Pijin clearly and properly, not the way I had learned to speak it in the bush.
>
> She took me into the kitchen and taught me to cook. We worked together in the kitchen, and she taught me figures and arithmetic. She taught me to make sponge cakes. She looked after me. Sister Cleaver and Sister [L.D.] Collins had been the two nurses there when I first went. After that, Sister White and Sister [I.] Svensen and Sister Frost came as well. They all looked after me and took care of me.[63]

---

62 ibid.
63 ibid , 33.

There is no way of knowing how many Tulagi residents had experience of servants back in Britain, Australia, New Zealand or Fiji, although given the middle-class origins of a good number of them, it seems likely that quite a few came from homes where there were servants.[64] For others, particularly the younger men, it was their first time being in a colonial master and servant domestic relationship. Some employers had prior experience with indigenous servants. Agnes Johnson, born in the New Hebrides in 1893 and resident on Tulagi for 23 years, was certainly one of these. What the servants thought of the 'masta' and 'misis' is also hard to know, except that some very long relationships developed. The rules of a household were those of the employer. Servants were bound under indenture contracts and could not leave of their own volition. It must have been hard for new servants to get used to foreign customs. Europeans breached Solomon Islands pollution taboos by allowing menstruating women to stay in the same house as men, which would have been difficult for Islanders to accept, and the servants would have been in the situation of having a woman walk over their heads in the house above if they were working or living downstairs (which is not acceptable even today to some Malaitans).

In 1901, Graham Officer reported an incident involving Woodford's wife, Florrie:

> Women must not pass in front of a tambu house. A man must not stand beneath a woman, or beneath where a woman has been e.g. at Tulagi ([according to] Mahaffy) while Mrs. Woodford was there and for a long time after she had left, no native would go beneath the house.[65]

In Solomon Islander communities, male and female spheres were separated to varying degrees and they often lived in separate houses. On some islands, menstruating women were separated from men. Childbirth, blood and bodily secretions had to be confined and compensation paid for breaches of pollution taboos. As anthropologist David Akin notes, for Kwaio Malaitans, older principles existed for 'adjusting, mitigating, or waiving ancestral taboos at home, in ways that allowed men to live a normal life when away'.[66] The first time that Malaitan men and women faced breaking these taboos in circumstances

---

64 Robinson 2008; Robinson 2015.
65 Richards 2012, Graham Officer Diary, 16 June 1901, 176.
66 Akin 2013, 23.

beyond their control was on labour recruiting vessels, where men had to share life close to women or have them walking about on the decks when they were below. Akin records how people

> negotiated with their ancestors new ground rules for proper behaviour abroad, to follow taboos when possible but to waive them when necessary. Like so many other things, taboo observation, and taboos themselves, changed over time and varied from person to person.[67]

Eventually, modifications were made to make living in an urban community possible; nevertheless, some things were always extreme and difficult for many Solomon Islander males. Emptying latrine cans used by women or dealing with females' garments or towels used during menstruation would also have caused issues since these were extreme violations of customs relating to female pollution.[68] Europeans feared that their servants were incapable of washing fine silks and undergarments and that close access to these clothes would ignite unwelcome passions. This was fortuitous because they likely would have interpreted a male servant's refusal to touch female garments as dereliction of duty rather than as adhering to their culture's religious rules.

In villages, Solomon Islanders, both men and women, were often naked or wore only small pubic covers. Foreigners soon got used to this, although around missions and government stations it was usual for Europeans or Melanesian church teachers to insist people cover their genitals. The issue of 'native' nakedness was addressed in Australian Papua when, in 1906, the first regulation passed by the new Australian administration was for all 'natives' (other than children) to be clothed in at least a loin-cloth while in public in Port Moresby. In 1920, due to fears that Papuans were suffering health issues from wearing wet clothes, a new regulation (which remained in force until 1941) forbade males and females in villages and labour lines from wearing clothes on the upper parts of their bodies. There were exemptions for those living in urban or mission station areas, police and village constables.[69] The Solomon Islands Government did not have similar regulations. Urban servants were sometimes dressed only in

---
67   ibid., 23; see also 204.
68   Interviews conducted in the 2010s by Christopher Chevalier with Solomon Islander men who were youths in the 1950s indicate their extreme discomfort with having to empty latrine cans used by women.
69   Wolfers 1975, 47–48.

lap-laps or *sulus*, although there are also photographs of males wearing shirts and women in full 'Mother Hubbard'–style dresses. Few indigenous males wore shorts or trousers; they were more expensive than *lap-laps* and the simpler garments were used to differentiate between 'natives' and Europeans. The ban on Solomon Islander males wearing shorts continued for a long time. Jonathan Fifi`i was angry because during the war members of the defence force, which was run by British officers and planters, could only wear khaki *lap-laps*, never trousers or shirts. And in his biography Sir Peter Kenilorea mentioned a dispute at King George VI School on Malaita in the early 1960s when students protested that they wanted to wear shorts, not *lap-laps*. They were not issued with shorts and shirts until 1964.[70]

Employers had to communicate with their servants in Pijin, which could easily degenerate into simplified English, which was used by European employers as though it were Pijin, although, unlike Pijin, it was not based on a Melanesian grammatical structure.[71] There would have been a great deal of miscommunication with newcomers, even if both parties eventually would have reached some linguistic understanding. It seems probable that some of the problems with servants experienced by Jessie Wilson and others related to their inability to communicate clearly in Pijin. Becoming fluent in Pijin was part of the process of learning to live in Solomon Islands. Dick Horton recounted an incident with Pijin from soon after he arrived:

> I'd not been in Tulagi for very long when I was invited up to dinner by the local doctor. In those days we had to be very pukka—black tie, black cummerbund, long mosquito boots and all the rest of it. Afterwards he suggested we had coffee outside on the lawn, and he told his boy to bring it. No coffee turned up, so he called him again. 'Simeon, where is fella coffee?' And he answered, 'Oh master, me sorry too much, arse piece belong coffee pot im e bugger-up finis'.
>
> This shook me rigid. I thought, 'Good lord, does he really use this language to his master?' But all he said was, 'I'm very sorry, the bottom of the coffee pot has burnt out'.[72]

---

70   Fifi`i 1989, 50; Kenilorea 2008, 85.
71   Mühlhäusler 1981.
72   Knox-Mawer 1986, 70.

Solomon Islanders had their own ways of dealing with illnesses, whether cuts or wounds, diarrhoea or chest infections, back pain, sprains or eye problems. Many had detailed knowledge of medicinal plants and Westerners are only now beginning to understand their abilities to deal with medical issues. There is no evidence that they shared this ability in domestic circumstances on Tulagi, but logic suggests that they did, and that some of the foreigners would have learnt local cures using various plants. Others would no doubt have scoffed at and rejected 'native' remedies. We are on firmer ground in the Pacific War, during which we know Solomon Islanders sometimes used indigenous remedies to assist American servicemen.[73] They very likely also passed some of their medical knowledge on to their domestic employers.

****

While undoubtedly many servants were kept very separate, close and abiding relationships seen to have develop between servants and their employers. Even Jonathan Fifi`i, who was physically injured by his employer, seems to have forgiven her and later appreciated her efforts to make him literate.[74] Nevertheless, Fifi`i's overall assessment of the British era is extremely negative.

He gives several examples of the behaviour of the Inspector of Labour, Monty Masterman—the worst type of colonial officer—who was pompous, incompetent and brutal. In one incident, Masterman supposedly got his comeuppance. The story concerns Masterman and Sau Beriboo, a strong, tough Kwaio man who worked for Dick Laycock on Tulagi. There had been a public holiday and Laycock had made his staff work through it. Sau asked for the next day off in lieu; Laycock refused and sent him off to Masterman with a note explaining Sau's effrontery. Masterman read it and is said to have slapped Sau. Fifi`i recounted that Sau grabbed Masterman's forearm and pulled him across the desk, pushing his face into the desk. Sau made his feelings very clear: 'You, Mr. Masterman, aren't half the man I am. I'd like to kill you.' Fifi`i recalled the incident:

---

73   Henderson and Hancock 1988, 271–73. Also based on conversations with David Akin, Brisbane, August 2016, and films of the customary use of plants from Kwaio, Malaita.
74   Fifi`i 1989, 32–33.

> Masterman gasped, with his face flattened onto the table: 'It's all right, son. It's all right. Don't tell anyone what's happened between us. I won't tell anyone. Don't tell anyone I hit you, and don't tell anyone you hit me. I can see how strong you are. Let's just keep it between us. You go back'. Masterman sat down and wrote a letter to Dick Leacock [sic]. Sau took it back. Dick Leacock read and said. 'All right, all you men have a holiday today. The Master said you are to have a holiday today'. Of course, by nightfall every Solomon Islander in Tulagi knew it.⁷⁵

It seems unlikely that this was true, although it is typical of the tales of bravado that circulated. Masterman would more likely have used the police to deal with Sau, quietly having him beaten up, although we can never know the dynamics of relationships between Solomon Islanders. If the Sau Beriboo story has any truth in it, the main reasons Masterman would have been conciliatory is probably that he did not want to lose face or he had a genuine fear of being hurt badly, then or later. We are on safer ground in predicting how the administration would react to inappropriate violence by a colonial official. In 1935, Masterman was investigated for brutally beating a prisoner who had 'grinned in a manner that is objectionable in a certain type of native'. Masterman said: 'I think very few of us are willing to tolerate direct impertinence from natives.'⁷⁶ Resident commissioner Ashley mildly admonished Masterman, saying:

> I am sure you regret your action and I realise that you did it in a fit of temper when, in this climate, it is not always easy to have under control, but I trust you will be more careful in future.⁷⁷

In most cases, we have only the employer's versions, which are inclined to stress good-natured relationships between employers and their staff, with Solomon Islanders kept in line with an occasional cuff over the ears. Both the Wilsons and Sandars mention keeping their servants for long periods and Spearline Wilson reemployed two of his Tulagi servants at Honiara during 1945–46. The Wilsons' servants wrote letters to the Wilson children when they were away in Australia at school and the fondness was reciprocated. But we need to balance this against the examples of sister Cleaver and Monty Masterman, who feature so strongly in Jonathan Fifi'i's memories. My conclusion is that Pacific colonial households were

---

75 ibid., 35–36.
76 Akin 2013, 288.
77 ibid.

different from those in the surrounding settler societies, but similar elements of paternalism, racism and brutality were found in both. There is, I think, a difference between a settler society where there is an almost total takeover of land and power from the indigenous people and a Pacific society such as Solomon Islands, where, despite large-scale land alienation in some areas, the foreign population was only ever a small minority who maintained their power largely through 'smoke and mirrors'—a classic magical technique of illusions with no substance. Solomon Islanders always had the ability to withdraw back to their villages, as they did with effectiveness during Maasina Rule.

Fifi`i deserves the last word:

> The rest of them were just as bad, acting as if they were a superior caste, and as if we were just animals, here in our own country—acting as if they were the rulers and we were the slaves.[78]

Europeans were never willing to surrender their dominant position or control over Pacific Islanders. It was part of the way they ruled colonies. The term 'invasion' is seldom used in the Pacific Islands to describe the colonial years, because in some areas the indigenous people never saw themselves as forced to relinquish control of their land or cultures. Nevertheless, a system of superiority was maintained by racist policies and intimidation. There was always a presumption of superiority. Certainly, this was the situation in Solomon Islands. There also were other aspects of these colonial relationships—sexual and racial attitudes—that fed into wider interpretations of imperialism and the prewar culture of the Tulagi enclave. These aspects will be discussed in the next chapter.

---

78   Fifi`i 1989, 35.

6

'... a pity you didn't wing him': Gender, sexuality and race

> Here at Tulagi, the Headquarters of Government and of the police establishment, you have failed to give adequate protection to white women, as recent records show, and you will continue to fail until unpractical idealism gives place to cold reason and stern justice, and the punishment is made to fit the crime.
> — Donald Mackinnon, BSIP Advisory Council, 1933[1]

Pacific colonial society

When I lived in Port Moresby in the 1980s, a common joke was that all expatriates fell into one of three 'M' categories: missionaries, mercenaries or misfits. It was also said that if the men were single and over 35, they were probably gay. Based on conversations in the 1970s and 1980s with gay expatriates who had friends whose experiences dated back to the prewar years, there is a good chance the 'gay' tag was also often relevant in New Guinea and Solomons Islands in the 1930s, although things were much more circumspect decades ago. Certainly, the three-M theory applied.

---

1   *WPHCG (S)*, 19 March 1934, MAC, 25 October 1933, 55.

Some Europeans arrived in the archipelago as heterosexual couples who had decided to take on an adventure by living in faraway islands. Among them were men and women driven by Christian fervour to spread the message of the Lord on a new frontier. There were also many single adventurers who thrived on living in a different culture. For others, the motivation was the chance of a job during hard economic times in Australia. They were ready to try their luck and expected conditions to be a little rough and the supply lines long. Separated from their families, they had no support during any domestic difficulties. For many city folks early in the twentieth century, it was like crossing a time warp to the years of their grandparents on the Australian colonial frontier. Solomons Islands was a British protectorate and, for some, it meant a trip around the world to the Antipodes, giving up cold, snow and sleet for heat, warm rain, cyclones and earthquakes. However, the shipping routes ran via Australia, from where supplies came, and even if expatriates arrived with no links to Australia, they soon found their way there, for medical care and for recreation. As the decades progressed, more and more government staff were recruited directly from Australia and, to a lesser extent, Fiji and New Zealand. Two of the four big trading companies originated from Australia and the other two also had Australian employees. As well, Chinese residents developed links with Australia to supplement existing connections with Rabaul, Hong Kong and Singapore.

Little is known about most of the European and Chinese children on Tulagi or of the Solomon Islander children who lived there. There were many child deaths from diseases such as malaria, and some expatriate parents went as far as to clothe their children from head to toe in mosquito netting for protection. Alexander ('Sandy') Robert Wilson, son of Spearline and Jessie Wilson, died on Tulagi in October 1926 at 13 months of age. Vera Clift lost her two-year-old son, Peter, to suspected malaria. Violet Laycock was always careful to give birth in Australia and not return to Tulagi until her children were thought strong enough to survive, usually at three or four months. Nevertheless, her daughter Eileen died on Tulagi from malaria, aged 18 months.[2] Even when children were brought up on Tulagi and began their education home-schooled with correspondence courses, they were eventually sent away to Australia to further their education. If they could afford it, women accompanied their children. Like their counterparts in expatriate plantation families, most of

---

2 Golden 1993, 327; Boutilier 1984a, 192–94.

the European children from Tulagi spent many years away at boarding schools, returning only during the long Christmas breaks. Once their son turned eight, Spearline and Jessie Wilson sent him to boarding school in Sydney. The Elkington children, Thomas and June, were both sent to Australia; Thomas went to live with his grandmother in Australia when he was five to attend primary school. After she died, he was sent to complete his education at Southport School (on what is now Queensland's Gold Coast) as a boarder. Thomas returned to Tulagi in 1926, and the next year, at age 11, June left Tulagi to attend the Garden House School in Mosman, Sydney. She had been home-schooled for the first few years of her education, using correspondence courses.[3]

Photographs of Spearline and Jessie Wilson's children have survived. Their lives on Tulagi appear to have been remarkably similar to those of children in tropical Australia. They had a 'red Indian' tent and a dolls' house and a large garden in which to play.

Plate 6.1 Spearline Wilson and his son Alexander ('Sandy') Robert, aged eight months

Sandy was born in Sydney on 25 September 1925 and died on Tulagi on 29 October 1926.

Source: UQFL, Wilson Papers and Photographs.

---

3   UQFL, Wilson Papers and Photographs, J.A. Wilson to Mary, 23 March 1932; Golden 1993, 92; Information from Ian Elkington, 15 February 2017.

TULAGI

Plate 6.2 Spearline and Jessie Wilson's children on Tulagi: Andrea Gordon (born 1931) and James Michael (born 1928), with their 'red Indian' tent
Source: UQFL, Wilson Papers and Photographs.

Plate 6.3 James Wilson on a garden bench at the family home in Tulagi
Source: UQFL, Wilson Papers and Photographs.

Plate 6.4 Jessie Wilson and her daughter Andrea Gordon visiting Sydney
Source: UQFL, Wilson Papers and Photographs.

Most employees spent their holidays (often called 'furloughs') away from the protectorate and, given the lengthy boat trips involved, much of their leave time was spent travelling, particularly if they returned to England. From 1926, the wives of government officers were given an annual fare to Sydney, which caused an exodus over Christmas and New Year. It was a chance to go shopping, seek medical care and catch up with family.[4] Judging by the length of leave periods recorded for BSIP officials, it was not unusual for staff to be away for three to six months. They could also take leave on half-pay to extend the period. Frances Blake, whose husband was an accountant in the Treasury, said they had three months' leave every two years and managed to arrange six months' leave to return to Britain every five years.[5] While they were away, their jobs were performed by assistants or staff seconded from other departments. The wives of public servants often went on leave three months before their

---

4   UQFL, Wilson Papers and Photographs, J.A. Wilson to Mary, 21 May 1926.
5   Boutilier 1984a, 188.

husbands and returned three months later. Many residents stayed for only one contract, moving on to better themselves or because they were unable to stand the tropics or the isolated lifestyle. There was a constant sense of impermanence. European society was held together by the half-dozen long-staying families and a group of resident bachelors.

Pacific colonial urban society had similarities with life back in Australia or Britain, although there were also unique features. In the Solomon Islands context, one has only to consider the mixed-race medical doctor Nathaniel Crichlow or the children of the leading mixed-race families (such as Geoff Küper, trained as a native medical practitioner, but always an outsider) to begin to appreciate the complexity. There were unacknowledged mixed-race children absorbed into villages or around Chinatown and several prominent mixed-race families and dozens of others, who fitted uneasily into British and Chinese racial and class systems.[6]

Descriptions of colonial society in Fiji show attempts to hold to British class conventions. The elite ignored lesser families, treating them as though they did not exist. Tulagi was probably always too small to enforce this depth of class-bound rules. It would, for instance, be hard to move to the other side of the street to ignore someone beneath contempt (as occurred in Suva) when the Tulagi street was a narrow coral path and you were both puffing your way up the ridge. In Fiji, CSR field engineers were regarded as inferior to chief engineers, who were permanent officers in the company, yet field engineers were not allowed to associate with those below them—the mechanics, stockmen and storekeepers.[7] Both Knibbs and Wilson had been field engineers in Fiji. On Tulagi, their long tenures erased their previous inferior status. However, there was a clear hierarchy in the domestic space, expressed in the architecture of the houses and interpersonal relations. The wives of senior administrators felt superior to the commercial company wives (except perhaps the wives of the BP, Levers and Carpenters managers) and both groups seem to have looked down on the plantation wives, who visited Tulagi on their way to and from the outer islands. Yet, there were also plantation wives who saw themselves as upper class and superior. Racial boundaries were stricter than social divisions, but still permeable.

---

6   Very little has been written on this aspect of Solomon Islands. Bennett's 2015 chapter on the Pacific War years concludes that there was little connection between servicemen and the local women, most of whom were evacuated into the centres of the islands during the war. Some cultural aspects of the separation would also have applied before the war.

7   Knapman 1986, 106.

Plate 6.5 Pop and Agnes Johnson on Tulagi in the 1930s
Source: Suzanne Ellis Collection.

Single white women were in short supply. If a public servant, missionary or planter wanted to marry, he usually had to find a wife while away on annual leave. The only local sources of wives were Tulagi Hospital, where nurses were appointed from 1914, or the daughters of plantation owners or managers. The hospital became known as the 'matrimonial bureau'—an indication that the nurses usually married quickly and moved on. During the hospital's first 15 years, only two nurses managed to fight off hopeful suitors.[8] For example, Jessie Watt arrived as a nurse in 1923 and was soon married to Spearline Wilson. Her letters home detail his courtship. Wilson visited her three times a day and, although she thought him 'a dear', she told a friend that she preferred men with dark hair, and he was fair-haired. Spearline kept wooing and eventually she succumbed, even though she admitted that there was no dearth of suitors. Another nurse married the Burns Philp manager, a man Jessie Wilson described as 'a perfect dear too, heaps & heaps of money'.[9] Clearly, he was considered a good catch. Inga (Ingrid) Svensen, daughter of Oscar Svensen, was also a nurse at Tulagi Hospital. She left Brisbane for the Solomons in 1934 to keep house for her brother on one of the family plantations. Inga had not been there long when both nurses at the hospital fell ill and resigned.

---

8   Boutilier 1984a, 188.
9   UQFL, Wilson Papers and Photographs, J.A. Wilson to Mary, February 1925[?].

A registered nurse, Inga was persuaded to take their place, until in 1937 she married Ernie Palmer, a prominent trader, labour recruiter and, later, planter. He, too, used heavy-duty wooing, learning to play golf to impress Inga and having Chan Cheong make her a beautiful sailing dingy for her birthday, for which Palmer lovingly completed the rigging.[10]

Other local white daughters also married Tulagi bachelors. For instance, three daughters of Sam and Edith Atkinson from the Western Solomons married Tulagi-based government officers.[11] Another local marriage was that of Jack Lotze, Carpenters' manager, to Dorothy Johnson, daughter of Pop Johnson, the Treasurer.

Plate 6.6 Agnes and Pop Johnson and their daughter Dorothy
Source: Suzanne Ellis Collection.

---

10 Golden 1993, 104; Struben 1963, 56.
11 Golden 1993, 362.

Plate 6.7 The marriage of Jack Lotze to Dorothy Johnson, Tulagi, 1931
Source: Suzanne Ellis Collection.

Plate 6.8 Jack and Dorothy Johnson and an unknown woman
Source: Suzanne Ellis Collection.

On Tulagi there were no 'aristocratic' Solomon Islanders comparable with the chiefly Fijian elite, although some of the native medical practitioners were high-ranking Fijians and their Solomon Islander counterparts carried status among their own people and foreign residents. Indigenous clergy were another in-between category of uncertain status. Jonathan Fifi`i mentions Joe Kona and Suda, both from Kwaio Malaita, who looked after him when he first worked on Tulagi as a boy. Suda, from west Kwaio, was the head dresser at the hospital. Although he was illiterate, Suda had worked his way up to be in charge of the hospital's dressing room—the equivalent of a casualty department. He fed Fifi`i, beyond what he received from his employer, and, as much as he could, provided guidance to the young Kwaio. Fifi`i arrived as a 10 year old in 1930, earning 5 shillings a month as a house servant. Back in Kwaio, his father needed shell wealth for a mortuary feast for Jonathan's grandfather. Fifi`i went to Suda, who gave him enough money to purchase two bags or rice and 12 big Dove tobacco twists, which his father was able to sell to obtain the necessary shell wealth.[12] There would also have been Solomon Islanders in the Tulagi enclave who were highly regarded in other ways, by possessing traditional knowledge, skills in healing, magic or fighting or coming from families whose members were prominent leaders.

Mixed-race relationships

Biographical sketches of the early European residents provide an essential account of the diverse group of individuals who made the Solomons their home. Intermarriage between expatriate families created an intricate web, and some of the plantation owners, managers and traders had local wives and mixed-race children, which added complexity to societal norms. Of course, many foreign men had relationships with local women, which they often chose not to acknowledge. For instance, when Thomas Edge-Partington, then aged in his 20s, was based on Gizo as Resident Magistrate (1904–09), he had a mistress from nearby Simbo Island. He was forced to apologise to both the Resident Commissioner and the High Commissioner for his (in Mahaffy's words) 'connection of an immoral kind'.[13] He also received an official reprimand from London.[14] His fall from grace offers

---

12 Fifi`i 1989, 34.
13 Mahaffy is quoted in Jackson 1978, 167.
14 CO, 225/87 170 (Microfilm, 2915), T.W. Edge-Partington to F.J. Barnett, 20 September 1909; WPHCA, 4/IV 836/1908, Arthur Mahaffy to HC, 22 December 1908, C.M. Woodford to Major, 30 September 1910.

a window into the existence of mixed-race relationships and the level of acceptance. Over centuries, the British Colonial Service had quietly encouraged colonial public servants to have concubines. Although it came too late to affect the assessment of Edge-Partington's behaviour, in 1909, the Marquess of Crewe, Secretary of State for the Colonies, issued the 'Crewe Circular', which made clear that such relationships were an offence against morality and would no longer be tolerated.[15] Nevertheless, Mahaffy noted that Edge-Partington had 'permanently impaired his influence with the natives' because he had reduced himself to the level of a disreputable trader. Edge-Partington—young and sociable, leading a solitary life and, other than his sexual liaison, an exemplary employee—was given a second chance. He could have been dismissed, but was forgiven, 'banished' to Malaita as the first Resident Magistrate and placed on probation. He married a British woman in 1913.

In the early years of the protectorate, only a few regulations directly governed European relationships with Solomon Islanders. Government policy opted for minimal administrative interference, particularly when it came to marriage, divorce and adultery. Customary behaviour varied island by island and the British had been unable to codify local conditions. Missionaries blessed the marriages of indigenous converts and usually did not concern themselves too closely with other sexual practices and types of relationships. Customary marriages could sometimes come into conflict with conversion to Christianity, and there were other conflicts when mission teachers with no civil licences took it upon themselves to conduct marriages.[16] Indigenous betrothal practices, which usually included an exchange of wealth items to bind the families, continued to operate with no reference to either civil or Christian authority. Most Europeans living with Solomon Islander women were in de facto relationships, choosing a middle way between customary practices and something approaching a Christian or modern civil marriage.

Britain passed the *Colonial Marriages Act 1865* to ensure that marriages contracted in its colonial possessions had the same validity as those in the United Kingdom. The 1893 order in council included provision for ministers of religion to celebrate marriages, if one marriage partner was a British subject. This provision was extended in 1896 to cover marriages between 'foreigners'—a term that included Solomon Islanders. In 1907, another order in council declared the protectorate a 'marriage district' and

---

15 Hyam 1986; Hyam 1990, 157–81.
16 Laracy and Laracy 1980, 133–35.

enabled civil marriages to be officiated by the Resident Commissioner or the Collector of Customs. Unlike in neighbouring Queensland, the BSIP laws never tried to limit or ban interracial marriages.

It is unknown how many mixed-race marriages occurred. Such couples lived all through the archipelago, except probably on Malaita or Choiseul, which had few foreign residents. Quite a few of the early traders came to brutal ends and the presence of a local wife could be a good safeguard by providing a close link to the people and a conduit for information. Taking a local wife was also a good way to learn local languages. Indigenous people may also have used marriages as a strategy to negotiate with Europeans.[17] There are examples of long-lasting relationships made in both customary and modern Christian styles, such as that between the Küpers of Santa Ana and the Wickhams in the north-west, and there were no clear class or racial patterns in those relationships. Even a few district officers and possibly one resident commissioner seem to have been involved in interracial relationships. Early traders often had indigenous wives and sometimes took advantage of local practices of polygyny. Graeme Golden lists 30 long-term mixed-race heterosexual relationships.[18] One marriage he missed was that of Lars Nielsen, the trader who began Gavutu and then sold out to Oscar Svensen in 1903. His great-great-grandson reports that Nielsen had a Malaitan wife, who lost contact with her husband when he returned to Norway. Their only child, a daughter, married into the Wickham and Pratt families from Western District.[19] The practice of having local 'wives' was quite common, even on Tulagi and close by in the Gela Group. Trader Julius W. Anderson, a Norwegian, operated his own engineering business on Tulagi before beginning work for Carpenters in about 1928, in charge of their workshop. He had a Gela wife and family

---

17 In *Illicit Love* (2015), a study of interracial sex and marriage in the United States and Australia, Ann McGrath makes the point that the Indigenous Australian women in many of the relationships made temporary alliances and often were already married to Indigenous husbands. Her interpretation is that this was part of the attempt to preserve sovereignty and exert a modicum of control on behalf of their people. Indigenous husbands likewise could exert some authority in these cross-cultural relationships. Nevertheless, McGrath's study is of settler societies where the colonisation process was of a different intensity. See also McGrath 1984, 2005.
18 I have not included those already named in this subsection of the text. Golden 1993: Major I. (Dick) Harper (pp 101, 184), John (Jack) Cooper (127), Arthur L. Threlfall (156), Thomas Woodhouse (202–04), T.G. Kelly (205, 215), Thomas Easson (212), Charles Atkinson (214), Edmund Peter Pratt (215–17), Jean Peter Pratt (218–19), George Creswell (223), Joe Biskin (231–33), Aubrey Griffiths (242), Harold Markham (244–47), William Bennett (250), Harold Beck (260), Tom Butler (287), Charles Olsen (288), Dick Richardson (290), C.R.M. (Roy) Gorringe (320), Ernie Palmer (103–05), William Macdonald (359), John Mathews (384–88), Harry Hoerler (398), James A. Buchanan (157) and Albert Molkin Andresen (183). For Palmer, see also Struben 1963.
19 Golden 1993, 68–69; Information from Justin Nielsen, 18 September 2016.

and owned property in Mboli Passage.[20] Dick Harper, a Gela plantation owner, married Enid Bennett, the part–Solomon Islander daughter of W.H. Bennett from Isabel.[21] William Dumphy, originally from Queensland, became a small-scale planter on Guadalcanal. He had a local wife and, after he died in the early 1920s, his daughter Maggie married Jim Buchanan, an English engineer in his 40s who had helped build Levers' Gavutu wharf in 1906. Buchanan owned a small plantation in the Gela Group and the couple had a daughter, Jean. Another Dumphy daughter, Bella, has already been mentioned; she too married an expatriate.[22]

Wilfred Fowler described a situation on Isabel in which a plantation owner, after a quick romance in Sydney, married and then deserted his new wife. She turned up at Tulagi and wanted to visit her husband. Refusing to heed warnings that it was not a good idea, she eventually reached Isabel, where she found him to be a hopeless alcoholic in relationships with several village women.[23] The sexual exploits of Jack Barley, a district officer and acting Resident Commissioner, have remained in Solomons' folklore. He was always concerned about depopulation and the Tulagi joke was that he was trying to rectify the problem all by himself.[24] While posted on Ontong Java in 1915–16, he had an affair with a local woman, who became pregnant, bearing his son, Jack Charles junior. According to some sources, Barley declared his love for this woman and was determined they should marry. Strongly advised against it by other government officers, he was forbidden by the Resident Commissioner.[25] The woman died soon after during an epidemic. Because of the official interference he encountered, Barley became more circumspect about revealing his later liaisons. However, he had at least two Solomon Islander children, Jack junior and Bill, and two other children he fathered to different women while based in Fiji. His Australian family is aware of even more children.[26] The relationships did no harm to Barley's BSIP career (1917–32) nor afterwards, when he was Resident Commissioner of the Crown Colony of Gilbert and Ellice Islands.[27] James Boutilier credits Za Za, a Simbo woman, with having relationships with five European men, one of whom

---

20   Golden 1993, 76. Anderson died from tuberculosis in Tulagi Hospital in 1935.
21   ibid., 101, 250–51.
22   ibid., 146, 157.
23   Fowler 1959, 211–23.
24   Akin 2013, 362–63, n. 59.
25   ibid., 362–63, n. 59; Butcher 2012, 171–72.
26   Butcher 2012, 171–72.
27   Boutilier 1984a, 196.

was Jack Barley. Bill Barley married Sumoli Wilomena Andresen in the 1930s. Jack senior was finally formally married in 1933, when he was 46, to a 24-year-old Queensland woman, Florence A. Doughty.[28]

Expatriate men had sexual relations with local women, particularly on islands where such relationships were accepted. Before he married Inga Svensen, Ernie Palmer, one of the expatriates who was closest to Solomon Islanders, availed himself of any sexual activity he was offered. On Makira, he was on friendly terms with Nafunenga, one of the leaders, who had an attractive daughter, Kavatnaasukulu, with whom Ernie had a relationship, for which he paid shell valuables to her father. Eventually, Nafunenga presented Palmer with an ultimatum: either marry his daughter or end the relationship, and all the wealth payments would be returned. Palmer chose to move on. Although he was fond of Kavatnaasukulu and she taught him a great deal about Makira, she always called him 'Sir' or 'Masta Palmer' and preferred to eat with his crew, slipping away into the shadows if he had expatriate visitors.[29]

Albert Molkin (Andy) Andresen, a Swede, arrived in the Solomons in about 1917, working first in the Western District, where he had relationships with local women, before leasing plantations on Guadalcanal, Ulawa and finally on Mandoliana Island in the Gela Group. His wife, Za Za, is one of the most fascinating serial wives of white men. Za Za was with the alcoholic Andresen from the 1930s until the 1960s. His daughter Sumoli was the child of his Ulawan wife, Tiganapalo. In the 1930s, when Sumoli married Bill Barley, Za Za arrived to attend the wedding. There are two versions of what happened next. One is that Za Za 'hit it off' with Andy Andresen and the other is that Sumoli arranged for Za Za to marry her father to look after him in her absence. Whichever is true, legend suggests they were married at the same ceremony as Sumoli and Bill, much to the consternation of the officiating missionary. Za Za kept the Andresen home spotless and always tried to curb his drinking—somewhat unsuccessfully—until his death in 1965.[30]

In 1933, Dr Sylvester Lambert mentioned an 'Austrian anthropologist' who had worked on Santa Ana and Choiseul, who was told to leave quickly or be charged with the rape of two Santa Ana girls, one aged

---

28 Akin 2009, Notes from Lambert, 27 May 1933.
29 Struben 1963, 32–33.
30 Bill and Sumoli Barley were the parents of Lady June Devesi, the wife of Sir Baddeley Devesi, the first Governor-General of Solomon Islands. Za Za lived at Mandoliana until she moved to Honiara in the early 1980s. Golden 1993, 183–85; Information from Transform Aqorau, 22 September 2016.

about eight and one 12 years old, whom Heinrich Küper had brought to Tulagi to report the behaviour. This was probably Hugo. A. Bernatzik, who published *Sudsee* in 1934, with an English translation the next year. For his reward, the anthropologist is said to have acquired gonorrhoea from the older girl.[31]

The best examples of prominent mixed-race families are the Wheatleys and the Wickhams from the Western District, the Campbells from Makira and the Küpers from Santa Ana, close to Makira. Short biographical sketches of the founders of these four families add to the complexity of life on Tulagi. They were constant visitors to the capital and some of them, particularly the Wheatley and Wickham families, were among the richest residents in the protectorate, yet they were never totally accepted because of their domestic arrangements. Although 'polite' Tulagi society was uncomfortable with them, they could never be ignored.

Norman Wheatley, born in Yorkshire in 1868, was apprenticed in his father's steelworks in Newcastle. Bad tempered, he attacked the foreman with an iron bar and fled. Wheatley reached the Solomons via Brisbane on a trading ship in the 1890s. He decided to leave the vessel when it reached idyllic Roviana Lagoon in the New Georgia Group. The resident trader had been killed and Wheatley volunteered to take over. Two years later, he discovered that the trading ship on which he had arrived had been captured at Bougainville and its crew killed. He then set up his own trading venture, under the protection of local bigmen, who benefited from access to his trade goods. He was successful but ruthless in the way he operated, using the bigmen to dispatch any rivals. Wheatley married Nutali and the couple had three daughters, Florence, Jean (Lina) and Annie. Florence and Jean both married planters, which helped create an important Western Solomons dynasty. Annie married Alemaena from Marovo Lagoon. Nutali left Wheatley and he next married Sambe Vindo, with whom he had six children. Two of these sons became native medical practitioners—the highest-status, best-paid government position that a prewar Solomon Islander could hold. Wheatley built a beautiful home at Laperti plantation on the shore of Roviana Lagoon and amassed thousands of hectares of land in the New Georgia Group and on Isabel. He was wealthy and prone to extravagant purchases during trips to Australia, including of a former Sydney Harbour ferry, which ended its days in Marovo Lagoon. His finances began to decline in the mid-1920s

---

31   Akin 2009, Notes from Lambert, 23 May 1933.

and he died in Tulagi Hospital in 1930. He was the arch-caricature of a Pacific planter: overweight, drank too much, swore like a trooper, had many children and behaved like a feudal lord.[32]

Francis (Frank) Wickham, who was born in Somerset, England, in about 1850, was another early arrival. Shipwrecked in Bougainville Strait about 1875, he was soon working for Alexander Ferguson, a trader. In the usual pattern, Wickham was able to set up as an independent trader and planter, owning several trading ships and significant amounts of land around Roviana and Marovo lagoons. He married three times to local women and had six children. Wickham shifted to Sydney in 1908, where he interested himself in the sporting careers of two of his sons, who became famous swimmers and divers. His son Alick 'invented' the 'Australian crawl' (freestyle) swimming style, which was in fact a New Georgia way of swimming.[33] Frank Wickham never returned to the Solomons and died in 1926. His family remains prominent in Solomon Islands today, with other descendants in Australia.[34]

Frederick (Fred) Campbell, an Australian from Wee Waa in New South Wales, was appointed as Commandant of the Armed Constabulary in 1912, serving at Auki and Tulagi, before he became District Officer for Makira in 1918. The next year he left government service and became a trader and plantation owner on Makira, marrying twice, first to Maria Kainaua and then to Kapinihare from Aona. There were no children from the first marriage and two boys, Jack and Pat, from the second. His marital infidelity ended the second marriage and, although he never remarried, Campbell had several relationships with local women on Makira. Campbell managed to straddle two worlds. In the 1920s, he was a member of the exclusive BSIP Advisory Council, which guided the Resident Commissioner, yet he maintained his indigenous family. We can imagine the conversations had (or perhaps avoided) when he served on the council with Reverend John F. Goldie, the Methodist leader, or with the Anglican Bishop of Melanesia. In the 1930s, Campbell was briefly Makira's District Officer again, once more blurring the boundaries. He died in 1953. His son Jack became president of the Makira Council and a member of the Legislative Council in the 1960s.[35]

---

32 Moore 2013, entry for Norman Michael Jackson Ernest Wheatley; Golden 1993, 227–30.
33 Osmond and Phillips 2006; Osmond 2006; see several entries under Wickham in Moore 2013.
34 Moore 2013, entry for Francis Wickham; Golden 1993, 206–08. Wickham' final wife, Sambe Vindo, survived him by many years and was still living in Dolovae village, Munda, in the 1980s when she was 100 years old. Information from Transform Aqorau, 22 September 2016.
35 Moore 2013, entry for Frederick Melford Campbell; Golden 1993, 305–07.

Plate 6.9 Frank Wickham, who married three local women and had six children
Source: PMB, AU PMB Photo 58_108.

Plate 6.10 Fred Campbell in 1913 while he was Commandant of the Armed Constabulary, playing tennis at Auki, Malaita, with Mary Edge-Partington and Captain Hancock of HMS *Sealark*

Campbell became a planter on Makira and married twice, first to Maria Kainaua and then to Kapinihare of Aona.

Source: BM, Thomas Edge-Partington Photographic Collection.

Heinrich Küper had been a German naval officer. He arrived in the Solomons via German New Guinea in 1912, then entered a trading and plantation partnership on Santa Ana. He managed to buy out his partner, married Augusta Kafagamurironga, the daughter of a local chief, and raised three sons and a daughter. Although initially their marriage 'contract' was based on customary exchanges, eventually Küper wanted a formal Christian ceremony. He went as far as to build a church where it could take place. Küper was interned during World War I, although in a very minimal manner. The Küpers were not involved in Tulagi society in the way the Campbells were, and lived closer to indigenous society.

However, the children were educated by the Melanesian Mission. The eldest son, Geoff, who had been initiated into his mother's descent group, was educated in New Zealand and trained in Suva as a native medical practitioner. One of the earliest Solomon Islanders to receive a high-level European education, while maintaining his indigenous culture, he reacted against the racial prejudice he faced from the colonial elite.[36]

There were other 'outsiders', those who 'batted for the other team'—a phrase from that era meaning homosexual. Homosexuality was illegal in British law and frowned on by the bulk of the expatriate population. Although some Solomons indigenous societies were accepting of homosexuality, others were not and saw it as offensive. For instance, there is little space for homosexuality in Malaitan society, although Malaitans were involved in homosexual activity on plantations. According to historian Judith Bennett, homosexuality among Solomon Islander male labourers was 'practically universal and tolerated' on plantations.[37] Dr Sylvester Lambert's observations in the 1930s back up this opinion:

> Europeans don't think that the primitive man goes homosexual. Humbug! Ask any of the big planters—and they're he-men if there ever were any—ask 'em about the native boys that weave their hips and ogle at the work-gangs going by. We call them 'queens', and they're nuisances we've jolly well got to get rid of it.[38]

In addition, Georgina Seton, a planter's wife, commented that she worried about homosexual threats to her young sons from labourers on their plantation.[39] Some Europeans and Chinese must have had discreet homosexual relationships with Solomon Islander men. There is enough evidence from around the Pacific to know that these relationships did occur, and some evidence from the Solomons.[40] It is also possible that there were homosexual relationships between some of the Chinese and between some of the Chinese and Europeans. In the early decades, there were Chinese *haus-bois* on Tulagi, like those found in northern Australia, particularly in Darwin, which had a large Chinese population. We know that homosexuality was accepted among the elite in premodern China and

---

36 Moore 2013, entries for Heinrich Küper and Augusta Küper Kafagamurironga; Golden 1993, 299–300, 103–06; Information from Doreen Küper, Brisbane, 19 August 2016.
37 Bennett 1987, 174, 182, 441, n. 56; Bennett 1993, 141, n. 74. See also Moore 2000b, 53–55.
38 Lambert 1946, 22–23.
39 Boutilier 1984a, 194.
40 Aldrich 2003, 246–75; Moore 2010–12, 36–37; Bennett 1987, 58, 174, 182; Moore 2000b, 57–59; Hilliard 1978, 155.

that domestic servants from southern China were open in their attitudes to homosexuality; it was a way for servants to wield power in domestic relationships.[41]

Our main evidence relates to indiscreet or improper 'relationships', such as those Reverend Charles Brooke had with Gela schoolboys, which led to his dismissal in 1874. In the 1890s, A.E.C. Forrest, an American lay member of the same mission, was dismissed for similar activities involving students on Santa Cruz. He remained on the island as a trader but was ostracised by other Europeans and eventually charged in 1901 with gross indecency. Forrest fled to the Torres Islands in the northern New Hebrides—close by but beyond the jurisdiction of the protectorate—where he took his own life in 1908.[42] The most prominent homosexual was Bishop Frederick M. Molyneux (1928–31), who was told to resign or face prosecution for his sexual relationships with schoolboys. He left quickly.[43]

Reports of homosexuals include Henry J. Townsend, who arrived in about 1878, after fleeing Samoa and Fiji because of his liking for men. He and a male 'native' friend landed at Uki to work for John Stephens, a trader's agent. Townsend was killed soon afterwards, for reasons other than his sexuality.[44] Another was cadet officer L.W. Keppel, who was accused of the homosexual rape of Ganga, a labourer from Rendova Island, at Auki headquarters on Malaita in 1911. He also left quickly, which seems to have been the standard method of dealing with cases of sexual misdeeds, although there were also more dramatic results.[45] In the early 1930s, Dr Lambert recorded that a prominent trader was about to be arrested for homosexual relations with Solomon Islanders, but chose to take '100 Iron Arsenic and Strychnine pills' rather than face the disgrace.[46]

While they were not necessarily practising homosexuals while in the protectorate, we can probably add to the list anthropologist Ian Hogbin and district officers Wilfred Fowler, Hector MacQuarrie and Michael Forster.[47] Undoubtedly, other expatriate men also fell into this category. If they were lucky, they ended up on islands where homosexuality was

---

41 Chaperlin 1930; Lowrie 2013.
42 Golden 1993, 32–33; Bennett 1981, 180.
43 Moore 2013, entry for Frederick M. Molyneux.
44 Golden 1993, 280.
45 ibid., 31; NASI, BSIP 14/40, T.W. Edge-Partington to C.M. Woodford, 27 December 1911.
46 Akin 2009, Notes from Lambert, 23 May 1933.
47 Laracy 2013, 243–56; Ian Hogbin, Interview with Clive Moore, Sydney, May 1978; Butcher 2012, 182, n. 878; MacQuarrie 1946.

accepted in local cultures. Some of the student partners mentioned above would have been older teenagers and young men in their 20s, although this does not abrogate the breach in duty of care nor that the sexual acts were illegal in British law.

It was unthinkable, given the racial and sexual beliefs and rules of the time, for European women to have sexual relationships with Solomon Islander men. I have not been able to locate any cases from Solomon Islands, although occasionally this did occur in other colonial realms, such as in neighbouring Queensland, where the government tightly controlled Indigenous interracial marriage, and in colonial Papua and New Guinea.[48] There also appear to have been occasional female visitors to Tulagi who were loose with their morals. Wilfred Fowler has left us a tantalising description:

> I had met women who had stopped off the mail-boat in Tulagi. One had been a dipsomaniac who had refused to leave Sterling's Hotel and had later spent a month in hospital; the others had been trollops free with their favours until they had set up house with someone or had been shipped back to Sydney.[49]

All of this serves as an introduction to the complexity of Solomons gender and sexual relations in the 1910s to 1930s, which will be teased out in the remainder of this chapter. An element of moral panic was played out over many years.

Sexual misadventures

Having so many young male servants around the house had some disadvantages. There was a discernible level of sexual and racial tension in Tulagi and the main concern was the possibility of the sexual assault of white women by black men. Sexual assault by white men of black women seldom rated a mention and, if it did occur, like the cases of homosexuality, the culprit was shipped out quickly before legal proceedings began. Although it was never exactly stated, a close reading of the diary of teenager Edna Campbell suggests that she was not allowed to walk about alone on Tulagi. Letters written by her aunt Jessie Wilson also contain references to attempts at molestation in the 1920s and 1930s,

---

48 McGrath 2015, 254.
49 Fowler 1959, 211.

and disciplinary regulations were passed in the same decades. She was personally involved in one incident and was always worried about break-ins when her husband was away, arming herself with a revolver.

Tulagi's foreign female population was small when the White Women's Protection Ordinance was passed in Australian Papua in 1926. This included the death penalty for rape or attempted rape of any white woman or girl, which was intended to discourage sexual misbehaviour by indigenous males. Indecent assault of a European woman could be punished with life imprisonment, accompanied by a whipping and hard labour. In comparison, the rape of a Papuan woman carried a sentence of one to four years' imprisonment with hard labour. The draconian 1926 ordinance was motivated by an attack on a European woman in a Port Moresby street in August 1925 and two more similar attacks in December of that year. After the first attack, lieutenant-governor Sir Hubert Murray was besieged by white men demanding action and claiming that more attacks were likely. Most of the settlers understood very little about Papuan cultures and viewed Papuan adult males as primitive and unable to control their sexual desires. The issue was also used to undermine Murray's policies towards Papuans—partly motivated by those who wanted more economic development and land alienation than Murray allowed. However, after the December 1925 attacks, Murray moved quickly and, by January the next year, had passed the White Women's Protection Ordinance. Superseding the relevant section of the Queensland Criminal Code (which operated in Australian Papua), the ordinance was among the most severe legislation of its type in the British Empire, equalled only by a 1903 ordinance in Southern Rhodesia.[50] It was used several times between 1926 and 1934: one Papuan was hanged, one was sentenced to hang but was reprieved and several were imprisoned for assault. The ordinance was not repealed until 1958.[51] It was mentioned in the BSIP Advisory Council debates in relation to similar issues at Tulagi and elsewhere in the protectorate. There can be no doubt that the expatriate population was aware of what had happened across the Coral Sea. Deep-seated European racism was at the base of the decisions taken, creating severe punishments for nonconsensual heterosexual activity between indigenous men and expatriate women in Australian Papua and Solomon Islands.

---

50   Behlmer 2018, 312, n. 72.
51   Inglis 1974; Inglis 1982.

I have been able to locate eight reports of attacks on white women in the BSIP between 1916 and 1937, which is more than are recorded for Australian Papua. Most of the attacks were on nurses at the hospital, which undercuts any argument that the cases related to expatriate male 'ownership' of indigenous women and could point to availability and proximity as the causes. However, this may be a faulty Eurocentric interpretation of what Solomon Islanders understood as a household. Perhaps some of the male doctors were at fault, causing payback to fall on the nurses. Nurse Edith Elliot was assaulted by a Solomon Islander in June 1916, as was nurse E.G. Ralph in November 1922. Then, the next year, during the night of 29 October, Maifurua, a Malaitan constable, was apprehended in a house, the conclusion drawn being that he had intended to assault a European woman.[52] The report indicated that there had been other cases. A year later (1924), Jessie Watt (later Wilson) described an incident with another nurse:

> We had a native boy in the house the other night. Sister Wright was awakened by feeling his cold hand on her knee & thinking it was a frog that had jumped up tried to brush it off, but as it persisted she grabbed her torch & off he went like a shot over the balcony & was off. We called the sentry who gave chase, but so far nothing has been discovered. So now we both sleep in the one room, & have made up our minds to marry the first man who asks us, because this is no place for unprotected women. We have a sentry back & front to guard us (native police) but we have a feeling that it must have been a sentry who came in![53]

There was an incident the next year involving Sister Betty Laycock, who had been resting when a Fijian entered her room.[54] The upshot was that nurses were issued with revolvers and given lessons in how to use them; nurse Watt said: 'We keep one under the pillow all the time.'[55] Later, as Jessie Wilson, she still slept with a gun under her pillow if she stayed at home when her husband was away, although she usually went to stay in another house at such times.[56]

---

52 UQFL, Wilson Papers and Photographs, J.A. Watt to Mary, 9 May 1923.
53 ibid., 18 June 1924.
54 Boutilier 1974, 14; Boutilier 1984a, 197.
55 UQFL, Wilson Papers and Photographs, J.A. Watt to Mary, 18 June 1924.
56 ibid., 26 May 1925.

There is other evidence of similar problems on Tulagi, and the matter was discussed by the Advisory Council several times between 1915 and 1935. While house servants were trusted, there were many reports of prowlers, who may have been innocent members of the armed constabulary on night patrol. Nevertheless, the constabulary was not entirely innocent, as the 1923 incident involving Maifurua suggests, and in 1921 they celebrated Christmas Eve by raiding Chinatown and doing considerable damage. The *Planters' Gazette* thundered that:

> Acts of violence, even to white women, take place with impunity, and nearly every resident has personal experience of the insolence, or worse, of the lazy, incompetent and brutal constabulary.[57]

Flogging for serious offences was allowed under the Preservation of Order Regulation No. 18 of 1922, which was modified in 1925. The regulation seems to have been introduced for similar reasons to the ordinance in Papua, although without the death penalty. The 1925 BSIP regulation applied alongside any previous law or regulation:

> Male persons sixteen years of age or over may be flogged; male persons under that age may be whipped only. Flogging is by means of the ordinary cat-o'-nine-tails, whipping by means of a tamarind rod or light cane, etc. The maximum number of strokes in case of flogging is limited to twenty-one; in case of whipping, six to twelve strokes according to age. A Resident Commissioner may substitute a whipping for a flogging, though the offender may be sixteen years of age or over. All cases of flogging must be carried into effect in the presence of a medical officer—who is empowered to order the flogging to be suspended either wholly or after partial execution should he consider the offender to be physically unfit to undergo the punishment.
>
> No female shall be sentenced to corporal punishment, and no person shall be sentenced to undergo corporal punishment more than once for the same offence.
>
> Corporal punishment may not be inflicted in public.[58]

---

57 *Planters' Gazette*, 6, May 1922, 14.
58 A. Young 1926, 175. A cat-o'-nine-tails is a leather whip with nine frayed ends used for severe physical punishment. It was used by the British Navy and Army and in some judicial punishments.

The 1925 flogging regulation was disallowed under a consolidation of the same regulation (No. 8 of 1930), replaced the same year with a new regulation enabling more severe punishment of offenders found illegally in dwelling-houses:

> Any person found in any dwelling houses or any verandah or passage attached thereto or in any yard, garden or land adjacent to or within the curtilage of such dwelling-house shall be liable on conviction thereof to imprisonment with or without hard labour for any term not exceeding one year, or if a male person under sixteen years of age, may be whipped in lieu of such punishment.[59]

In November 1932, Levers' manager Major Frank R. Hewitt raised the matter again at the Advisory Council. Hewitt doubted that imprisonment was sufficient deterrent. He believed that prison was regarded as work without pay. Based on his conversations with Solomon Islanders, Hewitt felt that only physical punishment was feared and that the Judicial Commissioner should be given the option to order whipping or flogging in all cases. Two plantation owners on the council, Donald Mackinnon from Vella Lavella and Geoff Clift from Fera on Isabel, along with other planters on Guadalcanal, supported Hewitt.[60] The Judicial Commissioner did not agree to the extension of flogging, arguing that this measure was usually reserved for crimes with violence. The High Commissioner concurred but asked for details of all cases in this category over the previous five years.[61] English law was clear on the matter. Unless modified by a regulation under the WPHC, rape or attempted rape was not punishable by whipping, although any 'attempt to choke, strangle or suffocate with intent to commit any indictable offence' was punishable in this way.[62] Whipping was not introduced for this offence as the High Commissioner's investigation did not establish any evidence of prior cases.

The matter was discussed widely among BSIP expatriates. Hewitt and others raised their concerns at Advisory Council meetings in 1933. Clearly, concerns about the vulnerability of white women existed among the small European community. Then two incidents occurred during 1933 that forced the issue. Two white women were raped by Solomon Islanders, one

---

59   *WPHCG (S)*, 29 January 1932, 1930 Regulation No. 8, Section 3, Subsection 2 was approved on 16 December 1930, MAC, 17 November 1931, 28.
60   ibid.
61   ibid., 17 December 1932, MAC, 3 November 1931, 122.
62   ibid., 28 March 1935, MAC, 23 October 1934, Report by the President, RC F.N. Ashley, 29.

a planter's wife in Western District and the other the wife of a protectorate official.[63] Both cases resulted in convictions and Ashley recommended that the option of flogging be added to the 1930 regulation. Mackinnon, representing the plantation sector, was scathing about the incidents:

> I refer to the wave of crime of a serious nature that has been sweeping through the Protectorate for more than twelve months. No more severe blow to our prestige, humiliating to our standard of ethics or demoralizing to our system of native control could be struck than that which violates our sacred trust, the safety and honour of our womenfolk. As men we have in the past and will continue in the future to take such personal risks as may be encountered in dealing with an uncivilized, or partially civilized native race. That risk is probably little more to-day then we should meet in our own country, but the women of our race, resident here, are not so fortunate. They are, of necessity, frequently left unprotected for varying periods, and are thus at the mercy of the house servants and other natives whose duties may take them to the homesteads. Savage primitive passions when aroused have led to abominable acts, humiliating to our pride and dignity as white men, and shameful and dangerous to the women who look to us for protection ...
>
> Here at Tulagi, the Headquarters of Government and of the police establishment, you have failed to give adequate protection to white women, as recent records show, and you will continue to fail until unpractical idealism gives place to cold reason and stern justice, and the punishment is made to fit the crime.[64]

Mackinnon wanted corporal punishment introduced for offences against white women, crimes of violence and consumption of alcohol. Other nonofficial members of the Advisory Council supported him. Clift called for the lash and imprisonment to be introduced for assaults with violence on women. Hewitt was worried that expatriate residents would take the law into their own hands and lynch one of the perpetrators. Strangely, Anglican Bishop Baddeley abstained from the debate, possibly compromised by his position and faith, unable to condone either leniency or violent punishment.[65]

---

63 Laracy and Laracy 1980, 141; *WPHCG (S)*, 19 March 1934, MAC, 25 October 1933, 55.
64 *WPHCG (S)*, 19 March 1934, MAC, 25 October 1933, 55.
65 ibid., 56–57.

Resident commissioner Ashley did not believe that the extra punishment would act as a deterrent and instead advocated radical changes to the conditions under which Solomon Islander males were employed.[66] Nevertheless, Ashley gave in and asked the Judicial Commissioner to investigate Mackinnon's claims, but he found no knowledge of one of the cases, which rather strained Mackinnon's credibility. The Criminal Law Amendment Regulation (No. 7 of 1934) was created to provide the penalty of flogging in certain cases of criminal assaults on women. Unlike Papua's White Women's Protection Ordinance, there was no specification of race in the regulation, although it did specify that a medical practitioner had to be present at the punishment, which meant it could only take place at Tulagi. There were very few doctors in the protectorate and the only certainty of finding one was at Tulagi Hospital. Hewitt objected to limiting the floggings to Tulagi.

Even with the revised regulation, the issue of prowlers and illegal entry into houses and grounds continued. In 1937, Jessie Wilson used her gun on an intruder she caught creeping into her bedroom one night. Her shot parted his hair, making him easy to identify in the morning as he could not hide the new track through his coiffure.[67] Resident commissioner Ashley wrote to her, unofficially, expressing his concern:[68] 'I suppose one in my position ought not to, but, I do say "bravo" for firing at the fellow, it is a pity you didn't wing him.'[69]

In similar circumstances, lieutenant-governor Murray in Australian Papua had acquiesced to pressure to introduce the death penalty. When expatriate women were evacuated once war began, the debate ceased. The 1934 regulation was repealed in 1951 by the Criminal Law (Amendment) (Repeal) Regulation. One grim reminder of these days was the whipping platform that either survived at Tulagi or was rebuilt in Honiara, as it existed at the police headquarters at Rove in the early 1950s, although it was never used after the war.[70]

****

---

66   ibid., 28 March 1935, MAC, 23 October 1934, 29; Thacker et al. 1936, 118.
67   Information from her granddaughter, Kate Broadhurst, 10 July 2015.
68   UQFL, Wilson Papers and Photographs, RC F.N. Ashley to J.A. Wilson, 9 March 1937, to F.A.G. Wilson, 8 March 1937.
69   ibid.
70   Laracy and Laracy 1980, 142; Information from Alan Lindley, Adelaide, who joined the BSIP Police Force in 1952.

Plate 6.11 Pop Johnson is in the centre of the photograph
Dorothy Lotze is on the right holding her umbrella while her husband, Jack Lotze, holds their baby, Ruth. Vic Sheridan is partly obscured on the right edge of the photograph. The scene is the wharf at Tulagi.
Source: Suzanne Ellis Collection.

Solomon Islanders observed strict rules and taboos about sexual contact between males and females, violations of which carried severe punishments, even death. However, this never inhibited adventurous males from engaging in '*krip*' (creeping in the night)—a common practice. Familiarity with Europeans in domestic situations on Tulagi and on plantations and missions, and a growing resentment of colonial inequalities, led some to test their rights of access to houses and their occupants. As foreigners were not part of the socio-legal system, severe punishments were irrelevant if *kriping* foreigners. There were certainly flirtations between Solomon Islander women and expatriate males: these led to casual sexual encounters and sometimes permanent marriages and families. There may also have been flirtations between indigenous males and expatriate men and women, and in the Papuan and Solomons contexts there seem to be examples of expatriate women being careless in their interactions with indigenous males.[71] In the Solomons, Georgina Seton, wife of a planter, said there were women 'with too few clothes' who liked to swim 'in the nuddy [naked] and constituted a menace to the safety

---

71 Ralston 1975, 60–62.

of other expatriate women'.⁷² Pop Johnson's granddaughter Suzanne Ellis remembers him saying that one reason young white girls should be sent away for education was to remind them that 'brown was not the norm'. The family had experience of mixed-race marriages. The brother of Pop's wife Agnes, Carl Cronstedt, married three New Hebridean women.⁷³ Clearly, expatriate residents were conscious of possible sexual encounters and all knew of long-term mixed-race relationships.

The surviving descriptions of muscular Solomon Islander males clad in skimpy, tight *lap-laps* may indicate that a few expatriate males and females achieved some degree of voyeuristic pleasure from the sight. Were domestic servants viewed as being of neutral gender, to be treated as predictable and beyond sexual or personal feelings? Some of the literature on Pacific and Asian domestic servants suggests that *haus-bois* were usually regarded as nonsexual. But nothing destabilised colonial power more than sexual encounters between indigenous servants and expatriate women and men. We will never know if Tulagi's night 'creepers' indicate a general change in behaviour towards foreign women. It is also possible that the incidents related to revenge on individual expatriate males who had transgressed with indigenous women and who were being punished via their own womenfolk. Although alcohol may have fuelled some aberrant behaviour, if we start from the premise that Solomon Islanders in the 1920s and 1930s behaved rationally within the limits imposed on them by their customary upbringing (which was morally strict) and their exposure to urban situations, there would have been predictable cultural consequences to personal interactions.

The same circumstances that provoked the draconian ordinance in Australian Papua existed on Tulagi. However, in Papua, Murray had much more power to rule and could pass special ordinances never possible in the BSIP, where decisions were checked by the High Commissioner in Fiji and ultimately by the Colonial Office in London. Passing a law as severe as the one in Papua would have been difficult in the protectorate. Racial ideology depicted Solomon Islanders as much lower on the human scale than Westerners and Darwinism gave justification to assumptions of biological superiority. 'Experts', including Woodford and some other officials and missionaries, seemed certain that Solomon Islanders were heading for

---

72 Boutilier 1984a, 197.
73 Information from Suzanne Ellis, 7 June 2016.

extinction.[74] Images of lustful but childlike savages were common in the literature of the time. Regardless of personal friendships that developed, it is not hard to imagine that European and Chinese residents were wary of rumoured propensities for violence and uncontrolled sexual passion by Solomon Islander males.

The evidence in Jessie Wilson's letters and other sources confirms that there were tensions at Tulagi that could easily lead to sexual misadventure. Gender and sexuality were only two of many social categories woven into the imperial agenda. There were differences in Solomon Islands and particularly in the Tulagi enclave, largely relating to the smallness of the foreign community, the difficult geography of a 900-island colonial territory and the lateness of the arrival of the colonial state, with no formal colonisation until the late 1890s. Manipulation of male labour, both in overseas colonies and within the protectorate, was one key to social changes, although it was hardly unique in the colonised world. The domestic scene around Tulagi was part of all this. Chapter 8 carries on the arguments about Pacific urbanisation and the type of societies that evolved.

---

74   Rivers 1922; Akin 2013, 9–10, 114–22.

7

Silk, white helmets and Malacca canes

> Dull leisure hours were not known at Gavutu, unless fever had lain one low. Business visitors and others enjoyed the company of these fine fellows. One of their number, a Sports Committee in himself, organized cricket, football, shooting parties, tennis, launch trips up miles of beautiful inland waters, and picnic parties. The new chum, distaining these for more inspiring adventure, could supply himself with refreshments, a bag, boat and rifle, and wander into the mangrove swamps of Gela, near at hand, to stalk the elusive alligator.
>
> — Joseph Dickinson, 1927[1]

This chapter focuses on the 1930s, before the Pacific War brought destruction. Tulagi was a small outpost of the great British Empire and Empire Day (24 May, Queen Victoria's birthday) was always celebrated. One clear indication of how rapidly change came to the protectorate is to compare Empire Day in 1914 with that in 1934. In 1914, the year before Woodford departed, a squadron of the paramilitary nationalist Legion of Frontiersmen[2] sailed to Levers' Ilu plantation on Guadalcanal, led by the government ship *Belema* and the Melanesian Mission's *Southern Cross*, accompanied by a flotilla of 10 launches and schooners. The squadron formed a guard of honour as the official party landed and festivities and a banquet proceeded in a transformed plough shed. Florrie Woodford presented the prizes after a competition at the rifle range—one of them to

---

1   Dickinson 1927, 32.
2   This was a paramilitary group formed in Britain in 1905, based on an idealised concept of empire.

her son, Harold. Dancing continued late into the night to the strains of a mandolin, the festivities ending with the national anthem and *Auld Lang Syne*. The next day, the same shed became a church for a commemorative service led by the Bishop of Melanesia before the vessels returned to Tulagi. It was a celebration conducted in isolation from the world. On Empire Day in 1934, by contrast, Royal Empire Society branches around the world held celebratory dinners. The speeches in Sydney were transmitted to Tulagi and wireless messages were sent from around the British Pacific, including from Tulagi.[3] The sense of isolation had been overcome, although the loyal sentiment was the same.

The only prewar census of the BSIP was in April 1931, which established the protectorate's population was 94,066: 89,568 Melanesians, 3,847 Polynesians, 478 Europeans, 164 Chinese, eight Japanese and one Malay. Tulagi and Gavutu harbours were the small hub of it all, with around 200 permanent foreign residents, a similar number of Solomon Islanders and an itinerant population of thousands of indentured labourers passing through. Outlying traders, planters and missionaries made trips to Tulagi to board the overseas steamers, purchase supplies, seek medical advice, pick up their mail, return labourers or just relax and socialise. Communications with the outside world had improved, not only because of radio transmissions but also through better passenger, postal and freight services. Although living conditions had become more comfortable, the costs of running a household were high.

In 1931, BP's headquarters at Makambo was managed by J.C.M. Scott, whose house perched atop the hill, and Levers' main base at Gavutu was under the control of Major F.R. Hewitt, whose home was down on the shore.[4] Ashley, Resident Commissioner since 1929, was ensconced in the second residency, which was being eaten by termites and was condemned. Demolished in May 1932, it had large rooms but smaller verandahs than its replacement and only one bathroom, in a concrete bunker underneath—the moisture attracting the termites to the floorboards above.

---

3 *SCL*, November 1914, 168–70; Hadlow 2016, 137.
4 Cameron 1923, 278.

7. SILK, WHITE HELMETS AND MALACCA CANES

Plate 7.1 The cooks at the squadron of the Legion of Frontiersmen's outing to Guadalcanal, 1914
Source: BM, Thomas Edge-Partington Photographic Collection.

Plate 7.2 The participants in the squadron of the Legion of Frontiersmen's outing, 1914
Charles and Florrie Woodford are in the centre of the second front row.
Source: BM, Thomas Edge-Partington Photographic Collection.

Plate 7.3 The armed constabulary marching with drums and bugles
Source: UQFL, Wilson Papers and Photographs.

Plate 7.4 The Tulagi Harbour in 1938, looking towards the port and Chinatown
Source: NASI, Nurse Talbot Collection, in ACOM Collection.

Plate 7.5 The Tulagi beachfront in 1939
Source: NASI, Nurse Talbot Collection, in ACOM Collection.

TULAGI

Plate 7.6 The third residency, completed in 1934, showing the armed constabulary guard house
Source: BM, Sir Ronald Garvey Photographic Collection.

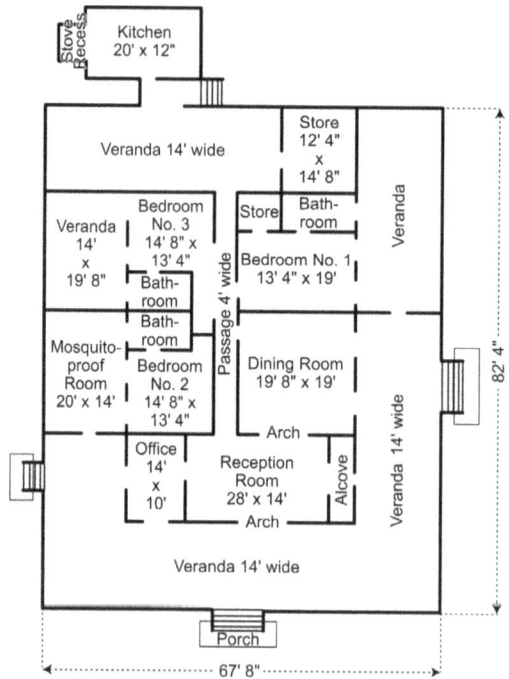

Figure 7.1 The third residency, 1934
Source: WPHC Archives, 3166, 1932 BSIP Residency Building at Tulagi, redrawn by Vincent Verheyen.

The final Tulagi residency was completed in 1934 at a cost of £2,850 and was again a Queenslander-style wooden structure with broad verandahs. The High Commissioner advocated for a concrete building with plaster walls but was politely overruled due to the costs. That would have required importing sand and gravel from Guadalcanal and carrying it up the ridge, which would have more than doubled the expense; furthermore, a timber lining was considered to be cooler. There were three bedrooms, each opening on to a private verandah that could be used for sleeping, if desired. One bedroom abutted a screened section of the verandah and was designated as private quarters for important guests 'from non-malarious countries'.[5] The house was built by three Chinese and six Solomon Islanders, as well as convict labour, who were used to level the site and fetch and carry—all supervised by a Chinese 'head mechanic'. The new residency was bigger than its predecessor, the main difference being the 4.3-metre-wide verandahs, which allowed greater focus on verandah living and entertaining. Similarly, the ceilings were 4.3 metres high, to aid air circulation. Each bedroom had a built-in wardrobe and its own bathroom with a plunge bath and shower, wash basin and flush toilet. There was a 24,200-litre water tank—twice the size of the previous one—and the toilets worked through a septic system. Reed shutters were provided around all the verandahs. The residency was the only government-owned house with electricity. The power plant also supplied the hospital and Carpenters' store.[6]

Social institutions and networks

When novelist Beatrice Grimshaw visited Tulagi in 1909, she described the port as a hard-drinking Pacific town dominated by men, where whisky flowed freely. When she returned in 1929, she noted that 'Tulagi had given up violent drinking, now, and there were a good many more white people'.[7] She was being kind to resident commissioner Kane, whose drunkenness sometimes prevented him from completing his duties.[8]

---

5   BSIP *AR* 1933, 12; WPHCA, 3166, 1932 BSIP Residency Building at Tulagi, See plans and Superintendent of Public Works Department to Government Secretary, 30 September 1932.
6   Horton 1965, 11.
7   Grimshaw 1931, 209, 213.
8   Boutilier 1983, 48–49; Boutilier 1984a, 186.

Outside domesticity, there was a set of social institutions in the Tulagi enclave similar to those in other Pacific colonies. In the main, they were very British with Australian tinges, and relied on class, race, gender and sexual concepts that were standard in imperial and dominion settings during the first half of the twentieth century. The variation was the extensive Chinese community. Although there are valid comparisons to be made with other urban centres in neighbouring colonies, Tulagi housed a government in miniature with a touch of 'Gilbert and Sullivan'. And we should not assume that we are dealing with a homogeneous expatriate community or that it was identical to urban communities in neighbouring colonies.

The Gela Group had been an Anglican preserve since the 1860s and 1870s, although—strangely for the period—Christianity was not central to the Tulagi community. In early decades, there was no formal Christian presence, probably because the Anglican base at Siota was nearby through Mboli Passage. There was constant traffic between Tulagi and Siota and, from 1911, an Anglican school operated on Bungana Island, about 9 kilometres from Tulagi. The government had erected a lighthouse on Bungana—the only one in the Solomons—to direct ships into Tulagi Harbour. In late 1919, the diocesan headquarters was moved from Norfolk Island to Siota, and a theological college for training clergy for the Solomons opened there in 1921. After long discussions during the 1910s and early 1920s, English officially replaced Mota as the language of instruction in the mission's schools in Solomon Islands, and in meetings and services. St Luke's Cathedral, beautifully constructed and decorated in local styles, was built at Siota in 1928, and was a beacon for Anglicanism until it was destroyed during the war. From the beginning of 1937, the Sisters of the Cross Order took over Bungana as a girls' boarding school and orphanage. Soon after, the Anglican headquarters was shifted from Siota to Taroaniara, close to Bungana.[9] Taroaniara's proximity to Tulagi and Bungana made it more convenient than Siota (see Map 1.2). In early decades, there were regular Anglican services held in the court house on Tulagi, and there is evidence of an SSEM gospel meeting on the island in 1928, although there were no early church buildings.[10]

---

9   Cross 1979, 21.
10 Maetoloa 1985; Fowler 1959, 178.

7. SILK, WHITE HELMETS AND MALACCA CANES

Plate 7.7 Anglican mission house at Bungana Island, 1906
Source: NASI, ACOM Collection, J.W. Beattie Collection.

Plate 7.8 The Anglican Melanesian Brothers when Charles Fox was a member, circa 1938
Source: NASI, Nurse Talbot Collection, in ACOM Collection.

Plate 7.9 The Anglican headquarters at Siota in the 1930s
Source: NASI, ACOM Collection.

Plate 7.10 The Anglican Christ the King Church, built on Tulagi in 1937
Source: NASI, ACOM Collection.

Missionaries constantly came to and from Tulagi as they picked up supplies and staff from the steamers and saw off colleagues travelling overseas. They availed themselves of the wireless telegraph and postal, banking and hospital services, and purchased supplies from Chinatown and the big trading companies. Starting in 1922, a member of the clergy always sat on the BSIP Advisory Council. The Marist Catholics leased land on Tulagi between 1915 and 1923, on the Sasape side of Chinatown, although their block was partly covered in mangroves. They seem never to have proceeded with any permanent presence until they constructed a church in 1936 on the site of what had been Elkington's Hotel.[11] Probably to counter this Catholic presence, the Church of England built its Christ the King Church on Tulagi in 1937. Map 8.1 (from 1942) shows the site of the Anglican Church on the beach between the Catholic Church and the prison. The Melanesian Brotherhood (an Anglican indigenous religious order) provided a service each day and had a base on the island. There were also monthly visits from the clergy at Siota. Once their church was complete, the Catholics based New Zealander Father James (Jim) Wall permanently on Tulagi. In the 1940s, Wall ministered to the Langalanga wharf labourers and other seamen at Honiara; it seems likely he did the same thing on prewar Tulagi.[12] There were also small chapels for the labourers on Makambo and Gavutu, built from local materials.[13] The Seventh-day Adventist Mission leased land on Tulagi (under the name Australasian Conference Association Limited), adjoining that of the Malayta Company. There is no evidence of churches on either block.

There were several ways to associate and seek camaraderie. A branch of the Masons began in 1934, with Anglican Bishop Baddeley serving until 1938 as the first Master of Lodge Melanesia. He was succeeded by J.C.M. Scott, BP manager at Makambo (in 1939), Spearline Wilson (1939–40), James Basil Hicks (1940–41) and M.J. Bernhardt (1941–49).[14] Once the war began in Europe, in 1939, a Red Cross Society was established to raise money. Fairs were organised for residents of the Tulagi enclave and nearby plantations, with £800 sent to England in April 1940. The next year, in October, Tulagi held its first (and last) agricultural show, exhibiting produce from across the protectorate.[15]

---

11   WPHCA, No. 2785 of 1936, A/Lands Commissioner A.H. Wilson to A/RC N.S.B. Kidson, 12 August 1936, Bishop W.H. Baddeley to HC WPHC, 1 September 1936 [telegram], A/RC N.S.B. Kidson to HC WPHC, 14 September 1936, A/HC C.J. Juxton T. Barton to Baddeley, 27 November 1936.
12   WPHCA, No. 2785 of 1936, Bishop W.H. Baddeley to HC WPHC, 1 September 1936 [telegram], A/RC N.S.B. Kidson to HC WPHC, 14 September 1936; O'Brien 1995, 226.
13   Fox 1938.
14   UQFL, Wilson Papers and Photographs, Programme for the Installation of R.A. Lawson, Masonic Temple, Honiara, 8 September 1967.
15   ibid., F.A.G. Wilson to J.A. Wilson, 27 September 1939, J.A. Wilson to Mary, 30 May 1940; Cross 1979, 27.

Plate 7.11 St Luke's Cathedral at Siota, dedicated in 1928
Source: NASI, ACOM Collection.

Plate 7.12 The altar of St Luke's Cathedral, Siota, when first built
Source: NASI, ACOM Collection.

Plate 7.13 The final ornate structure of the altar of St Luke's Cathedral, in the 1930s
Source: NASI, ACOM Collection.

The Chinese community—always a major part of Tulagi—was self-contained and continued its own religious and cultural rituals. There was no central Chinese temple, although there would have been small altars in houses and trade stores, and a branch of the Guomindang operated on Tulagi from the mid-1920s. There must also have been annual celebrations for Chinese New Year.

War service

One of the social links across the European community was war service—in British India, the Boer War, other parts of the British Empire and World War I. Although this network was informal, in the period during which Tulagi operated, it would have provided an essential social glue. Several men always used their war titles of captain or major—an assertion of rank and respect. Men with no rank to flaunt would still have shared a sense of camaraderie with the others. There are patterns elsewhere of war veterans looking after each other, and with no formal veterans' association in the Solomons, undoubtedly this occurred. They had something in common that others did not share or fully comprehend. Captain Norman Kidson, the long-serving Government Secretary in the 1920s and 1930s, and several times acting Resident Commissioner, gained his title from war service. Captain Ernest Nelson Turner, the Police Commandant, joined the Australian Army Flying Corps in 1915.[16] Levers' manager Major Frank Hewitt was awarded a Military Cross and resident commissioner Kane held a similar award. Major William V. Jardine Blake, Police Subinspector during the 1920s and acting Treasurer in the late 1930s, also used his military title, as did Major Eustace Sandars, who held many positions, including Government Secretary. Captain Francis Noel Ashley, Resident Commissioner between 1929 and 1939, always used his military title.

Some of the older men had served in India and the Boer War in South Africa. Owen G. Meredith, an Isabel planter, had property in Chinatown in the 1920s. He had been in the British India Army before heading to the Solomon Archipelago in about 1910.[17] Long-serving public servant

---

16 See National Archives of Australia and Archives New Zealand, *Discovering Anzacs*, 'NELSON-TURNER Ernest: Service Number—3753 Captain: Place of Birth—Bristol England: Place of Enlistment—Brisbane QLD: Next of Kin—(Sister) JAGON Minerva Victoria', available from: discoveringanzacs.naa.gov.au/browse/records/307051.
17 Golden 1993, 339.

Pop Johnson was in the British Army between 1896 and 1903, reaching the rank of sergeant in the Boer War.[18] William de Courcey Browne, later an employee of both Levers and BP, served in the Boer War as a trooper in the 2nd NSW Mounted Rifles.[19] William Bell, perhaps the most famous member of the protectorate staff due to his violent death in 1927, had fought in the Boer War.[20] Harold ('Marco') Markham, later a trader at Ontong Java and a convivial planter on New Georgia, arrived in the Solomons in 1908, having served as a trooper in the Boer War.[21]

Another Englishman, Philip Sydney Palmer, also served in the Boer War, then remained in South Africa and married Harriet Wheatley, sister of Solomons planter and trader Norman Wheatley. Harriet died during childbirth in South Africa, after which Palmer moved his two boys to England, where they were adopted by their grandfather and Palmer's brother, who was a Staffordshire doctor. Philip Palmer arrived at Tulagi in August 1910, moving to New Georgia, where he became Wheatley's partner on Laperti plantation for three years. Growing tired of Wheatley's relaxed, rather unconventional style, Palmer became an independent trader and owner of Kaola plantation on San Jorge Island, in narrow Otanga Passage between San Jorge and Isabel islands. In 1914, he sailed to Sydney to enlist in the Australian Light Horse, returning to the Solomons with his two sons, Ambrose Ernest (Ernie), born in 1904, and Phillip Francis Donald, born in 1906. After spending a short time with his brother-in-law, Palmer took his sons to Kaola, where he lived with Anne Nancy, an Isabel woman.[22] Ernie became famous as a labour recruiter and lived in the Solomons until his death in 1976. Philip junior became a plantation overseer and interisland skipper; he left the Solomons in about 1936 to marry and became manager of BP's Fanning Islands plantations in the Crown Colony of Gilbert and Ellice Islands .[23] Another son, Norman Kitchener Palmer, born in 1928, became the eleventh Anglican Bishop of Melanesia and the second Archbishop of the Anglican

---

18 ibid., 95–97; Frederick England Johnson, Boer War record, 5 November 1901, in the possession of Suzanne Ellis, Toowoomba, Queensland.
19 Golden 1993, 159, 248. See Australian War Memorial, *Pre First World War Conflicts Nominal Rolls*, 'William de Courcey Browne', available from: www.awm.gov.au/people/rolls/R1442317/.
20 Keesing and Corris 1980.
21 Golden 1993, 244.
22 ibid., 334–37; Moore 2013, entry for Norman Kitchener Palmer.
23 Golden 1993, 103–08.

Province of Melanesia. The Boer War carried through in his middle name. The blood of the Palmers and the Wheatleys was in his veins, through an illicit liaison Philip Palmer senior had with one of his nieces.[24]

Several of the BSIP colonial elite had served in World War I. Resident commissioner Marchant (1939–43) had received a bullet wound in his throat during the war, an injury that caused him considerable discomfort for the remainder of his life. Resident commissioner Kane served in World War I, as did resident commissioner Noel, who in 1919 was an officer in the British Army in India.[25] Ragna Hyne, Chief Magistrate in the 1930s, served in Wold War I.[26] Anglican Bishop Walter Baddeley (1932–47) had been in the Royal Sussex Regiment, 8th Battalion. He then joined the Royal Survey Regiment, reached the rank of acting lieutenant-colonel and commanded a battalion. Baddeley received a Distinguished Service Order, Military Cross and Bar, and was mentioned four times in dispatches. He never used his military title, which would have sat badly with being a bishop.[27] One important visiting official who also had war rank was Sir Harry Moorhouse, the 1928 WPHC Special Commissioner who investigated the Kwaio massacre. He had been in the British Army since the 1890s and returned to active service during World War I, reaching the rank of lieutenant-colonel. He served at Gallipoli in Turkey, where he was awarded a Distinguished Service Order.[28]

Other members of the permanent administrative staff left to serve in World War I or served in the war before arriving in the protectorate. For instance, Ralph B. Hill first arrived in the Solomons in 1909 and was District Magistrate for Gizo and Malaita until 1915, when he joined the British Army. He returned in 1920 as District Officer at Aola (1920–25)

---

24 Struben 1963, 5; Information from Transform Aqorau, grandson of Milton Talasasa, January 2017.
25 *Planters' Gazette*, 3, August 1921, 3.
26 *The Queenslander*, 21 December 1918.
27 See Moore (2013) for entries on William Sydney Marchant and Walter Hubert Baddeley. During the Pacific War, Baddeley remained in the protectorate, living at Tantalau in the Malaitan mountains in the early months, before returning to his Anglican headquarters at Taroaniara on Gela. After the Allies arrived, he was appointed Chaplain and Lieutenant-Colonel to the Fijian Battalion. Baddeley also held a position with the New Zealand Navy. His refusal to leave the Solomons increased his *mana* (spiritual power) both with Solomon Islanders (for whom he became a rare symbol of British strength) and with the Allied troops, particularly the Americans, who admired him. He was awarded an honorary doctorate in divinity from Columbia University in 1944 and the US Medal of Freedom in 1945.
28 See Alchetron.com, 'Harry Moorhouse', available from: alchetron.com/Harry-Moorhouse-1230903-W.

and Isabel (1927–29),[29] and also acted as Resident Commissioner. There were members of the joint Australian and New Zealand Army Corps (Anzac); Captain Turner, mentioned above, was one of these. Plantation manager Geoff Clift, who featured in the 1927 attack on the Kwaio, and his brother Dudley both enlisted when World War I broke out. They joined the Australian Light Horse Regiment; Dudley was killed in action in 1917 and Geoff returned to take up his old life.[30] Another Anzac was Spearline Wilson, who enlisted from Fiji, where he worked for the CSR. He joined the Australian Imperial Forces and went ashore at Gallipoli on the first day, was wounded, invalided out and then spent the rest of the war on the Western Front. His hearing was affected by his war service and for most of his life he wore hearing aids. Another man with a war injury was Leslie (Jerry) Keen, who served in the British Army during World War I. He suffered a serious head wound, which required the fitting of a steel plate in his skull. Trained as a fitter and turner, he was an ideal employee to take charge of a workshop and plantation, which was his position at Gozoruru and Hivo on Isabel. He and his wife, Amelia (Milly), then ran a trade store and he also worked as a labour recruiter.[31]

Other residents were also involved in the war. Bob Crookshank joined the British Navy in 1907, served in World War I and then moved to the Solomons and used his gratuity to purchase the lugger *Winton*. An excellent navigator, he set himself up as a trader and labour recruiter.[32] Kenneth Dalrymple-Hay (often just styled as Ken Hay) joined the Field Artillery Brigade in 1915.[33] C. Maxwell, a planter and trader from Isabel, and F. Ashton ('Snowy') Rhoades, manager of Lavoro plantation on Guadalcanal, both served in World War I.[34] Herbert Lockington (Bert) Freshwater arrived in the Solomons in 1913, working at Boroni plantation on Makira and later on another plantation on Uki Island. When war broke out, he returned to Australia, enlisted, fought in Europe and then returned to Uki and worked for the Melanesian Mission.[35] Cadet officer Kenneth C. Lillies, who was killed with William Bell in 1927, had served in World War I. Born in London in 1899, he had been a lieutenant in the British Army and subsequently was employed in the

---

29 Golden 1993, 409.
30 ibid., 164.
31 ibid., 341–43.
32 Struben 1963, 14.
33 See Australian War Memorial, Kenneth Dalrymple-Hay Service Record No. 9910.
34 *Planters' Gazette*, 6, May 1922, 4; Hadlow 2016, 125–26; Horton 1965, 22.
35 Golden 1993, 309.

Federated Malay States by the Telegraph Construction and Maintenance Company, before he joined the Colonial Service and was posted to the BSIP.[36] Major I. (Dick) Harper served in World War I before leasing land and operating a copra plantation on Mandoliana Island in the Gela Group from the early 1920s until 1942.[37] Charles Hubert Vivian (Viv) Hodges, born in 1899, enlisted in World War I from Australia and served on the Western Front. He arrived in the Solomons in 1921 and worked as an overseer and then plantation manager for Levers and for the Fairymead Sugar Company.[38] Jim Buchanan, an English engineer, had a business on Tulagi before he established small plantations in the Gela Group. He enlisted in World War I, after which he returned to his plantations. Niels R. Schroder, a relative of the successful early traders Oscar and Theodor Svensen, arrived in the Solomons in the 1900s. He enlisted in the Australian Imperial Forces in 1914, fought in France and returned to the islands after the war as a ship's captain and plantation manager and owner on Guadalcanal. Syd ('Pansy') Elder, well known as a ship's captain and engineer in the Solomons in the 1920s, had served as a seaman on a minesweeper during World War I.[39]

This incomplete list gives an idea of the war service of some of the European men in the protectorate. In such a small community, they probably all knew each other, and when their paths crossed in the Tulagi enclave, war and its physical and mental consequences would have been discussed. The camaraderie of war and the British Empire, combined with Christianity, the Masons, the Red Cross, the Guomindang and Chinese religious ceremonies and celebrations to create the mix of social relationships that made the Tulagi enclave work. Race, ethnicity and class were also distinguishing characteristics in the enclave's society.

---

36   Keesing and Corris 1980, 106–07.
37   Golden 1993, 101. Major was his Christian name.
38   ibid., 189.
39   ibid., 117, 157, 170, 172–73, 181.

TULAGI

Ethnicity and class in the British Pacific

Most of Tulagi's early settlers were of British origin, although often filtered through the Pacific and Australasian colonies. There were also Scandinavian,[40] German[41] and French[42] settlers, many of them ex-seamen. Some had left ships passing through the Solomons and settled, took up work with existing traders and saved or borrowed money to go into business for themselves and later obtained land for plantations. Many were either migrants from Europe or the children of migrants, and arrived in the Solomons via Queensland, that colony having provided assisted passages for migrants from Britain and Europe, particularly from Scandinavia and Germany.[43] Many residents had connections to New South Wales or Queensland, even dating back to the overseas labour trade days, which ended in the 1900s.[44] Others had Fiji labour trade connections: even Charles Woodford had travelled on a Fiji labour vessel and William Bell had been a recruiter and a government agent.[45] These early European residents were self-made men who rose or fell according to their abilities.

The most unusual expatriate resident was George Washington Ezekiel Richardson, also called 'Dick America', an African-American born in Philadelphia in about 1866. A sailor, he arrived in north Queensland and worked in Torres Strait, based on Thursday Island as a sailmaker, pearl-diver and lugger master. He arrived in the Solomons in 1905 and, after a beginning collecting and curing bêche-de-mer, he worked for Levers, settling on Santa Cruz Island with his local wife. The couple moved to

---

40   The Scandinavian element is extensive. Partly, it may relate to sponsored Scandinavian migration to Queensland in the 1870s and 1880s. See ibid., for Lars Nielsen (p. 68), Julius Walter Anderson (76), Solfren Nerdrum (131), J.G.B. Nerdrum (131), Carl Oscar Svensen (131–35), Theodor Svensen (131–35), Anton Daniel Olsen (151–52), Jack Svensen (153–55), Leif Schroder (170), Niels Reinhardt Schroder (172–73), Albert Molkin Andresen (183–85), Frederick Erickson (224), Charles Olsen (288), John Schroder (315–19), Bert Johnson (344), Julius Pien (372) and Paul Edward Allen Mason (Mikkelsen) (381–83). See also Hviding 2015a; Hviding 2015b.
41   See Golden 1993: for Fred Howard (p. 278), Charles Peter Munster (289), Harry Jacobson (291–92), Heinrich (Henry) Küper (292, 299–301), Franz Malcher (348–49), John Heinrich Mittelheuser (395), Frederick Christian Mittelheusler (397), Harry Hoerler (398) and Schwartz (398).
42   ibid., Jacques Benqui (p. 138), Charles Trachet (138), Jean Pouret (140), Edmund Peter Pratt (215–17), Jean Peter (Johnnie) Pratt (218–19) and William and Tom Dabelle (285–86).
43   Hviding 2015a; Hviding 2015b.
44   See Golden 1993: for W.R. Withrington (p. 71), John (Jack) Cooper (127), Theodor Svensen (131), Claude L. Bernays (158), John (Jock) Cromar (221–22), William Hamilton (225–26), James Gibbins (235), Oliver Burns (239–41) and Stanley Bateman (281). See also McLaren 1923; Cromar 1935.
45   See Golden (1993, 124) for J. Robinson. See also Clark 2011; Lawrence 2014, 76–78; Keesing and Corris 1980, 49.

Marou Bay, Makira, where he accidentally blew off his right arm while dynamiting fish. One of the legends about him is that he sent for an artificial arm by mail order and fitted it himself. He remained a small-scale, never very successful, trader and planter, remembered for his excellent collection of gramophone records. Powerfully built, a good singer and father of many children, he referred to himself as the 'biggest white man on Makira' and was said to be totally accepted among the white expatriate community. He died in 1949.[46]

In the colonial Pacific, the strictures of class divisions from the empire and its colonies and dominions did not always survive. An aristocratic background was not a good qualification for success. Having attended Eton or Oxford meant little when sailing in cyclonic weather or dealing with a crowd of angry Malaitan labourers. However, class backgrounds did play a role and, particularly in the BSIP administration, education was important. Some residents, including several resident commissioners and district officers, had a good education from the best schools in England and degrees from Oxford and Cambridge. A working-class, middle-class or upper-class background in British society and in the colonies was always a factor to consider, although some residents achieved status through their positions and hard work in the protectorate. It seems that several 'remittance men' lived in the protectorate, maintained financially by their upper-middle-class and aristocratic families—on the condition that they stayed far away. They drifted in and out of respectable circles. Equally numerous were 'beachcombers' from an earlier Pacific era who lived a frontier life, often drinking excessively.

There were residents with Australian pastoral backgrounds, either the children of landowners or ex-pastoral workers. Just as colonial east New Guinea attracted Australian adventurers, so too did the BSIP. These were places where a young man willing to work hard could make good. There was also a flow of settlers and workers back and forth between the two colonial territories. However, as with New Guinea, in the BSIP, they brought with them an element of Australian frontier racism, which certainly would have guided the attitudes of men who earlier had participated in the Queensland labour trade. The treatment of labourers

---

46   Golden 1993, 290.

on Solomons plantations was often brutal and owed much to the way Australians treated Aborigines, Torres Strait Islanders and immigrant Pacific Islanders, now known as Australian South Sea Islanders.

I know of only one person with a European aristocratic title in the protectorate: Spanish Castilian Baroness Eugênie lived on Guadalcanal in the 1900s. Her husband was Thomas Harding, an Englishman who was part-owner with George Darbyshire of Pennduffryn (later Berande) plantation between 1905 and 1909. Their living conditions were lavish, replete with a substantial house, elegant furnishings and a fine garden. The couple had met in South America. Baroness Eugênie (Mrs Harding) supposedly spoke eight languages and kept her coronet and jewels locked up in an overseas bank.[47] The most interesting long-term resident in terms of class background was Nicholas Charles Tindal, scion of an aristocratic English family. His father was a vice-admiral and his grandfather was Lord Chief Justice of England.[48] Just how Nick Tindal reached the Solomons is unclear, but it was probably through either his life as a seaman or his Australian connections. He settled in the Shortland Islands in the 1890s and married Minnie Thursa Louise, daughter of Melinda and John Champion Macdonald of Fauro, one of the earliest expatriate families. Minnie had married Edward Austen in Santa Ana in 1883—probably the first foreign marriage in the archipelago. After Austen died, she married Tindal. They became prosperous planters and traders. Both died in the 1900s, although the family connections with Solomon Islands continued until the 1970s. As early protectorate residents, the first Tindals carried considerable respect.[49]

The father of Commissioner for Lands Stanley Knibbs was a prominent Australian, knighted in 1923, but we can only speculate as to how this affected Stanley's social position on Tulagi. However, there were many who readily assumed a class status that a casual observer might have thought exceeded that of Tindal, the baroness or the son of a knight. One of these was Donald MacKinnon, who arrived in 1914 from Calcutta and took up

---

47 London 1915a, 369, 480; Golden 1993, 140–49.
48 The Tindal (Tyndall) family pedigree dates back to the eleventh century, descending from Anglo-Saxon nobility from Northumberland, Norman nobility and the royal Scottish house of Dunkeld. Nick Tindal's father was Vice-Admiral Louis Symonds Tindal (1810–76), son of Sir Nicholas Tindal (1776–1846), Lord Chief Justice of England (1829–45). His uncle, Charles Tindal, was a governor of the Bank of England, whose descendants formed an Australian branch of the family.
49 Golden 1993, 365–71. See also the entry for Nicholas Conyngham Tindal in Wikipedia, available from: en.wikipedia.org/wiki/Nicholas_Conyngham_Tindal.

land at Jurio on Vella Lavella. He became a well-known plantation owner, served on the Advisory Council during the 1930s and was awarded an Order of the British Empire in 1938.[50] MacKinnon was 'locally grown' upper class. Women seem to have stood by their class dignity more than did men, probably because their power was usually achieved by association with men rather than through a clearly defined job.[51] Men also needed to be physically fit and capable of manual labour as part of their occupations, whether they were sailors, surveyors or plantation managers. Although headquarters staff could be less active, there was little room for class differences when clearing jungle, launching canoes through the surf or marching long distances into the mountains.

European women usually did not have to undertake physical labour, although on plantations and mission stations this was more likely. It was possible to be a 'lady' in the Solomons. For instance, Vera Clift considered herself part of the Australian late colonial upper class. She was brought up on Bellevue pastoral station at Wivenhoe on the Brisbane River, Queensland, which in 1920 played host to Edward, Prince of Wales, later King Edward VIII.[52] The next year she visited the wife of acting resident commissioner Ralph Hill, when she met John McElhone (Jack) Clift, an influential plantation owner. Against her family's wishes, they married in the same year. She looked down on those she labelled Tulagi's 'dregs of Fiji'.[53] Her husband was from a prominent NSW pastoral and political family, from Breeza pastoral station near Gunnedah and Potts Point in Sydney. That they returned to Australia financially ruined by the Great Depression seemed not to have mattered in Vera's 1970s assessment of her high social position in the BSIP.[54] Like the others, Vera Clift often passed through Tulagi, where presumably she observed class boundaries. Georgina Seton (née Cameron), another leading expatriate woman, also had pastoral links, having been brought up by Scottish parents on Welltown pastoral station near Goondiwindi, Queensland, a property running 100,000 sheep.[55] In 1929, she married Carden Wyndham Seton, a planter from the Western Solomons. She was the only published woman

---

50   Golden 1993, 263.
51   Boutilier 1984a, 196–98; Bulbeck 1992, 85, quoting Daphney Bridgland in Papua New Guinea.
52   See the entry for Bellevue Homestead in Wikipedia, available from: en.wikipedia.org/wiki/Bellevue_Homestead.
53   Golden 1993, 163–69.
54   Rutledge 1974.
55   'Obituary of Donald McLeod Cameron', *Queensland Country Life*, 22 October 1943; Boutilier 1984a, 177.

author from the prewar protectorate, writing a novel set on a copra plantation. Both Setons were evacuated just before the Pacific War began and returned afterwards.[56]

Georgina Seton said: 'The upper middle-class, was represented in the Solomons by a good many of birth and breeding from England and Australia with titled relatives and good education.' She added that there were also expatriate women who were 'very unsuitable' and who 'played poker and did not pay their debts'. Seton said that Solomon Islanders could tell 'the difference between ladies and something-nothings', meaning low-class white women. Somewhat grudgingly, she also said that the 'right sort of woman of wherever status got the reputation she deserved. In the islands, class distinction disappeared, and recognition of character took over.'[57]

On Tulagi, the wife of the incumbent Resident Commissioner was always at the top of the female pecking order, followed by the wives of the Government Secretary, the Chief Magistrate and the Treasurer and Collector of Customs. Their only rival on the island was Dorothy Lotze, the wife of Carpenters' manager Jack Lotze; however, she was from commerce and younger, which would have counted against her. She was also the daughter of Pop and Agnes Johnson, which gave her a mixed status. The wives of the managers of BP, Levers and Morris Hedstrom also carried considerable social clout.

There were middle-class female missionaries in the protectorate, such as Gladys, Joan and Katherine Deck, and their cousin Florence Young, the founder of the SSEM, who visited the protectorate for a month each year between 1904 and the early 1920s. While the Deck and Young families had wealthy Quaker connections, and came from prominent families in Australia and New Zealand, mission women were workers in their own right and had less need to flaunt superior social status.

There were also 'rough types'. The pretensions to proper behaviour could fade quickly when faced with the dregs of the Pacific. Twenty-two-year-old Wilfred Fowler met one of the dregs when he first arrived at Tulagi in the late 1920s. He was in Sterling's Hotel when the following altercation took place, which seems to contain a self-deprecating reference to Fowler's rather prim and possibly 'camp' (homosexual) demeanour:

---

56   Seton 1944; Bennett 1987, 236, 289, 303; Golden 1993, 406.
57   Boutilier 1984a, 179.

As I turned to go, a gross giant of a man shuffled towards me. His paunch sagged over his belt and his shirt gaped open to his navel. He looked me up and down with affected surprise. 'Well, for God's sake, look who's here'. He declared in a melodious deep base voice. Then, as though amused by what he saw, he tapped my shoulder and bringing his face close to mine he whispered, 'She hadn't up to yesterday, pal, but I know she will tonight'. I could smell the stale sweat on him and I felt crowded by bulk. There was laughter, but someone shouted over the din, 'Sit down, Hector'. The drunken man looked back at me reluctantly as he rejoined his companions.[58]

Recreation

There were also particular events that drew residents together. Steamer day and the excitement of receiving visitors to the small community have already been mentioned. Some of the entertainment was aboard visiting ships. For instance, Joseph Dickinson arrived at Gavutu from Sydney on the ketch *Ruby* in the 1900s. The ship was immediately 'crowded by the white staff at Gavutu, and some eighty friends belonging to the crew'.[59] Parties were often held on board the larger vessels and groups from ships arranged excursions to local beaches or organised hunting and fishing parties.

One constant of Tulagi life was getting away from the tightly bound urban surrounds and enjoying the natural environment. This could be as simple as a family picnic close by on an undeveloped part of Tulagi. The Gela Group is beautiful; Mboli Passage is close by and a great place for recreation. Residents and visitors organised outings around Tulagi Harbour and into the passage. One fishing expedition from the *Ruby* consisted of five Europeans in a boat crewed by six men from Santa Cruz. They were 'equipped' with one dozen bottles of lager beer, two bottles of whisky, one dozen bottles of lemonade, veal, ham and pork pies, lobsters, cheese, pickled walnuts, six plugs of dynamite to obtain bait fish, fish hooks and lines and a Winchester rifle.[60] These were hardly starvation rations or inadequate equipment. It was standard entertainment to take visitors fishing, such as in 1939, when high commissioner Luke spent an afternoon fishing not far from Tulagi.[61]

---

58   Fowler 1959, 4.
59   Dickinson 1927, 30–31.
60   ibid., 33.
61   Luke 1945, 86.

Plate 7.14 Jack Barley and Stanley Annandale at a picnic in the Gela Group, 1910s
Source: BM, Thomas Edge-Partington Photographic Collection.

Plate 7.15 Pop Johnson, his children and friends at a picnic on Tulagi
Source: Suzanne Ellis Collection.

Ships became floating dining rooms. When BP's ship *Moresby* was in port for Christmas 1910, Captain William Voy prepared a floating banquet for the local elite. Woodford and his wife, Florrie, treasurer Frank Barnett, Dr S.C.M. Davies from the hospital, Dr A.B. Lewis of the Field Museum in Chicago, leading planter Norman Wheatley, district officers and other planters joined the crew for Christmas festivities. When resident commissioner Kane arrived in the Solomons, the *Planters' Gazette* of August 1921 carried news of a similar event, paid for by Morris Hedstrom and Company, on the *Minindi*, also under Captain Voy.[62] Similarly, when Ernie Palmer and Inga Svensen were married, the European population of Tulagi shouted them a party on board the *Malaita*.[63] And on his 1939 visit, high commissioner Luke was entertained at the residency and the Tulagi Club. He returned the hospitality with a dinner on his ship, *Wellington*.[64]

Sometimes trips away could be an adventure. Soon after her marriage, Jessie Wilson accompanied her husband on a surveying field trip to Guadalcanal. Although she enjoyed the adventure, eight weeks camped beside a river in the mountains became rather wearing:

> I enjoyed it tremendously for the first 6 weeks, but when it got to 7 weeks & then 8 & the biscuits ran out & we had no milk & not many tins of meat. I began to think of my nice comfy home & used to actually dream about things to eat—especially tomatos [sic] & peaches. You know we moved our camp up into the mountains towards the last & I had to walk three miles through the roughest country & waded 7 times through the river. Once it was up to my arm pits & I was terribly scared. Of course I was dressed for the part, khaki shorts & trousers—no stockings & very old shoes.[65]

A better solution to combat loneliness when her husband was away occurred when one of Jessie's friends married Bill Gibson, the manager of Rere plantation on the north-east coast of Guadalcanal. Jessie enjoyed spending time there: 'I loved the plantation life at "Rere". It is very much the same as farm life, excepting for the smell of copra that pervades the atmosphere.'[66]

---

62 *The Brisbane Courier*, 4 January 1911, [cutting], in PMB, Woodford Papers and Photographs, PMB 150, Reel 2, Bundle 8, 9/20; *Planters' Gazette*, 3, August 1921, 3–4.
63 Struben 1963, 62.
64 Luke 1945, 86.
65 UQFL, Wilson Papers and Photographs, J.A. Wilson to Mary, 8 April 1925.
66 ibid., 26 May 1925.

Plate 7.16 Jessie Wilson accompanied her husband on several surveying trips
Source: UQFL, Wilson Papers and Photographs.

Plate 7.17 Spearline Wilson and friends
Source: UQFL, Wilson Papers and Photographs.

Jessie does not mention the marital intrigue involved. Gibson, from London, had arrived in the Solomons in 1909, and with his partners accumulated land on Guadalcanal. He met his future wife during a trip to Sydney. She eloped with him to the Solomons, where they were married on Tulagi. Jessie would have been in the thick of it. In 1925, Gibson's wife returned to Sydney to reconcile with her parents, while her husband improved the previously primitive accommodation at Rere. Jessie Wilson's visit to Rere must have been soon after Mrs Gibson's return. Mrs Gibson did not like the isolation of Rere and the couple shifted to Aola, where life was more pleasant. Then Gibson became ill and they shifted back to Sydney, where he died in 1929. Their landholdings were wound up.[67]

Some of the regular Tulagi-based activities are almost invisible in the historical record, but logical when one considers the origins of the population. Australia's Melbourne Cup horse race in early November each year had its avid fans. They went down to the wireless station to listen to the radio broadcast or gathered around radios at home, ending up at the Tulagi Club or the hotels to continue the celebration.[68] The latest cricket scores from test matches in Australia were also passed on

---

67 Golden 1993, 159–61.
68 UQFL, Wilson Papers and Photographs, A.H. Wilson to F.A.G. Wilson, 9 November 1939.

this way. The official records also ignore Tulagi's eccentrics. Discounting the drunks, of whom there were many, others made Tulagi their home in personal ways. One of Spearline Wilson's letters mentions a Miss Hackett, who 'owned' Bangi Island, a few hundred metres offshore from the hospital, where she had a leaf house and spent relaxing afternoons in 1939.[69] One wonders if anyone told her that executions used to be carried out there? Likewise, early in his Tulagi years, Eustace Sandars had his own local-style house built:

> It was situated in the second little bay from the police lines towards the club; a charming little spot with the water lapping at the trees on the beach. It consisted of a large open living room and two small bedrooms, one on either end, a kitchen and a bit of corrugated iron on stilts and a couple of water tanks. Rather primitive but quite sufficient and very much cooler than any of the European built houses.[70]

There were always public places available for relaxation, mainly the hotels and the club. From the 1910s and 1920s, these were at the core of Tulagi's social life, just as similar places remain so in small Pacific towns today.

Alcohol

Alcohol was the social lubricant of choice and consumption began on the voyage from Australia to Tulagi. Sandars described the amount of alcohol consumed on the voyage from Sydney to Tulagi on the *Mataram* in 1928:

> The first night out from Brisbane was a late night with much drink, the fellows on board were great drinkers and mostly used to play poker well into the night, some who could drink no more went to bed and their place was taken by the long cook Jack who would play all night and make some attempt at cooking the next day.[71]

Sandars shared a cabin with Captain Swanson, an elderly seaman about to take command of the Resident Commissioner's steam yacht *Ranadi*, and who forced him to drink half a water glass of overproof rum in the evening before bed, to ensure sound sleep. Then in the mornings the passengers ambled to the saloon:

---

69 ibid., 6 October 1939.
70 PMB, Sandars, Papers on the Solomon Islands, 18.
71 ibid., 2.

> As soon as I got up in the morning the drill was to go up top and enter the saloon where everybody was in pyjamas drinking. The first morning I went up there some bright spark was drinking gin slings and his remark to the bartender as I entered was 'Give the poor bloody Pommy one Jim' to which one of the others replied 'Oh break it up. He ain't a bad sort of bastard when all is said and done'. The gin slings were absolutely marvellous, they put new life into one completely and after a second one, one was fit to jump over the moon … three of these and you were well on your way to being drunk for the rest of the day.[72]

When the overseas ships arrived at Tulagi, they were boarded by local residents, mainly the men, who treated the ship as a floating bar:

> Men in badly tailored tropical clothes came up the gangway, planters and traders meeting the ship for mail and cargo, men off schooners and out-of-works off the beach. They greeted the stewards boisterously and then sat around the smoking-room tables to drink.[73]

Ashore, there was a choice of commercial establishments where alcohol could be obtained or consumed. The Tulagi Club, with its wide verandahs and sports facilities, was the centre of the higher end of the Tulagi social scene. Members and visitors went there to read newspapers and magazines, to play sport and swim and to socialise and drink.[74]

Drinking was a major pastime for most of the expatriate men—often to excess. In the late 1920s, the Resident Commissioner's male typist was partial to a beer, even at 9 am, and used the office messenger to deliver cold beers from Chinatown.[75] Deaths from alcoholism sometimes occurred and 'drying out' alcoholics was one of the tasks at the hospital.[76] It is an education to read Golden's *The Early European Settlers of the Solomon Islands*. The number of alcoholics was high. There were always European men who 'went troppo', because of alcohol, isolation or from failure to adapt culturally. Alcoholism had a lot to do with this and was a constant problem among the employees based on Tulagi and for all expatriates in the protectorate. The single officers always made the Tulagi Club a comfortable extension of their social lives, although they were not

---

72 ibid., 3.
73 Fowler 1959, 3.
74 UQFL, Wilson Papers and Photographs, F.A.G. Wilson to Mary, 1933.
75 Fowler 1959, 8.
76 WPHCA, 1919/552, Annual Medical Report, 1918, 2.

the only residents who found access to alcohol tempting. In the 1920s, resident commissioner Kane was far too fond of alcohol. Legend has it that in 1921, the year he first arrived, he was too drunk to perform the marriage ceremony for Jack and Vera Clift, who had to stop off at Visale Catholic mission station on Guadalcanal to get a Catholic priest to do the honours, on their way to their new home on Aruligo plantation.[77] Dr C.R. Pattison, one of the government doctors, was likewise afflicted and had a fondness for sampling the hospital's medicinal brandy. Eventually, Pattison managed to run the government launch *Gizo* on to a reef, which ended his career in the protectorate.[78]

Plate 7.18 James Basil Hicks, Agnes Johnson, Dorothy Lotze, Vic Sheridan and a friend
Source: Suzanne Ellis Collection.

Newly arrived, Eustace Sandars had an unnerving experience with Jimmy Mutch from Aberdeen, foreman of the Public Works Department and a permanent occupant of the single officers' quarters:

> I was a bit tired after my first day and I turned in about 10 o'clock. I had been asleep for about an hour when there was a dreadful racket outside and a voice shouted down the verandah, 'Go to bed Jimmy put that sword away'. The sword was apparently intended

---

77 Boutilier 1984a, 186.
78 Boutilier 1974, 15.

for me and Jimmy Mutch was cutting the mosquito wire in my bedroom door to pieces with his sword. Jimmy said 'I don't like policemen I'm going to stick this B … in the guts'. I thought this was a nice start off. I moved myself very smartly on to the opposite verandah. In the meantime somebody had disarmed Jimmy and all became quiet again.[79]

This was not the only time Mutch attacked residents with a sword. Ernie Palmer told a story of Mutch attacking Monty Masterman with a two-handed Samarai sword, terrifying the Inspector of Labour, who was almost garrotted by a wire clothes line as he ran off.[80] Mutch had another eccentricity. While drunk, he loved to go down to the wharf at night, call out the police guards and drill them, much to the displeasure of their commandant. A decade later, he had not changed. Dick Horton provided a graphic description of Mutch, who was still living at the single officers' quarters. One night, dressed in his full whites and pith helmet, he tilted drunkenly at spectres with his sword.[81] Mutch lasted two more years, until Spearline Wilson took over lands and surveys and public works in 1939. Wilson managed to get the Resident Commissioner to persuade Mutch to resign.[82]

Other leading officials also succumbed to alcohol. Knibbs, mentioned earlier, who served the protectorate from 1913 to 1939, was clearly an alcoholic by the 1930s and was also persuaded to resign. Several sources say Kane was an alcoholic who neglected his duties and got into brawls.[83] In 1928, as a new government officer, Sandars had a surprise first meeting with his resident commissioner:

> The next day, the Resident Commissioner, Captain E. Kane was due to arrive back in his yacht 'Ranadi'. I arranged with Captain Swanson, who was to take her over, to go down to meet the ship which was due in about 9.30 p.m. We went down to the wharf and saw her tie up alongside and then went on board. Somewhat to my astonishment on the after deck were two people locked in deadly combat. One turned out to be Captain Kane, the Resident and the other the Second Engineer.[84]

---

79 Sandars, PMB, Papers on the Solomon Islands, 9.
80 Struben 1963, 42.
81 Horton 1965, 17. See also Lever 1988.
82 UQFL, Wilson, 1946, Lands and Public Works Department: A Brief History, 3.
83 Boutilier 1984a, 186.
84 Sandars, PMB, Papers on the Solomon Islands, 9.

Others of lesser official standing were also alcoholics.

There is also another aspect to 'going troppo', and that is 'going native'. Dress standards were usually kept up on Tulagi, but isolated Europeans on plantations often wore very little or clothed themselves in *lap-laps*. Charles Mumford, a down-on-his-luck plantation owner on Makira in the 1910s, fell into this category. He wore pyjamas all day, never washed, ate poorly, had homemade shoes and lived in an unfinished house with no walls.[85] Betel nut was free and could also become the drug of choice for isolated Europeans.

Visitors, science and the media

Empire Day was the most important annual celebration.[86] The day was marked with bonfires and fireworks and loyal declarations to the King and empire. There were also public holidays for the birthdays of the sovereign and the heir to the British throne.[87] The resident commissioners reigned supreme, except when the WPHC high commissioners came to inspect local affairs. The first to visit Tulagi was Sir Henry Moore Jackson, who came for three days in October 1903 to check on Woodford's temporary suspension of the labour trade. Other high commissioners visited if local circumstances demanded or when on circuit through their watery domain. British, German and Australian naval vessels called in regularly and occasionally dignitaries were on board. A few days before Jackson, the Governor of German New Guinea, Dr Albert Hahl, arrived from Herbertshohe on his steam yacht *Seestern* after inspecting the southern islands of his territory.[88]

Other important visitors have already been mentioned, such as Sir Hubert Murray, Lieutenant-Governor of Australian Papua in 1916, and in 1928 Lieutenant-Colonel Sir Harry Moorhouse, the retired Lieutenant-Governor of Nigeria.[89] Jessie Wilson described Moorhouse, who lived in the house next-door for two months: 'He is quite a simple old dear—plays his game of golf every day in the raggedest old clothes, like an ordinary

---

85 ibid., 302–03.
86 It was renamed Commonwealth Day in 1958.
87 Armstrong and Joy 1939, 92.
88 BSIP *AR* 1900–01, 1, 17–18, 1903–05, 30; Hahl 1980.
89 Nelson 1986; Knibbs 1929, 267–69; WPHCA, MP No. 698/1915 (1915), G21120 WP 12/1 579/15–777/15, J.H.P. Murray, Report of Alleged Shortage of Labour in Solomons and Proposal to Recruit Labour from German New Guinea, 29 April 1916; Moorhouse 1929.

person.'⁹⁰ The arrival of the British First Sea Lord, Admiral of the Navy, Earl John R. Jellicoe, in 1919 caused a flurry. He was inspecting Tulagi Harbour as a possible site for a major Pacific base. Rear-Admiral E.R.G.R. Evans, commander of the Australian Navy, arrived in 1930. Such occasions were accompanied by formal ceremonies and festivities, such as dances at the Tulagi Club. On these occasions, ships were dressed, flying their signal flags from their rigging.⁹¹

Other notable visitors had a more substantial impact on the Solomons, ensuring its place in world anthropology. In 1901, the Museum of Victoria sent Graham Officer to obtain artefacts. He visited Tulagi and Gavutu. Advised by Woodford to head for Guadalcanal and the Western Solomons, he obtained a large range of artefacts, including a war canoe.⁹² Other scientists visited, such as anthropologists A.M. Hocart, W.H.R. Rivers and G.C. Wheeler, who arrived in Tulagi in May 1909. They took advice from Woodford on fieldwork sites, choosing Simbo, Roviana Lagoon, the Shortlands, Kolombangara and Vella Lavella—all in the Western Solomons—which had significant impacts on anthropology worldwide.⁹³ Another famous anthropologist, Ian Hogbin from Sydney University, visited the protectorate regularly between 1927 and 1933, stopping off in Tulagi on his way to Rennell, Ontong Java, Malaita and Guadalcanal.⁹⁴ In 1928, Eugen Paravicini, an ethnologist from the Museum der Kulturen in Basel, Switzerland, visited the protectorate.

Many scientific visitors, as well as rich tourists who dabbled in artefact collection, also passed through Tulagi. It was quite usual for private yachts to arrive, some quite grand, carrying owners who were travelling the world in floating comfort. In the early 1930s, wealthy American Charles Templeton Crocker arrived to lead a scientific expedition. Crocker travelled on his own 125-ton, 34-metre-long and 7-metre-beam wooden-hulled, schooner-rigged yacht with an auxiliary engine, the *Zaca*. It was staffed with various scientific personnel, including anthropologist Gordon MacGregor of the Bishop Museum in Honolulu, Dr Sylvester Lambert of the Rockefeller Foundation in Suva, botanist Norton Stuart, Dr John B. Hynes and Malakai Veisamasama (both working with

90   UQFL, Wilson Papers and Photographs, J.A. Wilson to Mary, 17 July 1928.
91   Earl Jellicoe was visiting to assess the Gela Group as a site for a large British naval base. Fox 1962, 107; UQFL, Wilson Papers and Photographs, Edna Campbell Diary, 22 September 1930.
92   Richards 2012, 111–16.
93   Hviding and Berg 2014, 6, 9; Lawrence 2014, 209–15.
94   Beckett 1986; Beckett and Gray 2007.

Lambert) and Japanese photographer Toshio Asaeda.[95] Crocker did not stand on ceremony and while on board preferred to wear a *lap-lap* or a pair of shorts, with a bandana around his neck. The *Zaca* was luxurious: the gramophone had speakers wired throughout the ship, there was a powerful Morse code station and stewards to attend to every whim. The yacht arrived at Tulagi, then the expedition spent most of their time at Rennell, Malaita, Sikaiana, Makira and at Santa Cruz and nearby islands.[96] In 1932, Julius Fleischmann junior of Cincinnati topped them all by arriving on his extraordinary US$625,000 1,000-ton yacht, *Camargo*, stopping off at Tulagi before sailing north.[97] Today, the vessel would be worth about A$30 million. Tulagi's residents were amazed. The collections and writings of these men helped make Solomon Islands central in the early twentieth-century literature on nature, material culture and anthropology. Their presence in Tulagi would have stimulated local conversations about the natural and ethnographic history of the protectorate.

The Rockefeller Foundation assisted medical campaign in the late 1920s and 1930s attempted to eradicate yaws and hookworm and the Whitney South Sea Expedition passed through in the early 1930s, collecting bird and botanical species. Yaws has faded from memory as a significant disease in the Solomons, but before the Pacific War it was a terrible scourge, which the administration had no ability to combat. Yaws is a chronic disease of the tropics, contagious and brings disfiguring ulcer-like symptoms. This debilitating disease now can be cured with two injections of long-acting penicillin—a drug not available until the 1940s. Often nearly everyone in a village suffered from yaws. Small children would develop a rash covering their whole body and then lumps would start to erupt. The head, particularly around the nose and mouth, was often affected, then the disease spread to the rest of the body. Flies swarmed around the eruptions and the appearance was repulsive. It was almost a stage of growing up and parents accepted that their children would get the disease. It usually passed, and in about half the cases the skin would clear up again. In other cases, although the body healed, one sore would remain, almost always on the lower limbs, and gradually grow. Sometimes it would continue for years until part of the victim's foot had been eaten away or there would be a large ulcer on the calf. The smell was terrible and when one entered a village the stink from sores often pervaded the air.

---

95   Burt 2015, 59–61, 70; Anonymous 1934.
96   Lambert 1946, 335–55.
97   '*Camargo* in Solomons', *PIM*, 26 January 1932.

On Malaita and Makira in the 1920s, the infection rate was 60 to 65 per cent and up to 90 per cent among coastal people. The disease caused high infant mortality. Beginning in the 1920s, intravenous and intramuscular injections of neo-arsphenamine were used as a cure, aided substantially by the Rockefeller Foundation campaign. The director of the 1928–31 campaign was the already mentioned Dr Sylvester Lambert, with Dr Menzies in charge of one unit and Gordon White, assistant to Dr Hetherington from Tulagi Hospital, in charge of the other. Each European worked with two Islander assistants and a medical orderly. Native medical practitioners, missionaries and members of the foundation's medical team gave injections throughout the protectorate, which brought huge relief from the debilitating disease. For instance, during 1930, the Rockefeller campaign gave 32,702 anti-yaws injections to 18,704 Solomon Islanders and treated 12,904 cases of hookworm. Hookworm was difficult to treat for cultural reasons. Diagnosis involved a stool sample, which contravened taboos on contact with faeces.

The Christian missions also participated in the campaign. In 1929, the Methodist Mission gave 1,748 injections in the Gizo district and the Anglican Melanesian Mission gave 696 injections at Fuaambu on Malaita. Individuals travelled long distances to get their '*nila*' (needle). In 1932, 21,628 injections were given for yaws; however, the drugs used were not totally effective and the effort of the 1920s–1930s was partly wasted. Penicillin made the real difference.[98] The campaign staff constantly passed through Tulagi to collect supplies, for rest and recreation and on their way to other islands. One of them, Gordon White, stayed on and was appointed government yaws and hookworm officer during 1932; he was then acting dispenser at Tulagi Hospital, before joining Dr Lambert in a tuberculosis survey of the protectorate in mid-1933.[99]

The Whitney Expedition of the American Museum of Natural History began in the summer of 1920, funded by American businessman Harry Payne Whitney and his family. Its original purpose was to study the plants and birds of the Pacific Islands. This expedition visited hundreds of islands and was led by many different scientists and collectors over more than a dozen years. Administered by a committee at the museum, the expedition became a source of funds and equipment for collecting and research on

---

98   BSIP *AR* 1930, 13–14, 1931, 6; Boutilier 1974, 28.
99   CO, 225/276/18890, 1931933, Annual Medical and Sanitary Report, 1932, 225/281/38779, 1934, Annual Medical and Sanitary Report, 1933.

the Pacific Islands. The first leader was Rollo H. Beck, a veteran collector and naturalist, who hired Ernst H. Qualye and Charles Curtis. Together, they assembled most of the botanical collections for the expedition. They arrived on the sailing ship *France*, stopping at islands large and small. During 1929–30, the expedition worked in Solomon Islands, on Malaita and elsewhere. The main collection of botanical specimens was sent to the Bernice Bishop Museum, in Honolulu, Hawai'i.[100] These scientific visitors all mixed with the Tulagi residents during the 1920s and 1930s.

Contemporary media and literature

While the BSIP was too small to have its own newspaper (the closest it got was the short-lived *Planters' Gazette*, from 1920 to 1923, and church periodicals), the islands began to attract the attention of the media, particularly from Australia. News from New Guinea, Solomon Islands and the New Hebrides became a constant theme in the east coast Australian newspapers onwards from the 1860s, and from the 1870s to the 1900s, Australian papers carried a steady stream of stories about the labour trade to the Solomons. The islands also featured in the media at the time of the mass deportation of Pacific Island labourers between 1906 and 1908.[101] From the 1880s and 1890s, journalists began to visit the protectorate, reporting back to Australia through *The Argus* (Melbourne), the *North Queensland Register* (a Townsville weekly), *The Queenslander* (a Brisbane weekly), the *Sydney Morning Herald*, the *Sydney Mail* and the *Evening Star* (another Sydney paper).[102] Almost as soon as Woodford arrived in Tulagi in 1897, a special correspondent from the *North Queensland Register* visited and eulogised about the future of the protectorate.[103] The Solomons was an attractive prospect for a quick visit by journalists as the islands were on a regular shipping route out of Australian ports and could be linked with short visits to the New Hebrides, Australian Papua and German New Guinea. In the 1890s, the *Sydney Mail* artist Norman Hardy made such a trip and published articles, and later a book, on what he had seen along this route.[104] In 1906, Randolph Bedford, a Brisbane journalist, arrived on a vessel returning indentured labourers from Queensland to their home

---

100 Eyerdam 1933; Mayr 1931; Mayr 1943; Akin 2013, 108–14.
101 Corris 1972; Moore 2000a.
102 Lawrence 2014, 186, 208–14.
103 ibid., 186, quoting *North Queensland Register*, 21 July 1897, 12–13.
104 Quanchi 2014a.

islands. Bedford also visited the newly acquired Australian Territory of Papua and purchased land in Milne Bay. He published a series of articles in Brisbane's *Courier-Mail* and *The Queenslander*.[105]

In the immediate post–World War I period, when the Solomons was included in Australia's subimperialist designs, photographer and columnist Thomas McMahon made a similar trip, publishing hundreds of photographs of Solomon Islands in Australian, British and American magazines and illustrated newspapers.[106] He was followed shortly after by the American photographer and writer Merl La Voy, who then visited Sydney, where his photographs were published by the *Sydney Mail*.[107] Roviana Lagoon in the Western Solomons was visited regularly and much photographed.[108]

There were also literary and cinematic visitors. Jack and Charmian London arrived on board the schooner *Snark* in 1908. Jack London, the most popular (and extremely racist) American author of his time, published *The Cruise of the Snark* and *Jerry of the Islands* and his wife published *The Log of the Snark* and *Voyaging in Wild Seas, or, A Woman among the Head Hunters*.[109] American photographers and adventurers Martin and Osa Johnson, mentioned earlier, arrived in 1917, although Martin first visited the Solomons as crew on the *Snark* in 1908. The Johnsons' film footage contains the first 'moving pictures' from the Solomons and they also later wrote books including material gathered while they were in the protectorate.[110] English travel writer Charlotte Cameron passed through Tulagi in 1922 on a quest for information for a book on the Pacific.[111] Beatrice Grimshaw visited Tulagi in the 1900s and in the mid-1920s.[112] An accomplished, well-published writer, Grimshaw would have been regarded as a celebrity, and it is also likely that her Papua plantation novels—full of her antiquated racial attitudes—circulated in the Solomons. American artist Caroline Mytinger, another 1920s visitor, travelled through the archipelago with a female companion and

---

105 Boland 1979; Bedford 1906–07.
106 Quanchi 1994; Quanchi 1997; Quanchi 2010a; Quanchi 2014b.
107 Quanchi 2010b.
108 Wright 2013.
109 London 1911; London 1912, Ch. 6; London 1915[?]b; London 1917.
110 Behlmer 2018, 205. Johnson 1945. Their materials are preserved in the Martin and Osa Johnson Safari Museum, Chanute, Kansas, USA, available from: www.safarimuseum.com/. See also Ahrens et al. (2013).
111 *Planters' Gazette*, 5, February 1922, 14.
112 Boutilier 1984a, 191.

later published a best-selling account of their visit, *Headhunting in the Solomon Islands*.¹¹³ All of them began their journeys at Tulagi. Although writers, photographers and artists focused on portraits, material culture, customs and the 'native' way of life, the subtext was usually empire, British expansion and potential economic opportunities for Australians.¹¹⁴

Plate 7.19 High commissioner Sir Eyre Hutson visiting Tulagi in 1927
The flags of the BSIP and the Crown Colony of Gilbert and Ellice Islands are flying or are draped about.
Source: UQFL, Wilson Papers and Photographs.

There were a few local authors who would have attracted attention; their books have formed part of the sources for this volume. One was *Jock of the Islands: Early Days in the South Seas—The Adventures of John Cromar*, published in 1935, which recounted Cromar's voyages in the Queensland and Solomon Islands labour trade and his life as a planter.¹¹⁵ Stanley Knibbs was Cromar's editor—a not-so-obvious social link. Knibbs published his own book, *The Savage Solomons as They Were & Are*.¹¹⁶ The repetition of 'savage' and 'headhunter' in these titles shows that the authors and their

---

113 Mytinger 1930; Mytinger 1943.
114 Wright 2013; Quanchi 1995; Quanchi 2004; Quanchi 2014b.
115 Cromar 1935.
116 Knibbs 1929.

publishers knew how to titillate the reading market.[117] Several missionaries also wrote substantial books.[118] These books, along with those by Guppy and Woodford, circulated around the protectorate, as did hundreds of lesser-known publications that mentioned the Solomons. Although there was no public library, new books from near and far were available.

The Advisory Council

Until 1921, the Resident Commissioner had sole local authority over the protectorate, subject to approval by the WPHC High Commissioner. Then, on 25 April 1921, at the recommendation of high commissioner Sir Cecil Rodwell, a regulation was passed to provide for the creation of an advisory council. It consisted initially of the Resident Commissioner as president and not more than four members who were British subjects living in the BSIP, of whom one could be an official. The Resident Commissioner was empowered to request information and advice on any matters relating to the internal administration of the protectorate. The first meeting took place on 10 November 1921, with acting resident commissioner Jack Barley as president. Tulagi mustered all the pomp and ceremony it could manage. Captain Turner turned out a detachment of the armed constabulary and Barley took the salute. His opening speech was rich with classical allusions:

> We cannot expect, Gentlemen, to spring like Pallas Athene full-equipped from the head of Zeus; we must first learn to exercise our limbs and prove our strength before we aspire to the same rights and privileges as the grown-up children of our great Imperial family.[119]

In later years, the council was expanded to include the Resident Commissioner and seven members, three of whom could be officials. The official minutes of the meetings were published from 1926, and there were also substantial earlier reports in the *Planters' Gazette*. Author and adventurer Captain Alan Villiers, who arrived at Tulagi in the 1930s on his fully rigged sailing ship *Joseph Conrad*, left us a description of a ceremony held when the council met. It was

---
117 Dickinson 1927; Collinson 1926.
118 For instance, Codrington 1972; Fox 1924; F. Young 1926; Ivens 1927; Ivens 1930; Hopkins 1928.
119 *Planters' Gazette*, 5, February 1922, 4.

staged with all the pomp and show and banging of drums that could be mustered, and the sulu-dressed constables, all with fixed bayonets and very smart, lined up beside the weatherboard Parliament House for inspection. They seemed to enjoy it all, and the waters of Tulagi and Gavutu harbours sparkled below pleasantly in the sun.[120]

The 'Parliament House' was actually the court house. Villiers described the members as 'fine elderly gentlemen' who 'meet pleasantly together at intervals and discussed recommendations for the consideration of the High Commissioner of the Western Pacific at Suva in the Fijis'.[121] In the 1920s and 1930s, discussions of labour dominated council meetings. Their deliberations were published verbatim after 1930. Elderly they may have been, but there were some astute comments and understanding of both the economy and the society of the protectorate, tempered by a touch of conservatism and commercial reality.[122]

Plate 7.20 The new Anglican headquarters at Taroaniara, in the early 1940s
Source: NASI, ACOM Collection.

---

120 Villiers 1937, 179.
121 ibid.
122 The council did not meet between November 1941 and October 1945 due to World War II, and there were no Solomon Islanders on the Advisory Council until 1951.

Plate 7.21 The bishop's house at Taroaniara, in the early 1940s
Source: NASI, ACOM Collection.

Solomon Islanders in the Tulagi enclave

In writing about Tulagi, I have endeavoured to include everyone who lived on the island, including foreigners and Solomon Islanders. I featured expatriate women in Chapters 5 and 6. Including equivalent material on Solomon Islander residents has been difficult. How many Solomon Islanders lived permanently on Tulagi, Gavutu and Makambo? How did Solomon Islanders socialise with each other and the foreigners? What did they do in their time off? How did they interpret what they saw and how was that knowledge of events on Tulagi passed around the villages? Solomon Islanders were motivated by their own epistemologies (ways of knowing). Answers to these questions remain unresolved, although some things can be teased out.

TULAGI

When Woodford purchased Tulagi, it was uninhabited. Access remained controlled and yet, reading between the lines, Solomon Islanders were always there and involved in many different activities. They could not gravitate to this new centre of wealth and significance as freely as they did to mission and trading stations, or even to other government bases. Permanent indigenous settlement was never encouraged and there was a curfew. Yet, tens of thousands lived there or passed through as police, labourers, servants, ships' crews, mission workers, hospital patients and prisoners. We know that canoes from Gela constantly visited the administrative, mission and commercial islands and settlements.[123] Some photographs indicate local-style houses in Chinatown, which were probably the homes of employees of the retail outlets. Solomon Islanders worked in the stores and houses, assisted with boatbuilding and crewed the schooners and cutters.[124]

Plate 7.22 The seafront on Tulagi's inner side, in the 1930s
Source: UQFL, Wilson Papers and Photographs.

---

123 Richards 2012, 136.
124 Barge 1938, 117.

The earliest oral testimony from a Solomon Islander about Tulagi comes from Samuel Alasa`a from the Kwara`ae district on Malaita, when he was a young labourer in 1918. He was on the schooner *Maringe* under David Edward Davies, a returned soldier from World War I who committed suicide on the ship when it was anchored between Tulagi and Makambo. Tulagi officials, including the Resident Commissioner, were soon on board and, although the suicide was clear, there was a suspicion that the labourers and crew had a hand in ending his life after he had cut his own throat. Alasa`a spent a week in Tulagi prison awaiting his court appearance. He described the cells as basic, and food was mainly water and hard navy biscuits. His account shows only a limited knowledge of what occurred in the court. He mentions the *akalo* (his ancestors) and their part in controlling proceedings. He was also involved in a second court case, which in part involved pig theft and a sacrifice to his ancestors. On both occasions, the officials would never have realised the connections being made between ancestral religions and court processes.[125]

There can be no doubt that a few Solomon Islander leaders got their start in indigenous and mission affairs and government service after working in lowly jobs on prewar Tulagi. Sir Lloyd Maepeza Gina noted that Willy Paia, Ben Kevu, Alec Maena, Daniel Pule and Jonathan Leve, all from Munda, began their careers as government clerks on Tulagi. Silas Sitai from Santa Ana was appointed in 1939 as a clerk in the Resident Commissioner's office. In his spare time, Sitai learnt Morse code, which led to him being sent to Suva to train as a wireless operator during the Pacific War. His success in Tulagi in the 1930s led to a long career. In the 1960s and 1970s, he became a senior public servant and chairman of the Governing Council.[126] Another early Tulagi resident was E.S.D. (Dick) Richardson, the son of George Washington Ezekiel Richardson, also called 'Dick America', an African-American mentioned in Chapter 7 who lived on Makira. Dick Richardson joined the armed constabulary in June 1926 and served until 1934, when he resigned with the rank of corporal. He rejoined the police on 1 October 1939 as a constable first class and was promoted to sergeant-major two years later. He was the first Solomon Islander to be promoted to subinspector when he attained that rank on 1 January 1951. He retired from the force in 1959 at the age of 50, and shortly afterwards joined the Marine Department and was employed as master-at-arms in Honiara. He died in 1972.[127]

---

125 Burt et al. 2001, 104–11.
126 Gina 2003, 58; Moore 2013, entries for Alec Maena, Willie G. Paia and Silas Sitai.
127 *Solomon Islands Police Force Newsletter*, June 1972, 18.

Plate 7.23 Samuel Alasa`a was involved in a court case and spent a short time in prison on Tulagi in the 1920s

He later became secretary of the Kwara`ae Council of Chiefs. He is posed here in 1984 with a *subi* club and wearing the style of ornaments used in his younger days.

Source: Ben Burt Collection.

7. SILK, WHITE HELMETS AND MALACCA CANES

Plate 7.24 Shem Irofa'alu worked as a cook at the single officers' quarters on Tulagi

From To'ambaita Malaita, he became an important leader of the SSEM and later a key Maasina Rule leader. Wearing a white shirt and tie, he is in the bottom right of this 1920s photograph. Back row, left to right: Dick Lioiaa, Livae Liufakona, John Kanakwai, Livae Irokula, Isikiel Surioa, Mr Waite, Robert McBride, Northcote Deck, Joel Kanoli, Joseph Naute'e, James Oto'akaloa, Ma'arumae. Middle row, left to right: Peter Abu'ofa, Othanila, Stephen Meke, Mrs McBride, Mrs Northcote Deck. Front row, left to right: Benjamin Kanaa, Nathan Maitofana, Harry Fafanga, Stephen Kumalau, Samuel Laukana, Paul Iro'ota, Dauramo, Shem Irofa'alu.

Source: Deck 1928, facing p. 64. Full identification of individuals provided by Ian Frazer.

Jonathan Fifi'i (1921–89) from Kwaio district on Malaita was educated in Seventh-day Adventist schools at Sinalagu in Kwaio and at Marovo in the Western Solomons, before he worked on Tulagi between 1930 and 1941 as a house servant and cook. He became a sergeant in the Solomon Islands Labour Corps during the Pacific War and one of the 10 head chiefs of the Maasina Rule movement, from 1944 to 1952.[128] Fifi'i formed the first Malaitan Local Government Council at 'Aimela and was a teacher at the

---

128 Maasina Rule (1944–52) began in 'Are'are, Malaita, in early 1944, at a time when many Malaitans were working in the wartime Labour Corps on Guadalcanal and Gela. *Maasina* means 'his brother' or 'his sibling' or even 'his friend'. Maasina Rule aimed at a radical reorganisation of Malaitan society and wanted Malaitans to have more control over their own lives. The movement's members were influenced by American servicemen, including African-Americans, whose humane treatment of them and political advice encouraged them to make a stand against the old colonial system. The leaders spread a message of Malaitan independence across the island. Maasina Rule advocated improvements in agriculture, concentration into larger and cleaner villages and, later, noncooperation with the protectorate government and missionary societies. These teachings were coupled at some stages with hopes for American liberation and millenarian ideas, although this aspect of the movement was often fabricated or exaggerated by government officials, and later by anthropologists and historians influenced by government accounts. The movement spread quickly to all areas of Malaita and to neighbouring islands, particularly Makira and parts of Guadalcanal. For eight years, the movement dominated the political scene in the southern Solomons. It was an indigenous proto-nationalist movement grounded in a desire for self-government and self-determination. Akin 2013; Bennett 1987, 202–310.

council school there from 1952 to 1956. He also became a member and later president of the Malaita District Council and a member of the BSIP Governing Council and the Legislative Assembly.[129] 'Abaeata (Abaeatha) Anifelo from east Kwaio, Malaita—the son of Basiana, who was executed on Tulagi for his role in the 1927 assassination of William Bell, Kenneth Lillies and their police—became a boy bugler, drummer and policeman on Tulagi, rising to the rank of corporal. Later, he was an assistant district headman and then a central Federal Council leader during Maasina Rule. He was involved in negotiating the final settlement with the High Commissioner and the district officer and became an early Malaita Council delegate from Kwaio.[130] Shem Irofa'alu, who became the most important SSEM leader in north Malaita and a key leader of Maasina Rule, also lived on Tulagi. He had worked as a plantation labourer and at Auki, Malaita, where he was a cook for the district officer, before moving to Tulagi to work as a cook at the single officers' quarters.[131] Another prominent north Malaitan, Heman Ganisua Ioi, grandfather of Lady Margaret Kenilorea (née Kwanairara), was also employed on Tulagi in the 1930s, as was Salana Ga'a (Maega'asia) from west Kwara'ae, who later became the first president of the Malaita Council.

Plate 7.25 Silas Sitai from Santa Ana was a clerk in the office of the Resident Commissioner on Tulagi

He became a senior public servant and chairman of the Governing Council. This photograph is from 1957, when he was an administrative assistant at Kira Kira. He is standing with subinspector Dick Richardson and senior clerk Walter Togonu.

Source: PMB, Photo 66_0999, James L.O. Tedder Collection.

129 Fifi'i 1989.
130 Information from David Akin, 12 October 2018.
131 Moore 2013, entry for Shem Irofa'alu.

7. SILK, WHITE HELMETS AND MALACCA CANES

Plate 7.26 Salana Ga`a (Maega`asia) from west Kwara`ae, Malaita, worked on Tulagi as a *haus boi* and an orderly for two resident commissioners

He became the first president of the Malaita Council, and is shown here with HRH Prince Philip, Duke of Edinburgh, on Malaita in 1959.

Source: Clive Moore Collection.

TULAGI

Plate 7.27 As a teenager, Jonathan Fifi'i from east Kwaio, Malaita, worked as a *haus boi* on Tulagi

One of the 10 head chiefs for Maasina Rule, he became a member and then president of Malaita Council, the Member for Central Malaita in the Governing Council and the Member for East Kwaio in the Legislative Assembly. This photograph is from 1966 and was taken at Ngarinaasuru, behind Sinalagu Harbour, east Kwaio.

Source: Lot Page Collection.

Salana Ga'a said that at 12 years of age he began working as a *haus boi* for Gordon White on Tulagi in the 1920s, and then worked as an orderly for resident commissioners Ashley and Marchant. He became a member of the armed constabulary, as did Stephen Sipolo, a Malaitan from Ngongosila Island off east Kwara'ae, who joined in the mid-1920s and became a sergeant-major. Sipolo was based on Tulagi in the late 1930s and in the 1940s was a senior policeman on Makira and Malaita. He was dismissed in 1947 for his Maasina Rule connections and reluctantly became a Maasina Rule chief for Kwara'ae. Jailed with the movement's head chiefs, Sipolo was released in 1950. In 1960, Sipolo became Vice-President of the Malaita Council.[132] While there is no direct proof of the influence Tulagi had on men such as these, it must have been significant. They would have been able to view the colonial process and its foreign public servants at close quarters.

Fifi'i's autobiography has a substantial section on Tulagi. He described the 'colonial caste system' and was scathing about the assumed racial superiority of the Europeans he encountered. Undoubtedly, this influenced his involvement in Maasina Rule and his future political career. One person in his sights was Monty Masterman, the Inspector of Labour:

> Tulagi was strange place then. Let me recall some of the things that happened. Solomon Islanders, the young people of nowadays, wouldn't believe what it was like—the colonial caste system, with the white people all segregated up on the hill, with their hotel and their club; and the Chinese down in Chinatown, who weren't allowed to mix with Europeans. We Solomon Islanders were at the bottom of the heap …
>
> Let me give you an example of how the British acted, as if they were our lords and rulers. When I was working on Tulagi, I was given a bicycle to use, so I could ride to Chinatown to get bread. One day I was riding my bicycle, and I saw Mr. Masterman. He was the Commissioner of Labour. He was coming in my direction, and I was going towards him. He called out to me: 'Boy'! I came to him. 'Get down'! He told me to get off my bicycle. I got down. 'When you see a white man, you can't go past him on your bicycle. You get off and stand to attention until he goes past. Then you can

---

132 Information from Lady Margaret Kenilorea, Honiara, 7 May 2010; Moore 2013, entries for Salana Ga'a [Maega'asia] and Stephen Sipolo; Keesing 1980, 103.

get back on your bicycle. Because white people are the rulers here. You natives are nothing. If you see a white man, you have to give him proper respect.'[133]

In another example from the 1930s, Fifi`i mentions the cooks from the hospital playing soccer at lunchtime, when the ball was accidently kicked under Masterman's house, which was beside the playing field. Masterman called for his servant to retrieve it, but rather than return it he confiscated the ball and gave it to the police. The police insisted that the boys play a game with the ball as the prize. The cooks lost, and the police kept the ball.[134]

Masterman was an extreme, but he was far from alone in his racist attitudes and insistence on white supremacy. This thinking was built into the colonial system. Wilfred Fowler provided another example. He came across a staggering drunken European on the outskirts of Chinatown, whom he passed at the same time as did Johnny Sa`a, a petty officer on the government vessel *Tulagi*. Sa`a showed his concern and went to help the man, only to be brushed aside. The drunk then turned to Fowler:

'Did you hear what he called me,' he shrieked when he came up to me. 'He called me Peter! The bloody black bastard called me Peter.' He was almost in tears.[135]

In the 1920s and 1930s, there were as many permanent Solomon Islander residents in the Tulagi enclave as Europeans and Chinese—about 250. There were gangs of wharf labourers from Malaita, mainly from Langalanga Lagoon, who regularly worked to unload and load cargo when the overseas ships arrived. There were Solomon Islanders employed in the administration and by individuals. They were in the armed constabulary, ran messages from office to office, undertook minor clerical duties or were house servants. The postmaster even had a local assistant whose main job was to cancel stamps on letters. There is an indication of mixed-race children in Chinatown and another clue of the Islanders' presence exists in a photograph that shows houses built over the water, probably as accommodation for the Langalanga labourers.[136] The Johnsons' 1917 film seems to indicate Gela canoes beached to trade market produce at

---

133 Fifi`i 1989, 35.
134 ibid.
135 Fowler 1959, 120.
136 WPHC 10/XV/325/009. This also appears in other collections.

7. SILK, WHITE HELMETS AND MALACCA CANES

Tulagi and, as mentioned above, there was an SSEM gospel rally at Tulagi in 1928.[137] Clearly, some Solomon Islanders were well ensconced on Tulagi, although the photographic evidence is focused overwhelmingly on foreigners.

Solomon Islanders on Tulagi had to deal with sickness and death among their *wantoks*. Hundreds of prisoners and hospital patients passed through, and some died there. On 3 August 1930, young Edna Campbell was out walking with a friend; they went first to Chinatown and then through The Cut to the police barracks on the outer side of the island. A funeral was in progress for two men who had died that day. She also mentions visiting 'the village', an indication that there was a separate Solomon Islander settlement—presumably, the labourers' quarters.[138]

Depictions of Solomon Islanders at Tulagi vary considerably, from police to labourers, to 'boat-boys' and house servants. In 1927, Mytinger described her first view of labourers loading copra at Gavutu:

> I could see almost all of every one of them, for they were naked except for a strip of calico *lap-lap* rolled up around the loins, but there were no individuals or personalities. There was a double stream of spindly figures with big faces, each head made bigger by an enormous mound of tightly kinked hair on top of it, a rippling line of skin drenched in sweat and coconut oil to the richness of henna-coloured satin. As these figures sped past, the sunlight played over their sharp muscles exactly as it does over the coat of a chestnut racehorse. No white-skinned runners ever looked so dazzling. We had heard a lot about the laziness of these 'black swine' on the trip up, but I had never seen men of any colour work so fast. I had never before seen a mass of naked men working either fast or slow. These first Melanesians were surely unlike any other aggregate of men in the world.[139]

Mytinger had an outsider's view of the way the British treated Solomon Islanders and, on Gavutu, she could not help but contrast that with the way that Solomon Islanders, particularly Malaitans, were described as savages even while they were present. Yet, if one reads carefully, it is clear

---

137 Maetoloa 1985.
138 UQFL, Wilson Papers and Photographs, Edna Campbell Diary, 3 and 12 August 1930; Innes 2017, 42–43.
139 Mytinger 1943, 23–24.

that Solomon Islanders were incorporated into many activities. Sandars mentions golf, tennis and cricket as his main recreations, and that cricket games included Solomon Islanders:

> We had some very good cricket players, one particularly, I recollect was the launch driver Talena whom I grew to admire and dislike more everytime I played against him. He was a fast medium right arm bowler and extraordinarily accurate. I rather fancied myself with a bat but Telena [sic] was too much for me on almost every occasion I played against him.[140]

Edna Campbell also mentions watching a cricket match between 'the native boys' at the armed constabulary barracks.[141]

After the Anglicans built their Christ the King Church in 1937, daily services were taken by members of the Melanesian Brotherhood, which attracted Solomon Islanders resident on or transiting through the island. Reverend Charles Fox, the only European member of the order (1933–44), described their activities in 1938:

> When we came back from Rabaul, Brother Peter and I first spent a fortnight at Kopuria, the Brothers' Headquarters at Tulagi. It is in a mangrove swamp. From this swamp the Brothers issue daily in a small canoe to take services in the new church at Tulagi and in small native churches they have built at Makambo and Gavutu. They also visit the hospital and gaol. The daily attendance of workboys and houseboys, ships' crews and police is about fifty. They are also growing vegetables (tomatoes, cucumbers) for the white people on the hill behind the swamp. Brother Bartholomew Beve (Reefs [from Reef Islands]) is the Head Brother.[142]

Solomon Islanders also learnt to follow some of the less savoury practices of the Europeans and Chinese. In 1928, a regulation was passed to allow punishment for any Solomon Islander found to have consumed alcohol, as well as punishment for the supplier. Although it was illegal, some Solomon Islanders had access to alcohol—as also occurred in urban areas after the war—on Tulagi, Makambo and Gavutu, and could occasionally be found inebriated in their quarters. In discussions at the 1959 committee into alcohol consumption, BSIP Advisory Council member Mr Kondovar

---

140 Sandars, PMB, Papers on the Solomon Islands, 13.
141 UQFL, Wilson Papers and Photographs, Edna Campbell Diary, 26 July 1930.
142 Fox 1938.

said that although access was unusual in other parts of the protectorate, on Tulagi, Solomon Islanders had easy access to alcohol, which was sold to them by less scrupulous Europeans and Chinese.[143] It was also illegal to gamble, but they managed to do that as well and many became keen on games of chance.[144]

Xavier Herbert, always sympathetic to the local people, was probably correct in his assessment that the British were not so much wantonly cruel, but worse—they treated the Solomon Islanders as if they did not exist.[145] Racial segregation permeated Tulagi and was imbedded in colonialism. The hospital had segregated wards for Europeans, Asians and Solomon Islanders. The British behaved as superior beings and looked down on the Chinese and Solomon Islanders. At the top of it all, the resident commissioners figuratively and physically looked down on everyone from their house guarded by 'straight-backed native police clad in polished Sam Browne belts and spotless blue lava-lavas, armed with rifles and fixed bayonets'.[146]

There were occasions when Solomon Islanders witnessed behaviour they could not understand. In 1922, C. Maxwell, a trader and planter from Isabel, was arrested for murdering one of his labourers, with the charge later reduced to manslaughter. While an investigation was carried out over several weeks, and a judge imported from Fiji, Maxwell was confined under guard on his vessel at the Tulagi government wharf. He could exercise on the wharf, although not even his wife was allowed to speak to him. Solomon Islanders came from the surrounding Gela villages to view the spectacle of a captive white man—the first they had seen. The *Planters' Gazette* was outraged. The police were accused of 'strutting about delighted at the opportunity of displaying authority and domination over the white prisoner'.[147] The *Gazette* asked how European prestige could be maintained in the face of such indignity. One wonders what the villagers made of it all.

Although always polite to the senior members of the administration, the armed constabulary often saluted in an exaggerated manner, noisily slapping their buttocks after any salute, much to the amusement of the

---

143 *BSIPNS*, 31 March 1958.
144 Young 1928, 116; F. Young 1926, 145; Hodgson 1966, 42–44.
145 Keesing and Corris 1980, 208.
146 Ashby 1978, 60.
147 *Planters' Gazette*, 6, May 1922, 4.

European population, the police themselves and the watching indigenous population. Ostensibly polite, disciplined and proper, they may have been 'taking the mickey' out of established authority or were perhaps beginning a long tradition of colourful police parade behaviour that still exists today.[148]

It is not too long a bow to draw to conclude that the society of the Tulagi enclave influenced the future politicisation of Solomon Islanders. The worst example of all shows the barbarity of the British and their callous disregard of what we would now regard as common decency and humanity. When Basiana was hanged on Tulagi in 1928, his two sons were compelled by the British officials to watch the execution, to teach them a lesson. 'Abaeata Anifelo, about 14 years old, had been brought into the police as a bugler and drummer. His younger brother, Laefiwane, was only about seven years old. Understandably, the terrible memory remained with them all of their lives and they remembered their father, about to climb to the gallows platform, putting an ancestral curse on Tulagi.[149]

Solomon Islanders who lived on Tulagi or were in regular contact with the enclave understood the advantages of literacy and further education. They saw the benefits of medical treatment and learnt the way government processes worked. They resented and could not understand taxation, which seemed not to provide any benefits. They were infuriated by the actions of many of the expatriates and had to come to terms with the concept of prison for supposed wrongdoing. Exactly how, and how much, this resentment was articulated is difficult to know. David Akin explored this in his 2013 book on Maasina Rule, colonialism and *kastom* (traditional culture). Anthropologist Ian Hogbin, who was in To`abaita in north Malaita in 1933, wrote that he only ever heard the people express discontent over specific issues such as taxation and adultery laws, and that it was rare to hear anyone condemn the government as a whole. However, Akin takes a more strident view, saying that Malaitans resented British law 'as an alien imposition'. He provides an opinion from Aningari from To`abaita, to the effect that the heart of the problem was that Europeans demanded that Solomon Islanders should forget the ways of their ancestors and behave in ways that had evolved in Europe. Anthropologist Douglas

---

148 ibid., 7, August 1922, 7.
149 David Akin was a friend of the two brothers in their old age and both emotionally recounted this experience to him. See also Keesing and Corris 1980, 186–87.

Oliver (based on Bougainville) believed much the same thing, saying they were punished for acting 'like a Solomonese when [they] should have acted like a European'.[150]

This growing feeling of resentment came to a head with the Fallowes Movement (also called the Chair and Rule Movement), a 1930s political protest grouping associated with Richard Fallowes, an Anglican priest on Isabel between 1929 and 1934. The Anglican Church's system of government there included secular functions, which some district officers felt trespassed into areas more properly controlled by the government. The church had installed wardens in each village and Fallowes inflicted corporal punishment, with canings for some offences. He came under suspicion from Tulagi when he helped translate a petition asking that district officer Francis Filose, who had been removed in 1932 for brutality, be restored to his post. In early 1933, under investigation by the protectorate government, opposed by government headman Walter Notare and native medical practitioner George Bogesi, and suffering mental strain, Fallowes left for a holiday in Australia. On his return, he was arrested and prosecuted on 14 counts of common assault and convicted of three. He returned to Isabel but was still mentally stressed and went to Guadalcanal to recuperate. He left the protectorate in 1935, severely depressed.

Fallowes returned in 1938 and, after discussions on Isabel, he helped paramount chief Lonsdale Gado organise three big meetings, at Bughotu on Isabel and on Savo and Gela, which were attended by a broad range of leaders, from priests to police and traditional leaders. Participants came from Isabel, Malaita, the Gela Group, Savo, Russell Islands, Guadalcanal and Makira. The meetings were reminiscent of the Gela annual *Vaukolu* Anglican mission meetings of the 1880s and 1890s. At Fallowes' suggestion, a speaker was elected to conduct the meetings' business. The meetings produced lists of grievances against the government and missions and petitions, several of which were presented to resident commissioner Ashley. The government was requested to establish a technical school on Gela and a dispensary in each district, staffed by a native medical practitioner. Other requests were to build a government hostel in Tulagi, to allow the sale of cartridges, to stop married men signing back on to plantations for a second term and that Malaitans be given a higher wage

---

150 Oliver 1961, 227. See also Akin 2013, 88–89.

for plantation labour and as boats' crews. The Fallowes Movement also asked for the Sydney prices for copra and shell to be posted publicly, and that the protectorate never be handed over to Australia or any other power. One request demanded, rather wishfully, that all wages be increased from 10 shillings to £12 a month. Lesser demands related to marriage, adultery and rights of appeal in court, compensation and customary payments for funeral attendants. Fallowes was also defended against the lack of support he received from his mission.

The third meeting was at Gela in June 1939. High commissioner Sir Harry Luke visited the protectorate immediately afterwards and, before he even reached Tulagi, he faced demands at Makira and Guadalcanal, where the discontent included unhappiness about goldmining, which brought no return to the people. Luke received the Gela petition when he arrived at Tulagi. He was disturbed at the degree of discontent and blamed Fallowes, who had done no more than facilitate the existing discontent. Interestingly, Sir Harry makes no mention of Fallowes in his book, which includes diary entries from his 1939 visit.[151] Fallowes was deported on 29 July. The Fallowes Movement declined, but it had become known throughout the protectorate and was the precursor of future movements such as Maasina Rule.[152]

All of this was happening near and on Tulagi. Many Malaitans who later become involved in Maasina Rule and late colonial politics attended the Fallowes meetings. Jonathan Fifi'i and Basiana's son 'Abaeata Anifelo, Stephen Sipolo, Ariki Nono'oohimae, Harisimae and Hoasihau from 'Are'are (the last three the key founders of Maasina Rule) were all on Tulagi during the Fallowes Movement years. They attended the meeting Fallowes called on Tulagi at Sasape.[153] As Fifi'i recounted:

> He [Fallowes] spoke in Pijin, 'I'm an Englishman too. But I see the British Government here treating you badly. I see all sorts of wrongs being done to you. The Government only helps their fellow white people. You've heard the Government tell you, "Oh, that white man is crazy"! Well, I'm not crazy. My mind is working perfectly clearly, and I'm a well educated man. I'm not crazy.

---

151 Luke 1945.
152 Bennett 1987, 259–63; Akin 2013, 100–06.
153 Keesing 1980, 103–04; Akin 2013, 127.

> 'I see the way you live in poverty. The Government collects lots and lots of money as export duty on the copra you produce with your labour. Why doesn't the Government do anything for you? They haven't brought you any education. I've been teaching people that they should have leaders to represent them. But the Government says, "No, we won't allow it".'
>
> He was right. The Government sent word that we were not to believe what the crazy man was preaching to us. Mr. Ashley, the Resident Commissioner, said, 'He's crazy. You aren't to believe anything he tells you. I'm the Government and I have the power here. I treat you well. We're not destroying anything of yours, He's just lying to you'.[154]

Clearly, Fifi`i was watching closely and thinking about the process of colonialism. During the war, he learnt more about the outside world from the Americans, particularly the African-American servicemen. Then he became a leader of the Maasina Rule movement. Living on Tulagi was all part of the education and politicisation of Fifi`i and others.

There were also other results of discontent that were expressed in a more indigenous manner. Cults such as La`aka, a Malaitan indigenous mechanism for coping with the British presence, reached their height in 1939. La`aka was a powerful ancestress who spoke through the medium of Noto`i, a priest in the central Kwaio mountains, expressing discontent over the deaths of her descendants on plantations and at government hands. La`aka decried the growing power of the missionaries. District officer Bengough estimated that the La`aka cult had 2,000 followers—a large proportion of the inland population in that area. Her increased power can be interpreted as part of anticolonialism.[155] In the neighbouring Kwara`ae area, the Bulu cult was one of several attempts to resist the Christian missions. As anthropologist Ben Burt explains: 'They reflected the aspirations of those who wished to adapt to the changing times on their own terms, through a ritual system under their own control.'[156] Similar types of reaction occurred elsewhere in Solomon Islands.

The power of traditional leaders had been weakened by mission and government activities, although the level of the effect varied from island to island. In trying to access the effect of life in the Tulagi enclave, as

---

154 Fifi`i 1989, 40–41.
155 Akin 2013, 106–09, 371–72, n. 45; account by Siufiomea in Keesing 1980, 104–07.
156 Burt 1994, 139; see also 135–39.

Judith Bennett says, we should not 'impose values of a later age on the government of a colonial backwater'.[157] Interviews by Keesing, Burt and Akin in the 1970s and 1980s are not necessarily representative of the situation decades earlier, and we would be wrong to read too much from our own contemporary perspective on to Solomon Islands in the 1930s. Nevertheless, it is inescapable that the government viewed Solomon Islanders as inferior producers and consumers on the lowest rungs of British capitalism. A protectorate was—in theory—a lesser form of British territory, quite different from a protected state or a Crown colony, and should have been less exploitative, yet the British chose to ignore this legal difference. Nevertheless, between the 1890s and 1910s, many thousands of Solomon Islander men worked overseas and knew a great deal about life in Queensland and Fiji. Others had viewed the circumstances in the Tulagi enclave. They had rising expectations that were not matched by the way Britain ruled their islands.

****

The tropical beauty and fragrancy cloaked the controlled social structure of the capital. Tulagi was a British outpost of empire where capitalism, class, race, ethnicity and place of residence were ordered and controlled. There were expatriate social substrata that included Christian denominations and branches of the Red Cross, the Masons and the Guomindang, and of course Solomon Islanders had their own motivations and levels of understanding. Malaitans made up the majority of indentured labourers and were the dominant indigenous group in the Tulagi enclave. This pattern continued later in Honiara. Other relationships through common interest among the Europeans in the Tulagi enclave were not as easily discerned. The war veterans, particularly those from World War I, were one group with an invisible link, as were the alcoholics and those who lived with the 'Black Peril' (local women). Ceremonial occasions—such as the coronation of King George VI in 1937, visits by the high commissioners or the opening of the Advisory Council meetings—were usually marked with a parade, a church service and a reception at the residency. The officials lived high on the central ridge, potentates of their tropical isle, although even they could fall from grace due to hard-drinking or philandering. Soon, however, it was all to come to an end.

---

157 Bennett 1989, 210.

8

Evacuation, invasion and destruction

> Nobody knows what the future may hold, even from day to day. Go ahead and make arrangements for yourself that you think proper. But don't forget that if the worst comes to the worst, the British Empire is in your debt, and make your demands accordingly.
>
> — Spearline Wilson to his wife, Jessie, 28 January 1942[1]

Tulagi in 1942

By 1942, Tulagi's southern third was a tropical botanical garden dotted with spacious bungalows and auxiliary buildings. A *Walkabout* article from 1937 described the buildings as being surrounded by

> massed displays of gay crotons, exotic flowering shrubs, and riotous blossoming creepers. White-painted stones fringed the footpaths; the grass was cut short by natives swinging pieces of steel, like lengths of hoop-iron, to keep down the grass-seed … and well-trimmed hedges of hibiscus are on either hand. It was those glorious hedges of hibiscus, gay with flowers five or six inches across in pinks and reds and apricots, and the lovely perfumes of the frangipani that was growing everywhere in large trees, that brought to us the real breath of the Tropics.[2]

---

1 UQFL, Wilson Papers and Photographs.
2 Weetman 1937, 34.

Map 8.1 Tulagi in 1942, showing the trenches and gun emplacements
Source: Copy from Hugh Laracy, restored by Vincent Verheyen.

The permanent population of the whole Tulagi enclave just before the Pacific War was about 600 Europeans, Chinese and Solomon Islanders. The British Solomon Islands had become a 'copra protectorate', its economy relying almost totally on growing and processing coconuts. In 1940, the Advisory Council consisted of resident commissioner Marchant as president, Chief Magistrate and legal adviser, Ragna Hyne, Treasurer and Collector of Customs, Pop Johnson, and Government Secretary, Major Eustace Sandars. The nonofficial members were the Anglican Bishop of Melanesia, Walter Baddeley, and three business representatives, Eric P. Monckton (a plantation owner from Shortland Islands), Jack Lotze (manager of Carpenters on Tulagi) and Harold Corry (a plantation owner from Guadalcanal).[3] Roger Keesing and Peter Corris nicely described the Solomons and Tulagi as a world of 'caricature colonialists, of whiskey, quinine and coconuts'.[4] The British had created a small, mildewed centre of British administrative and commercial power and superiority, quite similar to settlements in other areas of the Pacific and the wider British

---

3 *WPHCG (S)*, 18 February 1941, MAC, 18 November 1940, 27.
4 Keesing and Corris 1980, 30.

Empire. All of this came to an end as the Japanese invasion became inevitable and Solomon Islands emerged as a crucial turning point in the Pacific War.

Preparing for evacuation

A few Japanese fishermen were already living in the Solomon Archipelago before Woodford took over as Resident Commissioner. Once Tulagi was settled there were always a small number of Japanese living there. Residents became uneasy about Japanese '*sanpans*' (fishing vessels), which appeared regularly in the 1930s; photographs of one ship and its crew from 1936 have survived.[5] As Japan expanded into Korea and coastal China, this Japanese presence in the Pacific Islands increased—part of *Nan`y-ō*, the Japanese vision of their rightful place in the South Seas.

Other foreign residents became suspicious that the Japanese residents were there to look at the lie of the land and sea on behalf of their government for future military purposes, and indeed there were Japanese residents who assisted the military advance.[6] Terushige Ishimoto, who lived on Tulagi for decades and then moved to Rabaul, was a guide for the 1942 Japanese invasion of Guadalcanal. Kwaiami, another Japanese who had lived on Tulagi and Makira, was with Japanese forces on Malaita.[7] The same suspicion was often voiced of prewar Japanese in New Guinea and Australia, although of course these Japanese residents may have been commandeered by military authorities who had discovered their special knowledge of geography, English and Pijin. The Japanese were more numerous in Australian mandated New Guinea than in Australian Papua or Solomon Islands, but even in the mandated territory they were economically marginal and in numbers only a small fraction of that of the more dominant Chinese population.[8]

---

5   Hadlow 2016, 157, quoting Reverend John Metcalfe on Choiseul.
6   Struben 1963, 54–55.
7   Lord 1977, 25–27.
8   Iwamoto 1999, 104–22.

Plate 8.1 A Japanese fishing boat at Tulagi, 1936
Source: BM, Robert Lever Photographic Collection.

This chapter concentrates on the early defence plans and the evacuation—the end of British rule. It does not examine Tulagi under the Japanese or after it was retaken by the Americans in August 1942, although those periods are covered in the photographs in the chapter. War in Europe in 1939 had few initial consequences for Solomon Islands, except when copra and rubber prices rose, which was short-lived once fewer ships were available to transport these primary products. Alarmed by the deterioration of events in Europe, Marchant, almost as soon as he arrived in Tulagi in 1939, began to prepare for invasion. He had been in World War I and knew what was needed. Solomon Islands was clearly in the path of the Japanese southward advance.

Plate 8.2 Japanese fishermen on Tulagi, 1936
Source: BM, Robert Lever Photographic Collection.

In September 1939, the WPHC passed a regulation to form a defence force, which was amended a year later. Resident commissioner Marchant was away from the protectorate between March and September 1941, leaving Pop Johnson in charge. Then, in late 1941 and early 1942, the WPHC passed additional regulations to enable the repression of sedition, detention of suspect individuals, forced but paid requisition of property and special court provisions.[9] Marchant was appointed lieutenant-colonel and Eustace Sandars commanding officer of the BSIP Defence Force, supported by district officers. Sandars had arrived in the protectorate in 1928 as a subinspector in the armed constabulary, progressing quickly to

9 Anonymous 1941, 114; Armstrong 1944, 78–83; Maude and Johnson 1945, 97.

become a district officer and a senior member of staff. David Trench and Martin Clemens were his defence force deputies, with Donald Kennedy and Michael Forster also involved—all with the rank of captain.[10] The number of deputy commissioners of the WPHC was expanded to include the BSIP Defence Force captains, who were also appointed special commissioners—able to hold courts with limited jurisdiction in criminal matters. The other captain was Spearline Wilson, another World War I veteran and the officer in charge of the possible future evacuation. He sent his wife and family to Sydney in 1939 for the sake of the children's education and also as a precaution against the possibility of war.

Plate 8.3 Martin Clemens and men from the BSIP Defence Force
Source: UQFL, Wilson Papers and Photographs.

Solomon Islanders knew the war was coming, even if they did not fully understand why or the full extent of what was about to occur. Jonathan Fifi`i, who was on Tulagi until just before the war, said:

> We heard that Japan was at war with England. People were saying that that war would come to us in the Solomon Islands. Solomon Islanders asked, 'What is the war about'? Why are they fighting'? The Europeans said, 'Japan wants to take control of lots of areas that are under the King. The war isn't far away. The Japanese are going to come here'.[11]

---

10 Baddeley 1942.
11 Fifi`i 1989, 41.

Looking back, it is easy to see the changes as Japan expanded its area of influence. Taiwan was under Japanese rule from 1895 until 1945 after China lost the first Sino-Japanese war and ceded control of the island, which became Japan's first overseas territory. When World War I broke out, on behalf of the Allies, Australia captured Rabaul (capital of German New Guinea) and the Japanese captured German Micronesia. After the war, Japan was awarded Micronesia and Australia was awarded German New Guinea, both as League of Nations mandated territories. In the 1930s, Japan began to expand militarily, annexing Manchuria in 1931, and the next year began to develop military defences in Truk (Chuuk) in the Caroline Islands, walking out of the League of Nations in 1934 after censure. Chuuk had the best anchorage in Micronesia, and Dublon Island in Chuuk Lagoon became Japan's Pearl Harbor for its fleet—a strategic base from which to cast covetous eyes on South-East Asia. In 1937, Japan invaded coastal China, initiating war in the Pacific. The WPHC authorities and the British Colonial Office watched with concern but, as with German aggression, they chose appeasement, not confrontation.

In World War II, Japan was an ally of the Axis powers, Germany and Italy. With the capture of South-East Asia in mind, Japan decided to make a preemptive strike to destroy America's Pacific fleet. The leadup to the loss and then recapture of Tulagi and Guadalcanal began on 7 December 1941, when Pearl Harbor, the American military base at Hawai`i, was bombed by the Japanese, bringing the United States into World War II. Pearl Harbor was the headquarters of the US Pacific Fleet and was the largest US military base beyond the American mainland.

Foreign residents in the Tulagi enclave and more widely in the protectorate watched preparations with sinking hearts. Prisoners helped build a maze of trenches and gun sites on Tulagi (see Map 8.1). Military squads were trained, including a Chinese squad.[12] In preparation for the upcoming war, Gavutu became an Australian naval base, a side product of which were the first aerial photographs of Tulagi Harbour. Sir Charles Burnett, Inspector-General of the RAAF, visited Tulagi by seaplane in May 1939. After discussions with Marchant and an inspection, he recommended that Australia establish an advanced operation base near Tulagi. Wing-Commander John Brogan, an Australian armed forces divisional works officer, and Group Captain John Margrave Lerew, who was the new

---

12   Horton 1970, 127.

commanding officer of No. 24 RAAF Squadron, arrived in July 1940. They chose Gavutu and its smaller neighbour Tanambogo Island (5.2 hectares) as their base. They then located a similar site at Port Vila in the New Hebrides and returned to the Solomons with a French surveyor named Louis Page. The plan was to clear mangroves and jungle on Tanambogo, which was accomplished in 10 days by Kennedy and a team of Malaitan labourers working from dawn to dusk. Brogan, Lerew and Page also mapped out the site for a naval base on Gela Sule, across the harbour. The next stage of the operation was to construct a link between the two islands, expanding the slender natural causeway that already existed. Then, beginning in March 1941, Levers supervised a new project that employed 32 Gela Islanders, organised by Jack Svensen, to enlarge the causeway to 22.8 metres long and 2.4 metres wide. The new Tanambogo base contained an administrative block, stores building, kitchen, sergeants' mess, quarters for the airmen, a store for marine equipment and a large T-shaped underground shelter.

Gavutu was also upgraded. A bomb storage area was dug on the north side and a fuel dump created on the south side. Gavutu later housed 409,000 litres of high-octane aviation fuel, with supplementary reserves held on Gela Sule. A radio station was built on the top of the island, enabling communication with Townsville, in Queensland, and a large tank was constructed nearby, allowing a gravity-fed water supply. Tanambogo also had a camouflaged radio transmitter, and a remote-controlled direction-finding station was set up on tiny Gaomi Island, off Gavutu. Levers' medical clinic was expanded into a small hospital and the base had its own barge and a crash boat for rescues.[13]

In July 1941, the RAAF moved some of its Port Moresby–based Catalina seaplanes to Gavutu, although most of the personnel did not arrive until after February 1942. Australia's Department of Air took over weather reporting, which linked weather stations between Netherlands New Guinea and New Caledonia. The first commanding officer, Major J. Edmonds Wilson, arrived at Gavutu in September 1941, along with Sargent T.E. Hore, to set up a weather station that relayed information back to the Port Moresby–based Catalinas. Arrangements were also made to transfer some of the commandos from Australia's No. 1 Independent Company, then in Kavieng, New Ireland, to Tulagi. This company was scattered through

---

13 Jersey 2008, 10–12.

the islands between Buka and the New Hebrides with the intention of training local defence forces and remaining behind after the evacuation to assist the Coastwatchers—the 'invisible army'[14]—to gather intelligence. The company arrived in early November, using a Sutherland seaplane, their own motorised 80-ton lugger *Induna Star* and a regular voyage of BP's *Malaita*. The commandos erected three Vickers machine guns on swivel mountings for antiaircraft use. They also began to train the BSIP Defence Force. The local officers were commissioned as second lieutenants on 16 December 1941, 10 days after the Japanese attack on Pearl Harbor. The commanding officer, with the rank of major, was 43-year-old Vivian Fox-Strangways, who came from an aristocratic military family that included the Earls of Ilchester. Resident Commissioner-designate of the Crown Colony of Gilbert and Ellice Islands, he was diverted to Tulagi once the Japanese began to invade the outer Gilberts in January 1942. Fox-Strangways was not happy with defence force standards, although as his soldiers had all functioned effectively within the armed constabulary, he may have underestimated their efficiency, particularly for bush patrols. There were also two American naval men based as observers at Gavutu, lieutenants George H. Hutchinson and Samuel P. Weller. The Japanese advanced south so fast that little training occurred. After a month, Fox-Strangways was ordered back to Australia and some of the officers left the protectorate or joined the Coastwatchers. By March 1942, the defence force was no longer functioning. It was reformed later in the war, serving honourably, based on experienced constables. Initially, Solomon Islanders were routinely denigrated as unsuitable for modern warfare. In fact, they turned out to be very effective and excellent practitioners of jungle warfare.

The seaplane base, the arrival of the commandos and the existence of the small defence force both calmed and alarmed Tulagi's residents. It offered some protection, but also signalled that the Japanese were heading south. Commercial interests would have been pleased by the activity as the Gavutu air base and the brief commando presence tapped into their local supply network. Levers continued to operate its store on Gavutu

---

14   The Coastwatchers were prewar planters, officials and missionaries, mainly from Australia and New Zealand, and Solomon Islanders, who went into hiding during the Japanese invasion and formed a secret communication system to monitor enemy shipping and planes for the Allies. They also rescued Allied personnel who were stranded. There were about 100 Coastwatchers in the South Pacific. Many were stationed in Papua New Guinea, with 24 in Solomon Islands, including two in Bougainville. Their activities were crucial to alerting the Allied forces of approaching Japanese bombing raids. Horton 1970; Lord 1977; Moore 2013, entry for Coastwatchers.

and other supplies were readily available from BP on Makambo and from Carpenters at Tulagi, plus the Chinatown stores. BP's ships continued to bring in regular supplies from Australia.

A 'scorched earth' policy was adopted: everything that could be of value to the Japanese was to be either removed or destroyed. The initial evacuations from Tulagi began in mid-December 1941—first, the women and children, followed by nonessential government and commercial company staff and equipment. Fears intensified after the attack on Pearl Harbor on 7 December, which brought the Americans into the war. Marchant knew via the BBC on 8 December that the Japanese had also landed on the Malay Peninsula. On that day, he sent a launch to Bungana to extinguish the lighthouse. Two days later, Bishop Baddeley arrived at Bungana to discuss evacuation plans with the Sisters of the Cross, asking that the entire school move to Taroaniara the next day. About 9 pm on 14 December, Marchant sent for Wilson because rumours were circulating that Japanese vessels had been sighted between Truk and Solomon Islands.

Marchant had heard that residents of Chinatown were becoming uneasy; it was much worse than that and panic had set in. The details below have been pieced together from a short account by Spearline Wilson, Marchant's brief diary entries, a report by Bishop Baddeley, government documents and secondary sources.[15] There were planned procedures and alarm signals to deal with attack and invasion, which everyone knew, but they counted for little once panic began. The first panic was quite premature, caused by Jack Lotze. Wilson described it this way:

> On going down to the wharf in the first instance, I realized that a considerable panic was in progress amongst Europeans, Chinese and natives. Chinese Government employees had fled, Natives, Government and otherwise, had rushed the wharf, making it problematic whether evacuation boats could have got away if necessary, and a number of Europeans were in a very excited state.
>
> I met Rev Father Wall on his way to the hospital, to assist in quieting patients who were said to be breaking out. On my explaining the real situation … he agreed to work with me, and sent Father MacMahon round to the hospital. I next saw Mr. Lotze, in a state of great excitement. He said he had heard a most alarming story, and was on his way to try and persuade Mr. F.E. Johnson to escape

---

15   UQFL, Wilson 1942, Notes on the Evacuation of Tulagi, 6 February; Marchant Diary, 2 Jan 1942 to 6 May 1943, NASI BSIP 5/IV/1; Baddeley 1942.

8. EVACUATION, INVASION AND DESTRUCTION

> with him on the 'Balus'. I talked him into a reasonable condition of mind, and then myself, Father Wall and Lotze went down to Chinatown.
>
> The place was completely deserted, except for Him Choy [Ye Cai], who had tried single handed to stop the panic. On failing to do this, he was on his way to report to the Government. At this stage Lotze went ahead on his bicycle.
>
> On reaching the W.R.C. [W.R. Carpenter and Company] wharf, I found the 'Balus' alongside, with a party of natives throwing stores on board. A number of Europeans were on the Bridge, including Lotze and Judd from Carpenters. J.C.M. Scott and A. Glen from B.P.s and Smith from Hollis Bros. They were apparently about to set out for an unknown destination.[16]

Wilson managed to get Lotze and Scott back on the wharf and used Carpenters' phone to call government secretary Kidson. He also located the Chinese community, which had fled across the harbour to Gela Sule, and got them to return to their homes. After that, everyone calmed down until well into January 1942.

Christmas passed uneventfully. The last steamer had gifted Tulagi with all its freezer stores, which kept them supplied with meat, fruit and vegetables. Johno Johnstone from Hollis Brothers' New South Wales Fresh Food and Ice Company acted like Father Christmas, giving Wilson a frozen turkey and a bottle of whisky, while his 'yellow friends' (the Chinese) presented him with a bottle of German wine. His comments on New Year's Day 1942 on events in the islands is probably typical:

> I must say that this war took me by surprise in the end. Like most people, I did not think the Japs would move until Germany had a certain victory. We have certainly had ourselves hoodwinked on this occasion. Actually, it is probably the worst of our under-estimations.[17]

Rabaul on New Britain (the capital of Australian New Guinea) was within a League of Nations mandated territory, which meant that Australia could not legally fortify the town. Tulagi's residents would not have known that Australia had already surreptitiously strengthened the Rabaul garrison, which included the New Guinea Volunteer Rifles along with the 2/22nd

---

16   UQFL, Wilson 1942, Notes on the Evacuation of Tulagi, 6 February.
17   UQFL, Wilson Papers and Photographs, A.H. Wilson to F.A.G. Wilson, 1 January 1942.

Infantry Battalion and the No. 24 RAAF Squadron. Australia had also discussed fortification with the Americans. A joint effort was made to expand Vunakanau airfield near Rabaul to take B-17 bombers, and the United States had readied a ship in San Francisco, carrying defence equipment. They were too late. The final evacuation of Rabaul began on 11 December 1941 and the Japanese began to bomb Rabaul on 4 January 1942.[18] By Friday, 23 January 1942, Rabaul was in Japanese hands. A scorched-earth policy was implemented at Samarai, the Australian Papua port in China Strait at the far east of the New Guinea mainland. Only the Anglican church there was spared.[19] South-east, in the BSIP, the expatriate population did not need the fall of Rabaul or the evacuation of Samarai to alert them to the coming invasion. Most had already fled or were on their way out. They packed only essential possessions and paid off their servants, sending them back to their home islands. After Christmas, Marchant took the *Tulagi* on a trip around the Gela Group, looking for the best places to hide.[20] The hospital's nursing staff had already left, which led Wilson to quip that the doctor, Crichlow, and the pharmacist, Stackpool, were now doubling as sister-in-charge and nurse.[21]

BP's *Malaita* left Sydney on 8 December, the day after the attack on Pearl Harbor. Carrying 76 passengers, seven of them Solomon Islanders returning home, the ship travelled via Queensland ports, Port Moresby and Samarai, arriving at Makambo at 10 pm on 13 December.[22] The *Malaita* left two days later, returning to Tulagi on New Year's Day. Six passengers disembarked, three of whom booked on the next *Morinda* voyage to Sydney. The *Malaita* cleared Makambo on 2 January, calling at protectorate ports as the ship proceeded to Bougainville, reaching Rabaul on 6 January. Fifty-six passengers boarded at Rabaul, including 28 captive

---

18   Stone 1994, 31–74; Townsend 2017, 152–54, 290–91.
19   In the event, it was not needed. The Japanese were turned back at Milne Bay and never reached Samarai.
20   UQFL, Wilson Papers and Photographs, A.H. Wilson to F.A.G. Wilson, 1 January 1942.
21   UQFL, Wilson Papers and Photographs, A.H. Wilson to F.A.G. Wilson, 1 January 1942. News of the bombing of Rabaul was received on 31 December.
22   In *Hell's Islands*, Stanley Jersey (2008) mentions some other evacuation dates, which are not in Marchant's diary. He discounts an account by Father Wall that *Trienza*, a Phosphate Commission vessel, helped evacuate Nauru's foreign population, assisted by the Free French destroyer *Le Triumphant*, taking them to Port Vila, then travelling back to Tulagi to evacuate civilians, and remaining there for three days. As the evacuation of Nauru did not occur until 23 February, Wall has his dates wrong. Jersey relies instead on Ken Hay's 1942–43 diaries, which say that his wife and other European women left a few days before 16 December. Jersey suggests that the evacuation occurred on 12 December and that perhaps *Trienza* was sent on a special voyage. See Australian War Memorial, Dalrymple-Hay 1942–43, Typed Transcript of a Diary as a Coastwatcher.

Japanese civilians who were locked in the hold and their 19 guards. The ship steamed south, taking on two passengers at Bougainville, four at Faisi, 21 at Gizo, one at Isabel, three at Russell Islands and 11 at Tulagi. Despite an attack from a Japanese seaplane off Bougainville, which caused no damage, the ship ferried 98 passengers to Sydney, arriving on 26 January.[23] BP's ships had been blacked out at night since 1940 and all had guns fitted for defence.[24]

Raids and evacuation

On 9 January 1942, a Japanese seaplane passed over Gavutu and the next day Japanese bombers were spotted over Buka, flying south. Two BP ships evacuated residents from Tulagi. The *Morinda* arrived on 11 January and left for Port Vila on 14 January. The *Malaita* left Tulagi the next day—the last ship to depart before the bombing began. At 12.35 pm on 22 January, a Japanese four-engine 'Mavis' seaplane dropped five bombs into the harbour, which were meant for Gavutu, and then machined-gunned weapons posts, strafed the *Kurimarau* and narrowly missed a Catalina seaplane as it took off to escape. The Japanese pattern often involved a circuit out of Rabaul, first flying south-east to bomb Ocean Island, the headquarters of the Crown Colony of Gilbert and Ellice Islands, before heading for Tulagi.[25] Coastwatcher Paul Mason on Bougainville was usually able to give sufficient notice of any Japanese aircraft heading south to allow the pilots to shift the Catalinas to Marau Sound or Aola on Guadalcanal. The Catalinas had the capacity to make long trips and occasionally they followed Japanese seaplanes back to Rabaul, attacking as the planes landed. They had amazing capacity and could fly for up to 19 hours at 90 knots (167 kilometres an hour).[26]

The 22 January raid on Gavutu terrified the remaining population of Tulagi. At dawn the next day, the Sisters of the Cross on Taroaniara saw canoes from Tulagi passing by, being paddled to home villages. There was no bombing on 23 January. On 24 January, Marchant ordered Pop Johnson, Nathaniel Crichlow, William Blake and Ragna Hyne to take the most valuable government records to Auki. Some other records were

---

23 Jersey 2008, 17.
24 UQFL, Wilson Papers and Photographs, F.A.G. Wilson to Mary, 4 April 1940.
25 Knox-Mawer 1986, 102.
26 Jersey 2008, 14; Horton 1970, 25, 46.

destroyed. The official final evacuation of Tulagi began on Saturday, 24 January, mostly to Auki.[27] Aiming to keep Lotze calm this time around, just after midnight on 24 January, Wilson woke the Carpenters' manager and advised him to go to see Marchant, which he did. However, later in the night, Lotze deserted his house and the business and went into hiding with his Solomon Islander labourers and Smith from Hollis Brothers. At 7 the next morning, Wilson failed to persuade one of Hollis Brothers' Chinese employees to keep the freezer engine operating. Marchant ordered Wilson to marshal Chinese women and children, most of whom had again fled to Gela Sule, from where they were encouraged to return by Wilson, Yip Choy and Quan Park. By daybreak on Sunday, 25 January, the Chinese were back on Tulagi. Marchant mentions that they were evacuated but does not say to where. Most ended up on Makira under the care of district officer and Coastwatcher Michael Forster.

On Sunday, Lotze and Scott were located hiding in Port Purvis, where they had sailed Levers' *Kombito* up a creek into the mangroves. Charles Widdy—Levers' manager at Gavutu (1939–42), later Solomon Islands Labour Corps commander and a wing-commander during the war—Lotze and Scott were on board. Their only interest was catching up with the 300-ton labour-recruiting vessel *Kurimarau*, which had evacuated civilians from Rabaul and was heading for Australia. Wilson was given permission to requisition ammunition from Carpenters' store. The *Morinda* was not due for another two weeks, which panicked the remainder of Levers' staff. Scott, Lotze and Glenn all left to join Widdy on the *Kombito*, still hoping to take passage on the *Kurimarau* when the ship reached the Russell Islands.

District officer A.N.A. (Nick) Waddell closed the Shortland Islands government station on 25 January and retreated to Gizo. Marchant had ordered Waddell to evacuate all Europeans—first to Gizo and then to Batuna on southern New Georgia. When a Japanese aircraft carrier was reported to be off Choiseul, they fled in small boats to Tulagi—a slow, lengthy trip. One group on the *Fauro Chief* decided to sail straight to Australia, miraculously making their way through the Great Barrier Reef and reaching Mackay, in Queensland, on 11 February.[28] As much as

---

27   Cross 1979, 56. Many of the expatriates escaping Tulagi had to wait, as the *Morinda*, their transport out of the protectorate, did not arrive until 7 February.
28   Jersey 2008, 28–34.

possible of the contents of BP's Gizo warehouse was distributed, then the town was set alight.[29] Widdy returned to Gavutu.[30] The expectation of attack was palpable.

On Monday, 26 January, a Japanese reconnaissance plane flew over Tulagi, which caused all remaining civilians to leave for the Russell Islands. The defence force left Tulagi for Malaita on 27 and 28 January. On 28 January, Faisi and Gizo were evacuated and all remaining stores destroyed. Malaitan labourers on Guadalcanal plantations were contacted and returned to their home island. Forlorn Tulagi, still in British hands (just), waited for the end. On 29 January, a Japanese plane strafed Tulagi. Marchant and his headquarters staff left for Auki on Sunday, 31 January, with some essential records, which were later transferred to the bush camp at Furi`isango in the hills behind Auki. Bishop Baddeley had collected up the Patteson mat and the Selwyn staff (both important relics from early bishops) and the Siota altar silver, which were transferred to Tantalau village on Malaita for safekeeping.[31] Spearline Wilson ensured that the furniture, regalia and ritual items from the Masons' lodge on Tulagi were shipped to Malaita and hidden in the bush behind the district officer's house at Auki.[32] Evacuees from the north-west arrived at Tulagi on 2 February. The Australian Government chartered the *Morinda* for a special evacuation voyage, leaving Sydney on 31 January and sailing straight to Tulagi. Trench and Clemens were aboard, returning from leave. The remaining foreign residents from Bougainville and all around the BSIP who wished to leave had made their way to Tulagi on a fleet of cutters and schooners. The ship arrived on 8 February, departing the next day. Spearline Wilson joined this final voyage, leaving Blake as the evacuation officer. The *Morinda* arrived at 10.20 am, which was bad timing, as the Japanese bombers usually arrived mid-morning each day. The military sent their crash boat—accompanied by Levers' *Kombito*, skippered by Ernie Palmer, with Father Wall also aboard (who was then based at the RAAF base at Gavutu)—to warn the ship to hide in Mboli Passage. Before the manoeuvre was complete, a Kawanishi seaplane arrived, sighted the ship and began a bombing raid. Captain S. (Stinger) Rothery was able to swing the *Morinda* wide of the bombs and strafing.

29   ibid., 25–27.
30   Taroaniara became the Melanesian Mission's headquarters again in late 1942, once the Japanese were expelled from the Gela Group.
31   Baddeley 1942, 4.
32   Information from Alan Lindley, 1 May 2016.

Luck was with the Tulagi evacuation as the *Morinda* was carrying tons of explosives and aviation fuel; and the plane did not use its machine guns on the small boats milling in Tulagi Harbour.

Blake's authority was ignored by Lieutenant Don Macfarlan, the naval liaison officer appointed to work with resident commissioner Marchant.[33] Macfarlan ordered the *Morinda* to dock at Gavutu, although the evacuees were waiting at Makambo or on their boats. Pandemonium ensued as they quickly reloaded their possessions and set off in a small armada towards Gavutu. Blake managed to shift some government records from Makambo to Gavutu on board the *Tulagi*, but when he arrived at Tanambogo an argument about evacuation was taking place, when they should have been following the prearranged plan. After the ship's narrow escape, Captain Rothery was contemptuous of a message he received from Tulagi, asking why he had docked at Gavutu before officially entering the port of Tulagi. He was also worried when he heard from Father Wall that there were 200 people waiting to board—far exceeding his passenger licence number. Most of them had no tickets and the government officials made no promise to pay. Pop Johnson's account presents the official version. Dick Horton, District Officer for Guadalcanal, recounted the saga differently, but of course his version was secondhand. Rothery decided he was in control and would sail at 5 pm. Finally, the Tulagi government said it would authorise transport of the unticketed evacuees. Johnson claimed that Rothery denied him and other officials the right to board, but then allowed on board military personnel who had escaped from New Guinea. Finally, the captain was persuaded to sail to the Tulagi wharf, where some of the cargo from Makambo was waiting. However, the prisoners, who usually did the loading, had already been released and the ship's crew refused to assist, presumably because it was against union rules. Loading commenced using commandos, SSEM staff and some of Levers' labourers.[34]

This continued by hand well into the night. The derricks were mounted on the other side of the ship and the captain would not allow them to be moved. Because a blackout was in force no one really knew what was loaded and the Kieta (Bougainville) government records were left on Makambo wharf. Rothery insisted that he would only carry the number of

---

33   Once Tulagi was evacuated, Macfarlan became a Coastwatcher at Berande plantation on Guadalcanal.
34   Horton 1970, 14–18.

passengers specified under the *Navigation Act*s, although in an emergency it was usual for this regulation to be waived. He said that without an extra lifeboat he could not exceed the quota, and none was available. Rothery counted heads and only allowed women and children and men with wives to board, leaving 23 Chinese and European civilians behind. This was the last ship leaving for Australia. A desperate rabble of 120 planters, missionaries, officials and three Japanese internees (long-term residents of the protectorate) with their six guards, as well as some military personnel from Bougainville, scrambled on board. At 9.10 pm, once the *Morinda* was laden with the legal number of passengers, their boxes and suitcases, government files, weapons and ammunition, Macfarlan ordered the ship to sail. On the way to Sydney, four extra passengers who had managed to evade the eyes of the captain were discovered. Two words come to mind: shemozzle and incompetence. The Resident Commissioner reported Macfarlan and Rothery to the Australian Prime Minister, to no avail.[35] However, Horton clearly disagreed with Johnson's version of events:

> The evacuation had been very nearly too late: it had been badly planned and badly organized, and the fault lay with the Government, whose attitude was inflexible and quite out of keeping with the facts. Even a modicum of foresight and planning would have avoided a situation which very nearly had most serious results and whose repercussions left a most unpleasant legacy.[36]

The Chinese

One of the myths of Solomon Islands history is that all the Chinese were left behind when foreign nationals were evacuated. Certainly, they were treated badly, but some of them chose to stay, and about one-quarter, including Quan Park and Yip Choy and their families, boarded ships travelling to Sydney or Nouméa during the first wave of the exodus.[37] One group of 24 people, including 22 Chinese, joined Isabel planter Charles Bignell, who sailed his schooner *Valere* to Santo and Port Vila. Another group escaped on *Hygenia II* just ahead of the Japanese.[38] Most of the Chinese children were evacuated. Considerable numbers of the Chinese adults hid in villages for the duration of the war, some initially in the

---

35 Jersey 2008, 36–40.
36 Horton 1970, 18.
37 Bennett 1987, 288.
38 Clarence 1982, 146.

Western District, but mainly on Makira under the supervision of district officer Forster. Johnny Chan Cheong, the Sasape boatbuilder, fled with his family deep into the jungle of Isabel, helping the Allies whenever he could. Quan Hong spent the war years on Makira. His younger brother Kwan Ho Yuan (Quan Haoyuan), along with Kwan Cho (Quan Zhu), sailed his trading ship *Auki* to Isabel, only to have it commandeered by the British Government. Kwan Ho Yuan accepted an offer from acting military governor David Trench to operate a tourist artefact shop at the American base that became Honiara, leaving his family on Makira. He worked as a middle man between the Americans who were keen to take home grass skirts, weapons and carvings and local villagers and members of the BSIP Defence Force and the Labour Corps who made the items in their spare time. The Gizo-based Chinese hid on Rendova, Ranongga and Choiseul until they were rounded up by the Coastwatchers, who arranged their transfer to Makira.

After the war, the British decided there would be no compensation payments for any prewar residents or companies, which ruined the Chinese traders and European owners of small plantations and businesses.[39] Quan Hong was typical. He began a business in Gizo in 1927 and built up his holdings to include four branch stores and three trading vessels used throughout the Western and Central districts. When the Japanese arrived, he lost everything. He and his family escaped to Rendova and then to Kirakira on Makira. After the war, he was refused permission to set up again in Gizo and returned to Hong Kong and Canton (Guangzhou) to establish a business, arriving back in Honiara in 1951.[40]

The temporary BSIP headquarters on Malaita

Scott had surrendered the keys to BP's Makambo base to Ken Hay, a plantation manager, who was given permission to act as the company's last remaining representative. Hay helped himself liberally and transported loads of supplies to Guadalcanal, where he was generous with his distribution. He and Macfarlan spent most of April shifting the stores to three locations inland on Guadalcanal.[41] Marchant also had to deal with

---

39 Willson et al. 1990, 98–99; Moore 2008; Laracy 1974; Bennett 1987, 152, 206, 208–09, 216, 224–25, 230, 236, 237–38, 249, 250, 252, 253, 254, 256, 268, 269, 271, 288, 319, 330; Willmott 2005, 19; Lord 1977, 161.
40 'QQQ's Milestone Celebration: A History in Its Own Making', *Solomon Star*, 8 February 2016.
41 Australian War Memorial, Dalrymple-Hay, 1942–43, Typed Transcript of a Diary as a Coastwatcher.

government officers who wanted to resign and enlist in Australia. In late February, district officers Dick Horton, Henry E. Josselyn and Martin Clemens all wanted to leave Auki to enlist. Marchant refused permission, because protectorate duties continued and the Coastwatcher system was being established. Horton insisted on resigning, much to Marchant's annoyance. In late February, Marchant was still trying to organise for key protectorate documents from the Secretariat, Treasury and Lands and Surveys Department to be evacuated to Port Vila and on to Australia. He succeeded in early March, just as heavy bombing of Tulagi began. The BSIP archives ended up in Sydney, under the care of Pop Johnson and Spearline Wilson for the duration of the war.

There were many more tasks to accomplish and Marchant needed all the staff he could muster. Carpenters' and BP's marine stores were blown up—probably far too soon, as this early move was later regretted. The Tulagi radio transmitter was transferred to Auki and a dummy structure substituted, which the Japanese kept attempting but always failing to bomb. Charles Bengough ran the Auki office and the radio link, continuing after Marchant and his party retreated to Furi`isango on 13 February.[42] Father Jim Wall rescued the remaining official records and the mail sacks deserted on Makambo wharf. They were taken to Auki, from where Josselyn bravely set off in a small boat to sail them to the New Hebrides, and eventually reached Sydney with them. Josselyn did not return until 7 August, when he and Widdy acted as guides for the US 1st Marine Raider Battalion, sent to retake Tulagi.[43] District officer Clemens was sent to the Eastern Solomons District to organise the evacuations to the New Hebrides, after which he was based at Aola on Guadalcanal until the Japanese arrived in June. He then shifted to the mountains around Gold Ridge, providing valuable Coastwatcher information.[44]

The Eastern Solomons District escaped the war. District officer Forster remained on Makira—shepherd to the Chinese who were evacuated there. District officer Colin Wilson remained on Vanikolo until 1944. Several gold prospectors, Fred Campbell and his young sons Jack and Pat, Bert Freshwater and rotund Ken Hay chose to stay put at the mountain fastness of Gold Ridge.[45] Kelemende Nabunobuno, one of the employees of the

---

42 Lieutenant-Colonel Bengough was killed when his aircraft was shot down at sea in August 1943. *PIM*, 17 February 1945, inside back cover.
43 Jersey 2008, 41; Horton 1970, 23–24.
44 Clemens 1998.
45 Moore 2013, entries for Frederick Melford Campbell, Jack Campbell and Kenneth Dalrymple-Hay.

Guadalcanal Sluicing and Dredging Company, also remained at Gold Ridge.[46] Courtesy of Hay and his access to the BP store at Makambo, these men lived in luxury, not wanting for material possessions, food or alcohol. They were able to watch the Japanese and American invasions and listen in on the radio to all the Coastwatcher and government information. It must have been like sitting in the back seats in a big theatre, watching the events far below.

Marchant also had to contend with various Europeans, missionaries, planters and Chinese merchants who had opted to stay but soon realised their error and wanted to leave the protectorate. He continued to move between his Malaita base and Tulagi, trying valiantly to control the situation from a distance, giving headmen and the native courts special powers. He offered to pay indigenous leaders 5 per cent of any loot they could locate. On 18 March, Marchant readied 10 protectorate youths and one from the New Hebrides to travel to Fiji for entry to the Central Medical School to train as native medical practitioners and to attend the Wireless School and Queen Victoria School. Transport proved slow to arrange; they did not depart until mid-April.

Heavy bombing began on 18 March. Marchant was not happy when he visited Tulagi again on 20 March:

> Found my house had been broken into—linen cupboard, office, bed room. All linen taken also some blankets. All this must have happened since Davis boarded up the bedroom door of 17th Apr as this was wrenched open.[47]

During March and April, the Japanese regularly bombed Tulagi, Makambo and Gavutu–Tanambogo. Initially, the attacks concentrated on Tulagi, aimed at the mock radio station and the hospital. Strangely, they ignored the recently established RAAF base on Tanambogo. However, it was not long before the Gavutu–Tanambogo air base was under attack. Some of the bomb craters left behind were huge: one on Gavutu measured 12.8 metres wide by 2.4 metres deep.[48] Limited protectorate services continued. On 6 March, Dr Thomson went to Gavutu to visit a patient, travelling there with district officer Bengough.[49] The Shortland Islands fell to the Japanese on 30 March. On 4 April, Marchant and his temporary

---

46   Jersey 2008, 45.
47   Marchant 1942–43: 20 March 1942.
48   Jersey 2008, 24.
49   Marchant 1942–43: 6 March 1942.

government retreated permanently from Auki inland to Furi`isango. At the end of April, there were reports of a large concentration of Japanese ships heading for the Solomons. On 18 April, Coastwatcher Donald Kennedy reported that a Japanese seaplane carrier, an escort frigate, a corvette and six Zeroes fitted with floats were in Thousand Ships Bay, Isabel, just under 100 kilometres from Tulagi. On 30 April, the Japanese dropped 26 bombs on the core islands in the enclave, damaging two Catalinas. One was towed into hiding at Aola and, remarkably, the next day Terry Ekins flew his Catalina to Rathmines on Lake Macquarie in New South Wales, without the use of the navigation instruments, which had been damaged in the attack.

In late March, Anglican Bishop Baddeley and the Bungana refugees left Taroaniara via Mboli Passage, initially to Siota and then to the hospital at Fauaabu, west Malaita.[50] As many as possible of the schoolgirls were sent to their home islands and villages, while the religious sisters moved to Aesasale, an Anglican village high in the central Malaitan mountains.[51] In late August, they moved to Qaigeo, a coastal village, and then to Fiu, Auki and to Aola on Guadalcanal, where they boarded USS *Barnett* to travel to the New Hebrides.[52]

Bishop Walter Baddeley described the evacuation:

> So we returned to Taroaniara, and then throughout the day at intervals we had a grandstand view of the dive-bombing of Tulagi—principally the wireless station, which we knew had not been inhabited or used since late January, three months before! During the afternoon the main body of the small garrison at Gavutu evacuated the place and crossed the Boli Passage en route to the schooners which had been prepared for their getaway—there being no intention of any definite effort to hold Tulagi-Gavutu, or even to delay the enemy. So at 5 p.m., most regretfully, I left Taroaniara for Siota, with a view to being ready to cross to Mala. Gordon, who has been No. 1 engine-boy on the *Southern Cross* for the past nine years, readily offered to stay on at Taroaniara and do such caretaking as was possible—two other lads remaining with him. At Siota several other volunteers offered to do the same. So at 7 p.m.—with the sky all lighted up with the burning oil dumps and stores at Gavutu and Tulagi—we set out for Government Headquarters at Auki.

---

50   Cross 1979, 48–53.
51   A detailed account is provided in ibid., 62–81.
52   ibid., 87–94.

> It was a rough passage of nearly seven hours. I admit that I sat with my head over my left shoulder, for I imagined there might be Jap destroyers in Indispensable Straits to cut off any who might be making a get-away from Gela. But nothing untoward happened, and as we entered the passage at Auki, I uttered a profound and reverent 'Thank God for that'. At this moment, Mr Bullen, who had travelled with me, 'came to' and exclaimed, 'Yes, I thought she (the *Patteson*, that is) was going right over twice out there in the middle'. I fear I had had no place in my mind for rough seas: he apparently had had no care for Japs![53]

The RAAF base at Gavutu–Tanambogo continued to operate until 2 May, when, mostly destroyed, it was abandoned to the imminent arrival of Japanese land forces. On the same day, there were heavy raids on the Gavutu–Tanambogo base and that night permission was given to withdraw. Detonation of all structures commenced, using 44-gallon drums of aviation fuel with gelignite strapped on.[54] The noise of the explosions was heard and the glow of the fires as they destroyed the base were visible from the west coasts of Guadalcanal and Malaita. All the charges were detonated and the last 53 military servicemen slipped away to the *Balus*, which was hidden in mangroves in Mboli Passage. The next day, they headed for Aola and south to Maura Bay, Makira, then moved on to Santo and Port Vila on Efate, both in the New Hebrides. The last of the RAAF staff left Tulagi Harbour just as four Japanese warships sailed in.

The 3rd Kure Special Naval Landing Force of the Japanese Army left Rabaul on 29 April, using the cruiser-minelayer *Okinoshima*, under the flag of Rear Admiral Kiyohide Shima. They successfully captured the Tulagi enclave on 3 and 4 May without any resistance. On 4 May, a US and Australian aircraft carrier task force on its way to Port Moresby launched an air attack on the Japanese at Tulagi, from USS *Lexington* and USS *Yorktown*. They caused damage but could not halt the takeover. The destroyer *Kitutsuki* was sunk in Tulagi Harbour and destroyers *Yuzuki* and *Okinoshima* were badly damaged, as were several landing craft and seaplanes.[55] West of the Solomons and south-east of the tail of New Guinea, between 4 May and 8 May, the Battle of the Coral Sea was fought

---

53 Baddeley 1942, 5–7.
54 Jersey 2008, 48.
55 Lord 1977, 11–16; Trench 1956a; Trench 1956b; Trench1956c; Noel Butlin Archives Centre, Burns Philp & Co. Archives, N115–250, Kenneth H. D. Hay to Chairman of Directors, Burns Philip (South Sea) Co. Ltd, 7 February 1942.

by American, Australian and Japanese ships and planes. It was the first sea battle fought entirely by aircraft with the ships all out of sight of each other. The battle is usually said to have been a tactical victory for the Japanese and a strategic victory for the Allies; the Japanese advance was checked and major aircraft carriers were damaged. The battle also strained the Japanese advance through the islands to the east, where they were involved in occupying the Solomon Archipelago.

The Japanese took over the smouldering wreck of what had once been a proud British port town. Having captured the Tulagi enclave, the Japanese established a seaplane base at the RAAF facilities on Gavutu–Tanambogo and in early June began to build an airfield at Lungga Point on Guadalcanal.

Meanwhile, the BSIP Government in exile was operating from Malaita. One task was to train Solomon Islanders as wireless operators. In 1942, Methodists Jacob Leti (Letesasa) and Simione Makini were sent to the new Wireless School in Fiji to attend a two-year course, as were another two from the Methodist system, Esau Hiele and Jobi Tamana. Leti and Makin failed to meet educational entry standards and were sent for two years to the Queen Victoria School at Nasinu, Fiji, before proceeding to the Wireless School. Makini qualified at the end of 1944 and was sent back to work for the BSIP administration. Leti was diagnosed with tuberculosis and sent to hospital in Fiji. Hiele proved a quick learner and soon mastered the new AWA equipment, and was then transferred to Gizo to take over the government wireless station there. Tamana was less successful and was discharged. Three more Solomon Islanders were sent to Fiji for training: Silas Sitai, Hugo Gigini and David Sade. Mark Rusa and Alec Lianga were recommended for training, as was Bill Bennett, who had already been trained in basic Morse code and wireless technology. Sitai did poorly and Bennett was considered intelligent but verbose (perhaps an indication of his future calling as a radio announcer). All three eventually passed the course and were sent home in March 1946. Many of these names are recognisable as members of the elite Solomon Islands families of the 1960s and 1970s.[56]

---

56 Hadlow 2015, 194–95; Hadlow 2016, 160–62; *WPHCG (S)*, 15 February 1939, MAC, 7 November 1938, 9, 6 April 1940, 52, MAC, 27 November 1939, 52, 14 October 1940, MAC, 1 July 1940, 214.

Around 100 Europeans and a similar number of Chinese remained in the protectorate after the Japanese invasion. The official contingent in Marchant's headquarters party consisted of Lieutenant Tom O. Sexton from the Royal Australian Navy Volunteer Reserve and Lieutenant H.W. Bullen (formerly of the Melanesian Mission) from the BSIP Defence Force, as wireless and cipher officers, and the protectorate officers who joined the Coastwatchers, although they were usually based at outposts. Also present for various periods were the Catholic Bishop and some of the priests and sisters, the Anglican Bishop and 15 of his staff (both men and women), Northcote Deck and five of his SSEM staff and a few of the planters.[57] Sexton was replaced with Captain Robert Taylor (the Tulagi wireless operator), who had been on leave, and they were also joined by Sergeant Clifford R. Kurtz from the US Army. With them was their team of Solomon Islander support staff, without whom nothing would have been possible. In early May, several boats set off south to Port Vila, where their passengers were able to board the *Manoora* for Sydney. The Chinese in the party were refused boarding and returned to Malaita. They stayed there or on Makira for the remainder of the war.[58]

Solomon Islanders

The Japanese remained in control of Tulagi for three months until American retaliatory raids on 7 and 8 August 1942. They had dug tunnels into the higher reaches of Tulagi and Gavutu, which they defended. During the final land onslaught, Japanese were incinerated in the tunnels when the Americans advanced with flame-throwers. Still unresolved is the question of the Japanese gold bullion, said by some to have been ransacked in Asia on their way south and stored in caves on Tulagi. It was real enough for prime minister Solomon Mamaloni, desperate to find funds for his ailing government in April 1996, to send police to search for it. Other Solomon Islanders have spent many years searching for the elusive booty.

---

57 Baddeley 1942, 2; Hadlow 2015, 174.
58 Jersey 2008, 53; Kwai 2017.

Plate 8.4 Members of the Japanese garrison on Tulagi, 1942
Source: US National Archives and Records Administration.

Plate 8.5 A camouflaged Japanese truck on Tulagi, August 1942
Source: US National Archives and Records Administration.

Plate 8.6 A Japanese 13 mm gun on Tulagi
Source: US National Archives and Records Administration.

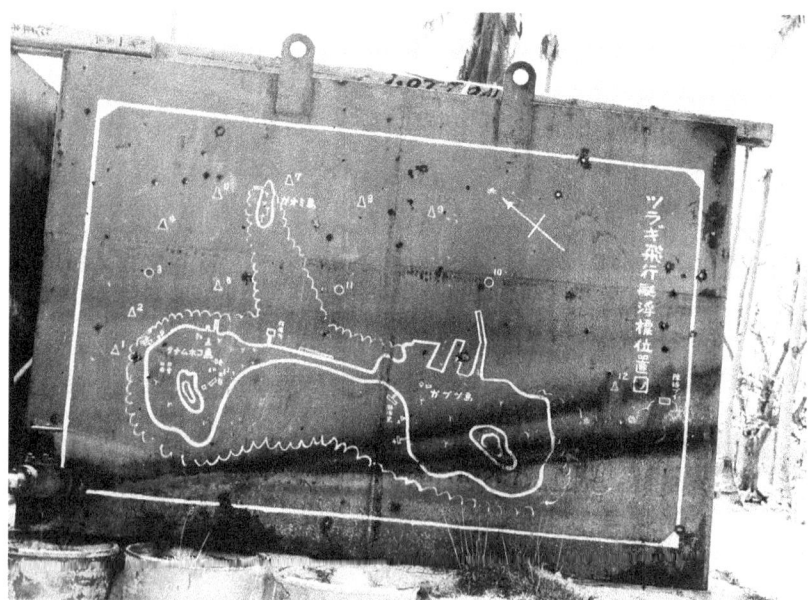

Plate 8.7 A Japanese plan of their flying boat facilities at Gavutu–Tanambogo
The Japanese characters on the right say: 'Tulagi Islands Flying Boat Buoy Locality Map.'
Source: US National Archives and Records Administration; translation by Morris Low.

Plate 8.8 A Solomon Islander trading on Tulagi, 1940s
Source: US National Archives and Records Administration.

How Solomon Islanders coped with the war has been covered in general in several publications, most recently in an account by Anna Kwai.[59] The administration used small government vessels such as *Hygenia II* and the auxiliary cutter *Wai-ai*, as well as the abandoned evacuation fleet in Tulagi Harbour, to return 1,500 labourers to their home islands. After this was accomplished, the fleet was sailed to Marau Sound and hidden in the mangroves, where most of the vessels survived the war. The Gela people continued to cooperate with the remaining military forces on Tulagi and Gavutu–Tanambogo, helping to unload supplies.[60] Once the Tulagi and Anglican headquarters in the Gela Group were deserted, the locals also began looting and then storing materials out of sight. Marchant recorded:

> Houses on Tulagi have been entered by Gela natives & wanton destruction of personal belongings carried out. It is not clear how much was stolen, but boxes opened & contents strewn on floor— it appears they were looking for money, liquor & clothing. Govt. Store also broken into with similar result.[61]

---

59 Laracy and White 1988; White et al. 1988; White and Lindstrom 1990.
60 Jersey 2008, 46.
61 Marchant 1942–43: 11 March 1942.

Most of the Gela people moved inland for the duration of the war. A small group of loyal parishioners remained in villages near the Siota and Taroaniara bases, although they could only watch when the Japanese pillaged the mission furniture, burnt books and smashed china.[62] The British lamented that some of the villagers on Guadalcanal, Savo and in the Gela Group were selling food to the Japanese after Tulagi was evacuated.[63] George Bogesi, a native medical practitioner from Isabel, stationed on Savo before the invasion, was reported to have approached the Japanese for payment for medical care he provided to survivors from a Japanese destroyer. He was interrogated and taken to Tulagi, where he acted as interpreter and tended wounded Japanese. Marchant believed that Bogesi had acted as 'scribe/cook to the Jap. Commandant'.[64] It seems likely that his medical skills were more in demand than his cooking. Later, Bogesi helped locate some of the Coastwatchers, probably out of hatred for one of them, Donald Kennedy.[65] The Japanese took Bogesi to Rabaul, returning him late in the war. The British prosecuted him for treason and imprisoned him in Australia. Like many Solomon Islanders, he was ambivalent about his role and his relationship with the British and the Japanese.[66] After all, both groups were invaders.

The constant bombing from air and sea, and the incursions by foreign troops on their lands, were disturbing and dangerous for Solomon Islanders, but large numbers of men joined the BSIP Defence Force and the Labour Corps. The question of collaboration has been raised, as it was wherever the Japanese advanced through Asia and the Pacific. The British arrogantly expected loyalty in their absence, when they had done little to deserve it, given the colonial relationship that existed with Solomon Islanders. While the Allied military tacticians may have felt confident, victory was by no means assured and the villagers could not predict the future of the war. Most sources report that Solomon Islanders remained loyal to the British. The biggest change was that they had seen their 'masters' turn and run in fear, after decades of assertions of superiority. The situation was similar all through the war-torn Pacific. European superiority could never be assumed again and no matter how much the colonisers tried to reinstate their old regime, something had changed. In the Solomons, the Maasina Rule years (1944–52), when Malaitans and others on neighbouring islands confronted the British with their own vision of a different future, were evidence of this change.

---

62 Baddeley 1942, 5.
63 Marchant 1942–43: 20 May 1942.
64 Marchant 1942–43: 27 May 1942, see also entry for 19 May 1942.
65 Laracy 2013, 211–28.
66 Moore 2013: entry for George Bogesi; Marchant 1942–43: 19 May 1942; Laracy 2013, 229–42.

Plate 8.9 A devastated Gavutu Island and the causeway to Tanambogo Island, 1942
Source: US National Archives and Records Administration.

Plate 8.10 The causeway between Gavutu and Tanambogo islands, 1942
Source: US National Archives and Records Administration.

Plate 8.11 Smoke from the American bombing on Tulagi, 7 August 1942

Source: US National Archives and Records Administration.

Plate 8.12 This photograph was taken after the Americans bombed Tulagi on 7 August 1942

The roof of the Tulagi Club and its adjacent tennis courts are visible to the left of the main fire, just behind the smaller area of smoke at the Point. The main fire is in the single officers' quarters. The cricket ground is visible to the right of the main fire and the Resident Commissioner's house can be seen in the upper right. Some of the hospital buildings are visible in the bottom right of the photograph, with a Red Cross symbol on the roofs.

Source: US National Archives and Records Administration.

Plate 8.13 Makambo Island being bombed, with Tanambogo Island burning in the background. The main Makambo wharf and the settlement area are visible
Source: US National Archives and Records Administration.

Ironically, the aerial photographs of Tulagi taken by the Australian defence forces just before the war and American photographs of Tulagi, Makambo and Gavutu–Tanambogo under bombardment are some of the best taken of the Tulagi enclave. War photography reveals greater detail of Tulagi than is readily available from written records. For example, a pre–American invasion aerial photograph is annotated with 'Blue Beach', a planned landing place, and is marked to show the Japanese antiaircraft batteries at the wireless station and the single officers' quarters, adjacent to the cricket ground. The photograph reveals the expansion of settlement in this area of the outer coast, which by 1942 was probably more significant than the original settlement on the inner coast.[67] Tracks crisscrossed the small island and extensive clearing and reclamation had been completed to create extra

---

67 Ever increasing numbers of wartime photos are available on the web, mainly searchable under 'Tulagi, 1942'.

facilities on the outer side of the island. Another photograph, of American marines wading ashore in a relaxed manner, suggests they were not in the first wave of arrivals. It shows the central ridge and the still undeveloped north-western end of the island. Other photographs taken on or just after the 7 August bombardment show the remains of Chinatown's wharves, the police, prison and hospital compounds and the Gavutu–Tanambogo and Makambo complexes. There are also photographs of buildings blazing after the American attack.

Once the Americans retook Tulagi in early August 1942, the harbour became a base for the American fleet and various facilities were rebuilt.[68] A Gela district officer was stationed there and, in a rudimentary way, the business of the BSIP Government continued, although the accommodation available to young district officer Cyril Belshaw when he arrived in 1944 was little better than that which Charles Woodford, the first Resident Commissioner, constructed in 1897.[69] From August 1942, the Americans and Australians, assisted by New Zealanders and some Pacific Islander troops, continued to pursue the Japanese north. By 1943, they were heading towards the Philippines along the north coast of New Guinea. Manila was recaptured in February 1945, Japanese cities were bombed and in August two atomic bombs were dropped, causing the Japanese to surrender. Isolated groups of Japanese remained on some western Solomon Islands until the end of the war. The last few soldiers hidden deep in the mountains did not surrender until the 1960s. No attempt has been made here to cover the military history of the Tulagi enclave. There are many excellent books about Solomon Islands during the Pacific War. The photographic essay below provides a short summary of the American occupation of Tulagi and Gavutu–Tanambogo.

---

68 Christ 2007.
69 Information from Cyril Belshaw, 20 January 2009.

8. EVACUATION, INVASION AND DESTRUCTION

Plate 8.14 The remains of Chinatown, with Makambo in the background, August 1942
Source: US National Archives and Records Administration.

Plate 8.15 Japanese and Korean prisoners-of-war on Tulagi, August 1942
Source: US National Archives and Records Administration.

Plate 8.16 An American machine-gun post on Tulagi
Source: US National Archives and Records Administration.

Plate 8.17 An American cargo ship at Tulagi wharf, 1944
Source: US National Archives and Records Administration.

Plate 8.18 Tulagi cricket ground turned into a tent town for the Americans
Source: US National Archives and Records Administration.

Plate 8.19 The US Navy Marine Corps Cemetery on Tulagi, on the edge of the former cricket ground. After the war, bodies were exhumed and returned to the United States
Source: US National Archives and Records Administration.

Plate 8.20 The marines' shower on the beach, Tulagi, May 1943
Source: US National Archives and Records Administration.

Plate 8.21 American ships gathered at Tulagi in March 1945 on their way to the Battle of Okinawa
Source: US National Archives and Records Administration.

Assessing Tulagi

Racial segregation on Tulagi was obvious in the separation of Chinatown and the segregated wards in the hospital.[70] The glaring anomaly in the European hierarchy was Dr Nathaniel Crichlow, who was of mixed Chinese and Scottish ancestry. Crichlow, despite his heritage, did not speak Chinese and seems to have been regarded as British (or rather, Scottish). His relationship with the local Chinese is unclear.[71] There were others in this in-between class. Appointed in the mid-1910s, Naphtali Kaisawani was a Fijian sergeant-major in the police, well-educated and

---

70 WPHCA, No. 800 of 1914, RC C.M. Woodford to HC WPHC, 3 April 1914, No. 2954 of 1926, Dr N. Crichlow to Government Secretary, 27 May 1926, HC WPHC to RC R.R. Kane, 15 October 1926; BSIP *AR* 1937, 20; Price 1977.
71 Bennett 1987, 184, 210, 398, 403; Golden 1993, 410; PMB, Sandars, Papers on the Solomon Islands, 21. Crichlow retired just before the Pacific War began, returning to Trinidad, where he became health officer for Trinidad Airport.

fond of Sherlock Holmes novels.[72] There were also other senior Fijians, mainly native medical practitioners from the 1930s on, who had high status in their own society. They were soon joined by the first Solomon Islanders trained as native medical practitioners. In the absence of European doctors, these men often had to perform medical examinations on and give advice and treatment to the expatriate community. Another 'in-between' man was Terusige Ishimoto, a Japanese tailor based in Chinatown, who was fascinated by Martin and Osa Johnson's motion picture camera and was himself the owner of an Eastman Kodak camera and a high-quality German camera. Osa Johnson describes Ishimoto's visits to her house in 1917. Presumably, he was one of the five Japanese noted as living in Tulagi in the early 1920s, and the one who developed photographic film commercially. He was certainly still there during the early 1930s, although by wartime, he was the Rabaul manager for a Japanese shipping company, Nanyo Boeki Kaisha (South Seas Trading) Limited.[73]

European racial attitudes were very Darwinian. Chinese and Japanese were viewed as inferior, as were Solomon Islanders—their complex societies underrated and seldom appreciated. The skin colour of Solomon Islanders varies from the honey brown of the Polynesians to the jet black of the people of the northern Solomon Islands, which Europeans used as a racial grading system. Pessimistic Darwinian beliefs depicted Solomon Islanders as a dying race and as a people who needed to be 'pacified' and Christianised. Generally, Solomon Islanders were seen as cannibalistic headhunting savages, hard to teach and incapable of being 'civilised'. Their loyalty to their extended families was never really understood. Their kinship concepts—particularly when brothers and sisters are not distinguishable from cousins—were not appreciated, nor was *wantokism*, the allegiances between speakers of the same languages.

How did expatriate men and women in the Tulagi enclave view Solomon Islanders? And did they view Solomon Islander men differently from the women? Not all Solomon Islander males were tough warriors uninterested in their appearance. All foreigners must have noticed a propensity of some young Solomon Islander men to be 'dandies', overly concerned about their physical presentation, while still being masculine. There are many

---

72   Knibbs 1929, 20–21.
73   Johnson 1945, 112; Muhlhauser 1924, 204; Lord 1977, 25–26. Another of the Japanese, Ito, was written about by MacQuarrie 1946, 66–84.

references to their large brushed-out coiffures, with a hibiscus flower stuck in the side. Men were often accused of applying peroxide to produce blond hair, although it is actually a genetic characteristic of Solomon Islanders. They were well-muscled and charming, so there would have been sexual attractions. Islander women and girls were demure, not boisterous like the males, yet they were still certain of their place in society. The boys, not the girls, were mainly the ones who received a modern education in mission schools and were literate. Females usually stayed in the village and remained separate from colonial society. Sometimes foreign women were outraged by the way Solomon Islander women were treated—particularly when they were isolated during menstruation and childbirth—and invoked the sisterhood to give them a right to intervene, which was not usually appreciated. Gender taboos were not understood, and when foreigners broke them, they did not realise the religious and social consequences.

Racism and colonialism were more powerful forces than sexism and gender in the lives of Solomon Islanders. In colonial society, the gender-power relations meant that interracial sex was acceptable if it was a European male with an Islander female. There were some quite celebrated relationships, and clearly the planters and traders, and some government officers, thought it normal to cohabit with local women. That Fred Campbell could sit on the Advisory Council and have an indigenous wife and children, or senior public servant Jack Barley could father several indigenous children, shows there was a degree of acceptance. Heterosexual relationships between expatriate males and local women always existed in the early Pacific communities, and in colonial and early twentieth-century Australia, where European men on the frontier had relationships with Indigenous women, both for sexual pleasure and to raise families.[74]

White women would have been ostracised if they had taken male Solomon Islander lovers. When white women arrived, did they ruin the cross-racial sexuality of empire? Did their presence cause a deterioration in race relations? Accusations that they did have been voiced for New Guinea and pre-cession Fiji. It has been argued that, once substantial numbers of European women lived in Fiji, their presence and their desire to establish domestic and family circumstances as close as possible to those from which they came, made European–Fijian friendships, associations and

---

74 McGrath 1984; McGrath 2005; Haskins 2001; Haskins and Maynard 2005; Conor 2013.

miscegenation disreputable.[75] Some earlier historians of Fiji and Papua New Guinea have concluded that European women interacted well with the indigenous peoples and felt a sense of mission in regard to health care and bringing 'civilisation'.[76] Interracial relations were complex and, in the Tulagi years, were influenced by pseudoscientific justification, practical experience and individual personalities. Racial attitudes are also mixed up with domestic relationships and the quite different cultural norms of the various groups. The racial superiority of Europeans was never questioned by Europeans, although from a Chinese or Solomon Islander perspective, it was presumably not accepted or even understood. European women were probably much closer to Solomon Islander women than men, but few indigenous women spoke Pijin and they were not usually employed as house servants. As Tulagi's expatriate women were mainly 'appendages' of their husbands and their jobs, not many were really independent or free to mix across racial, class and social divides.

How did Solomon Islanders view the Tulagi enclave and what was its effect on the protectorate after the Pacific War and on the independent nation since 1978? Tulagi was the headquarters of the colonial system and the bottleneck through which protectorate decisions passed. There was resentment about land alienation, the exploitative labour and taxation systems and the overriding of existing behaviours by protectorate regulations. There was relief from diseases such as yaws, although other prewar medical intervention was quite limited. There was relief from the tyranny of some leadership systems, such as the *ramo* on Malaita—warrior bounty hunters and assassins. We know that Melanesian clergy, police, medical staff, some government headmen and others engaged with Europeans in privileged ways and could enjoy high status among Solomon Islanders that was relatively new and novel. We know that such people could wield considerable power among Melanesians and Polynesians in the protectorate. At the same time, not all were respected and sometimes they came to be alienated from or resented by their home communities due to their close association with and perceived subservience to Europeans. Many of these individuals were the forebears of Solomon Islander elites and can still be linked to elite Solomon Islander families of today. The Tulagi enclave was a learning experience for Solomon Islanders

---

75   Young 1984; Young 1988. See also rejoinders and reviews in Knapman and Ralston 1989; Hoe 1984; Haggis 1990; Bulbeck 1993.
76   Keays 1995, 254–55.

and a means of understanding the colonial regime. Although small when compared with other Pacific territories, the enclave constituted the 'bright lights' of the prewar BSIP.

The Tulagi enclave prospered on a sheltered harbour, augmented late in the piece by Taroaniara and Tanambogo. In many ways, the enclave was unusual due to its small size and being spread over several islands. Particularly in the interwar years, Tulagi held an important place as a port town in the British Pacific. However, there were also similarities to north Australian colonial urban centres and to Port Moresby, Samarai and Rabaul in New Guinea, as well as Port Vila, Levuka, Suva and Nouméa. The class and racial hierarchies were maintained by geographic and social separation. Tens of thousands of Solomon Islander males passed through Tulagi at the start and end of their indenture agreements, availing themselves of the cheap trade goods in Chinatown. Numerically, although their presence was usually fleeting, more Solomon Islanders passed through Tulagi than anywhere else in the protectorate. There were tensions at Tulagi—more intense than in any other areas of the protectorate. These must have been constant points of discussion around the kitchen fires in the villages of Solomon Islands.

The Tulagi enclave was an artificial and restructured environment— islands extended, swamps filled, with paths, stairs and buildings in physical and symbolic places. Tulagi was physically altered to make it more serviceable and Gavutu and Tanambogo were joined. On Tulagi, The Cut through the island was the main physical change, the bridge over the top creating a special communication route that linked the homes of the higher echelon of administrative staff. The racial separation of Europeans, Asians and Solomon Islanders enabled the imposed colonial authority structure to emerge and operate. Part of the deliberate physical structure was practical—the need to improve communications and health—but Tulagi was also a classic imagining of the British Pacific, where power was exercised by using superior geographic sites, pleasing structures and tropical surrounds. Then, in 1942, after 45 years, old Tulagi came to an end. After a short hiatus, Honiara emerged as the next port, and capital of the protectorate.

Bibliography

Newspaper articles are listed in the bibliography only if the names of the authors are known. Anonymous articles are referenced in individual footnotes.

Ahrens, Prue, Lamont Lindstrom, and Fiona Paisley

2013   *Across the World with the Johnsons: Visual Culture and Empire in the Twentieth Century*. Farnham, UK: Ashgate Publishing.

Akin, David

1999   Compensation and the Melanesian State: Why the Kwaio Keep Claiming. *Contemporary Pacific* 11(1): 35–67.

2013   *Colonialism, Maasina Rule, and the Origins of Malaitan* Kastom. Honolulu: University of Hawai`i Press. doi.org/10.21313/hawaii/9780824838140.001.0001.

2015   List of BSIP Officers Posted to Malaita from 1909, and of Other Senior BSIP Officers. Unpublished ms in the possession of the author.

Aldrich, Robert

2003   *Colonialism and Homosexuality*. London: Routledge.

Allan, Colin H.

1957   *Report of the Special Lands Commission: Customary Land Tenure in the British Solomon Islands Protectorate*. Honiara: Western Pacific High Commission.

Amherst, W.A.T., and B. Thomson (trans and eds)

2010 [1901]   *The Discovery of the Solomon Islands by Alvaro de Mendaña in 1568*. London, Hakluyt Society. [2 vols]. Farnham, UK: Ashgate Publishing.

Amiot, I., and Christiane Terrier (eds)

2007   *Histoire, Cycle 3: Nouvelle-Caledonie*. Nouméa: CDP.

Anonymous

1934   The Templeton Crocker Expedition in Solomon Islands. *Science* 79(2050): 344–45. doi.org/10.1126/science.79.2050.344-a.

Anonymous

1941 Western Pacific. *Journal of Comparative Legislation and International Law* 23(2–3): 113–15.

Anonymous (by people of Levuka)

2001 *Levuka: Living Heritage*. Levuka, Fiji: Institute of Pacific Studies, University of the South Pacific and Levuka Historical and Cultural Society.

Aplin, Douglas

1980 *Rabaul: 1942*. Melbourne: 2/22 Battalion AIF, Lark Force Association.

Armstrong, A.L.

1944 Western Pacific. *Journal of Comparative Legislation and International Law* 26(1–2): 75–85.

Armstrong, A L., and G.A. Joy

1939 Western Pacific. *Journal of Comparative Legislation and International Law* 21(2): 90–94.

Ashby, Frederick

1978 *Blackie: A Story of the Old-Time Bushmen*. Wellington: Reed.

Association Salomon

2008 *Le Mystère Lapérouse ou le Rêve Inacheve d'un Roi* [*The Lapérouse Mystery or the Unfinished Dream of a King*]. Paris: Editions de Conti.

Bach, John

1986 *The Australia Station: A History of the Royal Navy in the South West Pacific, 1821–1913*. Sydney: UNSW Press.

Baddeley, Walter Herbert

1942 '*Behind It All Is God': The Melanesian Mission in War-Time—The Bishop's Report for 1942*. Sydney: The Australian Board of Missions.

Bambrick, Susan

1983 Knibbs, Sir George Handley (1858–1929). In *Australian Dictionary of Biography. Volume 9*, pp. 620–21. Canberra: National Centre of Biography, The Australian National University. Available from: adb.anu.edu.au/biography/knibbs-sir-george-handley-6985.

Barbançon, Louis José, Sylvette Boyer, and Bernard Fustec

2004 *Bourail: Il était une Fois—Histoire Singulière, Histoires Plurielles* [*Bourail: Once Upon a Time—Singular History, Plural Histories*]. Nouméa: Editions Thierry Darras.

Barge, J.F.

1938	Jottings from Tulagi. *Southern Cross Log*, August, p. 117.

Beattie, John W.

1909	*Catalogue of a Series of Photographs Illustrating the Scenery and Peoples of the Islands in the South and Western Pacific.* Hobart: J.W. Beattie.

Beckett, Jeremy

1986	Obituary: Ian Hogbin. *American Ethnology* 13(4): 799–801. doi.org/10.1525/ae.1986.13.4.02a00120.

Beckett, Jeremy, and Geoffrey Gray

2007	Hogbin, Herbert Ian Priestley (1904–1989). In *Australian Dictionary of Biography. Volume 17*, p. 539. Canberra: National Centre of Biography, The Australian National University. Available from: adb.anu.edu.au/biography/hogbin-herbert-ian-priestley-12644.

Bedford, George Randolph

1906–07	Around the Coral Sea: This Being the Record of My Journeyings in the Coral Sea, c. 1906–07. Manuscript. London: Conru Africana and Oceanic Art. Available from www.kevinconru.com/.

Behlmer, George K.

2018	*Risky Shores: Savagery and Colonialism in the Western Pacific.* Stanford, CA: Stanford University Press.

Bell, Peter

1984	*Timber and Iron: Houses in North Queensland Mining Settlements, 1861–1920.* Brisbane: University of Queensland Press.

Bennett, Judith A.

1974	Cross-Cultural Influences on Village Relocation on the Weather Coast of Guadalcanal, Solomon Islands, c. 1870–1953. MA thesis, University of Hawai`i, Honolulu.

1981	Oscar Svensen: A Solomons Trader among 'the Few'. *Journal of Pacific History* 16(4): 170–89. doi.org/10.1080/00223348108572426.

1987	*Wealth of the Solomons: A History of a Pacific Archipelago, 1800–1978.* Honolulu: University of Hawai`i Press.

1993	'We do not come here to be beaten': Resistance and the Plantation System in the Solomon Islands to World War II. In *Plantation Workers: Resistance and Accommodation*, edited by Brij V. Lal, Doug Munro and Edward D. Beechert, pp. 129–86. Honolulu: University of Hawai`i Press.

2015   The Solomon Islands: Off the Radar. In *Mothers' Darlings of the South Pacific: The Children of Indigenous Women and U.S. Servicemen, World War II*, edited by Judith A. Bennett and Angela Wanhalla, pp. 228–42. Honolulu: University of Hawai`i Press.

Bernatzik, Hugo A.

1935   *Südsee: Travels in the South Seas*. Translated and edited by Vivian Ogilvie. London: Constable & Co. Ltd.

Blake, Thom

n.d.   Historical Monetary Data for Australia. [Online]. Available from: www.thomblake.com.au/secondary/hisdata/query.php.

Boland, Rodney G.

1979   Bedford, George Randolph (1868–1941). In *Australian Dictionary of Biography. Volume 7*, pp. 241–42. Canberra: National Centre of Biography, The Australian National University. Available from: adb.anu.edu.au/biography/bedford-george-randolph-5181.

Bolton, Geoffrey

2000   *Edmund Barton*. Sydney: Allen & Unwin.

Boutilier, James A.

1974   The Role of the Administration and the Missions in the Provision of Medical and Educational Services in the British Solomon Islands Protectorate, 1893–1942. Annual Meeting of the Association for Social Anthropology in Oceania, held at Asilomar, Pacific Grove, California, in March 1974. Manuscript. Deposited in Anglican Church of Canada, Church House Library, Toronto.

1978   Missions, Administration, and Education in the Solomon Islands, 1893–1942. In *Mission, Church, and Sect in Oceania*, edited by James Boutilier, Daniel Hughes and Sharon Tiffany, pp. 139–61. Ann Arbor: University of Michigan Press.

1983   The Government is the District Officer: An Historical Analysis of District Officers as Middlemen in the British Solomon Islands Protectorate, 1893–1943. In *Middlemen and Brokers in Oceania*, edited by William L. Rodman and Dorothy Ayers Counts, pp. 2–67. Lanham, MD: University Press of America.

1984a   European Women in the Solomon Islands, 1900–1942: Accommodation and Change on the Pacific Frontier. In *Rethinking Women's Roles: Perspectives from the Pacific*, edited by Denise O'Brien and Sharon W. Tiffany, pp. 172–201. Berkeley, CA: University of California Press.

1984b 'The Law of England Has Come': The Application of British and Custom Law in the British Solomon Islands Protectorate, 1893–1942. Paper presented at the Association for Social Anthropology in Oceania Annual Conference, Molokai, Hawai`i, 28 February – 3 March.

Bowe, F.

1899 Diseases of Polynesians, As Seen in Queensland. *Transactions from the Intercolonial Medical Congress of Australasia*, pp. 59–63. Melbourne: Intercolonial Medical Congress of Australasia.

Bradbury, R., and R.J. Traub

2016 Hookworm Infection in Oceania. In *Neglected Tropical Diseases: Oceania*, edited by A. Loukas, pp. 33–68. Cham, Switzerland: Springer International Publishing. doi.org/10.1007/978-3-319-43148-2_2.

Braga, Stuart

2004 Deck, John Northcote (1875–1957). In *The Australian Dictionary of Evangelical Biography*. Sydney: Evangelical History Association. Paper copy held by the author.

British Colonial Office

1925 *The British Colonial Office List, or General Register of the Colonial Dependencies of Great Britain*. London: HM Stationery Office.

Brooke, Charles H.

1881 *Percy Pomo: Or the Autobiography of a South Sea Islander*. London: Griffith & Farren.

Brown, Paul H.

2007 Taem Blong Iume: Some Notes on People and Events in the Post World War II British Solomon Islands Protectorate by a Proud Former Resident. Unpublished ms in the possession of the author.

Buckley, Kenneth, and Kris Klugman

1981 *The History of Burns Philp: The Australian Company in the South Pacific*. Sydney: Burns Philp & Co. Ltd.

1983 *'The Australian Presence in the Pacific': Burns Philp, 1914–1946*. Sydney: George Allen & Unwin.

Bulbeck, Chilla

1992 *Australian Women in Papua New Guinea: Colonial Passages, 1920–1960*. Melbourne: Cambridge University Press. doi.org/10.1017/CBO9780511518263.

1993 New Histories of the Memsahib and Missus: The Case of Papua New Guinea. *Journal of Women's History* 3(2): 82–105.

Burt, Ben

1994 *Tradition and Christianity: The Colonial Transformation of a Solomon Islands Society.* Chur, Switzerland: Harwood Academic Publishers.

2015 *Malaita: A Pictorial History from Solomon Islands.* London: British Museum.

Burt, Ben, and Michael Kwa'iola (eds), with contributions from the Kwara'ae Chiefs

2001 *A Solomon Islands Chronicle, as Told by Samuel Alasa'a.* London: British Museum Press.

Burton, Antoinette

2010 Rules of Thumb: British History and 'Imperial Culture' in Nineteenth- and Twentieth-Century Britain. In *The New Imperial Histories Reader*, edited by Stephen Howe, pp. 41–54. London: Routledge.

Butcher, Mike

2012 *'... when the long trick's over': Donald Kennedy in the Pacific.* Bendigo, Vic.: Holland House Publishing.

Buxton, P.A.

1925–26 The Depopulation of the New Hebrides and Other Parts of Melanesia. *Royal Society of Tropical Medicine and Hygiene Transactions* 19: 420–55. doi.org/10.1016/S0035-9203(26)92580-7.

Cahill, Peter

2012 *Needed—But not Wanted: Chinese in Colonial Rabaul, 1884–1960.* Brisbane: CopyRight Publishing.

Cameron, Charlotte

1923 *Two Years in the Southern Seas.* London: T. Fisher & Unwin Ltd.

Carter, Jennifer M.T.

1999 *Painting the Islands Vermilion: Archibald Watson and the Brig Carl.* Melbourne: Melbourne University Press.

Cauville, Gérard, Rémy Le Goff, and Maïlys Imbach

2006 *Le Mémorial de la Boxe Calédonienne de 1914 à nos Jour* [*The New Caledonian Boxing Memorial from 1914 to Our Day*]. Nouméa: Editions Teddy.

Chaperlin, H.

1930 Asiatic Menace in Pacific: What Chinese Traders are Doing in the Solomons. *Pacific Islands Monthly*, 16 December.

Christ, James F.

2007 *Battalion of the Damned: The 1st Paratroopers at Gavutu and Bloody Ridge, 1942*. Annapolis: Naval Institute Press.

Clarence, Margaret

1982 *Yield Not to the Wind*. Sydney: Management Development Publishers Pty Ltd.

Clark, Jennifer

2011 *Kauri, Coal and Copra: 19th Century Voyages of Captain James Robinson around the South Pacific*. Auckland: Jennifer Clark.

Clemens, Martin

1998 *Alone on Guadalcanal: A Coastwatcher's Story*. Annapolis: Naval Institute Press.

Codrington, Robert Henry

1972 [1891] *The Melanesians: Studies in their Anthropology and Folk-Lore*. New York: Dover Publications.

Collinson, Clifford W.

1926 *Life and Laughter Midst the Cannibals*. London: Hurst & Blackett.

Conor, Liz

2013 'Black Velvet' and 'Purple Indignation': Print Responses to Japanese 'Poaching' of Aboriginal Women. *Aboriginal History* 37: 51–76. doi.org/10.22459/AH.37.2013.03.

Corris, Peter

1972 'White Australia' in Action: The Repatriation of Pacific Islanders from Queensland. *Historical Studies* 15(58): 237–50. doi.org/10.1080/10314617208595469.

1973 *Passage, Port and Plantation: A History of Solomon Islands Labour Migration, 1870–1914*. Melbourne: Melbourne University Press.

Cowling, W.E.

1984 The Unacknowledged Element: The Domestic Servant in a Colonial Economy and Society (Papua New Guinea between the Two World Wars). BA Hons thesis, Macquarie University, Sydney.

Cromar, John

1935 *Jock of the Islands: Early Days in the South Seas—The Adventures of John Cromar*. London: Faber & Faber.

Cross, Gwen

1979 *Aloha Solomons: The Story of a People's Courage and Loyalty*. Suva and Honiara: Institute of Pacific Studies and Solomon Islands Extension Centre, University of the South Pacific.

Daly, Henri

2002   *Nouvelle-Calédonie: Porte-avions Américain dans les Mers du Sud— La Guerre du Pacifique 1941–1945* [New Caledonia: American Aircraft Carriers in the South Seas—The Pacific War 1941–1945]. Nouméa: SEHNC.

Daws, Gavan

1967   Honolulu in the 19th Century: Notes on the Emergence of Urban Society in Hawaii. *Journal of Pacific History* 2: 77–96. doi.org/10.1080/00223346708572103.

2006   *Honolulu: The First Century*. Honolulu: Mutual Publishing.

Daws, Gavan, and Bennett Hymer (eds)

2008   *Honolulu Stories: Voices of the Town through the Years—Two Centuries of Writing*. Honolulu: Mutual Publishing.

Deck, John Northcote

1928   *Seeing Greater Things: Some of the Horizons of Faith*. London: Pickering & Inglis.

De Groen, Frances

1998   *Xavier Herbert: A Biography*. Brisbane: University of Queensland Press.

Delathière, Jerry

2000   *Ils ont Créé La Foa: Familles Pionnières de Nouvelle-Calédonie* [They Created La Foa: Pioneer Families of New Caledonia]. La Foa, New Caledonia: Mairie de La Foa.

2004   *La Foa: 120 Ans d'Histoire Municipale* [La Foa: 120 Years of Municipal History]. Nouméa: Agence Demain.

Dickinson, Joseph H.C.

1927   *A Trader in the Savage Solomons: A Record of Romance and Adventure*. London: H.F. & G. Witherby.

Douglas, Ngaire

1996   *They Came for Savages: 100 Years of Tourism in Melanesia*. Lismore, NSW: Southern Cross University Press.

2004   Towards a History of Tourism in Solomon Islands. *Journal of Pacific Studies* 26(1–3): 29–49.

Dutton, Tom

1985   *Police Motu: Iena Sivarai (Its Story)*. Port Moresby: University of Papua New Guinea Press.

Edridge, Sally

1985　　　*Solomon Islands Bibliography to 1980*. Suva, Wellington and Honiara: Institute of Pacific Studies, University of the South Pacific, Alexander Turnbull Library and Solomon Islands National Library.

Epstein, A.L.

1969　　　*Matupit: Land, Politics, and Change among the Tolai of New Britain*. Canberra: Australian National University Press.

Eyerdam, Walter J.

1933　　　Among the Mountain Bushmen of Malaita. *Natural History* 33(2): 430–38.

Festetics de Tolna, Rudolph

1903　　　*Chez les Cannibales: Huit Ans de Croisière dans l'Océan Pacifique et Indien á Bord du Yacht le Tolna* [*The Cannibals: Eight Years of Cruising in the Pacific and Indian Ocean aboard the Yacht Tolna*]. Paris: Plon-Nourrit.

Fifi`i, Jonathan

1989　　　*From Pig-Theft to Parliament: My Life between Two Worlds*. Translated and edited by Roger M. Keesing. Honiara and Suva: Solomon Islands College of Higher Education and Institute of Pacific Studies, University of the South Pacific.

Fowler, Wilfred

1959　　　*The Island's Mine*. London: Constable.

1969　　　The Young Dick. *Queensland Heritage* 2(1): 23–35.

Fox, Charles

1924　　　*The Threshold of the Pacific: An Account of the Social Organization, Magic and Religion of the People of San Cristoval in the Solomon Islands*. London: Kegan Paul, Trench, Trubner.

1938　　　Letter to the editor. *Southern Cross Log*, August, p. 118.

1955　　　*A Dictionary of the Gela Language*. Auckland: Auckland Unity Press.

1958　　　*Lord of the Southern Isles: Being the Story of the Anglican Mission in Melanesia, 1849–1949*. London: Mowbray.

1962　　　*Kakamora*. London: Hodder & Stoughton.

Frazer, Ian L.

1990　　　Maasina Rule and Solomon Islands Labour History. In *Labour in the South Pacific*, edited by Clive Moore, Jacqueline Leckie and Doug Munro, pp. 191–203. Townsville, Qld: Department of History and Politics and the Centre for Melanesian Studies, James Cook University.

Gina, Lloyd Maepeza

2003   *Journeys in a Small Canoe: The Life and Times of a Solomon Islander*. Edited by Judith A. Bennett and Khyla J. Russell. Suva and Canberra: University of the South Pacific and Pandanus Books.

Gisburn, Harold G.D.

1956   *British Solomon Islands Protectorate: Its Postage Stamps and Postal History*. Southampton, UK: J. Sanders (Philatelist) Ltd.

Godfrey, Richard

1928   Diary of the Rev. Richard Godfrey, Priest of the Melanesian Mission, First Voyage of S.T. Southern Cross, 1928, Synod Trip. Project Canterbury, Oceania. Available from: anglicanhistory.org/oceania/godfrey_synod1928.html.

Golden, Graeme A.

1993   *The Early European Settlers of the Solomon Islands*. Melbourne: Graeme A. Golden.

Grimshaw, Patricia

1931   *Isles of Adventure: From Java to New Caledonia but Principally Papua*. Boston: Houghton Mifflin Company.

Groves, William C.

1940   *Report on a Survey of Education in the British Solomon Islands Protectorate*. Tulagi: British Solomon Islands Protectorate.

Guppy, Henry B.

1887   *The Solomon Islands and Their Natives*. London: Swan Sonnenschein, Lowrey & Company.

Hadlow, Martin Lindsay

2015   *Radio Broadcasting: 63 Years On and Counting!* Honiara: SIBC Voice of the Nation. Available from: www.sibconline.com.sb/sibssibc-63rd-anniversary/.

2016   Wireless and Empire Ambition: Wireless Telegraphy/Telephony and Radio Broadcasting in the British Solomon Islands Protectorate, South-West Pacific (1914–1947): Political, Social and Developmental Perspectives. PhD thesis, University of Queensland, Brisbane.

Haggis, Jane

1990   Gendering Colonialism or Colonising Gender? Recent Approaches to White Women and the History of British Colonialism. *Women's Studies International Forum* [SI: British Feminist Histories] 13(1–2): 106–15.

Hahl, Albert

1980 *Governor in New Guinea*. Translated and edited by Peter G. Sack and Dymphna Clark. Canberra: Australian National University Press.

Haskins, Victoria

2001 On the Doorstep: Aboriginal Domestic Service as a 'Contact Zone'. *Australian Feminist Studies* 16(34): 13–25. doi.org/10.1080/08164640120038881.

Haskins, Victoria, and John Maynard

2005 Sex, Race and Power: Aboriginal Men and White Women. *Australian Historical Studies* 36(126): 191–216. doi.org/10.1080/10314610508682920.

Heath, Ian

1974 Charles Morris Woodford of the Solomon Islands: A Biographical Note, 1852–1927. MA qual. thesis, The Australian National University, Canberra.

1979 Land Policy in Solomon Islands. PhD thesis, La Trobe University, Melbourne.

1981 Solomon Islands: Land Policy and Independence. *Kabar Seberang: Sulating Maphilindo* 8–9: 62–77.

Henderson, C.P., and I.R. Hancock

1988 *A Guide to the Useful Plants of Solomon Islands*. Honiara: Research Department, Ministry of Agriculture and Lands.

Hermant, P., and R.W. Cilento

1928–29 *Report of the Mission Entrusted with a Survey on Health Conditions in the Pacific Islands*. Geneva: League of Nations.

Hernsheim, Eduard

1983 *South Sea Merchant*. Translated and edited by Peter G. Sack and Dymphna Clark. Boroko, PNG: Institute of Papua New Guinea Studies.

Herr, R.A., and E.A. Rood (eds)

1978 *A Solomons Sojourn: J.E. Philp's Log of the Makira 1912–1913*. Hobart: Tasmanian Historical Research Association.

Hilder, Brett

1961 *Navigator in the South Seas*. Adelaide: Rigby.

Hilliard, David

1978 *God's Gentleman: A History of the Melanesian Mission, 1849–1942*. Brisbane: University of Queensland Press.

Hodgson, Reginald

1966   *Reminiscences: Missionary Priest in Melanesian Mission.* Project Canterbury, Oceania. Available from: anglicanhistory.org/oceania/hodgson_reminiscences.html.

Hoe, Suzanna

1984   White Women in the Colonies: Were They Responsible for Setting up Racial Barriers? *Bikmaus* 5(2): 80–88.

Hopkins, Arthur I.

1928   *In the Isles of King Solomon: An Account of Twenty-Five Years Spent amongst the Primitive Solomon Islanders.* London: Seeley, Service & Company.

Horton, Dick C.

1965   *The Happy Isles: A Diary of the Solomons.* London: Heinemann.

1970   *Fire Over the Islands: The Coastwatchers of the Solomons.* Sydney: Reed.

Hunt, Doug

2007   Hunting the Blackbirder: Ross Lewin and the Royal Navy. *Journal of Pacific History* 42(1): 37–53. doi.org/10.1080/00223340701286826.

Hviding, Edvard

2015a   Adventurous Adaptability in the South Sea: Norwegians in 'the Terrible Solomons', ca. 1870–1930. In *Navigating Colonial Orders: Norwegian Entrepreneurship in Africa and Oceania*, edited by Kirsten A. Kjerland and Bjørn E. Bertelsen, pp. 187–218. Oxford: Berghahn Books.

2015b   Norwegian Shipping and Landfall in the South Sea in the Age of Sail. In *Navigating Colonial Orders: Norwegian Entrepreneurship in Africa and Oceania*, edited by Kirsten A. Kjerland and Bjørn E. Bertelsen, pp. 173–86. Oxford: Berghahn Books.

Hviding, Edvard, and Cato Berg

2014   The Ethnographic Experiment in Island Melanesia. In *The Ethnographic Experiment: A.M. Hocart and W.H.R. Rivers in Island Melanesia*, edited by Edvard Hviding and Cato Berg, pp. 1–43. New York: Berghahn Books.

Hviding, Edvard, and Cato Berg (eds)

2014   *The Ethnographic Experiment: A.M. Hocart and W.H.R. Rivers in Island Melanesia.* New York: Berghahn Books.

Hyam, Ronald

1986 Concubinage and the Colonial Service: The Crewe Circular (1909). *Journal of Imperial and Commonwealth History* 14(3): 170–86. doi.org/10.1080/03086538608582718.

1990 *Empire and Sexuality: The British Experience*. Manchester: Manchester University Press.

Inglis, Amirah

1974 *'Not a White Woman Safe': Sexual Anxiety and Politics in Port Moresby, 1920–1934*. Canberra: Australian National University Press.

1982 *Karo: The Life and Fate of a Papuan*. Port Moresby and Canberra: Institute of Papua New Guinea Studies and Australian National University Press.

Inglis, Christine

1972 Chinese. In *Encyclopaedia of Papua and New Guinea*, edited by Peter Ryan, pp. 170–74. Melbourne: Melbourne University Press in association with University of Papua New Guinea.

Innis, John

2017 *Guide to Guadalcanal Battlefields*. Brisbane: Self-published.

Ivens, W.G.

1927 *Melanesians of the South-East Solomon Islands*. London: Kegan Paul, Trench, Trubner & Co.

1930 *The Island Builders of the Pacific*. London: Seeley, Service & Co.

Iwamoto, Hiromitsu

1999 *Nanshin: Japanese Settlers in Papua and New Guinea*. Canberra: The Journal of Pacific History.

Jack-Hinton, Colin

1969 *The Search for the Islands of Solomon, 1567–1838*. Oxford: Clarendon Press.

Jackson, K.B.

1978 Tie Hokara, Tie Vaka: Black Man, White Man—A Study of the New Georgia Group to 1925. PhD thesis, The Australian National University, Canberra.

James, Clifford S.

1949 *Diseases Commonly Met with in Melanesia: Their Diagnosis, Prevention and Treatment*. 3rd edn. Auckland: Melanesian Mission.

Jersey, Stanley Coleman

2008 *Hell's Islands: The Untold Story of Guadalcanal*. Austin: A&M University Press.

Johnson, Donald D., assisted by Phyllis Turnbull

1991   *The City and Country of Honolulu: A Government Chronicle*. Honolulu: University of Hawai`i Press.

Johnson, Osa

1945   *Bride in the Solomons*. London: George G. Harrap & Co.

Johnson, R. W., and Neville A. Threlfall

1985   *Volcano Town: The 1937–43 Rabaul Eruptions*. Bathurst, NSW: Robert Brown & Associates.

Johnston, William R.

1973   *Sovereignty and Protection: A Study of British Jurisdictional Imperialism in the Late Nineteenth Century*. Durham, NC: Duke University Press.

Joyce, Roger B.

1971   *Sir William MacGregor*. Melbourne: Oxford University Press.

Kakau, Serge

1998   *Découverte Photographique de la Nouvelle-Calédonie, 1848–1900* [*Photographic Discovery of New Caledonia, 1848–1900*]. Nouméa: Actes Sud.

Keays, Susan C.

1995   Sinabada or Misis: The Experiences of Expatriate Women in Colonial Papua and New Guinea, 1872 to 1942. PhD thesis, University of Queensland, Brisbane.

Keesing, Roger M.

1980   Antecedents of Maasina Rule: Some Further Notes. *Journal of Pacific History* 13(2): 102–07. doi.org/10.1080/00223348008572392.

1986   The Young Dick Attack: Oral and Documentary History on the Colonial Frontier. *Ethnohistory* 33(3): 268–92. doi.org/10.2307/481815.

Keesing, Roger M., and Peter Corris

1980   *Lightning Meets the West Wind: The Malaita Massacre*. Melbourne: Oxford University Press.

Kenilorea, Peter

2008   *Tell It As It Is: Autobiography of Rt Hon. Sir Peter Kenilorea, KBE, PC, Solomon Islands' First Prime Minister*. Edited by Clive Moore. Taipei: Centre for Asia-Pacific Area Studies, Academia Sinica.

Kirk-Greene, Anthony

1999   *On Crown Service: A History of HM Colonial and Overseas Civil Services, 1837–1997*. London: I.B. Tauris Publishers.

Knapman, Claudia

1986 *White Women in Fiji, 1853–1930: The Ruin of Empire?* Sydney: Allen & Unwin.

Knapman, Claudia, and Caroline Ralston

1989 Historical Patchwork: A Reply to John Young's 'Race and Sex in Fiji Re-visited'. *Journal of Pacific History* 24(2): 221–24. doi.org/10.1080/00223348908572616.

Knibbs, S.G.C.

1929 *The Savage Solomons as They Were & Are: A Record of a Head-hunting People Gradually Emerging from a Life of Savage Cruelty & Bloody Customs, with a Description of Their Manners & Ways & of the Beauties & Potentialities of the Islands.* London: Seeley, Service & Co.

Knox-Mawer, June

1986 *Tales from Paradise: Memories of the British in the South Pacific.* London: Ariel Books, BBC Publications.

Kuo, Mei-Fen, and Judith Brett

2013 *Unlocking the History of the Australian Kuo Min Tang, 1911–2013.* Melbourne: Australian Scholarly Publishing.

Kwai, Anna

2017 *Solomon Islanders in World War II: An Indigenous Perspective.* Canberra: ANU Press. doi.org/10.22459/SIWWII.12.2017.

Lagarde, Louis

2016 The Legacy of Planter Jean My: Analysis of Two Private Colonial Homes in Southern Melanesia. *Journal of Pacific History* 51(2): 143–68. doi.org/10.1080/00223344.2016.1193271.

Lal, Brij V.

1992 *Broken Waves: A History of the Fiji Islands in the Twentieth Century.* Honolulu: University of Hawai`i Press.

2016 *Historical Dictionary of Fiji.* Lanham, MD: Rowman & Littlefield.

Lambert, S.M.

1934a British Solomon Islands Health Surveys, 1933. *Journal of Tropical Medicine and Hygiene* 37(60): 81–85, 100–04, 119–23, 134–39.

1934b *The Depopulation of Pacific Races.* Special Publication 23. Honolulu: Bernice P. Bishop Museum.

1946 *A Doctor in Paradise.* 4th edn. London and Melbourne: J.M. Dent & Sons Ltd and Georgian House.

Laracy, Hugh M.

1974   Unwelcome Guests: The Solomons' Chinese. *New Guinea* 8(4): 27–37.

2013   *Watriama and Co: Further Pacific Islands Portraits*. Canberra: ANU Press. dx.doi.org/10.22459/WC.10.2013.

Laracy, Hugh M., and Eugénie Laracy

1980   Custom, Conjugality and Colonial Rule in the Solomon Islands. *Oceania* 51(2): 133–47. doi.org/10.1002/j.1834-4461.1980.tb 01963.x.

Laracy, Hugh M., and Geoffrey White (eds)

1988   Taem Blong Faet: World War II in Melanesia. '*O*'*O: A Journal of Solomon Islands Studies* 4[SI]. Honiara: University of the South Pacific Honiara Centre.

Lawrence, David R.

2014   *The Naturalist and his 'Beautiful Islands': Charles Morris Woodford in the Western Pacific*. Canberra: ANU Press. doi.org/10.22459/ NBI.10.2014.

Lawrence, David, Kylie Moloney, and Christine Bryan

2015   The Charles Morris Woodford Papers and Photographs at the Pacific Manuscripts Bureau and the Pacific Research Archives, Australian National University. *Journal of Pacific History* 50(4): 519–32. doi.org/10.1080/00223344.2015.1024094.

League of Nations Mandated Territory of New Guinea (LNMTNG)

1925–40   *Annual Reports*. Geneva: League of Nations.

Lever, Robert A.

1988   Tulagi: The Capital that was Abandoned. *Journal of the Overseas Pensioners' Association* 56. Website discontinued. Copy held by the author.

London, Charmian

1915a   *The Log of the Snark*. New York: Macmillan.

1915[?]b   *A Woman among the Head Hunters: A Narrative of the Voyage of the Snark in the Years 1908–1909*. London: Mills & Boon Ltd.

London, Jack

1911   *The Cruise of the Snark*. London and New York: Mills & Boon Ltd and Macmillan.

1912   *South Sea Tales*. London: Mills & Boon Ltd.

1917   *Jerry of the Islands*. London: Mills & Boon Ltd.

Lord, Walter

1977   *Lonely Vigil: Coastwatchers of the Solomons.* New York: Viking Press.

Lowrie, Claire

2013   White Men and their Chinese 'Boys': Sexuality, Masculinity and Colonial Power in Singapore and Darwin, 1880s–1930s. *History Australia* 10(1): 35–57. doi.org/10.1080/14490854.2013.11668 445.

Luke, Harry

1945   *From a South Seas Diary, 1939–1942.* London: Nicholson & Watson.

McArthur, Norma

1961   *Report of the Population Census of 1959, British Solomon Islands Protectorate.* Honiara: Western Pacific High Commission.

Macdonald, Barrie

1982   *Cinderellas of the Empire: Towards a History of Kiribati and Tuvalu.* Canberra: Australian National University Press.

McElwaine, P.A., and W.K. Horne

1930   Western Pacific. *Journal of Comparative Legislation and International Law* 12(2): 139–40.

McGrath, Ann

1984   'Black Velvet': Aboriginal Women and their Relations with White Men in the Northern Territory, 1910–1940. In *So Much Hard Work: Women and Prostitution in Australian History*, edited by Kay Daniels, pp. 237–67. Sydney: Fontana.

2005   Consent, Marriage and Colonialism: Indigenous Australian Women and Colonizer Marriages. *Journal of Colonialism and Colonial History* 6(3). doi.org/10.1353/cch.2006.0016.

2015   *Illicit Love: Interracial Sex and Marriage in the United States and Australia.* Lincoln: University of Nebraska Press. doi.org/10.2307/j.ctt1d98bzf.

McIntyre, W. David

1960   Disraeli's Colonial Policy: The Creation of the Western Pacific High Commission, 1874–1877. *Historical Studies Australia and New Zealand* 9(35): 279–94. doi.org/10.1080/10314616008595177.

1967   *The Imperial Frontier in the Tropics, 1865–75: A Study of British Colonial Policy in West Africa, Malaya and the South Pacific in the Age of Gladstone and Disraeli.* London: Macmillan. doi.org/10.1007/978-1-349-00349-5.

2012 The Partition of the Gilbert and Ellice Islands. *Islands Studies Journal* 7(1): 135–46.

Mackenzie, S.S.

1987 [1927] *The Australians at Rabaul: The Capture and Administration of the German Possessions in the Southern Pacific. Volume X: The Official History of Australia in the War of 1914–1918.* Brisbane: University of Queensland Press.

McLaren, Jack

1923 *My Odyssey.* London: Ernest Benn Ltd.

MacQuarrie, Hector

1946 *Vouza and the Solomon Islands.* Sydney: Angus & Robertson.

Maetoloa, Meshach

1985 The Remnant Church. In *New Religious Movements in Melanesia*, edited by Carl Loeliger and Garry Tromph, pp. 120–48. Suva and Port Moresby: University of the South Pacific and University of Papua New Guinea.

Markus, Andrew

1994 *Australian Race Relations, 1788–1993.* Sydney: Allen & Unwin.

Maude, H.E., and C.W.S. Johnson

1945 Western Pacific. *Journal of Comparative Legislation and International Law* 27(1–2): 95–99.

Mayr, Ernst

1931 Birds Collected during the Whitney South Sea Expedition XVII: The Birds of Malaita Island (British Solomon Islands). *American Museum Novitates* 504: 1–26.

1943 A Journey to the Solomon Islands. *Natural History* 52: 30–37.

Mitjà, O., and M. Marks

2016 Yaws in Oceania: New Tools for the Global Eradication Campaign. In *Neglected Tropical Diseases: Oceania*, edited by E. Loukas, pp. 143–152. Cham, Switzerland: Springer International Publishing. doi.org/10.1007/978-3-319-43148-2_5.

Moore, Clive

1984 Queensland's Annexation of New Guinea in 1883: The Clem Lack Memorial Oration. *Royal Historical Society of Queensland Journal* 12(1): 26–50.

1985 *Kanaka: A History of Melanesian Mackay.* Port Moresby: Institute of Papua New Guinea Studies and University of Papua New Guinea Press.

1997	Queensland and its Coral Sea: Implications of Historical Links between Australia and Melanesia. In *Northern Exposures* (Occasional Paper 19, Papers from the 1996 Symposium of the Australian Academy of the Humanities), edited by Malcolm Gillies, pp. 17–44. Canberra: Australian Academy of the Humanities.
2000a	'Good-Bye, Queensland, Good-Bye, White Australia; Good-Bye Christians': Australia's South Sea Islander Community and Deportation, 1901–1908. *New Federalist* 4: 22–29.
2000b	*Sunshine and Rainbows: The Development of Gay and Lesbian Culture in Queensland.* Brisbane: University of Queensland Press.
2001	Herbert, Robert George Wyndham (1831–1905), and Bramston, John (1830–1921). In *Who's Who in Gay and Lesbian History: From Antiquity to the Second World War*, edited by Garry Wotherspoon and Robert Aldrich, Vol. 1, pp. 207–08. London: Routledge.
2003	*New Guinea: Crossing Boundaries and History.* Honolulu: University of Hawai`i Press.
2004	*Happy Isles in Crisis: The Historical Causes for a Failing State in Solomon Islands, 1998–2004.* Canberra: Asia Pacific Press.
2004–05	Working the Government: Australia's South Sea Islanders, their Knowledge of and Interaction with Government Processes, 1863–1908. *South Pacific: Journal of Philosophy and Culture* 8: 59–78.
2007	The Misappropriation of Malaitan Labour: Historical Origins of the Recent Solomon Islands Crisis. *Journal of Pacific History* 42(2): 211–32. doi.org/10.1080/00223340701461668.
2008	No More Walkabout Long Chinatown: Asian Involvement in the Solomon Islands Economic and Political Processes. In *Politics and State Building in Solomon Islands*, edited by Sinclair Dinnen and Stewart Firth, pp. 64–95. Canberra: Asia Pacific Press.
2010–12	Changes in Melanesian Masculinity: An Historical Approach. *South Pacific: Journal of Philosophy and Culture* 11: 28–41.
2013	*Solomon Islands Historical Encyclopaedia, 1893–1978.* [Online]. Available from: www.solomonencyclopaedia.net.
2015	The Pacific Islanders' Fund and the Misappropriation of the Wages of Deceased Pacific Islanders by the Queensland Government. *Australian Journal of Politics and History* 61(1): 1–19. doi.org/10.1111/ajph.12083.
2017	*Making Mala: Malaita in Solomon Islands, 1870s–1930s.* Canberra: ANU Press. doi.org/10.22459/MM.04.2017.

Moorhouse, H.C.

1929   *British Solomon Islands Protectorate. Report of Commissioner Appointed by the Secretary of State for the Colonies to Inquire into the Circumstances in which Murderous Attacks took Place in 1927 on Government Officials on Guadalcanal and Malaita. Presented by the Secretary of State for the Colonies to Parliament by Command of His Majesty*. London: HM Stationery Office.

Mortensen, Reid

2000   Slaving in Australian Courts: Blackbirding Cases, 1869–1871. *Journal of South Pacific Law* 4: 7–37. Available from: eprints.usq.edu.au/5513/.

Moyen, Remy

2004   *Les Evènements: Arrêt sur Images, 1984–1989* [*The Events: Freeze Frame, 1984–1989*]. Nouméa: Les Editions du Lémurien.

Muhlhauser, G.H.P.

1924   *The Cruise of the Amaryllis*. London: John Lane, Bodley Head Ltd.

Mühlhäusler, Peter

1981   Foreigner Talk: Tok Masta in New Guinea. *International Journal of the Sociology of Language* 28: 93–113. doi.org/10.1515/ijsl.1981.28.93.

Mullins, Steve

1995   *Torres Strait: A History of Colonial Occupation and Culture Contact, 1864–1897*. Rockhampton, Qld: Central Queensland University Press.

2019   *Octopus Crowd: Maritime History and the Business of Australian Pearling in the Schooner Age*. Tuscaloosa, AL: University of Alabama Press.

Munro, Doug, and Stewart Firth

1986   Towards Colonial Protectorates: The Case of the Gilbert and Ellice Islands. *Australian Journal of Politics and History* 32(1): 63–71. doi.org/10.1111/j.1467-8497.1986.tb00341.x.

Mytinger, Caroline

1930   With Brush and Palette in the South Seas: An Artist Visits the Melanesian Islands to Paint the Natives. *Natural History* (July–August): 349–66.

1943   *Headhunting in the Solomon Islands*. London: Macmillan.

Nelson, Hank N.

1982   *Taim Bilong Masta: The Australian Involvement with Papua New Guinea*. Sydney: ABC.

1986	Murray, Sir John Hubert Plunkett (1861–1940). In *Australian Dictionary of Biography. Volume 10*, pp. 645–48. Canberra: National Centre of Biography, The Australian National University. Available from: adb.anu.edu.au/biography/murray-sir-john-hubert-plunkett-7711.

Neumann, Klaus

1992	*Not the Way It Really Was: Constructing the Tolai Past*. Honolulu: University of Hawai`i Press.
1996	*Rabaul Yu Swit Moa Yet: Surviving the 1994 Volcanic Eruption*. Melbourne: Oxford University Press.

Newbury, Colin

1973	Treaty, Grant, Usage and Sufferance: The Origins of British Colonial Protectorates. In *W. P. Morrell: A Tribute—Essays in Modern and Early Modern History Presented to William Parker Morrell*, edited by G.A. Wood and P.S. O'Connor, pp. 69–84. Dunedin, NZ: University of Otago Press.

O'Brien, Claire

1995	*A Greater Than Solomon Here: A Story of Catholic Church in Solomon Islands*. Honiara: Catholic Church Solomon Islands Inc.

O'Brien, Patty

2006	*The Pacific Muse: Exotic Femininity and the Colonial Pacific*. Seattle, WA: University of Washington Press.

Oliver, Douglas L.

1961	*The Pacific Islands*. Rev. edn. Cambridge, MA: Harvard University Press.

Oram, Nigel D.

1972	Samarai. In *Encyclopaedia of Papua New Guinea*, edited by Peter Ryan, pp. 1028–29. Melbourne and Port Moresby: Melbourne University Press and University of Papua New Guinea.
1976	*Colonial Town to Melanesian City: Port Moresby 1884–1974*. Canberra: Australian National University Press.

Osmond, Frederick Gary

2006	Nimble Savages: Myth, Race, Social Memory and Australian Sport. PhD thesis, University of Queensland, Brisbane.

Osmond, Gary, and Murray G. Phillips

2006	'Look at That Kid Crawling': Race, Myth and the 'Crawl' Stroke. *Australian Historical Studies* 127: 43–62.

Paravicini, Eugen

1931   *Reisen in Den Britischen Salomonen* [*Travelling in the British Solomon Islands*]. Leipzig: Verlag Huber.

Patarin, Pierre

1997   *Messageries Maritimes: Voyageurs et Paquebots du Passé* [*Maritime Couriers: Travellers and Passengers of the Past*]. Rennes: Editions Ouest-France.

Penny, Alfred

1887   *Ten Years in Melanesia*. London: Wells, Gardner, Darton & Co.

Pirie, Peter

1972   The Effects of Treponematosis and Gonorrhoea on the Populations of the Pacific Islands. *Human Biology in Oceania* 1(3): 189–206.

Price, Charles

1974   *The Great White Walls Are Built: Restrictive Immigration to North America and Australia, 1836–1888*. Canberra: Australian Institute of International Affairs in association with Australian National University Press.

Price, Charles, with Elizabeth Baker

1976   Origins of Pacific Island Labourers in Queensland, 1863–1904: A Research Note. *Journal of Pacific History* 11(1–2): 106–21.

Price, Geoffrey

1977   Letter to the editor. *Solomons News Drum*, 3 June.

Quanchi, Max

1977   The Glorious Company: The Polynesian Company in Melbourne and Fiji. MA thesis, Monash University, Melbourne.

1994   A Trip through the Islands in 1918: The Photography of T.J. McMahon. *Meanjin* 53(4): 715–22.

1995   T.J. McMahon: Photographer, Essayist and Patriot in Colonial Australia, the Pacific and Empire. In *Messy Entanglements*, edited by Alama Talu and Max Quanchi, pp. 49–62. Brisbane: Pacific History Association.

1997   Thomas McMahon: Photography as Propaganda in the Pacific Islands. *History of Photography* 21(2): 42–53.

2004   Jewel of the Pacific and Planter's Paradise: The Visual Argument for Australian Sub-Imperialism in the Solomon Islands. *Journal of Pacific History* 39(1): 43–58.

2006   Photographing Samarai: Place, Imagination and Change. In *Social Change in the 21st Century*, edited by C. Hall and C. Hopkinson. Brisbane: Queensland University of Technology. Available from: eprints.qut.edu.au/6415.

2010a	A Collector of Images: The Pacific Archive of Photographer Thomas McMahon. In *Hunters, Collectors and Exhibitions: Oceanic Collections in Australia*, edited by Susan Cochrane and Max Quanchi, pp. 161–81. Newcastle upon Tyne: Cambridge Scholars Publishing.
2010b	Merl La Voy: An American Photographer in the South Seas. In *Coast to Coast*, edited by Prue Ahrens and Chris Dixon, pp. 117–37. Newcastle, UK: Cambridge Scholars Publishing.
2014a	Norman H. Hardy: Book Illustrator and Artist. *Journal of Pacific History* 49(2): 214–33.
2014b	Thomas McMahon's Pacific Neighbours: An Early Australian Photojournalist. In *Shifting Focus: Colonial Australian Photography 1850–1920*, edited by Anne Maxwell and Josephine Croci, pp. 218–29. Melbourne: Australian Scholarly Publishing.

Quanchi, Max, and Max Shekleton

2015	*Postcards from Oceania: Port Towns, Portraits and the Picturesque during the Colonial Era*. Suva: University of the South Pacific.

Queensland Kanaka Mission

1904–06	*Not in Vain: What God Hath Wrought amongst the Kanakas. Queensland. Report of the Queensland Kanaka Mission*. Sydney: South Sea Evangelical Mission.

Quinlivan, Paul J.

1988	Phillips, Sir Frederick Beaumont (1890–1957). In *Australian Dictionary of Biography. Volume 11*, pp. 214–15. Canberra: National Centre of Biography, The Australian National University. Available from: adb.anu.edu.au/biography/phillips-sir-frederick-beaumont-8034.

Radi, Heather

1979	Bruce, Stanley Melbourne (1883–1967). *Australian Dictionary of Biography. Volume 7*, pp. 453–61. Canberra: National Centre of Biography, The Australian National University. Available from: adb.anu.edu.au/biography/bruce-stanley-melbourne-5400.

Ralston, Caroline

1975	'White Woman with a Towel…': A Series of Shabby Episodes. *New Guinea and Australia, the Pacific and South-East Asia* 10(2): 57–62.
2014 [1978]	*Grass Huts and Warehouses: Pacific Beach Communities of the Nineteenth Century*. Brisbane: Pacific Studies Series, University of Queensland ePress.

Rannie, Douglas

1912   *My Adventures among South Sea Cannibals*. London: Seeley, Service & Co. Ltd.

Reiger, Kerreen M.

1985   *The Disenchantment of the Home: Modernizing the Australian Family, 1880–1940*. Melbourne: Oxford University Press.

Richards, Rhys

2012   *Head Hunters Black and White: Three Collectors in the Western Solomon Islands 1893 to 1914; and the Diary of Graham Officer, Collector of Museum Objects in the Solomon Islands in 1901 for Museum Victoria in Melbourne*. Wellington: Paremata Press.

Rivers, W.H.R. (ed.)

1922   *Essays on the Depopulation of Melanesia*. London: Cambridge University Press.

Robinson, Shirleene

2008   *Something like Slavery? Queensland's Aboriginal Child Workers, 1842–1945*. Melbourne: Australian Scholarly Publishing.

2015   'Always Good Demand': Aboriginal Child Domestic Servants in Nineteenth- and Early Twentieth-Century Australia. In *Colonization and Domestic Service: Historical and Contemporary Perspectives*, edited by Victoria K. Haskins and Claire Lowie, pp. 98–110. New York: Routledge.

Robson, Richard W.

1944   *The Pacific Islands Year Book, 1944*. Sydney: Pacific Publications.

1965   *Queen Emma: The Samoan–American Girl Who Founded an Empire in Nineteenth Century New Guinea*. Sydney: Pacific Publications.

Rodman, Margaret C.

2001   *Houses Far from Home: British Colonial Space in the New Hebrides*. Honolulu: University of Hawai`i Press.

Roe, David

1993   Prehistory without Pots: Prehistoric Settlement and Economy of North-West Guadalcanal, Solomon Islands. PhD thesis, The Australian National University, Canberra.

Rolland, Jean

2002   *Les Rails Calédoniens, 1892–1953* [*The Caledonian Rails, 1892–1953*]. Nouméa: Editions Jean Rolland.

Rolls, Eric

1992   *Sojourners: The Epic Story of China's Centuries-Old Relationship with Australia*. Brisbane: University of Queensland Press.

Romilly, Hugh Hastings

1887   *The Western Pacific and New Guinea: Notes on the Natives, Christian and Cannibal, with Some Account of the Old Labour Trade*. London: John Murray.

Russell, Tom

2003   *I Have the Honour to Be: A Memoir of a Career Covering Fifty-Two Years of Service for British Overseas Territories*. Spennymoor, UK: The Memoir Club.

Rutledge, Martha

1974   McElhone, John (1833–1898). In *Australian Dictionary of Biography. Volume 5*, pp. 150–52. Canberra: National Centre of Biography, The Australian National University. Available from: adb.anu.edu.au/biography/mcelhone-john-4087.

Sandars, George Eustace Drysdale

1971   Letter to the editor. *British Solomon Islands Protectorate News Sheet*, 31 March.

Scarr, Deryck

1967   *Fragments of Empire: A History of the Western Pacific High Commission 1877–1914*. Canberra: Australian National University Press.

1980   Viceroy of the Pacific: The Majesty of Colour—A Life of Sir John Bates Thurston. *Pacific Research Monograph No. 4*. Canberra: The Australian National University.

1984   *Fiji: A Short History*. Sydney: Allen & Unwin.

Seton, Georgina

1944   *Bring Another Glass: A Mystery Story of the Solomon Islands*. Sydney: Angus & Robertson.

Shlomowitz, Ralph, and Richard Bedford

1988   The Internal Labor Trade in New Hebrides and Solomon Islands, c. 1900–1941. *Journal de la Société des Océanistes* 86: 1–85.

Siegel, Jeff

1985   Origins of Pacific Island Labourers in Fiji. *Journal of Pacific History* 20(2): 42–54.

Singe, John

1979   *The Torres Strait: People and History*. Brisbane: University of Queensland Press.

Sinker, William

1900 *By Reef and Shoal: Being an Account of a Voyage amongst the Islands in the South-Western Pacific.* London: Society for Promoting Christian Knowledge.

Standley, R.H.

1981 *My Heart's in the Islands.* Oxford: Beckett Publications.

Stone, Peter

1994 *Hostages to Freedom: The Fall of Rabaul.* Yarram, Vic.: Oceans Enterprises.

Stuart, Ian

1970 *Port Moresby: Yesterday and Today.* Sydney: Pacific Publications.

Sturma, Michael

2002 *South Sea Maidens: Western Fantasy and Sexual Politics in the South Pacific.* Westport, CT: Greenwood Press.

Swindon, G.J.

1994 HMAS Adelaide and the 1927 Malaita Expedition. *Naval Historical Review: Official Journal of the Naval Historical Society of Australia.*

Tedder, James L.O.

2008 *Solomon Islands Years: A District Administrator in the Islands, 1952–1974.* Stuarts Point, NSW: Tuatu Studies.

Tennent, John W.

1999 Charles Morris Woodford C.M.G. (1852–1927): Pacific Adventurer and Forgotten Solomon Islands Naturalist. *Archives of Natural History* 26(3): 419–32.

Thacker, R.S., J.S. Neill, and R.D. Blandy

1936 Western Pacific. *Journal of Comparative Legislation and International Law* 18(2): 116–19.

Thomas, Tim

2014 Objects and Photographs from the Percy Sladen Trust Expedition. In *The Ethnographic Experiment: A.M. Hocart and W.H.R. Rivers in Island Melanesia*, edited by Edvard Hviding and Cato Berg, pp. 252–81. New York: Berghahn Books.

Threlfall, Neville A.

2012 *Mangroves, Coconuts and Frangipani: The Story of Rabaul.* Rabaul, PNG: Rabaul Historical Society.

Townsend, Ian

2017   *Line of Fire*. Sydney: Fourth Estate.

Trench, D.C.C.

1956a   Marchant on Malaita. *Corona* 8(5): 106–08.

1956b   Marchant on Malaita. *Corona* 8(6): 230–33.

1956c   Marchant on Malaita. *Corona* 8(7): 58–61.

Tulagi Club

1934   *Rules of the Tulagi Club*. Guadalcanal: Melanesian Mission.

van der Veur, Paul W

1966   *Search of New Guinea's Boundaries: From Torres Strait to the Pacific*. Canberra: Australian National University Press.

Villiers, Alan John

1937   *Cruise of the Conrad: A Journal of a Voyage Round the World, Undertaken and Carried Out in the Ship Joseph Conrad, 212 tons, in the Years 1934, 1935 and 1936 by Way of Good Hope, the East Indies, the South Seas and Cape Horn*. New York: Charles Scribner's Sons.

Waters, Christopher

2016   The Last of Australian Imperial Dreams for the Southwest Pacific: Paul Hasluck, the Department of Territories and a Greater Melanesia in 1960. *Journal of Pacific History* 51(2): 169–85. doi.org/10.1080/ 00223344.2016.1195595.

Watson, I. Bruce

1991   Australians Living Plantation Lives, Southwest Pacific c. 1900– 1975. *Journal of the Royal Australian Historical Society* 77(1): 50–68.

Watters, David, with Anna Koestenbauer

2011   *Stitches in Time: Two Centuries of Surgery in Papua New Guinea*. Bloomington, IN: Xlibris Corporation.

Weetman, Charles

1937   Tulagi. *Walkabout*, 1 October, pp. 33–35.

Wetherell, David

1996   *Charles Abel and the Kwato Mission of Papua New Guinea, 1891– 1975*. Melbourne: Melbourne University Press.

White, Geoffrey M., and Lamont Lindstrom (eds)

1990   *The Pacific Theatre: Island Representations of World War II*. Melbourne: Melbourne University Press.

White, Geoffrey M., David Gegeo, David Akin and Karen Watson-Gegeo (eds)
1988 *The Big Death: Solomon Islanders Remember World War II*. Honiara: Solomon Islands College of Higher Education and University of the South Pacific.

Whiteman, Darrell L.
1983 *Melanesians and Missionaries: An Ethnohistorical Study of Social and Religious Change in the Southwest Pacific*. Pasadena, CA: William Carey Library.

Willmott, Bill
2005 *A History of the Chinese Communities in Eastern Melanesia: Solomon Islands, Vanuatu, New Caledonia*. Macmillan Brown Working Paper Series No. 12. Macmillan Brown Centre for Pacific Studies, University of Canterbury, Christchurch.

Willson, Margaret
1989 The Generous Face: Concepts of Personhood and Trade among the Papua New Guinea Chinese. PhD thesis, London School of Economics, London.

Willson, Margaret, Clive Moore and Doug Munro
1990 Asian Workers in the Pacific. In *Labour in the South Pacific*, edited by Clive Moore, Jacqueline Leckie and Doug Munro, pp. 78–107. Townsville, Qld: Department of History and Politics and Centre for Melanesian Studies, James Cook University.

Wolfers, Edward P.
1971 *The Significance of Protectorate Status*. Washington, DC: Institute of Current World Affairs.
1975 *Race Relations and Colonial Rule in Papua New Guinea*. Sydney: Australia and New Zealand Book Company.

Woodford, C.M.
1890 *A Naturalist among the Head-Hunters: Being an Account of Three Visits to the Solomon Islands in the Years 1886, 1887 and 1888*. London: G. Philip.

Wright, Christopher
2013 *The Echo of Things: The Lives of Photographs in the Solomon Islands*. Durham, NC: Duke University Press. doi.org/10.1215/9780822377412.

Wu, David W.H.
1982 *The Chinese in Papua New Guinea, 1880–1980*. Hong Kong: Chinese University Press.

Young, A.K.

1926   Western Pacific. *Journal of Comparative Legislation and International Law* 8(2): 174–76.

1928   Western Pacific. *Journal of Comparative Legislation and International Law* 10(2): 114–16.

Young, Florence S.H.

1926   *Pearls from the Pacific*. London: Marshall Brothers Ltd.

Young, John M.

1966   Australia's Pacific Frontier. *Historical Studies* 2(47): 373–88.

1984   *Adventurous Spirits: Australian Migrant Society in Pre-Cession Fiji*. Brisbane: University of Queensland Press.

1988   Race and Sex in Fiji Re-visited. *Journal of Pacific History* 23(2): 214–22. doi.org/10.1080/00223348808572593.

Newspapers and magazines

The Brisbane Courier
British Solomon Islands Protectorate News Sheet
Chinese Times [Sydney]
Daily Mail [Brisbane]
Evening Post [Wellington]
Fiji Times [Suva]
Mackay Mercury and South Kennedy Advertiser [Mackay, Qld]
North Queensland Register [Townsville, Qld]
Pacific Islands Monthly [Sydney]
Pacific Islands Year Book [Sydney]
Planters' Gazette [Gizo]
Queensland Country Life
The Queenslander [Brisbane]
Solomon Islands Police Force Newsletter [Honiara]
Solomon Star [Honiara]
Solomon Voice [Honiara]
Solomons News Drum [Honiara]
Southern Cross Log [Auckland and London]
Sun [Sydney]
Sydney Mail
Sydney Morning Herald
Western Pacific High Commission Gazette

Unpublished manuscripts

Akin, David

2009 Notes from the May–June 1933 Diary of Sylvester M. Lambert, University of California San Diego, Special Collections, MSS 682, folder 22. Unpublished ms in the possession of the author.

Barrett, Helen Hugo

1946–88 Papers from her years in Solomon Islands. In the possession of the author.

Marchant, William S.

1942–43 Diary for 2 January 1942 to 6 May 1943, transcribed by J. French, aide-de-camp to the High Commissioner, 29 December 1962, Solomon Islands National Archives, BSIP 5/IV/1. Unpublished ms.

Struben, Roy

1963 South Seas Cannonade: A Biography of Ambrose Ernest (Ernie) Palmer, 1904–1976—A Legend in the British Solomon Islands Protectorate and the South Pacific (from a draft manuscript given to Paul H. Brown by Ernie and Ingie Palmer). Copy of unpublished ms in the possession of the author.

Other sources

British Museum (London)

Edge-Partington, Thomas. Photographic Collection.
Garvey, Sir Ronald. Photographic Collection.
Lever, Robert. Photographic Collection.
Melanesian Mission Photographic Collection.

British Solomon Islands Protectorate

1896–1945 *Annual Reports.*

1896–1978 Archives. Held in the National Archives of Solomon Islands, Honiara.

1911 *Handbook of the British Solomon Islands Protectorate, with Returns up to 31st March 1911.* Tulagi.

1923 *Handbook of the British Solomon Islands Protectorate, with Returns up to 31st March 1922.* London: HM Stationery Office.

1923–38 *Blue Books.*

1933–36 *Agricultural Journal.* Volumes 1–3.

Fryer Library, University of Queensland

Wilson, Alexander H.

1942   Notes on the Evacuation of Tulagi, 6 February.

1946   Lands and Public Works Department: A Brief History.

1972   Notes for James Boutilier.

Wilson, Alexander H. and Jessie A.

　　　　Papers and Photographs, also including material from their daughter Andrea Gordon Bannatyne.

Pacific Manuscripts Bureau (Canberra)

Sandars, George Eustace Drysdale

1966[?]   Untitled ms on his Solomons years. In Papers on the Solomon Islands, 1928–1943, Film 553.

Woodford, C.M.

n.d.   Charles Morris Woodford Papers and Photographs, PMB 151, 1021, 1290, 1381, 56, 58.

Other archives and libraries

Admiralty Record Office, London

British Admiralty

1885–96   Royal Navy Australian Station, Correspondence Respecting Outrages on British Subjects (New Guinea and Solomon Islands).

Anglican Church of Melanesia, Honiara

The ACOM Solomon Islands Collection is housed in the Solomon Islands National Archives.

The Nurse Talbot Collection is within the ACOM Collection.

ANU Archives and Noel Butlin Archives Centre

Burns Philp & Co.

n.d.   Archives. Burns Philp and Company (Sydney Office and Branches), N115. Noel Butlin Archives Centre, The Australian National University, Canberra.

Woodford, C.M.

n.d.   Charles Morris Woodford papers on the Solomon Islands and other Pacific countries, ANUA 481. ANU Archives, Canberra.

Archives New Zealand

Barnett, Frederic Joshua

1917   Last Will and Testament and Probate Documents, Ref. AAOM 6029, Box 322. Archives New Zealand, Wellington.

Australian War Memorial

Dalrymple-Hay, Kenneth Houston

1942–43   Typed Transcript of a Diary as a Coastwatcher, 3DRL/6122. Unpublished ms. Australian War Memorial, Canberra.

National Archives, United Kingdom

Colonial Office Records

1878–1951   *Western Pacific: Original Correspondence and Reports.* Available on microfilm through the Australian Joint Copying Project in the National Library of Australia and various other libraries.

National Library of Australia

1909   Photographs R32 Sundry 1.11, Solomon Islands 11, Coaling Station, Gavutu Island. National Library of Australia, Canberra.

Solomon Islands National Archives

BSIP and Solomon Islands Government Archives, and the Anglican Church of Melanesia (ACOM) Collection, Honiara.

United States National Archives and Records Administration (College Park, MD)

University of Auckland

Western Pacific High Commission Archives. University of Auckland Archives, Auckland.

University of Queensland

Smith, Sydney Mercer

1898   Diary of the Voyage of the Fearless. Unpublished ms. Anthropology Museum, University of Queensland, Brisbane.

University of Sydney

Elkin, A.P.

     Papers, Box 159, File 4/1/49. University of Sydney Archives, Sydney.

Index

Page numbers in **bold** refer to maps, tables and plates.
The glottal stop (`) is ordered as the last letter in the alphabet.

Abbott, A. Hedley, 102, 164
Abel, Charles, 9
Adams, John Edward (Bill), 233
Akin, David, 278–79, 368, 372
Alasa`a, Samuel, 357, **358**
Alemaena, 299
Alexander, Captain G.G., 195
Aliang, Johnnie, 272
Allan, Sir Colin, 51
Allardyce, K.J., 130
Aloysius, 273
Amalgamated Wireless (Australasia) (AWA) Ltd, 175, 264
Amherst, William T.-A., Baron of Hackney, 47
Anderson, Julius W., 296
Anderson, Pastor, 227
Andresen, Albert Molkin (Andy), 298
Andresen, Sumoli Wilomena, 298
Andresen, Tiganapalo, 298
Andresen, Za Za, 297, 298
Aningari, 368
Annandale, Stanley, 338
Anuta (Cherry) Island, 66
Argus, The, 350
Asaeda, Toshio, 348
Ashley, Francis Noel, 146–48, 152, 161–62, 165, 206, 223, 247, 270, 282, 310, 311, 316, 327, 363, 369, 371

Atkin, Joe, 34
Atkinson, Edith, 292
Atkinson, Sam, 292
Auki (`Aoke), *see* Malaita
Austen, Edward, 334
Austen (née Macdonald), Minnie Thursa Louise, 334
Australia, 1, 11, 17, 24, 46, 47, 50, 54, 56, 74, 84, 96, 107, 111, 112, 149, 154, 159, 164, 189, 195, 199, 217, 230, 235, 236, 237, 239, 241, 252, 253, 264, 266, 278, 299, 300, 303, 330, 331, 335, 336, 341, 342, 369, 370, 381, 386, 389, 391, 400
Australian Army, 330, 331, 380, 383–84
Australian Broadcasting Commission, 264
Australian Crawl (freestyle) swimming stroke, Solomon Islands origins, 300
Australian South Sea Islanders, 334
Commonwealth Institute of Science and Industry, 160
deportation of Solomon Islanders, 125, 126
frontier sexuality, 411

German New Guinea, capture of, 9, 102
High Court Mabo and Wik judgments, 48
Indigenous population, attitudes to, 48–49, 333–34
media, 350–51
merchant companies, 109–10
Navigation Acts, 389
Pacific interests, 53–54, 63, 77, 102
Royal Australian Air Force, 243–44, 327, 379–80, 384
Royal Australian Navy, 196, 237–41, 347, 396
schools, 282, 286, 287
settler society, 48, 49, 50, 53
shipping services, 82–93
White Australia Policy, 9, 10, 62, 114, 115, 126
See also British New Guinea; German New Guinea; New Guinea Mandated Territory; New South Wales; Papua, Territory of; Queensland
Australasian Colonial Conference, 59
Australian United Steam Navigation Co., 82

Ba`etalua, Head Warder, 166
Baddeley, Bishop Walter H., 225, 310, 325, 329, 374, 382, 393
Banks Group, 82
Barley, Bill, 297, 298
Barley (née Doughty), Florence A., 298
Barley, Jack Charles, 139, 146, 152, 297–98, **338**, 353, 411
Barley, Jack Charles Jr, 297
Barley (née Andresen), Sumoli Wilomena, 298
Barnett, Frank, 71, 104, 141–42, 156, 246, 266, 339
Barnett, Kate, 266

Basiana, 168, 228, 229–30, 239, 242, 360, 368
Bates, Issac Grainger, 156
Baura, bugler, 168
bêche-de-mer, 58, 119, 332
Beck, Rollo H., 350
Bedford, Randolph, 350
Bell, Lieutenant-Colonel George John, 237
Bell, William R., 142, 156, 157, 227, **228**, 229–30, 231, 242, 328, 330, 360
Bellona Island, 66, 104
Belshaw, Cyril, 404
Bengough, Charles V.F., 371, 391, 392
Bennett, Bill, 395
Bennett, Enid, 297
Bennett, Judith, 232, 248, 303, 372
Bennett, W.H., 297
Beriboo, Sau, 281
Bernatzik, Hugo. A., 299
Bernhardt, M.J., 325
Bevan, Sister, 180, 185
Beve, Brother Bartholomew, 366
Bignell, Charles Edward, 112
Bignell, Charles, 91, 112, 189, 204, 232, 234, 236, 389
Bignell, Kathleen, 91, 112, 188–89, 201, 204, 209, 232, 234, 253
Bignell, Margaret, 112, 232
Blake, Frances, 289
Blake, Major William V. Jardine, 264, 272, 327, 385, 387, 388
Boer War, South Africa, 157, 159, 327–29
Bogesi, Native Medical Practitioner George, 369, 400
Bonnard, F.A.H., 227, 229, 230, 232–33
Bosden, Sister, 180
Bougainville, 1, 49, 65, 384, 387, 388
Bougainville Strait, 41, 300
Boutilier, James, 146, 248, 297–98

Boyle, Mrs, 205, 206, 265
British Government
    Admiralty, 59, 237
    Air Ministry, 244
    Armed Forces, 78, 235, 330, 328, 329
    Berlin Conference (1884–85), 57, 59
    Berlin Convention (1899), 65
    British Broadcasting Commission, 264
    British Settlement Act (1887), 64
    Colonial and Indian Exhibition, 61
    Colonial Office, 54, 55, 57, 59, 63, 73, 77, 114, 147, 149, 154, 231
    Colonial Service, 146, 148–49
    colonial territories, 57, 60, 116, 146, 147, 148, 155, 195, 242, 331, 346, 382
        British New Guinea, *see* separate entry
        British Solomon Islands Protectorate, *see* separate entry
        Crown colonies, 52, 372
        Hong Kong, 91, 116, 119, 120, 218, 223, 224, 235, 286, 390
        Protectorates, 24, 27, 49–54, 372
        South Africa, 157, 159, 327–29
    colonialism, 11, 24, 48–69, 368, 372, 409–14
    Crewe Circular (1909), 295
    Foreign Jurisdiction Act, 52, 56, 64
    Foreign Office, 54, 55
    Imperial Service Order, 160
    Order of the British Empire, 335
    orders in council, 50, 52, 56, 57, 64, 65, 67, 154, 295
    Pacific Islanders Protection Acts (1872 and 1875), 55, 64
    Royal Navy, 330, 347
        Australian Station (RNAS), 47, 54, 57, 63, 88, 236, 240
    Secretary of State for the Colonies, 47, 67, 68, 69, 73, 93, 148, 180, 295
    Unionist Government, fall of, 114
    Warren Fisher Committee report, 149
    See also London
British Melanesia, concept of, 49, 59, 60, 102
British New Guinea, 77, 192, 333
    Administrators, 60, 61, 62
    Crown Colony, 49, 53, 65
    Deputy Commissioners WPHC, 60, 61
    Lieutenant-Governor, 62, 346
    offered to Queensland, 60
    Port Moresby, 8, 9, 25, 50, 59, 61, 62, 134, 265
    Protectorate, 53, 59, 60, 61
    See also Papua, Australian Territory of
British Solomon Islands Protectorate (BSIP), 63, 64, 65, 66, **67**, 73, **150–51**
    Advisory Council, 12, 68, 129, 140, 159, 300, 306 307, 309, 324, 335, 353–54, 366–67, 374, 411
    Armed Constabulary and Prisons Department
        Armed Constabulary, 74, 76, 79, 105, 124, **127**, **135**, 138, 155, 156, 163, 165–72, **167**, **168**, 169, **170**, 185, 200, 227, 229, 230, 231, 233, 237, 239, **243**, 307, 308, **318**, **320**, 353, 357, 363, 364, 365, 366, 367

Commandants, 102, 151, 155, 156, 163, 233, 239, 300, **302**, 327
District prisons, 168, 169
Special Constables, 232–37, 239, 241
Subinspectors, 163, 327, 357, 377
Tulagi prison, **14–15**, 74, 76, 101, 105, 138, 165, 169–70, **171–72**, 357
whipping platform, 311
census (1931), 316
Colonial Service, 140–97
Criminal Law (Amendment) Regulation (No. 7, 1931), 311
currency, 94, 95
death penalty, 169, 172
Deputy Governor, 68
discriminatory legislation, 25
economy, 73, 77
Education Officer, 164
Empire Day, 315–16, 346
Governing Council, 68, 69, 357, 360
Government Entomologist, 104, 164
Governor, 51, 69
High Commissioner, *see* WPHC
Honiara, *see* separate entry
Labour Department, 101, 103, 110, 127, 128, 157, 158, 164, 178, 235, 345, 363
Lands and Surveys Department, 49, 80, 162, 190–97, **191**, 235
  Commissioner of Lands, 150, 156, 160, 162, 194, 252
  Crown Surveyor, 102, 160, 162, 194, 195
  Government Surveyor, 194, 195, 252
  Land Regulation (1914), 193
  mining, 80, 160, 196
  Phillips Lands Commission (1922), 192, 193, 195, 196
  Special Lands Commission (1957), 51–52
Legal and District Administration Department
  District Magistrate, Resident Magistrates, *see* District Officers
  District Officers, 25, 78, 95, 138, 142, 146, 149, 150, 152, 153, 154, 155, 158, 160, 163, 164, 166, 169, 181, 194, 210, 220, 227, **228**, 233, 235, 237, **258**, 296, 297, 300, 304, 329, 330, 333, 334, 339, 360, 369, 371, 377, 378, 386, 387, 388, 390, 391, 404
  Judicial Commissioners (Chief Magistrates), 101, 139, 156, 169, 267, 309, 329
Legislative Assembly, 69
Legislative Council, 68, 300, 360
lobbying to become a Crown colony, 67–68
Marine Department, 357
Medical Department, 176–89, 294
  hospital, **7**, 80, **81**, 101, 102, 105, 112, 133, 138, 241–42, 150, 158, 178, **179**, **181**, **184**–89, 300, 343, 349, 384, **402**, 404, 409
  nurses, 180, 265, 276–77, 307
  Resident Medical Officer, 162
  Senior Medical Officers, 180, 181, 184, 186
  Travelling Medical Officer, 180
  See also medical doctors; hospitals, non-government

INDEX

Military Governors, 141, 147, 390
population
    Chinese, 6, 119, 120, 218, 316
    European, 72, 265, 316
    Japanese, 113, 316
    Malay, 9, 316
    Melanesian, 316
    Polynesian, 316
    Solomon Islander, 123
Port and Marine Department, 4, 111, 322, 382
ports of entry, 83, 87, 180
postal service, 93, **192**, 235
Preservation of Order Regulation (No. 18, 1922; No. 8, 1930), 308, 309
proclamation of BSIP (1893), 48, 64, 65–66
public holidays, 346
Public Works Department, 101, 105
    Superintendent, 156, 160
Resident Commissioner's Department
    Deputy Commissioners, 63, 71, 73, 78
    Government Secretaries, 139, 141, 145, 146, 156, 163, 165, 327
    Resident Commissioners, 12, 67, 68, 73, 88, 97, 139, 140–48, 208, 294, 297, 353, 396, 399
    See also Ashley; Kane; Marchant; Noel; Woodford, Charles Morris
residency, *see* Tulagi
self-government, 69
Supreme Court of Appeal, Suva, 169
Sydney office, 162, 391
Treasury, Customs and Postal Department, 80, 93, **95**, 149, **152**
    head tax, 128, 129, 140, 242
    Treasurer and Collector of Customs, 141, 156, 159
    WPHC transferred to Honiara, 68
    See also Tulagi
Brogan, Wing-Commander John, 79, 380
Brooke, Rev. Charles, 34, 36, 304
Browne, William de Courcey, 327
Browning, Rev. C.W., 41
Bruce, R., 236
Bruce, Prime Minister Stanley, 236
Buchanan, Bella, 297
Buchanan, Cyril, 174
Buchanan, Jean, 297
Buchanan, Jim, 297, 331
Buchanan (née Dumphy), Maggie, 297
Buka, 65, 385
Bula, Reuben, 41
Bullen, Lieutenant H.W., 396
Burnett, Sir Charles, 379
Burns Philp & Co., 17, 94, 97, 110
    BP Magazine, 91
    Burns Philp (South Seas) Co. Ltd, 109
    See also Fiji
    copra plantations, 84, 88, 109
    copra storage, 109
    Faisi branch, 109
    Gizo branch, 110
    government subsidies, 84
    Makambo Island, 4, 17, 28, 42, **84–86**, 87, 88, 91, 92, 93, 95, 100, 105, 106, 109, 110, 111, 112, 124, 125, 126, 128, 131, 132, 140, 142, 197, 202, **215**, 227, 230, 235, 244, 247, 252, 256, **260**, 269, 276, 316, 325, 355, 357, 366, 382, 384, 388, 390, 391, 392, **403**, **405**
    managers of the Tulagi Club, 208
    Picturesque Travel, 91

shipping, 74, 82, **84**, 85, **86**, 109, 126, 382
Shortland Islands Plantations Co., 109
Solomon Islands Development Co., 109, 110
tourism, 17, 21, 24, 88, **89–90**
See also New Guinea Mandated Territory
Burt, Ben, 371

Cambridge, Rolfe, 234
Cameron, Charlotte, 351
Campbell, Edna, 269, 305, 365, 366
Campbell, Frederick, 133, 166, 233, 264, 299, 300, **302**, 391, 411
Campbell, Jack, 300, 391
Campbell, Kapinihare, 300
Campbell, Maria Kainaua, 300
Campbell, Pat, 391
Cape Marsh, see BSIP, Legal and District Administration Department; Russell Islands
Capricornia, 186
Carment, Dr Andrew G., 184
Caroline Islands, 56, 63, 379
Catholic mission, 96, 174
See also Tulagi
Central Islands Province, Solomon Islands, 1, 21, 41
Chester, Edward C., 195
China, invasion by Japan, 379
Chinese, 4, 9, 91, 92, 103, 113–21, 197, 202, 213–27, 321
A Guo (Ye Koh), 117 (Map 2.1), 218 (Figure 4.12 code)
Ah Choi (A Cai), 118
Ah Tam (Ya Tan), 114
Akun, Aloysius (Alois), 214, 216, 220
Australian Territory of Papua, in, 9
BSIP Defence Force members, 379

Chan (Chen), Aloysius, 214, 214
Chan Cheong (Chen Chang, or Zhang), Johnny, 118, 121, 200, 217, 291, 390
Chan Dung (Chen Deng), 117 (Map 2.1), 218 (Figure 4.12 code)
Chan Wing (Chen Rong), 216
Chinatown, 4, 6, 24, 101, 105, 113–21, **115**, **117**, 187, 199, 213–27, **215**, **218**, **221**, **223**, 252, 265, 270, 365
Chinese Nationalist Party, 222
Chinese Times, 217
Ching Fook Ye (Ching Fook Yo, Cheng Fuyou), 117 (Map 2.1), 218 (Figure 4.12 code)
Chow (Zhou), 220
Chow Kai (Zhou Qi), 220
complaints against, 222, 224
consular officials visit, 217, 223
counties and districts of origin, 114, 117
dialects, 115
Djienbien Young (Dianbin Yang), 223
Doo (Du), Sam, 206
domestic servants, 303
evacuation, 386, 389–90, 391, 396
gambling, 222
Gizo stores, 225
government storekeeper, 101
Guangdong Province, 114, 117, 217, 390
Guomindang (Kuomintang), 217, 222, **223**, 225–26, 326, 372
Him Choy (Ye Cai), 383
Ho Chi Tak (He Zhide), 118
Ho Man (Ho Nan, He Min), 118
Hong Kong, 91, 120, 218, 223, 390
Huong Lee [Wangli] Co., 113
jetties, **115**, 117, 200, **215**, **216**, **218**, 220, 221

INDEX

Kwan Cho (Quan Zhu), 390
Kwan Ho Yuan (Quan Haoyuan), 390
Kwong Cheong (Guang Chang) & Co., 118
Kwong Yong Cheong (Guang Yin Chang) Co., 118
Leong Ben, 216
Leong Tung (or Tong) (Liang Dong), 118
Lin, Mr, Chinese Consul-General, Australia, 217
Lo King (Lu Jing), 118
Man Cheong (Min Chang) & Co., 120
merchant companies, 111–21, 227
mixed-race, 225, 290
Nam Cheong (Nan Chang), 117 (Map 2.1), 218 (Figure 4.12 code)
Neong Kong (Long Gang), 117 (Map 2.1), 218 (Figure 4.12 code)
opium use, 222
petitions against, 120
QQQ Holdings Ltd, 118
Quan Chow [Guan Zhou] Co., 134, 135
Quan Hong (Guan Houyuan), Augustine, 118, 216, 390
Quan Park Yee (Guan Baoyi), 117, 118, 225, 386, 389
Quan Sung Wai (Guan Songwei), 117, 118
Rabaul connection, *see* German New Guinea
restaurants, 214
Sam Doo's Hotel, Tulagi, 206
segregation of at Tulagi hospital, 185
servant at Tulagi Club, 268
Seto Cheong (Situ Chang), 117 (Map 2.1), 218 (Figure 4.12 code)
sewing and washing services, 270
Shanghai, 118
Suete (Shunde), 118
Sweetie Kwan Wing Leung Ltd, 118
trading licences, 222
trading schooners, 119, 220, 224, 244
Wang, James (Wang Desheng), James, 118
women, 120, 386
Yap (Yam) Tim (Ye Tian), 117 (Map 2.1), 218 (Figure 4.12 code)
Yee Poy (Yi Bo), 220
Yip Choy (Ye Cai), 216, 386, 389
Yip Sing (Ye Xing), 216
Yip Yuk (Ye Yun), 118, 216
See also British Government, colonial territories
Chamberlain, Joseph, 73, 148
Choiseul, 1, 65, 104, 177, 298, 390
Christianity, 17, **20**, **21**, 96, 157, 286, 295–96
See also Catholic Mission; Methodist Mission; Melanesian Mission (Anglican); Queensland Kanaka Mission; Seventh-day Adventist Mission; South Seas Evangelical Mission
Christmas Island, 54
Chuuk (Truk), 379
Clarence, Margaret, *see* Bignell, Margaret
Cleaver, Nurse H.M., 276–77, 282
Clemens, Martin, 378, 387, 391
Clift, Dudley, 330
Clift, Edward Geoffrey (Geoff), 189, 231–32, 233, 236, 309, 330
Clift, John McElhone (Jack), 233, 234, 335, 343
Clift, Peter, 286
Clift, Vera Muriel, 266, 344

453

coconut (copra) plantations, 42, 76, 77, 79, 87, 88, 97, 98, 103, 108, 109, 127–34, 139, 193, 374
   prices, 102–03, 155, 204, 370, 376
   village-based, 42, 58, 116, 119, 133, 219, 220, 224
   See also Burns Philp; labour; Levers
Colley, Peter, 247
Collins, Sister L.D., 277
Comins, Rev. Richard, 39, 66
commercial companies, *see* merchant companies
Cookson, Arnold, 174
Coral Sea, 1, 9, 54, 82, 102, 306, 394
Corfield, Nurse, 180
Corris, Peter, 232, 240, 374
Corry, Harold C., 224–25, 374
Courier-Mail, 351
Courteney Dr C.A., 177
Crichlow, Dr Nathaniel, 158, 180–81, **183**, 290, 384, 385, 409
Croan, Miss, 271
Crocker, Charles Templeton, 347
Cromar, Jack (Jock), 352
Cronstedt, Agnes Wilhelminia Watt, 159
   See also Johnson, Agnes
Cronstedt, Axel Frederik Auguste, 159
Cronstedt, Carl, 313
Cronstedt (née Ellis), Ester 159
Crookshank, Bob, 330
Cruise of the Snark, The, 351
Cullen, Peter, 206
Cunningham, D., 236
Curtis, Charles, 350

Dalrymple-Hay, Kenneth, *see* Hay, Ken
Darbyshire, George, 334
Davies, David Edward, 357
Davies, Dr S.C.M., 180, 339

De Havilland DH50A sea-plane, 243
De Heveningham, N.W.P., 156, 267
Deck, Gladys, 336
Deck, Joan, 336
Deck, Katherine, 336
Deck, Norman, 176
Deck, Northcote, 104, 176, 396
Des Voeux, Sir William, 61
Dickes, Alan W., 234, 235
Dickinson, Joseph, 100, 266, 337
Dolphin Island, *see* Gavutu
Douglas, Hon. John, 61
Duff (Wilson) Islands, 66
Dumphy, Bill, 226, 297
Dumphy, Maggie, 297

Early European Settlers of the Solomon Islands, The, 232, 343
Edge-Partington, Mary, **258**, **302**
Edge-Partington, Thomas, 104, 142, 294–95
Ekins, Terry, 393
Elder, Syd (Pansy), 232, 331
Elkington, June, 287
Elkington (née Bathe), May Elisabeth Ann, 203, 205, 265
Elkington, Thomas H.G., 203, 205
Elkington, Thomas Jr, 203, 205, 287
Elliot, Edith Elizabeth, 180, 185, 235
Ellis, Jack, 92, 200, 217
Ellis, Suzanne, 313
Emmanuel, Joseph (Portuguese Joe), 41
England, Mary Ann, 159
Erskine, Commodore James Elphinstone, 61
European lifestyles, 285–86, 346
   class systems, 72, 104, 225, 290, 332, **333**–37
   etiquette, 247, 266, 322
   children, *see* Tulagi
   cost of living, 261, **267**
   fashions, 200, 246–47, 270, 271, 343, 346

INDEX

holidays, 91, 266, 281, 289–90, 346, 369
heterosexual relationships, 112, **249**, **257**, 286, **288**, **289**, **291**, **292**, **293**, 294–303
homosexual relationships, 285, 303–05
medical care, 176–89
mixed-race relationships, 181, 225, 290, 294–305, 313, 372
'Red Sea' or 'Gulf' rig, 88, 247
war service, 327–31
Evans, Rear-Admiral E.R.G.R., 347

Fallowes, Rev. Richard, 369–71
Fataka (Mitre) Island, 66
Ferguson, Alexander, 41, 300
Ferry, F., 236
Festetics de Tolna, Comte Rodolphe, 104
Fifi`i, Jonathan, 276–77, 280, 281, 283, 294, 357–58, **362**, 363–64, 370, 378
Fiji, Crown Colony of, 1, 44, 46, 47, 48, 56, 57, 62, 68, 152, 157, 192, 195, 307
  Burns Philp (South Seas) Co. Ltd, 109
  Central Medical School, 392
  Chief Justice, 57
  Chief Medical Officer, 62
  Colonial Service, 149
  Colonial Sugar Refining Co., 107, 160, 162, 290
  Council of Chiefs, 49
  Court of Appeal, 169
  Fiji Medical College, 177
  Government Agents, 58, 63, 157
  Governors, 57, 59, 60
  Indo-Fijians, 10
  labour trade, 34, 43, 55, 58, 74, 83, 125–26
  Lautoka, 133, 185
  Levuka, 8, 10, 11, 28, 56, 106, 113, 133, 265, 413
  Morris Hedstrom & Co., 109
  Nasinu, 395
  Native Lands Ordinance (1880), 192
  proclamation of colony, 48–49
  Queen Victoria School, 392, 395
  Suva, 6, 8, 10, 11, 25, 32, 47, 61, 68, 73, 74, 79, 91, 95, 106, 132, 133, 169, 177, 189, 194, 225, 231, 237, 266, 290, 303, 347, 354, 357, 413
  Wireless School, 392, 395
film, 105, 110, 351, 364
Filose, F.G., 235, 369
firearms, 73, 74, 80, 125, 165, 166, 229, 236, 307, 337
Fitton, S., 235
Fleischmann, Julius Jr, 348
Fletcher, Sir Murchison, 223
Floyd, Lieutenant-Commander, 65
Forrest, A.E.C., 303
Forster, Michael J., 153–55, 161, 304, 386, 390, 391
Fowler, Wilfred, 137, 204–05, 210, 218–19, 297, 305, 336–37, 364
Fox, Rev. Charles, **323**, 366
Fox-Strangeways, Major Vivian, 381
Freeman, Kathleen, *see* Bignell, Kathleen
French, 332
French Government, 48, 55, 60
  New Caledonia, *see* separate entry
Freshwater, Herbert Lockington (Bert), 330, 391
Fulton, George, 106
Fyfe, Bill, 205

G.J. Waterhouse & Co., 82
Ga`a, Salana (Maega`asia), 360, **361**, 363
Gado, Lonsdale, Isabel paramount chief, 369

455

Ganga, 304
Gaomi, 380
Gaskell, Edith, 234
Gaskell, Richard, 234
Gaskell, Richard Luke Jack (Dick), 234
Gavutu, *see* Levers Pacific Plantations Ltd
Gela (Flores or Florida) Group, **xxvii**, 1, 24, 28, **29**, 32, **33**, 36, **37**–**38**, **39**, **40**, 41, **43**, 72, 102, 112, 118, 234, 304
    Bungana Island, 4, **40**, 41, 42, 100, **323**
        lighthouse, 4, 111, 322, 382
        Melanesian Mission school and orphanage, 111, 322
    Gavutu Island, *see* Levers
    Gela Pile (Little Gela) Island, 28, 106
    Gela Sule (Big Gela) Island, 4, 15, 28, 36, 72, 106, 111, 380, 383
    Kona, Joe, 294
    labour trade participation, 43–44
    Lavinia massacre, 44
    Makambo Island, *see* Burns Philp
    Mandoliana plantation, 234, 331
    Mboli Passage, 21, 34, 65, 72, 106, 112, 297, 322, 337, 387
    Mendaña expedition (1568), 28, 46
    population, 43
    Port Purvis, **30**, 65, 106, 142
    Sandfly incident, 44
    Sandfly Passage, 28, **30**, 112, 234
    Siota, **35**, 65, 106, 111, 176, 322
    Tanambogo Island, 4, 17, 388, 413
    Taroaniara, 111, 227, 247, 322, **324**, **354**, **355**, 382, 385, 393, 400, 413
    trade with foreigners, 31, 41, 42
    See also Melanesian Mission

Germans
    internment of, 102
    labour recruiting by, 44
German New Guinea, 9, 10, **62**, **67**, 84, 102, 115, 116, 302, 333
    borders, 63, 66, 76–77
    Chinese, 10, 113, 114–16
    Neu Guinea Kompagnie, 59
    quarantine, 80
    Rabaul (Herbertshohe), 82, 87, 114, 115, 116, 117, 346
    Schutzgebiet, 59
    smallpox epidemic, 76
    See also New Guinea Mandated Territory
German Samoa, 47
Gibson, Bill, 339
Gibson, Captain, 65
Gigini, Hugo, 395
Gilbert and Ellice Crown Protectorates/Colony, 44, 47, 54, 57, 78, 79, 82, 103, 141, 142
    Colonial Service, 149
    Crown Colony, 53, 65, 69, 153, 200, 381, 385
    Fanning Islands plantations, 328
    Ocean (Banaba) Island, 8, 385
    Protectorates, 53, 64, 149
    removed from WPHC, 69
    Resident Commissioners, 54, 79, 153, 297, 381
Gina, Sir Lloyd Maepeza, 357
Gizo, *see* BSIP; New Georgia
Glen, A., 383
Gold Development Ltd, 175
Golden, Graeme, 232, 248, 296, **343**
Goldie, Rev. John, 222, 300
Gordon, Sir Arthur Hamilton, 59, 60
Great Depression, 91, 111, 130, 132, 133, 140, 149, 156, 164, 168, 175, 195, 223, 224, 335
Griffith, Sir Samuel, 63
Grimshaw, Beatrice, 321, 351
Groves, William C., 164

Guadalcanal Island, 1, 15, 28, 29, 32, 83, 104, 111, 138, 196, 235, 261, 331, 347
   Aola, **45**, 46, 94, 111, 120, 233, 235, 329, 339, 385, 391
   Aruligo plantation, 234, 344
   Berande (Pennduffryn) plantation, 83, 175, 334
   Gold Ridge, 233, 391–92
   Guadalcanal Sluicing and Dredging Co., 392
   Honiara, *see* separate entry
   Ilu plantation, 315
   Ivatu plantation, 224
   Lavoro plantation, 235, 330
   Marau Sound, 72, 385
   Pennduffryn, *see* Berande
   plantation labourers evacuated, 387
   Point Cruz, 15, 142
   Rere plantation, 339
   Visale Catholic Mission, 174
   Weather Coast, 235
Gunther, Dr John, 177
Guppy, Henry, 46, 353

Hackett, Miss, 342
Hahl, Governor Albert, 116, 346
Halliday, S.A., 236
Hancock, Captain, **302**
Hanscombe, L.J., 234
Harding, Baroness Eugénie, 334
Harding, Thomas, 334
Hardy, Norman, 350
Harisimae, 370
Harper, Major Richard (Dick), 234, 297, 331
Harrison, Captain G.H., 236, 240
Havousi, Joseph, 65–66
Hay, Kenneth, 300, 390, 391
Headhunting in the Solomon Islands, 351
health, 76, 80, 176, 178, 186, 189, 281, 299, 348, 349
   alcoholics, 92, 146, 157, 160, 185, 196, 197, 224, 232, 297, 298, 321, 342–46, 372, 383, 392
   Atebrin (quinacrine), 188
   Hansen's disease colony, Fauaabu, Malaita, 177
   malaria, 79–80, 161, 177, 187–88, 213
   quarantine, 76, 80, 83, 184, 186
   quinine, 188
   Spanish influenza pandemic, 181, 184–85
   yaws, 178, 186, 348–49
Heath, Ian, 97
Herbert, Xavier, 186, 246, 247, 367
Hetherington, Dr Harry B., 162, 181, 186, 213, 277, 349
Hewitt, Major Frank R., 106, 309, 316, 327
Hewitt, Mrs, 272
Hicks, James Basil, 325, **344**
Hiele, Esau, 395
Higginson, R.C., 156
Hill, Ralph B., 146, 329, 335
historiography
   colonisation, 24, 48–69, 247, 283
   discriminatory legislation, 25, 306, 311
   gender, 25, 247
   heritage studies, 24
   invasion, concept of, 48–49
   race relations, 411, 412
   sexuality, 247, 285, 313
   urbanisation, 27
   white women in the Pacific, 25, 247, 248, 411–12
Hoasihau, 370
Hocart, A.M., 347
Hodges, Charles Hubert Vivian (Viv), 331
Hoeler, Willlie, 268
Hogbin, Ian, 157, 206, 246, 304, 347, 368

Hollis Brothers, 217, 233, 393, 386
Holt-MacCrimmon, Dr Lucy, 177
Honiara, 4, 12, 15, 17, 21, 24, 28–29, 68, 118, 121, 142, 148, 162, 166, 214, 216, 233, 282, 311, 325, 357, 372, 390, 413
Hore, Sargent T.E., 380
Horton, Dick C., 189, 210–11, 247, 280, 345, 388, 391
hospitals, non-government, 96, 177
Hubbard, P.C., 156
Huddy, J.J., 106
Hugo, Captain P.B., 239
Hutchinson, Lieutenant George H., 381
Hutson, Sir Eyre, 200, **352**
Hynam, Bill, 171
Hyne, Ragnar, 156, 329, 374, 385
Hynes, Dr John B., 347

India, 114, 327, 329, 334
indentured labour, *see* labour
Ioi, Quarter-Master Heman Ganisua, 165, 360
Irofa'alu, Shem, **359**, 360
Isabel, 1, 32, 41, 63, 65, 66, 111, 121, 176, 224, 327, 328, 330, 367, 385, 390, 393, 396
    Fallowes Movement (Chair and Rule Movement), 369–71
    Fera plantation, 309
    Fulakora plantation, 112, 253
    Gozoruru plantation, 330
    Hivo plantation, 234, 330
    Kaola plantation, 328
    San Jorge Island, 236, 328
    Thousand Ships Bay (Tanabuli Harbour), 142, 393
Ireland, 78, 145, 180
Ishimoto, Terusige, 375, 410
ivory (sago palm) nuts, 58, 80, 224

Jackson, Sir Henry Moore, 346
Jackson, K.B., 97
James, Dr Clifford, 177

Japan, 87, 375, 379
    See also World War II
Japanese, 9, 28, 105, 113, 177, 348, 375, **376**, **377**, 410
Jellicoe, Admiral of the Navy Earl John R., 347
Jerry of the Islands, 351
Jock of the Islands—The Adventures of John Cromar, 352
Johnson (née Cronstedt), Agnes Wilhelminia Watt, 159, **254**, 256, 266, 278, **291**, **292**, 313, 336, **344**
Johnson, Dorothy, 292
    See also Lotze, Dorothy
Johnson, Frederick E. (Pop), **158**, 159–62, **254**, 256, **291**, **292**, **312**, 313, 328, 336, **338**, **344**, 374, 377, 385, 388, 391
Johnson, Martin, 105, 351, 364, 410
Johnson, Osa, 105, 119, 247, 351, 364, 410
Johnson-Kaine, Florence Edna, 177
Johnston, Ross, 55, 64
Johnstone, J.A. (Johno), 205, 233, 383
Josselyn, Henry E., 391

Kaisawani, Sergeant-Major Naphtali, 409
Kalekona, 36
Kanda, 268
Kane, Richard Rutledge, 6, 145–46, 163, 208, 230, 236, 239, 242, 321, 327, 329, 339, 344, 345
Kavatnaasukulu, 298
Keen, Amelia (Milly), 330
Keen, Leslie (Jerry), 330
Keesing, Roger, 232, 240, 372, 374
Kenilorea (née Kwanairara), Lady Margaret, 360
Kenilorea, Sir Peter, 280
Kennedy, Donald, 378, 380, 393
Keppel, L.W., 304

Kevu, Ben, 357
Kidson, Captain Norman S.B., 146, 156, 205, 230–31, 236, 327, 383
King, Charles, 234, 235
King, Felix F., 194
Knibbs, Mrs, 271
Knibbs, Sir George Handley, 160, 334
Knibbs, Stanley G.C., 102, 157, 160–62, 194–95, 196, 219, 252, 271, 273, 290, 345, 352
Koenig, Charlie, 206
Kondovar, 366–67
Küper, Augusta Kafagamurironga, 300
Küper, Native Medical Practitioner Geoffrey, 290, 303
Küper, Heinrich, 299, 300–01
Kurtz, Sergeant Clifford R., 396
Kwai, Annie, 399
Kwaiami, 375
Kwaio massacre (1927), 199, 227–43, **240–41**

labour, 32, 43, 56, 58, 66, 73, 83, 88, 94, 127, 128, **129**, **131**, 132, 232, 233
    beach bonus, 129, 130
    Chinese employers, 120
    deaths, 132, 178, 365
    deportation of labourers from Australia, 62, 125, 126
    enlistment boycotts, 133
    Government Agents, 44, 58, 64
    head tax, 129, 130
    kidnapping, 34, 55
    'passage masters', 130
    Pijin English, 130, 165, 412
    Protectorate internal labour trade, 127–33, 346
    returned to home islands, World War II, 399
    wages, 128, 129, 133
    wharf labour, 124–25, 132, 364

See also BSIP, Labour Department; Fiji; Queensland
Laefiwane, 368
Lambert, Dr Sylvester, 147, 153, 162, 298, 303, 304, 347–48, 349
languages, 270, 296, 334
    Austronesian, 32
    Chinese, 226
    English, 322
    Gela, 32, 36
    Mota, 39, 96, 322
    Pijin English, 130, 150, 155, 165, 226, 280, 370, 375, 412
Laracy, Eugénie, 248
Laracy, Hugh, 146, 248
Laukoma, Dudly, 36
La Voy, Merl, 351
Lawrence, David, 97, 98
Laycock, Sister Betty, 307
Laycock, Eileen, 286
Laycock, Richard C. (Dick), 92, 111, 112, 189, 199, 217, 281
Laycock, Violet, 111, 286
League of Nations Mandated Territories, 9, 10, 57, 87, 102, 114, 116, 196, 375, 379, 383
Leauli, Native Medical Practitioner Eroni, 189
Leembruggen, E.L., 195
Legion of Frontiersmen, 315, **317**
Lerew, Group-Captain John Margrave, 379, 380
Leti (Letesasa), Jacob, 395
Leve, Jonathan, 357
Lever, Robert A., 104, 164
Lever, William, 106
Levers Pacific Plantations Ltd, 17, 77, 82, 106, 112, 177, 196, 240, 331, 332, 380
    Gavutu Island, 4, **22**, 28, 31, 41, **42–43**, 72, 74, 83, 88, 91, 92, 93, 94, 95, 100, 106, **107**, **108**, 109, 110, 111, 112, **122**, 125, 128, 131, 132, 140, 142, 174, 197, 202, 227, 230, 232,

247, **255**, 256, 269, 272, 275, 296, 297, 315, 316, 325, 337, 347, 354, 355, 365, 366, 379, 380, 381, 385, 386, 387, 388, 392, 393
    Pacific Islands Co. Ltd, 77, 106
    Unilever, 107
Levuka, *see* Fiji
Lewis, Dr A.B., 339
Lianga, Alec, 395
Lightning Meets the West Wind, 232
Lillies, Kenneth C., 227, 229, 230, 330, 360
Lingutu, Marovo Lagoon, *see* New Georgia
Lobu, Alfred, 41
Log of the Snark, The, 351
London, 46, 47, 56, 61, 69, 73, 94, 140, 146, 149, 175, 176, 313, 330, 341
London, Charmian, 83, 351
London, Jack, 83, 351
Lord Howe, *see* Ontong Java
Lotze (née Johnson), Dorothy 159, 292, **293**, **312**, 336, **344**
Lotze, Jack, 159, 271, 292, **293**, **312**, 336, 374, 382, 383, 385
Low, Nurse E.L., 184
Loyalty Islands, *see* New Caledonia
Lucas, Walter H., 97, 104
Luke, Sir Harry, 162, 337, 339, 370

McDonald, D.R., 156
Macdonald, John Champion, 113, 334
Macdonald, Melinda, 334
Macdonald, William, 113
Macfarlan, Lieutenant Don, 388, 389, 390
MacGregor, Gordon, 347
MacGregor, Dr Sir William, 63, 97
McIntyre, David, 56
Mackinnon, Donald, 308, 334–35
McLaren, Jack, 270
MacMahon, Father, 382

McMahon, Thomas, 351
MacQuarrie, Hector, 138, 146, 304
Maena, Alec, 357
Mahaffy, Arthur William, 78–79, 148, 155, 278, 294, 295
Mahaffy, Rev. Sir John, 78
Maifurua, 307
Making Mala: Malaita in Solomon Islands, 1870–1930s, xxv
Makini, Simione, 395
Makira (San Cristobal) Island, 1, 46, 49, 66, 72, 104, 113, 189, 251, 300, 333, 356, 349, 357, 363
    Boroni plantation, 330
    Chinese community, evacuated to, 386, 389–90, 391, 396
    District Officers, 233, 235, 300
    Kirakira, 94, 154, 181, 390
    Waimamura plantation, 264
Malaita Island, 1, 21, 32, 46, 63, 66, 71, 142, 152, 177, 239, 240, 295, 347, 348, 349, 359, 360, 363, 387
    Auki (`Aoke), 4, 94, 102
    Bula cult, 371
    Coleridge Bay, *see* Fauaabu
    District Officers, 25, 152, 154, 158, **258**, 329, 371
    Fauaabu, 46, 177, 393
    Furi`isango, Protectorate headquarters (1942–43), 387
    King George VI School, 280
    Kwaio massacre (1927), *see* separate entry
    La`aka cult, 371
    labour recruiting, 131
    Langalanga Lagoon, 32, 66, 104, 325, 364
    Maasina Rule, 359, 360, 363, 368, 371, 283, 400
    Malaita District Council, 359, 360, 363
    Manaba plantation, 236
    Sinalagu Harbour, 46, 229–30, 238–40, 359

Spanish influenza epidemic (1919–23), 185
Malamu, 273
Malayta Co. Ltd, 164, 177, 217, 233, 234, 236, 325
Mamaloni, Prime Minister Solomon, 396
Marchant, William Sydney, 147, 329, 363, 374, 376, 377, 384, 385, 386, 388, 389, 390–91, 392, 400
Marconi Wireless Co., 173, 174, 175
Marfee, 187
Markham, Harold (Marco), 328
marriage, 112, 292, **293**, 294, 295, 296, 334, 339, 344, 370
   Colonial Marriages Act (1865), 295
   interracial, 294–305, 313, 372, 411
Marshall Islands, 63, 65
Marshall, Dr Russell, 177
Mason, Paul, 385
Masterman, Stanley (Monty), 139, 164–65, 235, 244, 272, 281–82, 345, 363
Mather, John, 233
Maxwell, C., 330, 367
Maybury, Dr Lysander Montague, 177
medical doctors in BSIP, 39, 147, 153, 158, 162, 176–77, 180, **183**, 184, 185, 186, 213, 277, 303, 304, 339, 347, 349, 392, 409
   Native Medical Practitioners, 177, 189, 290, 294, 299, 303, 349, 369, 392, 400, 410
Melanesian Mission (Anglican), **20**, 34, 64, 96, 330
   bishops, 34, 36, 55, 104, 189, 225, 300, 304, 310, 316, 325, 328–29, 374, 382, 387, 393, 396
   Bungana mission and girls' school, 41, 111, 322, **323**
   Christ the King Church, Tulagi, **324**

Gela Group, 27, 31–32, 34, 36, 40, 41, 322
Hautabu, Guadalcanal, 96, 177
Hospital of the Epiphany, Fauaabu, Malaita, 177
Maravovo, Guadalcanal, 96, 177
Melanesian Brotherhood, 325, **323**, 365
Mota language, lingua franca, 39, 322
Siota, 4, **35**, 39, 41, 65, 106, 111, 176, 179, 322, 325, **326**, 387, 393, 400
Sisters of the Cross, 322, 382, 385
St Barnabas' College, Norfolk Island, 34, **35**, 36, 322
St Luke's Cathedral, Siota, 322, **326**
St Luke's School, Siota, 39
Taroaniara, 111, 227, 247, 322, **324**, **354**, **355**, 382, 385, 393, 400, 413
theological college, 322
Vaukolu congress, 36, **37–38**, 369
Welchman Memorial Hospital, 96, 177
Mendaña expedition (1568), 29, 46
Menzies, Dr, 349
merchant companies, 24, 106–21, 227
   See also Burns Philp; Chinese, merchant companies; Levers; Morris Hedstrom; W.R. Carpenter
Meredith and Clift, 121, 218 (Plate 4.12 code)
Meredith, Owen G., 121, 327
Messrs McLeod, Bolton & Co., 220
Messrs Thomas De La Rue & Co. Ltd, 94
Methodist Mission, 77, 96, 174, 177
   Solomon Islander wireless operators, 175
   wireless telegraphy, 174

Micronesia, 54, 370, 379
Mills-Parker, Dr Dorothy, 177
Minns, C.E., 226, 234
Molyneux, Bishop Frederick M., 304
Momo, 172
Monckton, Cecil, 173
Monckton, Eric P., 374
Mono Island, Treasury Islands, 65
Montgomery, Bishop H.H., 104
Moorhouse, Lieutenant-Colonel Sir Harry, 242, 329, 346–47
Morris Hedstrom & Co., *see* Fiji; Tulagi
Muhlhauser, Lieutenant G.H.P., 276
Mumford, Charles, 346
Murray, Sir Hubert, 97, 266, 306, 346
Mutch, Jimmy, 196, 344–45
Mytinger, Caroline, 275, 351–52, 365

Nabunobuno, Kelemende, 391
Nafunenga, 298
National Fisheries Development Ltd, *see* Tulagi
natural history collecting, *see* scientific expeditions
Naturalist Among the Headhunters, A, 46
Nauru Island, 1, 142
Netherlands, 108
Netherlands New Guinea, 50, 380
Nevison, N.L., 195
New Caledonia, 11, 48, 58, 234, 357, 380, 413
New Georgia Group, 1, 65, 104, 328, 347
  Gizo Island, 4, 78, 94, 109, 118, 180, 214, 329, 385, 387, 390
  headhunting, 79, 87, 165,
  Kokeqolo, 96, 174, 177
  Laperti plantation, 299, 328
  Lingutu plantation, 142
  Malavare plantation, 235
  Marovo Lagoon, 96, 142, 152, 155, 174, 177, 299, 300, 359
  Rendova Island, 304, 390
  Roviana Lagoon, 41, 46, 66, 96, 174, 299, 300, 347, 351
  Seghe plantation, 235
  Simbo Island, 294, 297, 347
  Vella Lavella Island, 79, 309, 335, 347
  whaling, 50
New Guinea Mandated Territory, 87, 102, 114, 164, 380
  Burns Philp & Co., 110
  Chinese, 114
  Japanese, 375, 379
  Nanyo Boeki Kaisha (South Sea Trading) Ltd, 410
  New Britain, 9, 383
  Rabaul, 116, 119, 134, 175, 189, 214, 216, 217, 218, 219, 224, 286, 366, 375, 379, 383, 384, 385, 386, 394, 400, 410, 413
  See also World War II
New Hebrides, 36, 44, 63, 64, 83, 84, 159, 389
  Anglo-French agreement (1878), 58
  Anglo-French Joint Naval Commission (1888), 58–59
  British Consul, 61
  Condominium (1906), 1, 46, 49, 50, 56, 57, 58
  independence, 59
  Port Vila, 8, 59, 82, 87, 134, 380, 389, 396, 413
  removed from WPHC, 69
New South Wales, 47, 53, 58, 61, 84, 112, 287, 335, 347, 393
  2nd New South Wales Mounted Rifles, 328
  Breeza pastoral station, 232, 335
  proclamation of Crown Colony, 53

Sydney, 27, 47, 53, 54, 58, 65, 73, 80, 82, 83, 84, 87, 91, 93, 94, 95, 96, 97, 100, 103, 106, 111, 112, 114, 119, 159, 160, 162, 169, 184, 189, 202, 206, 217, 223, 224, 226, 232, 236, 237, 239, 261, 263, 264, 266, 268, 271, 287, 289, 297, 299, 300, 305, 316, 328, 335, 337, 341, 342, 347, 350, 351, 370, 378, 384, 385, 387, 389, 391, 396
New Zealand, 34, 48, 50, 51, 53, 54, 56, 141, 149, 154, 174, 184, 266, 278, 286, 303, 325, 336, 330
   Australia and New Zealand Army Corps (Anzac), 330
   Melanesian Mission, 34
   proclamation of colony, 48
   troops, 404
Newman, Jack, 91, 92, 199
newspapers and periodicals, 350
Nielsen, Lars, 41, 42, 72, 296
Niue Island, 54
Noel, Owen Cyril, 147–48, 329
Nono`oohimae, Ariki, 370
Norfolk Island, 34, **35**, 36, 82, 96, 322
North Queensland Register, 350
Norway, 87, 234, 296, 332
Notare, Walter, 369
Noto`i, 371
Nukumanu (Tasman) Atoll, 65

O'Sullivan, Dr J.E., 180
Officer, Graham, 98, 278, 347
Oliver, Douglas, 368–69
Olsen, Anton Daniel, 234
Ontong Java (Lord Howe) Atoll, 65, 104, 152, 297, 328
Osborne, Arthur E., 158, 174, 175, 180
Oxford University, 78, 142, 152, 333

Pacific Islands Co., *see* Levers Pacific Plantations Ltd
Pacific Islands Monthly, 157, 224
Pacific War, *see* World War II
Page, Louis, 380
Paia, Willie, 357
Palmer, Ambrose Ernest (Ernie), 92, 146, 236, 292, 298, 328, 339, 345, 387
Palmer, Anne Nancy, 328
Palmer (née Svensen), Ingrid (Inga), 339
Palmer, Norman Kitchener, 328
Palmer, Philip Francis Donald, 328
Palmer, Philip Sydney, 188, 236, 328
Papua, Territory of, 9, 60, 62, 84, 192, 203, 333, 351, 384
   Burns Philp & Co., 110
   clothes, regulations, 279
   Port Moresby, 9, 266, 279, 285, 306, 380, 384, 394, 413
   Samarai Island, 8, 9, 28, 134, 203, 345, 384, 413
   White Women's Protection Ordinance, 25, 306
Papua New Guinea
   See British New Guinea; German New Guinea; New Guinea Mandated Territory; Papua, Territory of
Paravicini, Eugen, 219, 347
Patteson, Bishop John, 34, 55
Pattison, Dr C.R., 185, 344
Peacock, Pastor G., 227
pearling, 113
Penny, Rev. Alfred, **34**, 36
Philip, HRH Prince, Duke of Edinburgh, **361**
Philippines, 9, 113, 186, 404
Phillips, Frederick Beaumont (Monty), 195–96
Philp, J.E., 83, 100, 111, 126
photography, 26, 103–05, 200, 247, 254, 256, 270, 280

Pijin English, *see* languages
Pitcairn Island, 57
Plant, Rev. John H., 36
Planters' Gazette, 6, 96, 308, 339, 350, 353, 367
Pogula, 172
Pule, Daniel, 357

Qualye, Ernst H., 350
Queensland, 8, 10, 61, 63, 84, 133, 156, 203, 287, 296, 335, 350, 386
    annexation of south-east New Guinea (1883), 53
    Bellevue pastoral station, 335
    Brisbane, 53, 83, 84, 189, 203, 291, 299, 335, 342, 350, 351
    deportation of Solomon Islanders, 126
    Government Agents, 58, 64
    Government Resident, 61
    Governor, 62
    labour trade, 27–28, 34, 43, 54, 58, 63, 66, 125–26, 333, 350
    migrants, 332
    pastoralists, 335
    Polynesian Labourers Act (1868), 56
    Premiers, 61, 63
    Thursday Island, 8–9, 61
    Torres Strait, 54, 61, 332, 334
    Welltown pastoral station, 335
Queensland Kanaka Mission, 42, 164
    See also South Seas Evangelical Mission
Queenslander, The, 350, 351

Rabaul, *see* German New Guinea; New Guinea Mandated Territory
racial attitudes, 97, 113, 120, 217, 220, 222, 283, 303, 306, 313, 333–34, 364, 367, 409, 410–11
Radcliffe-Brown, Professor Alfred R., 157
Ralph, Nurse E.G., 184, 307
Ranongga, 390
Ratcliffe, Francis, 270
recreation, 91, 204, 210, 211, 263, 264, 269, 270–71, 337, 341, 350–53
    alcohol, 102, 146, 157, 160, 185, 196, 201–11, 232, 247, 267, 297, 298, 321, 342–46, 372, 383, 391, 392
        Solomon Islanders, access to, 213, 224, 336, 366–67
    dinner parties, 271–72, 339
    hotels, 91, 105, 140, 203–06
    photography, 103–06, 403–04
    radios, 263, 264, 342
    Tulagi Club, *see* Tulagi
Reef Islands, 1, 55, 65, 66, 366
Rennell Island, 66, 104, 347, 348
Resident Commissioners, *see* BSIP; WPHC
Rhoades, F. Ashton (Snowy), 330
Richardson, E.S.D. (Dick), 357, **360**
Richardson, George Washington Ezekiel (Dick America), 332–33
Rippon, Marquess of, 47
Rivers, W.H.R., 347
Rodwell, Sir Cecil H., 121, 138, 353
Romilly, Hugh H., 60
Rose, George, 104
Rothery, Captain S. (Stinger), 387, 388, 389
Royal Geographical Society, 46, 47
Rusa, Mark, 395
Rushton, Nurse, 180
Russell Islands (Cape Marsh), 32, 142, 163, 196, 233, 270, 385, 386, 387
    Banika plantation, 232
Russell, Tom, 164–65

Sa`a, Petty Officer Johnny, 364
Sade, David, 395
Sakurai, Dr, 177
Samarai, *see* British New Guinea

Samoa, 44, 47, 54, 106, 126
San Cristoval Estates Ltd, wireless telegraphy, 174
Sandars, G.E.D. (Eustace), 137, 146, 163, 168, 171, 188, 210, 268, 282, 327, 342, 344, 345, 366, 374, 377, 378
Sando, Harry W., 195
Santa Ana Island, 46, 83, 104, 113, 298, 302, 334, 357
Santa Catalina (Owa Riki) Island, 251
Santa Cruz Group, 1, 48, 49, 63, 64, 65, 66, 82, 104, 180, 234, 235, 304, 332, 337, 338
Santa Isabel Island, *see* Isabel
Sapibuana, Charles, 34, 36
Savage Solomons as They Were and Are, 352
Savo Island, 21, 41, 138, 163, 369
Sayers, Dr Edward, 177
Schroder, Niels R., 331
scientific expeditions, 44, 46, 339, 347, 348, 349, 350
    Rockefeller Foundation Assisted Medical Campaign, 147, 186, 347–49
    Whitney South Sea Expedition, 349–50
    Woodford, Charles M., 44, 46, 47, 50, 72
Scott, J.C.M., 316, 325, 383, 386, 390
Scratchley, Sir Peter, 61
Seddon, R., 236
seismic activity, 251
Selwyn, Bishop John, 36
Seton, Carden Wyndham, 335–36
Seton (née Cameron), Georgina, 303, 312–13, 335–36
Seventh-day Adventist Mission, 177, 217, 325, 359
Sexton, Lieutenant Tom O., 396

sexuality
    assaults, 305–11
    mixed-race relationships, 181, 226, 285, 290, 294–305, 372
    moral panic, 25, 247
    rape, 240, 298, 304, 309
    taboos, 278, 279, 312, 349
    See also European lifestyles
Seymore. A.W., 146
Shatz, Charlie, 206
Sheridan, Vic, **344**
ships:
    Advent Herald, 227, 229
    Amelia, 42
    Auki, 227, **229**, 390
    Balus, 383
    Belama, 169, 315
    Camargo, 348
    Carl, 55
    Christine, 46
    Clansman, 158
    Daphne, 164
    De Tolna, 104
    Duranbah, 87
    Evangel, 164
    Fauro Chief, 386
    France, 350
    Gizo, 344
    Helena, 66
    HMAS *Adelaide*, 163, 236, 237, **238**, 239, 240
    HMAS *Biloela*, 239
    HMAS *Sydney*, 238
    HMCS *Ranadi*, 88, 163, 236, **238**, 239, 342, 345
    HMCS *Tulagi*, 88, 384
    HMS *Beagle*, 61
    HMS *Cormorant*, 36, 61
    HMS *Curaçoa*, 65
    HMS *Emerald*, 36
    HMS *Goldfinch*, 65
    HMS *Lark*, 46
    HMS *Pylades*, 72
    HMS *Rapid*, 74

HMS *Sandfly*, 36, 44
HMS *Sealark*, 302
HMS *Torch*, 74
Hygenia, 178, 232, **238**
Hygenia II, 181, 389, 399
Induna Star, 381
Jessie, 234
Joseph Conrad, 353
Kitutsuki, 394
Kombito, 386, 387
Kulambangara, 82
Kurimarau, 385, 386
Lahloo, **77**, 87
Lavinia, 34, 44
Lindsay, 234
Makambo, 87, 88, 91
Malaita, 87, 88
Malaita II, 88, 381, 384, 385
Manoora, 396
Maringe, 357
Marsina, 88, 184
Mataram, **86**, 88, 244, 342
Meg Merillies, 61
Minindi, **84**, 88, 339
Minota, 112
Moresby, 112, 339
Morinda, 384, 385, 386, 387, 388, 389
Narova, 42
Newfoundland, 112
Okinoshima, 394
Patience, 44
Ravu, 112
Ruana, 227, 229
Rubiana, 42
Ruby, 337
Seestern, 346
Snark, 83, 351
Southern Cross, 104, 315
Star of Fiji, 113
Susquehanna, 234
Titus, 74, 82
Tulagi, 364, 388
Upolu, 82
USS *Lexington*, 394
USS *Yorktown*, 394
Valere, 389
Wai-ai, 399
Wellington, 339
Wheatsheaf, 227, 229
Winton, 330
Ysabel, 82
Yuzuki
Zaca, 347
Shlomowitz, Ralph, xxv
Shortland Islands, 46, 49, 65, 66, 82, 104, 196, 214, 243, 347, 374
    Commonwealth Bank of Australia agency, 95
    District Officers, 180
    Faisi Island, 87, 94, 95, 109, 180, 385, 387
    Fauro Island, 46, 334
Sibolo (Sipolo), Sergeant-Major, 166, 363, 370
Sikaiana (Stewart) Islands, 66, 92, 104, 234, 348
Singapore, 116, 119, 214, 286
Singhalese (Sri Lankan), 9
Sitai, Silas, 357, **360**, 395
Solomon Islander society, 27, 410
    ancestral communication, 357
    ancestral curses, 368
    compensation payments, 170
    children, 178, 240, 348
    education, modern, 411
    entrepreneurship, 224, 225
    fishing, **43**
    gender differences, 411
    hawker licences, 225
    headhunting, 79, 87
    land alienation, discontent over, 195–96
    land tenure, 190, 193
    pollution taboos, 278, 279, 312, 349
    reaction to colonialism, 368–72, 409–14

sexual rules, 312
store licences, 225
trade networks, 134
trade with foreigners, 41–42
village-based copra and trochus shell production, 224
wantokism, 240, 242, 410
women, 240, 294, 295, 297, 298, 300, 411
Solomon Islanders in the Tulagi enclave, 4, 153, 355–56, 367, 412
  alcohol, access to, 213, 224, 366–67
  ancestral curse on Tulagi, 368
  Armed Constabulary, *see* BSIP
  artefact sales, 91–92
  barracks, 105, 110, 138, 155, **167**, 169, 178, 185, 365, 366
  bicycles, 363–64
  boat crews, 111, 125, 276, 337
  BSIP Defence Force, 377–**78**, 381, 387
  castor oil as a purgative, 275
  clerks, 357, 364
  clothes, 279–80
  colonialism, 409–14
  commodities purchased, 125, 213
  corporal punishment, 275
  cricket games, **209**, 366
  deaths, 185, 241, 242, 365
  deported labourers return from Australia (1900s), 62, 125, 126
  employed in Chinatown, 214
  Fallowes Movement, 369–71
  fishing, **262**
  gambling, 222, 367
  gospel rally, 322, 365
  hospital orderlies, 184, 187
  hospital patients, **181**
  house servants, 252, 261, 264, 267–83, **269**, **274**, 305, 359, 364
  houses, **6**, **221**

indenture contracts, 4, 120, 124, 125–26, 278
krip, 312
labourers, 4, 123, 124, 321
  See also labour
Melanesian Brotherhood, **323**, 325, 366
mixed-race relationships, 95, 181, 225, 226, 285, 290, 294–305, 364, 372
morse code, learning of, 357
Native Contracts' Regulation (No. 2, 1896), 94
Native Medical Practitioners, 177, 290, 294, 299, 303, 369, 392, 400, 410
prisoners, **123**, 124, **243**, 262, 268, 282
sewing machines, 272
sexual attacks by, 305–11
sickness, remedies, 281
status, 294
trading, 32, 23, 133, 263, 364
violence against, 275–77
wages, 273
waiters at Tulagi Club, 210
wharf labourers, 124–25, 364
wireless operators, 176, 395
women, 178, 240
Solomon Islands and Their Natives, The, 46
Solomon Islands Historical Encyclopaedia, 1893–1978, xxv
South Seas Evangelical Mission, 164, 176, 331, 322, **359**, 360, 365, 388
  Malayta Co. Ltd, 164, 174, 177, 217, 233, 234, 236, 325
  See also Queensland Kanaka Mission
Spencer, C.E., 196
Spencer, Professor Walter Baldwin, 98
Stackpool, Francis (Frank) T., 186, 383

467

Stirling, A.W., 23
Stephens, John, 304
Sterling, Bobby, 205–06, 234
Stone, R.W., 186
Stuart, Norton, 347
Suda, 294
Sudsee, 299
Sun (Sydney), 232–33, 234
Suva, *see* Fiji
Svensen, Inga (Ingrid), 291, 298
    See also Palmer, Inga
Svensen, Jack, 180, 235, 380
Svensen, Oscar (Captain Marau), 41, 42, 106, 112, 126, 235, 291, 331
Svensen, Theodor, 180, 235, 331
Swanson, Captain, 268, 342, 345
Sweden, 87, 159, 298, 332
Sydney Mail, 103, 350, 351
Sydney Morning Herald, 350
Symes, R.C., 217

Taiyo Ltd fish cannery, *see* Tulagi
Talena, 366
Tamana, Jobi, 395
Tambokoro, 72
Tanambogo Island, *see* Gela Group
Taylor, Robert S., 158, 175, 396
Temotu (Trevannion) Island, 66
Temotu Province, Solomon Islands, 49
Thomson, Dr, 392
Threlfall, Arthur L., 226
Threlfall (neé Dumphy), Isobel (Bella) 226
Thursday Island, *see* Queensland
Thurston, Sir John, 47, 62, 63
Tikopia Island, 1, 66
Tindal (née Macdonald), Minnie Thursa Louise, 334
Tindal, Nicholas Charles, 334
Togonu, Walter, **360**
Tonga Group, 54, 106, 156
tourism, 88, **89–90**, 91
Townsend, Henry J., 304

Trader in the Savage Solomons, A, 109
traders, 31, 34, 41, 42, 58, 72, 74
    See also merchant companies
Treasury Group, 65
Trench, David, 378, 387, 390
trochus shell, 42, 119, 189, 219, 220, 224
Troup, Ian, 235
Truk, *see* Chuuk
Tubo, 268
Tulagi, **xxviii**, **2–3**, **5**, **6**, 31, 50, 72, **73**, 74–76, 79–80, **96**, 103, 139, 187, 200, **217**, 245, **263**, **319**
    agricultural show, 325
    aircraft, first, 243–44
    Australasian Conference Association Ltd, 325
    boarding house, 205, 206
    Catholic church and land lease, 324–25
    children, 111, **117**, 119, 126, 154, 164, 176, 208, 219, 225, 240, 252, 263, 266, **269**, **274**, 275, 282, 286, **287**, **288–89**, 290, **291**, 294, 297, 299, 300, 303, **312**, **338**, 346, 364, 378, 382, 386, 389, 411
    Chinatown, *see* Chinese
    Christ the King Cathedral, 17, **20**
    Christ the King Church, **324**, 325
    Commonwealth Bank of Australia agency, 94, 95
    curfew on Chinese and Solomon Islanders, 120, 221
    electricity, 259, 321
    Elkington's Hotel, 91, 105, **202**, **203**, 203–05, 233
    enclave, concept, 4
    engineering workshops, 93, 116, 199, 253, 296, 331
    European domestic life on Tulagi, 25, 200, 247–83
        See also European lifestyles
    evacuation, 382, 384–87

executions, 172, 342
gardens, 76, 140, 248, 262, 263, 264, 373
Gavutu, *see* Levers
golf course, 210, 211, **212**, **213**, 251
harbour, 24, **26**, **78**, **81**, **139**, **318**, **356**
hospital, *see* BSIP, Medical Department
houses, 100–02, 200, 203–06, 247–83, 250
King George V cricket ground, **209**, 211
lighthouse (Bungana), 4, 111, 322, 382
lighting, 259, 321
Makambo, *see* Burns Philp
Malayta Co. Ltd, 217, 325
Masons' Lodge Melanesia, 325, 372, 387
McMahon Community High School, 17
Melanesian Brotherhood, 325, 366
Morris Hedstrom & Co., 105, 109, 111, 113, 121, 125, 200, 336, 339
Mothers' Union and Women's Resources Centre, 15, 17, **20**
National Fisheries Development Ltd, 15
New South Wales Fresh Food and Ice Co., 217, 233, 259, 383
population, 6, 100, 119, 200, 316, 364, 374
port of entry, 32, 125
prison, 124, 200, 241, 262, 268
Radio Tulagi, 92, 229, 316
Red Cross Society, 325, 372
residency, **7**, **8**, **13**, 21, 74, **75**, **76**, 99, 100, 103, 105, 123, 147, **248–49**, 252, 255, 271, 316, **320**, 321
restaurants, 199, 205, 206, 214

sail makers, 92
Sam Doo's Hotel, 206
sanitation, 80, 124, 178, 321
Sasape, 17, 92, 111, 118, 121, 200, 217, 265, 370, 390
Seventh-day Adventist Church, **21**
Seventh-day Adventist Mission, 325
shipping services, 82–93
single officers' quarters, 101, 250, 344, 345
slipway, 200, 216
Solomon Tayo Ltd, 15, **16**
Sterling's Hotel, 205–06, 226, 336–37
Telekom, **18**
telephone system, 200
tennis courts, 211, **212**
'The Cut', **19**, 102, 138, 140, 142, **143–45**, 200, 250, 365, 413
Top Office, 139, 148
town planning committee, 134
Tulagi Club, 91, 96, 102, 105, **127**, 138, 154, 199, 200, 201, 205, **207**, 208–11, **212–13**, 250, 268, 269, 339, 341, 343, 347
Vanita Motel, **18**
W.R. Carpenter & Co., 87, 93, 94, 111, 112, 121, 199, 200, 217, 219, 292, 321, 336, 374, 381, 383
water tanks, 137, 178, 250, 321
wharf, 74, **122**, **136**, 139, **407**
wireless station, 102, 105, 138, 158, 173–76, **213**, 341, **253**
See also BSIP; Solomon Islanders on Tulagi; recreation; women
Turner, Captain Ernest Nelson, 163, 239, 270, 327, 329, 353
Turner, G.R., 194
turtle shell, 58, 119, 254

Uki ni masi (Uki) Island, 46, 72, 83, 330
Ulawa Island, 72
Ulgau, Tom, 34
Unilever, *see* Levers
Unites States, 108, 332, 347, 359
    African-American, 332–33
    copra purchases, 87, 103, 108
    Honolulu, 6, 91
    See also scientific expeditions; World War II
urbanisation, 8–12

Vanikolo, 1, 87, 94, 174, 177, 391
Vanikolo Kauri Timber Co., 177
Vanuatu, *see* New Hebrides, Condominium
Veisamasama, Malakai, 347
Villiers, Captain Alan, 353
von Norbeck, Baron, 72
Voy, Captain William, 339
Voyaging in Wild Seas, or, A Woman among the Head Hunters, 351
Vuria, 36

W.E. Smith & Co., 94
W.R. Carpenter & Co., *see* Tulagi
Waddell, A.N.A. (Nick), 386
Walkabout, 373
Wall, Father James (Jim), 325, 383, 387, 388, 391
Wealth of the Solomons, 232
Weetman, Charles, 124, 250–51
Welchman, Dr Rev. Henry Palmer, 39
Weller, Samuel P., 381
West, J.C., 235
Western Pacific High Commission (WPHC), 6, 32, 44, 47, 57
    abolished, 69
    Chief Judicial Commissioner, 57
    decision to shift BSIP capital, 28–29
    Deputy Commissioners, 47, 54, 56, 61, 63, 78, 378
    High Commissioner's Court, 57, 59
    High Commissioners, 52, 57, 67, 79, 231, 294, 309, 353
        See also Des Voeux; Fletcher; Gordon; Hutson; Jackson; Luke; Rodwell; Thurston
    Resident Commissioners, *see* BSIP; Gilbert and Ellice Islands Protectorates
    shift to BSIP, 63
    Special Commissioners, 329, 378, 413
    Superintendent of Telegraphs and Telephones, 173
    Supreme Court of Appeal, 169
    wireless transmissions, regulation of, 173
whaling, 33, 50, 58
Wheatley, Annie, 299
Wheatley, Florence, 299
Wheatley, Harriet, 328
Wheatley, Jean (Lina), 299
Wheatley, Norman, 298–99, 328, 339
Wheatley, Nutali, 299
Wheatley, Sambe Vindo, 299
Wheeler, G.C., 347
White, Charles Havelock Gordon, 234, 235, 349, 363
Whitney, Harry Payne, 349
Wickham, Alick, 300
Wickham, Francis (Frank), 41, 299, 300, **301**
Widdy, Charles V., 231–32, 239, 386, 387, 390, 391
Williams, Group-Captain, 243
Wilmot, W.F. (Bill), 234
Wilson, Alexander (Sandy) Robert, 286
Wilson, Alexander H. (Spearline), 102, 145, 157, 160, **161**–63, 194, 196, 206, 252, **253**, **257**, 263, 282, 286, **287**, 290, 325, 329,

341, 342, 345, 373, 378, 383, 384, 387, 391
Wilson, Andrea Gordon, **288**, **289**
Wilson, C.E.J., 236, 239
Wilson, Colin, 391
Wilson, Major J. Edmonds, 380
Wilson, James Michael, **288**, **289**
Wilson (née Watt), Jessie, **182**, 186, 206, 211, 245, 246–47, 251, **253**, **257**, 263, **269**, 270, 273, 286, 287, 291, 305–06, 307, 311, 314, 339, **340**
wireless station, *see* Tulagi
Wolfers, Edward, 53, 64
women
    Europeans in Tulagi enclave, 25, 146, 165, 211, 222, 247–83, 290, 291, 307–11, 334, 335–36, 381
        See also historiography; Tulagi, children
    Solomon Islanders, 42, 153, 179, 240, 298
Woodford, Charles Morris, 24, 27, 28, 31, 42, 44–47, **45**, 71, 83, 93–94, 97–100, **99**, 102, 103, 117, 141, 148, 155, 190, 193, 194, **249**, 255, 262, 265, 268, 313, 315, **317**, 339, 347, 352, 356, 404
    photographs by, 103–04, 105
    scientific expeditions by, 44, 46, 47, 50, 72
Woodford (née Palmer), Florence (Florrie) M., 47, **249**, 265, 278, 315, **317**, 339
Woodford, Harold, 316
World War I, 9, 102, 108, 147, 152, 157, 174, 231–32, 234, 235, 376
    Gallipoli, Turkey, 329, 330
    Germans interned, 302
    veterans, 327–31, 372, 378
World War II, 4, 6, 15, 28, 68, 163, 180, 281, 373–413

Allied counterattack, 396, 403
British relations with Solomon Islanders, 399–400
BSIP Defence Force, 377, 381, 390
BSIP headquarters shifted to Furi`isango, Malaita, 390–96
BSIP Labour Corps, 359, 386
BSIP Sydney office, 162, 391
Coastwatchers, 381, 390, 392, 396, 400
commandos, 380, 381
evacuation, 148, 162, 375–93, 399
Gavutu Island, 379, 380, 381, 385, 395, 399, **401**, 403, 404, 413
Japanese military forces, **23**, 96, 375, 379, 384–85, 385, 387, 394, 396, **397**, **398**, 404, **405**
New Guinea Mandated Territory, 383–84
Shortland Islands evacuated, 386
Solomon Islanders, 392, **399**, 400
    Maasina Rule, *see* Malaita
Tanambogo Island, 380, 388, 392, 394, 395, 399, **401**, **403**, **404**, **413**
    Gavutu Island, causeway to, 17, 42, 380, 413
Tulagi enclave bombing of, **401**, **402–03**, **405**
Tulagi fortifications, **374**
United States military forces, 379, 391, **406–09**
wireless operators, training, 395
See also New Guinea Mandated Territory; Papua, Territory of; Tulagi
Workman, Charles Rufus Marshall, 120, 142, 180
Woser, Walter, 36

Yield Not to the Wind, 112, 232
Young, Florence S.H., 42, 336

`Abaeata (Abaeatha) Anifelo, 168, 360, 368, 370
`Aimela, 359
`Aoke Island, 104
`Oloburi, 240

www.ingramcontent.com/pod-product-compliance
Lightning Source LLC
Chambersburg PA
CBHW040209020526
44112CB00040B/2854